THE SECULAR AND THE SACRED

THE SECULAR

and

THE SACRED

NATION, RELIGION AND POLITICS

Editor

WILLIAM SAFRAN

FRANK CASS
LONDON • PORTLAND, OR

First published in 2003 in Great Britain by
FRANK CASS PUBLISHERS
Crown House, 47 Chase Side, Southgate
London N14 5BP

and in the United States of America by
FRANK CASS PUBLISHERS
c/o ISBS, 5824 N.E. Hassalo Street
Portland, Oregon, 97213-3644

Website: www.frankcass.com

British Library Cataloguing in Publication Data

The secular and the sacred: nation, religion and politics
  1. Religion and politics 2. Nationalism – Religious aspects
  3. Religion and state
  I. Safran, William
  322.1

ISBN 0-7146-5368-3 (cloth)
ISBN 0-7146-8301-9 (paper)

Library of Congress Cataloging-in-Publication Data

The secular and the sacred: nation, religion, and politics / edited by
William Safran.
    p. cm.
Includes bibliographical references and index.
  ISBN 0-7146-5368-3 (cloth) – ISBN 0-7146-8301-9 (pbk.)
1. Religion and politics–Congresses. I. Safran, William.
BL65.P7 S43 2003
322'.1–dc21

2002073783

Typeset in 10/12pt Times NR by Vitaset, Paddock Wood, Kent
Printed in Great Britain by
MPG Books Ltd, Bodmin, Cornwall

Contents

List of Tables

Acknowledgements

This book is based on a selection of papers presented at a conference on Religion and Politics held in Haifa, Israel in 1998, as well as additional contributions. I wish to thank all the contributors for their efforts at thematic coherence, their patience in responding to the criticisms and suggestions of the anonymous reviewer, and their good-natured adherence to the editorial demands of the publisher. My thanks also go to Sally Green and Sian Mills, project editors, for their encouragement, and to Lisa Blackwell, copy editor, for her skill and precision.

1

Introduction

WILLIAM SAFRAN

The place of religion in politics is at once a reflection of the extent of free choice of expression and the matrix around which a national culture and identity develop. Religion has functioned as a mechanism of social control, a rival to the welfare state and a brake to modernization. Many generations ago, religion and politics were inseparable; indeed, the state was, more often than not, a secular manifestation of the dominant faith. Many rulers of antiquity argued that they derived their authority and legitimacy from God, not from the people they ruled, and justified their absolute power on the basis of their divine right to rule. The Jewish nation and, subsequently, the Jewish state, were based on a contract with God, made through Moses, that committed them to obey revealed law; similarly, the Greek state's security and prosperity depended upon the grace of the various gods.

During the Middle Ages, a distinction was made between the cross and the sword, that is, between the spiritual and the terrestrial power; yet the supremacy of the Church in Europe was unchallenged by a secular state, because the state in the modern sense did not yet exist. In fact, the early Christian churches insisted that their sovereignty was supranational. The Holy Roman Emperor was anointed by the Pope; during the Protestant Reformation later on, monarchs, basing themselves on the principle of *cujus regio, ejus religio*, decided which religion was to be 'established', and they became its heads and 'defenders'. Certain nations were so deeply imbued with a collective religious faith that they came to be identified in terms of it. Spanish, Irish and Polish nationalisms were congruent with Roman Catholicism and equated with it. Until the Revolution of 1789 (and except for a brief interlude in the seventeenth century), 'Frenchness' was defined so thoroughly in terms of Catholicism that France was considered 'the eldest daughter of the church'. Analogous situations are found in other countries: thus, Russian and Greek nationalisms have been closely associated with Eastern Orthodoxy; and the 'Arab nation' is difficult to imagine without Islam.

The coupling of religion and nationhood – and the role of religion in nation-building efforts in the past – applied largely to the pre-democratic age, and applies today to many non-Western societies that have not yet modernized (such as Iran, Pakistan and Saudi Arabia). How strongly, however, does it apply to modern polities? What is the relationship between nationalism and religion? To what extent is religion compatible with democracy? These are some of the basic questions that inform the essays that follow. The answers depend on what religion we are discussing as well as on the nature of the political system. When we think of modern democratic states, we refer to secularized societies to which religions, or rather, a plethora of competing and sometimes cooperating religious establishments, have accommodated to changes because they have been republicanized.

The relationship of religion to freedom and democracy has been a matter of controversy throughout history. The Bible calls upon Moses to 'proclaim liberty throughout the land unto all the inhabitants thereof' (Leviticus 15:1). That call specifically applied to slaves, who were to be freed during the Jubilee year. Throughout the generations, Jews have thanked God for delivering them 'from slavery to freedom'. Unfortunately, the linkage between religion and either freedom or democracy has been noticeably weak historically. Many religions – most prominently Christianity and Islam – have found ways to justify slavery; and to the extent that religions have been hierarchically organized, they have had little use for democracy. Until recently, Church establishments preferred monarchical forms of government as best suited to protect their privileges.

According to Locke, the typical religion, understood as an all-embracing *Weltanschauung* claiming a superior, if not absolute, truth, is not compatible with individual freedom, democracy and, above all, tolerance. In reality, however, the role of institutionalized religion in the promotion of democracy has been uneven. It is generally accepted that Protestant minority or 'dissenter' sects have played a significant role in economic and political development. We have been led to believe that Protestantism has been the major religious progenitor of democracy; according to Max Weber's analysis, there has been a clear 'developmental' causal chain from the 'Protestant ethic' to individualism, capitalism and democratic governance.[1] Some observers argue that not all Protestants (not even all Calvinists and Puritans) shared that productivist ethic and identify it with other religions – R.H. Tawney with the Catholicism of Renaissance Italy and Werner Sombart with Judaism.[2] To Marx, Judaism was the religion of money and the embodiment of collective greed, and hence the religion of capitalism; to many anti-Semites, it was the faith that led to Bolshevism; to still others, the socioeconomic marginality of Jews forced them to foster economic innovations that led to capitalism; to others again, a secular translation of the divine commandment to do good deeds (*mitsvot*) led Jews to embrace socialism. To many contemporary observers, the ethic of hard work is incarnated in Chinese Confucianism – although there is uncertainty about the extent to which it is associated with democracy.

It should be noted that the Protestants' original stress on the primacy of the individual as the interpreter of religious truth did not necessarily translate into political individualism, that is, the promotion of individual freedom. On the contrary, the German Evangelical Lutheran establishment was marked by its authoritarian character and was intimately associated with the Prussian autocracy; the Roman Catholic establishment was closely allied with the absolute monarchies in France, Spain and Portugal; and neither establishment had much difficulty in supporting Hitler and countenancing his massacre of the Jews. After World War II, both of these churches embraced democracy as well as the welfare state in Europe; furthermore, they were influential in promoting decolonization, land reform and grassroots democracy.

In short, some religions are the harbingers of democracy and progress, whereas others are not. It may be argued that in a number of countries neither capitalism nor democracy could develop because the beliefs associated with the religions that dominated there were incompatible with an autonomous and progressive civil society. For example, premodern Catholicism was marked by features that were not conducive to what is now called 'democratization'; these included hierarchical institutions that regulated nonparticipant and highly inegalitarian societies and perpetuated the belief that this life was a vale of tears. Such a situation is widely believed to prevail in Muslim societies, owing to the fatalism – the belief that everything is God's will ('insh'allah') – that is considered an important element of Islamic culture.

All countries discussed in this volume once constituted, *grosso modo*, nations that were defined, in turn, in terms of religion. A specific religion once determined the norms of individual and social behaviour of a country's citizens (or rather, 'subjects'); the state's leadership worked closely with the religious establishment in exercising surveillance over public morality, providing education and establishing personal status laws. Those who were outside the framework of the dominant religion were, at best, tolerated, and, at worst, socially ostracized, legally handicapped, forcibly converted, ghettoized or expelled.

That is no longer true in the countries under review. Members of all religions are equal before the law, provided, of course, that their practices do not clash with the dominant political values of the state. Religious conflict is no longer pursued by means of crusades, theological disputations or holy wars; blasphemers or heretics no longer are burned at the stake; and adherents of minority religions are no longer publicly molested and can openly practise their beliefs. Owing to the rapid pace of secularization and the decline of the peasantry, churches are losing members and are increasingly on the defensive. Moreover, owing to the influx of new populations and the spread of democracy, religious pluralism is now widely accepted.

The countries examined in this collection share a number of features: they are democratic, at least in the formal constitutional sense; they are committed to the principle of the free exercise of religion; the adherence of their citizens to a religion is increasingly voluntary, and, at least officially, 'exit' is possible.

Although one or another religion may be dominant, it has lost its monopoly over defining the proper path to morality or spirituality; and – largely as a result of the weakening of central ecclesiastical authority – there is increasing pluralism even *within* religions. Educational curricula and personal status increasingly are defined by the state (whether embodied in a central government or regional authorities) rather than religious institutions, within varying parameters ranging from those of secular France to selectively 'theocratic' Israel. Finally, religious public-policy agendas are promoted by democratic and peaceful means, such as interest groups, social movements, political parties and elections. In some countries, religious groups enjoy official legitimation and their participation in the political process – via confessional political parties, trade unions, or 'recognized' charitable associations – is institutionalized; in others, religious groups have the same opportunity as other sectors of civil society to exert pressure on the public authorities by informal means. In some societies, adherence to a religion is less a matter of theology than kinship or other ascriptive ties. In short, in all these countries *laïcité* is the dominant norm, although it may not be expressed in terms of the Jacobin dogma of republican France. This norm is reflected in the affirmation of fundamental rights, the religious neutrality of the state (at least in practice), freedom of religion and non-religion, and the autonomy of the individual conscience.

This is not to suggest that all countries have a uniform approach to religion. In six countries – the United States, France, Turkey, India and, more recently, Italy, Spain and Poland, religion has been 'disestablished' at least in some formal sense. In Greece, Israel (Northern) Ireland and the former Yugoslavia this has not yet been accomplished, in part because the very identity of these states continues to be defined in terms of a specific religion.

The British case is more complex: while there are two 'established' religions, the non-established religions operate on a roughly equal playing field. Anglicanism may be the norm applied to the Crown, but it has gradually ceased to be the decisive indicator of Britishness (or even Englishness), and the continued reality of two established Churches has not had a chilling effect on the free exercise of a great variety of non-established religions. Yet religious equality has not yet been fully achieved: the 'lords spiritual' of only two religions have special representation in the House of Lords; and it is only very recently that former Catholic priests obtained the right to sit in the House of Commons.

In two of the countries under discussion – Spain under General Franco and France under Marshal Pétain – religious institutions once functioned as handmaidens of autocratic government – but they were politically deinstitutionalized as these countries returned to democracy. In fact, as democratization appeared inevitable, the Catholic Church in both countries adapted to the situation, if only in order to preserve what was left of its authority. In Spain, moreover (as Víctor Urrutia argues), the Church anticipated democratic reforms toward the end of the Franco regime by supporting greater pluralism within civil society.

The essays presented here portray connections between religion on the one hand and ethnicity or nation on the other that reflect a considerable diversity, which can be summed up as follows:

1. religion mixed (or fused) with ethnicity – in the cases of Greeks, Poles, Bosnians, Northern Irish Catholics and Israeli Jews;
2. religion as transnational but as constituting, at the same time, a major element of national identity – in the cases of Turks, Serbs and Croats;
3. religion as pluralistic, transethnic and nonpolitical – in the cases of the United States, France, India and, increasingly, Great Britain and Spain.[3]

The cases of (former) Yugoslavia and Northern Ireland illustrate the fact that religion cannot always be separated from ethnonationalism – that, indeed, the two have had a reciprocal influence. Yet there is no exact congruence between the two; for example, there are Albanian Kosovars who are Roman Catholic and Croatians who are Protestant. Similarly, in Ulster there are Catholics who wish to remain citizens of the United Kingdom and Protestants who would adjust without much difficulty to union with the Irish Republic. Furthermore, both religious and national identities are shaped by collective memories, especially a memory of cruelties perpetrated by one religious group against another. In addition, both religious and national identity may be reinforced, if not created, by institutional engineering and public policies.

Yugoslavia was established as a successor state that was from the beginning multiethnic, multilingual and multireligious. Under President Tito, religious pluralism was tolerated, because it did not interfere with 'nation-building' – i.e., the creation of a transethnic and transreligious Yugoslav political community based on Marxism, structured along federal lines and consolidated by means of a charismatic leader aided by the police. The intertwining of religion and ethnicity was exemplified by the Bosnian Muslims. The transformation of Bosnia-Herzegovina into a constituent republic under Tito led to the creation of a Bosnian Muslim *nationality*. This did not seem to matter too much, because the members of the various religious groups got along well in Sarajevo, the Bosnian capital. It was remarked that, 'the major difference between the Catholics, Eastern Orthodox, Muslims, and Jews [in that city] was that the Christians don't go to their churches, the Muslims don't go to the mosque, and the Jews don't go to synagogue'.

Since the disaggregation of Yugoslavia, members of the various (Serbian, Croatian and Bosnian) communities seem to have turned to religion in order to provide an underpinning to their collective *ethnic* identities. The reassertion of such identities was stimulated and exploited by Serbian leader Slobodan Milošević, whose oppressive cultural policies against the Albanian Kosovars fed the religious consciousness of the latter.

The interface between religion and politics is clearly apparent in Spain, where three religious groups lived in harmony for many generations; after the Inquisition, however, the country became so solidly Catholic that its culture and identity could not be disjoined from Roman Catholicism. During the fascist Franco regime, Catholicism became, in effect, an institutional component of the state. In the context of post-Franco democratization, several processes were inaugurated, among them secularization and the creation of a pluralistic society, a development that resulted in a gradual and partial 'privatization' of religion. This process, however, stopped short of clear separation of Church and state, since special formalized relationships were set up between the state and the Catholic Church on the one hand, and the other 'rooted' religions, such as Judaism, Islam and Protestantism, on the other.

Greece and Poland bear comparison because in both countries national and religious identities have tended to merge. Just as Greek Orthodoxy is a marker of 'Greekness', 'to be Polish is to be Catholic'. Both countries are committed to freedom of religion; but that commitment is limited in practice. Greek Orthodoxy enjoys a preferential status, while other religions have encountered official obstacles in their legitimation, if not their observances: for example, as Adamantia Pollis points out, the Eastern Orthodox leadership has been pressuring the public authorities to reinstate the mention of religion on identity cards. Muslims and Jews enjoy special legal status as well; but this means less than meets the eye. The Greek attitude to Islam is coloured by the country's more or less antagonistic relations with Turkey; and freedom of worship for Jews is not a significant public issue, since there are few Jews left in the country after the genocide committed during World War II (in which the role of the Greek Orthodox establishment was not negligible).[4] Nevertheless, religious pluralism (or at least tolerance) is making steady progress, in part because of increasing secularization, and in part because of the influence and 'surveillance' of the European Union and the Council of Europe.

The role of religion in Poland is more complex. For many generations, the Church played a dominant role in the development of Polish national conscious-ness and, indeed, the Polish state.[5] Poland developed as a distinct political entity when under the leadership of Duke Mieszko I, it embraced Christianity. The aristocracy and landed gentry were almost exclusively Catholic and (for the most part) Polish, and the Black Madonna of Częstochowa became a powerful symbol of Catholic as well as Polish collective identity. From the fourteenth century on, many Jews and German Protestants settled in Poland and played crucial roles in the country's economic development; the Jews maintained their own social and cultural institutions, and, during the seventeenth and eighteenth centuries, enjoyed considerable communal autonomy. Most Jews spoke their own language; as Isaac Bashevis Singer, the Nobel Prize-winning author, once said, 'to me, the Vistula speaks in Yiddish'. With the restoration of Polish independence after World War I, Poland was committed to religious freedom and pluralism, but non-Catholics continued to be the objects of discrimination. Owing to ethnic cleansing, boundary changes and expulsions, post-World War II Poland became a fairly homogeneous state; yet although Catholics now accounted for more than 95 per cent of the population, their religion was eclipsed by Communist ideology. Nevertheless, public hostility to Communist rule was so strong that Catholicism became the only credible counter-ideology to Marxism-Leninism, and the only way in which Polish nationalism could be expressed (albeit not always openly) to the point that it was embraced even by many secular Poles.

After decommunization, the appeal of Catholicism began to diminish, especially among the educated urban bourgeoisie. As the country democratized and embraced market liberalism, secular political culture spread quickly, and so did hostility toward the Catholic Church. Today, Poland is officially as much committed to religious pluralism as it is to democracy; yet the Roman Catholic leadership remains powerful and continues to attempt to impose Catholic values upon the country that are not always conducive to democracy. On the one hand, such imposition now seems easier than it was before World War II, since the proportion of non-Catholic inhabitants, who once accounted for 30 per cent of the population, was reduced to less than 5 per cent. On the other hand, the norms of democracy, pluralism and secularism are likely to gain dominance with the decline of the peasantry, the pressures of modernization and the enticement of Polish membership of the European Union.

One of the most obvious connections between religion and nation is found in the State of Israel; indeed, the very existence of that country arises out of the matrix of Judaism, both in its original homeland and in the diaspora. Many of Israel's internal conflicts are due to religion; and its capital is a spiritual centre for three monotheistic faiths. The country was re-established as a *haven* for Jews (regardless of the condition of their religious observance); at the same time, it is regarded by many of its Jewish inhabitants, and most of its supporters in the diaspora, as a Jewish *state*.

Israel's culture is marked by the Jewish historical and religious experience; its official language is a modernized version of the language of the Hebrew Bible, which is an important part of the curriculum even in the predominantly secular 'state schools'. The personal status laws, public holidays and rules pertaining to marriage and burial are heavily influenced by Judaism; and the national anthem refers to the Zionist dream and 'the Jewish soul' that beats in the heart of its citizens. At the same time, Israel is a modern society; its elite is strongly marked by Western democratic values, and the majority is secular.

This ambiguity has given rise to many religious–secular conflicts and has raised the question to what extent an especially legitimated and officialized Judaism is compatible with democracy. It is argued that certain orthodox Jewish norms are difficult to combine with the standard liberal catalogue of individual rights, especially those relating to women and aspects of individual lifestyle; moreover, the Jewish character of Israeli culture might be difficult to preserve in the face of a rapid growth of the (predominantly Muslim) non-Jewish minority, unless democratic principles were jettisoned. The clash between the observant and the secular Jews – the former constituting the demographic power-house and the latter the country's political and economic elite – has produced a low-intensity *Kulturkampf*, which, as Ira Sharkansky shows, revolves around questions of education, conversion, the definition of 'who is a Jew' and the political role of the rabbinate. Yet it is difficult to factor out the Jewish identity of the majority of Jewish Israelis (including ostensibly secular ones) and equally difficult to imagine a 'post-Jewish' Israel.

In France, the revolutionaries of 1789 attempted to do away with religion; Jacobin ideologues, viewing the Catholic church as a reactionary and undemocratic interposition between the individual and the sovereign state, replaced it for a while with a 'religion of reason'. After its legitimacy was restored by Napoleon and placed under the surveillance of the state, the Catholic Church could not be easily 'republicanized', and it tried intermittently to undermine the republican regimes that followed. Since 1905 (in the wake of the Dreyfus Affair), religion has been separated from the state; the conflict between them, however, has not yet been fully resolved. On the one hand, France is officially committed to *laïcité* (secularity); on the other hand, it is committed to religious pluralism. The former is reflected in the continuing de-Christianization of French society, the latter in the fact that France has become a multiethnic and multireligious mosaic. However, the Catholic heritage is so deeply embedded in French culture that it continues to persist, albeit in a secularized form; conversely, there are now so many Muslims in the country that fears have spread about the chilling impact of Islamic fundamentalism on republican values.

Half a century ago, religion was the major divisive force in Imperial India. When the country gained independence, it was the conflict between Hindus and Muslims that led to a civil war, population exchanges and territorial division. Today, religious, ethnic and linguistic differences are not nearly so divisive as they are in European countries; indeed, pluralism is one of the national unifying elements of the country. According to some of the country's leaders, India was seen, ideally, as 'a composite culture (Hindu, Muslim, Buddhist, even Western) historically merging into an harmonious whole' and it was held that 'the only true Indian was one who acknowledged India to be his or her holy land. The creed was unimportant.'[6] Officially, India is committed to secularism; its constitution guarantees the freedom and equality of all its religions; and religious autonomy institutionally is buttressed by meaningful federalism. Yet religion has not been totally depoliticized; occasionally 'Hinduness' is asserted by certain political leaders, and there are confrontations between Hindus on the one hand, and Muslims and Christians on the other. While the various religious communities in India fight for as much autonomy as possible, *vis-à-vis* the state, Islamic parties are openly committed to a theocracy in which *sharia* law prevails.

Since the revolution undertaken by Kemal Atatürk, Turkey has been committed to a democratic regime associated with secularism. The vast majority of the population is Muslim, and this proportion is growing, as is the political power associated with it, despite the progressive Westernization of the country. It is ironic that in Turkey it is the military – an institution not often associated with democracy – that, as Joseph Szyliowicz shows, functions as the handmaiden of the government in protecting the constitutional principle of *laïcité*, and in that role it has staged coups d'état to prevent the major Islamist party from achieving control over the country. Far from being hostile to Islam, however, the government has attempted to insure religious pluralism while promoting the stability of the state and civil society and staying out of the Arab–Israeli and other regional conflicts.

In many respects, the United States constitutes a special case. It was the first country committed to religious liberty and equality. Reflecting the religious diversity of its settlers, many of whom had fled their homelands because of religious persecution, as well as the deism of many of its founders, its constitution provided for a wall of separation between Church and state. From its very inception, the federal government was 'almost completely divorced from formal religion'.[7] As in France, no religion formally is recognized, and public life is informed, at least officially, by a 'civil religion'. However, whereas in France the dominance of 'civil religion' is reflected in the fact that marriages performed by clergy are not officially recognized, clergy in the United States have been delegated the authority to perform this rite of passage in the name of the state. At the same time, just as in France Catholicism is woven into the fabric of the country's life and culture, American social life was dominated for many generations by White Anglo-Saxon Protestants (WASPs), and American political culture continues to be heavily informed by WASP values. Although some observers insist that all religions enjoy equal protection – and one sociologist has even argued that Protestantism, Catholicism and Judaism are the three 'American' religions and, as such, are on an equal footing[8] – Christianity is clearly dominant. This fact is reflected in the political clout of the 'moral majority' and the 'Christian Coalition'; in the frequent display of religious symbols on public property; in Sunday closing laws; and the exercise of Church pressure with regard to the issuing of liquor licences. The influence of religion is often observed in the domain of education, specifically, with respect to government aid to parochial schools; prayer in public educational institutions; and the introduction of a particular religious dogma in the school curriculum, sometimes surreptitiously and sometimes openly. The influence of religious lobbies is also reflected in continuing attempts by federal and state legislatures to permit the teaching of 'creationism' in public-school biology classes and to legalize sectarian prayers at school athletic events; and in recent efforts by some state authorities to require the posting of the Ten Commandments in public-school classrooms. So far, the Supreme Court has been a guardian of the 'wall of separation' between state and religion, as stipulated in the First Amendment; but that wall is in the process of being undermined by stealth, or worse, is being frontally attacked by the Christian Coalition, which would like to accord Christianity formal (and preferential) legitimation. At this writing, such attempts are impeded by the growth of a society marked by an increasing religious diversity and the persistence of a healthy democratic pluralism.

Unlike France, Turkey and Israel, the United States has neither religious nor anti-religious parties. Nevertheless, well-organized religious communities play a significant role in influencing public policies. Religious groups take an active part in elections; moreover, the Republican party is strongly influenced by Christian movements (in particular the Protestant fundamentalist ones concentrated in the Southern 'Bible Belt').

Before the Civil War, there was a widespread belief among the founding elite that Anglo-Saxon Protestants would make better citizens because they were better equipped to understand liberty, so that constitutional democracy was often confounded with WASP culture.[9] This has long since ceased to be the case; the values of constitutional democracy have become embedded in the majority of an increasingly multireligious society.

It is evident from the foregoing that religions are not static. Their institutional and doctrinal development depends to a considerable extent on 'opportunity structures', including the political context in which they operate and the changes within the societies in which they function. In several of the countries dealt with in this volume, the sociopolitical position of the churches has been challenged by several developments. One of them is the growing distinction between the traditional organized religions and individual beliefs outside them, a phenomenon reflected in the growth of parallel belief systems – often labelled cults, sects, or superstitions. Curiously, this is said to be particularly true of the young, precisely that sector of the population that is most susceptible to the influences of modern secular culture.[10] Another development is the growth of the welfare state, itself a consequence of the politicization of the masses and their socio-economic demands, many of which were once met (or expected to be met) by religious institutions. Reacting both to the flight of many enfranchised industrial workers from organized religion and to growing competition among religions present in the country in question, the major churches embraced the welfare state and developed social doctrines focused on the here-and-now. This change, in turn, enabled Christian democratic parties to enter into coalitions with socialists.

This adaptability of religion suggests a degree of instrumental behaviour on the part of their leaders. Indeed, there are many examples of the instrumental use of religion:

1. In Poland, as was pointed out, the Catholic Church was used (even by non-believers) to oppose Communism; and the moment Communism collapsed, the Church's influence began to decline.

2. In Israel, certain Jews have resorted to an ultra-Orthodox definition of Judaism in order to oppose the existence of the State of Israel, which they consider anathema.

3. In the immediate postwar years of the German Federal Republic, many inhabitants of, say, Bavaria or Württemberg would identify as adherents of a religious community – say, as Roman Catholics – rather than as members of a nation whose image had been severely tarnished. In short religion served as a convenient instrument (however temporary) of 'Selbstentdeutschung'.

4. In Yugoslavia, Milošević invoked the memory of the historic Eastern Orthodox presence in Kosovo to promote Serbian nationalism and his own political career.

5. In Northern Ireland, anti-papism is occasionally invoked in order to preserve the political control (and the economic privileges) of the Protestants.

6. In the United States, the policies embraced by President George W. Bush (including 'faith-based initiatives' relating to welfare) suggest that religious values are being manipulated to promote a reactionary economic and social agenda.

Instrumental behaviour can be said to characterize the overall position of religions in most of the countries dealt with here (with Turkey and Serbia constituting exceptions). The leaders of the dominant religions in these countries are officially committed both to democracy and to religious freedom. They have tried hard to efface the negative image of their churches that existed before and during World War II – e.g., in Spain and France as in Germany and Italy. All the major religions dealt with in this book – except in Turkey and, in part, in Greece and Israel – have been 'republicanized', and all have accepted the welfare state. Indeed, religious institutions in some countries (e.g., France and Spain) may even be in the forefront in providing assistance to the poor and the homeless and in fighting for the rights of immigrants.

What of the future? It is not entirely clear how the process of globalization will affect the relationship between religions and states. To the extent that globalization refers to secularization, national collective identity will doubtlessly come to depend less on religion; indeed, it may be argued that ethnic (or ethnonational) identity will be a substitute for a waning religious belief. National identity, however, may itself be increasingly eclipsed by one or another supra-national one. To the extent that globalization implies the growth of supranational or transnational authority, the sovereignty of individual states will be reduced, and their power to 'deal' with one or another religion – either to control it or to hold it to their national values, including democratic ones – will be weakened. Whether this development will revive religious sentiment by making it less dependent on national politics is a question that awaits an answer.

NOTES

1. Max Weber, *The Protestant Ethic and The Spirit of Capitalism*, trans. Talcott Parsons (New York: Charles Scribner's, 1958).
2. R.H. Tawney, *Religion and the Rise of Capitalism*, 3rd edn (New Brunswick, NJ: Transaction Publishers, 1998), esp. pp. 261–2; Werner Sombart, *The Jews and Modern Capitalism*, trans. Samuel Z. Klausner (New Brunswick, NJ: Transaction Books, 1982). Weber, too, finds elements of the productivist ethic among Jews; however, while showing similarities to the Puritan and Calvinist ethic, it was more traditionalist. See Weber, *Protestant Ethic*, note 58, pp. 270–1.
3. Cf. the typological division of the position of religions in Europe posited by Jean Baubérot, 'Quatre modèles possibles en Europe: ethno-religion, religion civile, pluralisme, laïcité', Yves

Léonard (ed.), *Religions et sociétés*, *Cahiers français*, no. 273 (Paris: Documentation Française, 1995), p. 29.

4. The existence of a Sephardic museum in Athens, where there are only a few thousand Jews left, is of little more than symbolic (if not touristic) value.

5. See Norman Davies, 'Polish National Mythologies', in Geoffrey Hosking and George Schöpflin (eds), *Myths and Nationhood* (New York: Routledge, 1997), esp. pp. 141–8.

6. Martin Fuller, *Political Stability and Religion: Fundamentalism in Perspective*, Wilton Park Paper 119 (London: HM Stationery Office, May 1996), p. 21.

7. Merle Curti, *The Growth of American Thought*, 2nd edn (New York: Harper, 1951), p. 135.

8. Will Herberg, *Protestant, Catholic, Jew*, rev. edn (Garden City, NY: Doubleday Anchor, 1960).

9. See Dale T. Knobel, *Paddy and the Republic: Ethnicity and Nationality in Antebellum America* (Middletown, CT: Wesleyan University Press, 1986), p. 12.

10. Yves Lambert, 'Une définition plurielle pour une réalité en mutation', *Religion et société*, 273, octobre–décembre (1995), pp. 10–11.

2

Religion and Politics in American Democracy

HORST MEWES

Our civilization and our institutions are emphatically Christian. From the discovery of this continent to the present hour, there is a single voice making this affirmation ... that this is a Christian nation.

(Justice David Brewer writing for the majority, in *Church of the Holy Trinity* v. *United States*, 1892)

neither the State nor the Federal Government can constitutionally aid all religions as against non-believers, and neither can aid those religions based on a belief in the existence of God as against those religions founded on different beliefs.

(*Tarcosa* v. *Watkins*, 1961)

INTRODUCTION: RELIGION AND AMERICAN POLITICAL VALUES

Proponents of theories of American 'exceptionalism' point to an apparent paradox central to American society and its political system. The United States is, on the one hand, by any measure the most modernized, secularized society among developed Western democracies today. It is committed to such typically modern goals as economic growth, free-market capitalism, scientific and technological progress, radical individualism and a culture of hedonistic mass-consumption. On the other hand, and paradoxically, with regard to the cultural status, social significance and political importance of religion, the modern United States defies all past predictions and assumptions of general theories of modernization and secularization.[1] Where the latter predicted the demise or radical diminution of traditional religions under the pressures of secular modernism, the United States even today is by many accounts the most religious society among modern Western democracies.[2] This apparent paradox is an appropriate starting point for a discussion of religion and politics in America.

Such a discussion is further confounded or complicated, however, by another prominent feature of the United States constitutional and social system, namely what has variously been called its 'civil religion', or the American Creed. Essentially consisting of faith in the fundamental political ideals embedded in the Declaration of Independence, as well as the principles of the Constitution and the Founding Fathers, this political creed is said to have taken on many of the communal and symbolic functions associated with traditional religion.[3] Mainly, it serves to unify a factious free society around common political ideals legitimated by divine inspiration and, most importantly, thereby lending 'sacred character to civic obligations'.[4] Consequently, any discussion of religion and politics in the United States must distinguish between the role of its *civic religion*, on the one hand, and the political attitudes and degrees of involvement of 'traditional', non-political *religious denominations*, on the other. Historical experience warrants this distinction. Ever since the early nineteenth century many mainstream Protestant religions did indeed fervently support the emerging American civil religion, blending religious faith with political nationalism in 'God's chosen nation' and the 'shining city on the hill', while other religious denominations did not join in a practice they considered blasphemy. Some recent writers have added to the confusion. Ralph Bellah and others, who have popularized the concept of civic religion in contemporary political literature, claim that civic religion 'provides a *religious dimension for the whole fabric* of American life, including its political sphere' (my italics).[5] If taken to this extreme, however, the notion of a civic religion eliminates the basic principle of American politics, the separation of Church and state. The concept of a civic religion, by institutionalizing the worship of the principles of the democratic state into something of a church, or at least a semi-religious practice, in effect obscures the history of the relation between private religions and politics in the United States. Equally important, the comprehensive use of 'civil religion' to denote the American Creed hides the historical influence of traditional religion, especially radical Protestantism, upon basic American political values.

For this reason our discussion of politics and religion will not primarily focus on America's *civic religion*.[6] Instead, we will consider some key facets of the interactions of American politics based on a *secular* constitution, and essentially *private religions* whose practice is protected by the First Amendment.[7] Compared to most other modern democracies, the key to understanding the continuing strength of American religion lies precisely in the *private* nature of religious communities in a civil society largely independent of the state.[8] It has been claimed that this, 'more than anything else, made the United States a new thing on earth, setting new tasks for religion, offering it new opportunities'.[9]

To repeat, America's unique position or 'exceptionalism' among modern developed democracies is said to rest to a great extent on the fact that the United States 'has been' and still is 'the most religious country in Christendom'.[10] The United States is, in short, an 'outlier' among Western democracies because it is 'the *most religious*, optimistic, patriotic, rights-oriented, and individualistic'.[11]

Due to its 'Protestant-inspired moralism', American public and political discourse tends to be 'also more moralistic in both its social criticism and political
rhetoric'.[12] Even American disdain for state-authority is, in one of its manifestations, the result of the priority of 'obedience to conscience' over obedience to
government and its laws.[13] If Edmund Burke was correct in asserting that the
original Americans were the Protestants of Protestantism and the Dissenters of
Dissent, the religious origins of individualism sustained and, in turn, were
supported by its other modes rooted in Lockean rights to life, liberty and
property.[14]

Politically speaking, the heart of the thesis of American exceptionalism
is the claim that the United States 'remains the least *statist* Western nation in
terms of public effort, benefits and employment'.[15] Again, historically one of the
main causes of this pervasive anti-statist disposition is said to be the 'unique
character of American religion' fostering the legendary American ideology of
radical individualism supported by self-evident rights.[16] Lipset and others
refer here to America's radically Protestant roots and the highly individualistic
notion of 'freedom of conscience'. Part of this inheritance, however, is also its
concomitant voluntaristic congregationalism, resulting in the crucial fact,
emphasized already by Tocqueville in the 1830s, that American individualism
took the form of active participation in pre-political voluntary associations.
Chief among these are religious congregations. Even today those American
citizens actively involved in their small, local religious communities far
outnumber those actively participating in political organizations. Religious
congregations, rather than politics, are the predominant form of popular
participation in American civil society.[17] And, with few exceptions, citizen
'movements' rather than political parties have been the preferred method of
national political action.

All of this is largely beyond dispute. However, the signal importance allotted
to religion by proponents of American exceptionalism is an insufficient
explanation of the roles religions have played in American life. For one, religion
must be placed in the context of the uniquely American version of the process
of modernization, and the accompanying secularization of society, culture,
politics and economics. 'Exceptionalists' argue that the unusual strength of
religion in contemporary America has 'falsified' both the modernization and the
secularization theses, insofar as they forecast the demise or debilitating weakening of religion.[18] But the complex history of the interaction between religion
and politics in America is not adequately explained merely by pointing to the
'survival' of religion under the onslaught of modernization and secularization.
If religion has both thrived in and influenced modern American society, and if
religious issues and concerns have indeed been 'politicized', United States-
modernized secular culture has also profoundly changed 'traditional' religion.
For one, American modernization, in conjunction with the secularization of
public life, has meant the rapid pluralization of religious denominations,
churches and sects. Moreover, it has led to a variety of reactions to

modernization by various religious organizations, issuing in fundamental conflicts pervading the entire politics of religion. Indeed, these reactions can be categorized broadly in terms of religion's attitudes towards the secularization of everyday life, responses to growing religious and cultural pluralism, and their views towards the increasing liberalism of American life. Religions reacted differently to the increasing inclusion of groups, like former black slaves, women, religious minorities like Jews, and other ethnic groups, under the rubric of equal 'men' famously endowed with the individual rights to life, liberty and the pursuit of happiness promised in the Declaration of Independence.

The point is that American modernization and secularization also meant greater egalitarianism of the American republic. Thus, entirely aside from theological and doctrinal conflicts between Christian denominations, as well as other non-Christian religions, religions were forced to articulate their disposition toward the growing democratic republic. They were forced to take positions regarding the need to spread republican virtue, public education, and extending equality of individual freedoms. Consequently, religions' attitudes toward *modernization* were interwoven with their attitude towards *democratization*, or the various implications of true popular sovereignty. Politically, modernization included the elimination of traditional social hierarchies, the expansion of equal rights to previously excluded parts of the population. Indeed, it has been pointed out that 'evangelical Christians became a powerful agent of democratization in the first fifty years of the new nation'.[19] A proliferation of new preachers with little or no formal training taught a gospel supportive of the spiritual aspirations of the poor and the humble. Hierarchy and deference diminished in significance. The, so-called, Second Awakening during the first half of the nineteenth century, stressing the providential mission played by American evangelical Christianity, was a key factor in the popularization of a uniquely American brand of religious republicanism. Regarding the expansion of equal individual rights, the more 'radical' fringes of Protestant sects, led by the Quakers, played a significant, often leading role in expanding basic rights.[20] In the mid-eighteenth century, Philadelphia Quakers under the leadership of Anthony Benezet were already calling for the abolition of slavery. And Philadelphia Quakers, organized under the Society for Promoting the Abolition of Slavery, with Benjamin Franklin as its President, sent the first official petition to the First United States Congress in favour of abolishing slavery. Later, abolitionists were split between those, like Frederick Douglass, primarily arguing against slavery as political, constitutional republicans, and William Lloyd Garrison, condemning the Constitution on religious grounds. By having incorporated slavery into the Constitution, the latter was said to be anti-republican as well as anti-Christian, and thus 'null and void before God'. Abolitionists as Christians had to 'obey God and ... Christ our leader', rather than the Constitution.[21] The Constitutionalists, inspired most prominently by Abraham Lincoln and his advocacy of 'civil religion', ultimately carried the day.

Without religiously motivated activists dominating the abolitionist movement, the early women's rights movement, as well as the temperance movements, down to Martin Luther King, Jr, and the Civil Rights Movement of the 1960s, the expansion of basic rights would not have taken place in the United States.[22] To cite merely a few examples: Lucretia Mott of Philadelphia, a Quaker, was both a leading abolitionist and an early spokesperson for women's rights. The same is true for the Quakers Sarah and Angelina Grimke. And, the first organizational meeting of the women's rights movement, issuing its now famous Declaration of Principles, was held in a Wesleyan Methodist chapel in Seneca Falls, New York, in 1848. However, if one focuses on the maverick activities of more 'radical' religious activists outside the 'mainstream' denominations, one must see them against the background of a majority of religious denominations either opposed to or apathetically neutral toward the expansion of individual rights. Instead, they reflected the prevailing public opinion concerning the traditional social place of women and racial hierarchies. Angelina Grimke, for instance, had been expelled from the Presbyterian Church over the issue of slavery before joining the Society of Friends.

In fact, religious activists did not only, or even primarily, engage in expanding republican rights, or pursue the teaching of republican virtues, as was the case with many women's Benevolence Societies and Christian Temperance Unions. Profound social and economic changes in the United States, including periodic massive nineteenth-century immigration by non-Protestant denominations also produced considerable hostility between religious sects.[23] In other words, the growth of the new American democratic republic meant not only the democratization of religion, but also the growing self-assertion and self-defence of separate religious groups directed against each other. Most important, America changed from a prominently Protestant nation to a multireligious republic where today the Catholic religion has become the single largest denomination, including approximately 25 per cent of the total population of those identifying with a church.[24] Throughout the nineteenth century, the main form of political activism by religious groups consisted of the often-virulent anti-Catholicism by a significant part of Mainline Protestant churches.[25] Conflict over education, and especially public support of parochial schools, led to events like the Philadelphia Bible riots of 1844, where 30 died and hundreds were wounded in battles between Catholics and Protestants over what version of the scriptures ought to be taught in public schools.[26] In the middle of the century, the American Party, dominated by the so-called Know-Nothings, was expressly motivated by nativist, anti-Catholic sentiments. Although their presidential candidate Millard Fillmore garnered only 22 per cent of the vote in the race of 1856, the Know-Nothings elected eight governors, a number of mayors in major cities, as well as at least 100 Congressmen, before being absorbed by the Republicans.[27] The politics of Protestant-dominated nativism, or rejection of new immigration, mixed with the imported ethnic hatreds between various European nationalities, as well as their rival religious affiliations coagulated into an explosive cauldron of politically assertive fear, hatred, intolerance and prejudices. The paranoia and excesses aside, there were some real differences between republicanism and prevailing Catholic doctrines in the nineteenth century. Popes Gregory XVI and Pius IX had spoken out against the dangerous doctrine of liberty of conscience, and also the 'detested liberty of the press', a mainstay of democratic republicanism. As late as 1899, Leo XIII condemned 'Americanism', in *Testem Benevolentiae*, as a sacrilegious accommodation to modernism.[28]

Another major point of contention between religions was of course the great issue of slavery. In brief, religious denominations split along the great divide of the Civil War. The schisms were to last until well into the twentieth century. Presbyterians split along North–South lines in 1837, Methodists in 1845, Baptists in 1845. The Southern Baptist Convention became the dominant church of the South, and in the second half of the twentieth century the largest Protestant denomination of the United States, all the while upholding white supremacy and white dominance until the Civil Rights Movement of the 1960s.[29] As northern churches increasingly turned against the 'slave power', and some organizations like the Church Anti-Slavery Society of 1859 actively fought it, southern churches defended slavery on religious, Christian grounds. This, despite the fact that earlier southern Christians had actively converted black slaves and educated them with the help of scripture readings, in some cases encouraging biracial worship. Black Christian churches proliferated. After the development of an extensive black 'invisible Church', African-American open congregations began to emerge after 1760. African-American Baptists gathered in South Carolina in 1775, Black Methodists in Philadelphia in 1794. Bishop Allen of the African Methodist Episcopal Church in 1830 organized the first 'Negro Convention' of church leaders to coordinate their fight against slavery. But the enormous conversion of slaves and former slaves to Christianity did not prevent Southern religious leaders from defending that inhuman institution in religious terms. The defence of southern state's rights mixed with a defence of Southern culture and religious faith. The South stood for Christianity, the North for atheism. In 1864, southern Presbyterians argued that 'it is the peculiar mission of the southern Church to conserve the institution of slavery'. The war was a struggle 'not alone for civil rights, and property, and home, but the religion, for the Church, for the gospel'.[30]

Many of these inter- as well as intra-denominational religious divisions and their political manifestations were to last well into the twentieth century. However, with the rapid development of a capitalist economy after the Civil War, these interdenominational conflicts were increasingly superseded by a major new division crossing most traditional denominational lines. The new crucial religious struggle, both theological and political, was to become that between religious modernists and liberals, on the one side, and religious biblical literalists and orthodox fundamentalists, on the other. Late nineteenth- and early twentieth-century modernists were not necessarily singing the praise of modern trends. Rather, their theological orientation demanded concern with the economic and social *problems* emerging in modernity. The most prominent example was the Social Gospel Movement. Condemning fashionable Social Darwinism, they essentially argued for the necessity of Christian community in modern capitalism. Without being socialist, they were social communitarians, advocating governmental care for a society inspired by Christian values of neighbourly love. Some, such as Washington Gladden, took great interest in workers' rights to organize and strike. Others emphasized the problem of the maldistribution of wealth, advocating social and economic equality based on Christian principles. As the forerunners of the later National Council of Churches and the social teachings of the American Catholic Bishops Conference, the Social Gospel Movement inspired much of twentieth-century religious involvement in social and economic reforms.[31]

The opposition between modernists and biblical literalists dominates the entire twentieth century until our own days, and is marked by periods of political activism and retreat mainly by religious fundamentalists. In many ways it is this very struggle itself which has guaranteed the persistent vitality of religious-political controversy in the United States. This enduring and very contemporary religious divide is also marked by a proliferation of new religiously based interest groups or single-issue activist groups, which in many cases have become more significant politically than the traditional denominations. Aside from denominational organizations, special agenda associations rather than political parties have always played the most important role in the active political and social engagement of American religions. Organizations like the early American Temperance Society (claiming 8,000 local chapters after 1826), the American Sunday School Union (1824) and the National League for the Protection of the Family (1896), set the pattern. The first major organization of fundamentalists, the World's Christian Fundamentals Association, was already founded in 1919. But special agenda groups, often umbrella agencies for interdenominational cooperation, proliferated especially rapidly between 1945 and the 1990s, to more than 500. Most, if not all, of these, including political lobbies and religiously based public affairs organizations, reflect the basic divide between modernists and fundamentalists, a cultural realignment frequently referred to as the modern 'culture war'. On the fundamentalist side, the basic orientation of special agenda groups is a commitment to the 'principle that law and public policy in our country should be in harmony with the fundamental biblical principles of the Judeo-Christian civilization'.[32]

In stark contrast to fundamentalists' desire to 'restore traditional moral and spiritual values' in American families, government, schools and mass media, the United States has over the last decades not only witnessed growing secularization of public life and culture, but has also been subject to a growing pluralism of religious denominations, churches, sects and groupings. In partial response, the legal system, led by the Supreme Court, has begun to foster an attitude of 'state neutrality' towards religions in general. Public manifestations of any religion are increasingly challenged, and often excluded from public life. This has brought the charge that government, rather than defending the equal right to practise religions, has turned against all public manifestation of religion in general. The sum total of all these, often contradictory, trends makes for a very complex picture of religion and politics in America. But the trends reveal at least that, on the one hand, religion has remained vital in American society under the predominant condition that the majority of denominations have largely accommodated themselves to modern life. On the other hand, fundamentalists of all religious faiths have become increasingly active in the course of the twentieth century, and again in recent decades, in vehement opposition to this accommodation. The profound tensions inherent in the complex processes of secularization of modern life, issuing in what fundamentalists call the doctrine of 'secular humanism', and what its proponents prefer to call a liberal, rights-based, diverse and tolerant pluralistic democratic society, thus continue to influence American politics.

Broadly speaking, two basic patterns of interaction between religion and politics have thus marked American history. In one, various religious denominations and sects have acted in their own, narrowly defined interests explicitly directed against those of other groups. These interests could be either specifically theological, or they could reflect other regional, economic, racial or ethnic interests concerning various sects. Religious struggles of Protestants against Catholics throughout the latter half of the twentieth century, as well as religious groups' defence of ethnic superiority or of certain economic groups (such as farmers or labour unions), fall within this category. With the rise of industrial capitalism, religious denominations and churches split largely along economic interests and class divisions, as well as overlapping ethnic identities. Party affiliations and their periodic 'realignments' are notoriously based on such divisions throughout American history. On the other hand, some religions would struggle for the identity of America as the embodiment of certain values, often equating America's basic political values with those of religious faith. Thus, more 'radical' religious groups would fight for the abolition of slavery or racial discrimination, the equality of women, or even general public morality in the name of the American Political Creed based on divine law. In other words, religions would intervene in the public sphere either to defend their own specific group interests, or to fight for values perceived to be universal in both a religious and a political sense. The difference between these two broadly conceived types of religious politics touches upon basic questions of the nature of democratic republicanism. In fact, these two ways of religious politics, i.e., public involvement for exclusive *particular* or all-inclusive *universal* interests and values, amount to two fundamentally opposed perceptions of the role of religion in the American republic. It is probably not coincidental that both of these views were articulated at the beginning of American political history, attesting to the continuity and persistence of the problems. Rather than assessing the significance of religion exclusively in terms of processes of modernization and secularization, these theories focus on the role and function of religion in *republican* government and society.

RELIGION IN A MODERN DEMOCRATIC REPUBLIC: TWO THEORIES

As initially indicated, the place of religion in American politics has since the constitutional founding been conceived in two ways fundamentally opposed to each other. It pays to focus upon these two conceptions since they are still rival forces active in contemporary American politics. These theories both address the *normative* function of religion in democracy (i.e., what the role of religion ought to be), and provide a standard by which the *actual history* of religion in American democracy may be understood. Both are still present today in the ongoing 'culture war' between the *fundamentalists* of various religious denominations and the more 'liberal' and secular mainstream of American political and popular culture.

One view regards religion as the moral and cultural mainstay of modern democracy and its civil society. It maintains that in a liberal democracy, based on private freedoms, private morality must necessarily support public morality, or the distinct virtues of democratic citizenship. Within the framework of a separation of Church and state, private religion serves as the most influential force in the formation of private morality. Consequently, private religion becomes the breeding ground for public and political standards of conduct. Pre-political and voluntary religious communities constitute the training grounds for political community spirit. Thus, even a system of avowedly secular politics ultimately is reliant upon a religious society. The view that the 'American Creed' is a distinct fusion of its pre-political religious roots and its political, constitutional form in a uniquely American 'political religion' is a national variant of this first thesis. The American Creed claims that in the singular case of the American democracy, religion and popular government have fused into one cultural foundation. But regardless of whether religion remains private, or religious sects have fused with a unifying public, political religion or creed, the crucial role of religion as source and support for public morality is maintained. As such, religion is also the single most important source of cultural and social unity and harmony.

The second, rival thesis about religion in American democracy denies it this fundamental public function. Instead, it relegates various religious denominations to the status of 'factions' or interest-groups which, like all such groups, act upon their own self-interest 'adverse' to the interest of others as well as the common good. Consequently, no one of these religious factions is relied upon to support and sustain universal standards of public morals. Such standards are instead viewed to be grounded in a secular, political capacity or 'virtue' of self-government, based on a rational view of individual self-interest together with the 'permanent and aggregate interests of the community'.[33] In contrast, religious factions must be prevented from forming a potentially oppressive 'majority faction' by their proliferation in a large, 'extended' republic. Just as with other forms of freedom, religious liberty is mainly protected by religious diversity and the mutual counterbalancing of innumerable religious sects.

The first thesis of religion as the necessary prerequisite of democracy was advocated by President George Washington in his Farewell Address and elaborated most famously by Alexis de Tocqueville in his *Democracy in America*. In contemporary America, it is still defended by a host of religiously inclined 'communitarian' critics of modern liberal democracy.[34] It even echoes in politically active fundamentalist calls for a 'Christian nation'. According to Washington, 'religion and morality are indispensable supports' of political 'prosperity'.[35] If morality is indeed 'a necessary spring of popular government', and morality cannot be maintained without religion, then a wall of separation between 'private and public felicity' cannot be maintained without detriment to democracy.[36] Clearly, this view of the fundamental importance of religion and its inducements to virtuous conduct and character was inherited from traditional doctrines of republicanism. While classic republicanism and its primarily Roman sources insisted upon its own 'political' virtues, derived from love of country and friendship with one's fellow citizens, modern Christian republicans saw no basic problem in adapting Protestant Christianity to the requirements of political republicanism. This disposition was epitomized in the early stages of the American Revolution by Samuel Adams' call for an American 'Christian Sparta'.[37] According to this view, religious education and practices would be of basic political value even if religious sects were essentially private organizations and concerns. Private morality rooted in religious faith is the prerequisite of public republican virtue and self-government.

This view of the supporting role of religion for popular sovereignty was both normatively affirmed and empirically observed by Alexis de Tocqueville during the 1830s. Religion was crucial for democracy because it helped prevent its worst tendency, extreme individualism. Born of the belief in individual equality, individualism for Tocqueville was the strong proclivity for individuals to withdraw from involvement in and interaction with fellow citizens in society. Equality of condition leads men to the 'erroneous judgment' that they 'owe nothing to any man, they expect nothing from any man; they acquire the habit of always considering themselves as standing alone, and they are apt to imagine that their whole destiny is in their own hands'.[38] This attitude could lead men, 'living apart', to be 'as a stranger to the fate of all the rest; his children and his private friends constitute to him the whole of mankind'.[39] Men are divorced from their fellow citizens, and while he still has his family, 'he may be said … to have lost his country'.[40] According to this view, religion serves to combat this politically destructive tendency of democracy by the simple means of teaching the community of all men in the eyes of God, and the superiority of God (and eternal life after individual death), together with all of his creation. Religion, in other words, elevates individuals above their own private needs and wants, their petty daily material desires and passion, by making them aware of the value of eternity and the larger community of their fellow citizens and human beings as God's creatures. Understood in these terms, religion is viewed not as a cultural artifact, but a human need rooted in human nature required to combat another human proclivity adverse to community, especially in a community of free, self-governing men and women. Human nature decrees that religion is necessary to sustain free, democratic nations. The 'discharge of political duties' and the 'care to attend to public affairs' will, without the basic immaterial and transcendent perspective of religion, appear nothing but a 'troublesome impediment' to the individual isolated in his circle of friends and to private aspirations for material advancement.[41]

The second thesis of the role and function of religion was first advanced most prominently by James Madison in *Federalist*, number 10. Madison argued that a free people, even if united for the purpose of justice and protection of rights, would inevitably produce a society of factions. The latter are groups, either a minority or majority of the whole, motivated by some 'common impulse' of passion or interest, adverse to the rights of other citizens or the common interest. Madison's view of general human nature is such that he assumes men's different interests and passions to 'inflame them with mutual animosity' and dispose them not to cooperate for the common good, but instead 'vex and oppress each other'.[42] Indeed, 'a zeal for different opinions concerning religion' is merely one of many causes dividing men into such hostile factions. Given these human tendencies in free society, Madison insists, contrary to the proponents of the public role of religion, that, 'we well know that neither moral nor religious motives can be relied on as an adequate control' of such factious proclivities.[43]

Instead, it is the 'extent and proper structure' of the Union, which will prevent religious oppression by a majority faction. Without going into the details of Madison's representative republic, it is the variety and great number of parties and religious sects that will guarantee religious liberty. Thus, 'the variety of sects dispersed over the entire face' of the nation will prevent a religious sect which has 'degenerated into a political faction' from destroying natural freedoms, including the freedom of conscience.[44] Because of the latter freedom, religion is 'wholly exempt' from the power and cognizance of Civil Society. In his argument against the legal and political establishment of religion in Virginia, Madison not only defends the '*equal* title to the free exercise of Religion according to the dictates of conscience' which would be destroyed by arming Christian religion 'with the sanctions of a law'.[45] He in addition argues that civil magistrates may not 'employ Religion as an engine of Civil policy'.[46] Such would be 'an unhallowed perversion of the means of salvation'.[47] Religion being 'wholly exempt from the cognizance of Civil Society' thus implies not only the prohibition of the political establishment of, but any kind of political *utilization* of, religion. This would include the use of religion for the purpose of instilling republican virtues, attitudes or public morality.

JUDICIAL 'INCONSISTENCY': THE RIVALRY BETWEEN SEPARATION AND ACCOMMODATION

Religion as the private source of republican public morality and politics, requiring a certain measure of political 'accommodation' to the needs of religion? Or, to the contrary, the complete prohibition of religion as any 'engine of civil policy', calling for 'strict separation' of Church and state by governments and courts? Until well into the first half of the twentieth century, American society, backed mainly by predominant public opinion rather than decisions of the Supreme Court, largely subscribed to the first version of religion's public role. Since World War II, however, Supreme Court decisions mirroring wider changes in an increasingly secular and pluralistic society have increasingly affirmed, but not decisively or conclusively decided upon, the notion of the 'secular character of the state'.[48] As pointed out, the development of the basic struggle between religious modernists and fundamentalists points back to the late nineteenth century. It includes famous fundamentalist setbacks, like the repeal of national Prohibition by constitutional amendment in 1933, as well as the 1925 Scopes trial over the teaching of evolution. The struggle was undoubtedly rejuvenated by rapidly accelerating secularization and commercial-ization of society after World War II. In addition, however, the changing attitude of the Supreme Court since the late 1940s contributed its part to the recent revival of political evangelism. But today, the more precise meaning and implications of the proper relation between Church and state in the context of the unchallenged principle of their 'separation' still has not been settled. In this specific sense, it can certainly be claimed that the 'religious question' is still very much at the centre of modern American democracy. The 'inconsistency' noted in a series of recent Supreme Court cases attests to this fact.

Regarding constitutional standards and their political implications, the meaning of the separation of Church and state, expressed in the First Amend-ment's prohibition of laws establishing a religion, or its free exercise, was left unclear by the fact that originally it applied to Congress only, and not the states. Where they survived from colonial times, state establishment of religions was not finally abolished until a few decades into the nineteenth century.[49] The Northwest Ordinance of 1787 endorses religious instruction as a goal of government policy. It was not until 1940 that the Supreme Court decided to apply the First Amendment's religion clauses to the states by incorporating them under the Fourteenth Amendment protection against state governments (*Cantwell* v. *Connecticut*).[50] The 1947 case of *Everson* v. *Board of Education* is generally said to have been the 'turning point' towards strict separationism. It established the principle that 'Neither a state nor the federal government can pass laws which aid one religion, aid all religion or prefer one religion over another'.[51] In 1948, in *McCollum* v. *Board of Education*, teaching by religious organizations offering 30 minutes a week of religious instruction in public schools during normal hours was held to be unconstitutional. Everson was confirmed and established the principle that a 'wall of separation' between Church and state 'must be kept high and impregnable'.[52]

Over the next decades, the Supreme Court continued the trend towards establishing a 'secular public sphere' devoid of religious influences. In 1962, in *Engel* v. *Vitale*, the Court declared government-written prayers in public schools to be unconstitutional. A year later, reading the Bible in public schools as a devotional exercise was deemed unconstitutional (*Abington Township School*

Dist. v. *Schempp*). In 1968, an Arkansas statute prohibiting the teaching of theories of evolution was held unconstitutional. Programmes of public aid to private religious schools were banned in 1971. In the same year, the case of *Lemon* v. *Kurtzmann* established the so-called Lemon test, a set of criteria required to pass the Establishment Clause muster: 'First, the statute must have a secular legislative purpose; second, its principal or primary effect must be one that neither advances nor inhibits religion; finally, the statute must not foster "an excessive entanglement with religion"'.[53] This implied that the Establishment Clause of the First Amendment was written, not to protect religion from the state, but to further the 'secular legislative purposes' of the state. In 1980, a Kentucky law allowing the posting of the Ten Commandments in public schools was held unconstitutional. An Alabama statute setting aside daily periods of silence for meditation or voluntary prayer in public schools was banned in 1985. In 1987, the Supreme Court in *Edwards* v. *Aguillard* eliminated a Louisiana statute requiring the teaching of both creation science and evolution.

Despite this new trend towards secularization of the public realm and 'strict separationism', the Court, in other rulings, has also ignored its own Lemon criteria and continued to judge according to the standards of accommodationism of religious practices involving governments. For instance, in 1952 (*Zorach* v. *Clauson*) the Court declared constitutional the practice of 'release time' for religious education in New York City. It endorsed Sunday closing laws in 1961. In 1968, New York was allowed to continue providing secular textbooks to parochial students. State tax exemptions for religious property were upheld in 1970. The motto 'In God we Trust' on government coinage was held to be constitutional, as were government-paid chaplains in the military. In 1988, federal funds were allowed for religious organization promoting government-sponsored programmes promoting chastity among teenagers.[54] In 1984, a city government was allowed to erect city-sponsored Christmas displays. The displays were declared constitutional because their advancement of religion was seen to be 'indirect, remote and incidental', and their main purpose was said to be engendering 'a friendly community spirit' in tune with the season.[55] Prayers at the opening of legislative sessions were held constitutional because of their 'unambiguous and unbroken history of more than 200 years', which had made them 'part of the fabric of our society'.[56]

Over the last decades it became clear that the disposition of the Supreme Court was indeed inconsistent: it attempted simultaneously to continue the age-old 'traditions', providing religious support for American government and its political creed, while also trying to live up[57] to the new religious pluralism of modern America by limiting government to purely secular purposes. As noted above, in some decisions the Court went so far as to assert that certain religious practices were justified so long as they conformed with the traditions of the American 'civil religion'. Such practices would in effect have resembled the official 'establishment' of a (civil) religion as criterion for the behaviour of all other, 'private' religious practices. In a 1981 decision, Justice Byron White

revealed the court's inability to decide once and for all between 'accommodationism' and 'strict separationism', when he wrote that 'we are divided
among ourselves, perhaps reflecting the different views on this subject of the
people in this country'.[58] Justice Powell admitted that 'our decisions in this area
... draw lines that often must seem arbitrary'.[59] Justice White was correct in
pointing to the differences in views among the American people. These
differences were beginning to be embedded in party politics as well. Polling data
of the 1996 presidential election indicated that the *core* of the Democratic Party
had become 'secular, made up of nonreligious voters and religious "modernists."
In sharp contrast, the core of the Republican Party is made up of religious
traditionalists who are strongly pro-life, especially compared to their modernist
counterparts.' Accordingly, it could be argued that party politics in presidential
contests have 'become referendums on values and religious beliefs'.[60]

RELIGION AND THE ACCOMMODATION OF DIVISION

In a manner of speaking, American religions have thus survived the process of
modernization and secularization. Mainstream, middle-class religious denominations ranging from Christian Protestantisms and Catholicisms to Judaisms,
constituting the majority of the population, have done so largely by 'accommodating to the spirit of the times'.[61] Mainstream religion has clearly been
'secularized' and supports the goals and aspirations of a predominantly
a-religious modern society. America's religious mainstream, although still
identifying itself in terms of a 'Judeo-Christian' tradition, has also adopted the
values of tolerance and openness towards the expanding religious, cultural and
ethnic diversity or pluralism of the modern United States, denominations
themselves have become less important as all-encompassing communities and
sources of individual identity. Instead, frequently interdenominational religious
interest groups, politically pursuing specific issues and goals, have proliferated.
Here, again, religions follow the general trend: American politics as a whole has
moved away from being centred on strong, coherent political parties to the
politics of 'single-issues' and 'special-agenda' groups.
    But while mainstream religions have largely accommodated themselves to a
predominantly secular society, religious fervour has moved to a minority of
largely anti-modernist sects consisting of rapidly growing evangelists, born-
again Christians and fundamentalists of various non-Christian denominations.
Hence, instead of traditional hostilities and cleavages between various non-
Christian, Christian and Jewish denominations, sects or churches, religions
today are severed by interdenominational divisions reflecting their modernistic
orientation or their religious and social fundamentalism. In tune with this basic
division, the politically most prominent phenomena of recent religious political
involvement have been Jerry Falwell's 'Moral Majority' and its successor
Christian Coalition under one-time presidential candidate Pat Robertson, and

its participation in the Republican Party. But, the recent fate of this 'right-wing' of the Republican Party also manifests the dilemma of the fundamentalists: Republican party leaders have used evangelical fundamentalist voting support without turning their social and religious goals into concrete legislation. In the eyes of fundamentalist leaders, the 'culture war' over the American collective identity has been lost. Demands for a separate, third party of their own have become frequent, but hardly more feasible. Much of the religious fundamentalist activism has moved from a national to the local or state level. Here the issues of 'family values', community morality, the content of education, attitudes towards gays, as well as the issue of abortion will continue to be pursued with varying intensity. Here limited victories are possible: as recently as autumn 1999, the Kansas state-elected Board of Education voted to eliminate the testing of theories of evolution on mandatory state tests. This measure in effect supports the agenda of Christian fundamentalists by overtly discouraging the teaching of theories of evolution in Kansas schools.[62]

Significantly, then, in recent history two different, albeit related modes of religious politics were enacted on the stage of American politics. First, the Southern Christian Leadership Conference under the leadership of Martin Luther King, Jr, largely dominated the politics of the late 1950s and early 1960s. Affirming the divine roots of American values of equal individual rights to freedom, King and his supporters expressed the dual universality of human rights and dignity, in both American constitutional law and individual faith. (The affirmation of these American values did not preclude a critique of, and political attack upon, the social and economic injustices of the realities of American life.) It can be claimed that King's and the Civil Rights Movement's near-universal appeal was less based on its (narrower) Baptist articles of faith than on a broader and more popular (secularized) faith in human rights. Nonetheless, that fact does not alter its essentially universal appeal, both political and religious. The universal dimension of its ideals helped it transcend party politics, although it was mainly backed by the liberal branches of both Democratic and Republican parties.

The Civil Rights Movement also was backed by the Fourteenth Amendment of the Constitution in its militant opposition to many (southern) state laws. Public sentiment, not exclusively limited to the northern states, had also shifted in its favour. Subsequently, however, as some observers have pointed out, it is of great political as well as cultural significance that American liberalism has essentially abandoned any interest in the Civil Rights Movement's unique blend of religious politics.[63] The Moral Majority of fundamentalist Christians, on the other hand, while also concerned with the basic American identity as a community of values, interpret those values more narrowly in terms of literal biblical commands and imperatives inaccessible to most constituents of the American 'community'. Its attacks upon 'secular humanism' bespeak an image of human freedom closer to the old-testament Protestantism of early, colonial America than to the expansion of equal rights dominating American history since then. Christian and other fundamentalists, rather than confronting American injustices with American political ideals inherent in its founding documents, instead confronts its alleged moral disintegration with the standards of what has long ceased to be a shared religious faith. The two-party system, and the fundamentalist plan to dominate the policy platform of the Republicans, also did not work in their favour. The complex federal structure of the United States government will undoubtedly sustain evangelical policies in many locales. Nationally, though, the gulf between today's fundamentalists and American social and economic realities is, if anything, widening.

To return to the modernization theme, America is thus 'exceptionalist' in two different ways. For one, here, unlike in the other modern European democracies, a measurable number of survivors of pre-modern religions, like the evangelical and Catholic fundamentalists, and, on a much smaller scale, forms of Jewish orthodoxy, persist in politically fighting the trends of modern secularism. But these groups, however large numerically, cannot be said to have 'survived' modernism. On the other hand, here, also unlike in most other modern democracies, religious groups like the Civil Rights Movement could view basic American political values as divinely inspired, or at least compatible with the dicta of divinely inspired faith. Both modes of religious politics can lead to religiously inspired, and either exclusive or inclusive, nationalism. Ironically, with the continuing secularization of American society both such faiths will be ever more difficult to sustain.

In conclusion, we can assume that in the immediate future American religions will continue to be involved in politics, be it local or national, because both of these fundamentally different perspectives on America have endured. Both, despite their vast differences, address the same question: by attempting to establish the precise meaning of 'separation of Church and state', protagonists are essentially trying to establish the fundamental place of religion in modern democracy. Which of the basic theories – Madison's or Washington's, or the Supreme Court's strict separationism and a purely secular state, or accommodationism and religion's support of republican citizenship, perhaps in the form of the American civil religion – will prove to be possible or necessary under modern circumstances? In the 1914 edition of his massive study of late nineteenth-century America, James Bryce once again phrased the question in a manner reminiscent of Tocqueville in the 1830s. He asked whether 'morality with religion for its sanction' which had hitherto been the basis of free government could indeed be replaced by a regime without religious faith and instead based exclusively on 'custom, sympathy', and 'insight into the self-interest intrinsic to orderly self-government, rule of law and restraint'.[64] Bryce wondered whether a society of commerce and 'a people consumed by a feverish activity', living in a 'huge but delicate fabric of laws and commerce and social institutions' could survive if its traditional foundations would 'crumble away'.[65] He allowed that 'history cannot answer this question'.[66] Neither, by all accounts, can contemporary Americans.

NOTES

1. Kenneth D. Wald, 'Social Change and Political Response: The Silent Religious Cleavage in North America', in George Moyser (ed.), *Politics and Religion in the Modern World* (London and New York: Routledge, 1991).
2. Statistics have long shown that modern Americans in greater numbers than citizens of most European democracies show faith in God, attend religious services and consider religion more important in their lives. Cf. the numbers in Seymour Martin Lipset, *American Exceptionalism* (New York: W.W. Norton, 1996), pp. 61 ff.
3. The young Abraham Lincoln referred to reverence for the law as the 'political religion of the nation'. Cf. The Address to the Young Men's Lyceum of Springfield, Illinois, in *Selected Speeches and Writings of Abraham Lincoln* (New York: The Library of America, 1992).
4. Wald, 'Social Change and Political Response', p. 252.
5. Cited by Lipset, *American Exceptionalism*, p. 84.
6. But two modern Supreme Court decisions have made it very difficult to clearly separate religion from American civil religion. In *Marsh* v. *Chambers* (1983) and *Stein* v. *Plainwell Community Schools* (1987) the Court for the first time mentions 'the American civil religion' as the standard by which religious invocations and benedictions on public occasions are judged. They are allowed if they do not 'go beyond' that civil religion and preserve 'the substance of the principle of equal liberty of conscience'. But aside from the problem of defining precisely the content of civil religion, this use of a rather amorphous term to 'authenticate' religious symbols and ceremonies in public life raises the question of whether the Court isn't unwittingly establishing a public religion antithetical to the establishment clause. Cf. Arlin M. Adams and Charles J. Emmerich, *A Nation Dedicated to Religious Liberty: the Constitutional Heritage of the Religion Clauses* (Philadelphia, PA: University of Pennsylvania Press, 1990), pp. 83–7.
7. The First Amendment of the United States Constitution states that 'Congress shall make no law respecting an establishment of religion, or prohibiting the free exercise thereof.' Article VI of the Constitution also states that 'no religious Test shall ever be required as a Qualification to office or public Trust under the United States'. However, the prohibitions of the First Amendment did not initially apply to the state governments, see below.
8. This is already substantiated by Tocqueville, who, when questioning 'faithful of all communions', found that 'they all agreed with each other except about details; all thought that the main reason for the quiet sway of religion over their country was the complete separation of church and state'. Quoted in Leonard W. Levy, *The Establishment Clause* (Chapel Hill, NJ: The University of North Carolina Press, 1994), p. 246.
9. Garry Wills, *Under God, Religion and American Politics* (New York: Simon & Schuster, 1990), p. 383.
10. Lipset, *American Exceptionalism*, p. 19.
11. Ibid., p. 26.
12. Ibid., pp. 20, 27.
13. Ibid., p. 21. For the signal importance of the battle between the authority of organized church and individual 'liberty of conscience', cf. Richard L. Bushman, *From Puritan to Yankee* (New York: W.W. Norton, 1967).
14. Lipset, *American Exceptionalism*, p. 60.
15. Ibid., p. 289.
16. Ibid., p. 33.
17. But while community involvement 'in the broader sense of a relationship between the faithful and the larger community is a regular … part' of organized religion, it constitutes 'a quite small part' of almost all religions. Participation inside religious communities is much higher. Cf. Robert Booth Fowler, 'Religion and the Escape from Liberal Individualism', in Charles W. Dunn (ed.), *Religion in American Politics* (Washington, DC: Congressional Quarterly Press, 1989), p. 46.
18. Cf. Wald, 'Social Change and Political Response', and Lipset, *American Exceptionalism*, p. 62.
19. Michael Schudson, *The Good Citizen: A History of American Civic Life* (New York: Free Press, 1998), p. 93.
20. Ibid.
21. Cf. Rogers M. Smith, *Civic Ideals* (New Haven, CT: Yale University Press, 1997), p. 247.
22. One can make this claim even about the 'Great Awakening' and its influence on the American

Revolution. Cf. Gordon S. Wood, *The Creation of the American Republic, 1776–1787* (New York: W.W. Norton, 1969).

23. The most massive immigration of Catholics was between the 1830s and 1850s, at which point over 5 million had immigrated. Before 1850, half of the Catholic immigrants were Irish. In the late 1830s, there were about 15,000 Jews in the United States. Through German Jewish immigration by the 1880s, the number had increased to 300,000, and to over 4 million by the 1920s.

24. Mainline Protestant churches, including such denominations as Episcopalians, Presbyterians, Methodists, wings of the Lutherans and Baptists, as well as Congregational and Unitarian denominations, are said to comprise around 33 per cent of church members today. Evangelical or 'fundamentalist' Protestants have increased their share to over 25 per cent of the Christian population. Today Jews constitute about 2–3 per cent of the entire adult population. Significantly, American religious pluralism today includes, since the late 1980s, over 4 million Muslims, with over 600 mosques or Islamic centres nationwide. This makes Muslims larger than the Episcopal Church, the Presbyterian Church and the United Church of Christ. In the 1990s, Hindus grew close to a million members, with over 40 temples. In addition, well over 200 contending denominations, mostly Christians, have been identified in the United States. That does not include about 1,200 identifiable groups categorized as 'small, occult, non-Christian' sects. Cf. James Davison Hunter, *Culture Wars: The Struggle to Define America* (New York: Basic Books, 1991), pp. 72–3; also, Wald, 'Social Change and Political Response', p. 248, and Martin Marty, 'North America', in John McManners (ed.), *The Oxford Illustrated History of Christianity* (Oxford: Oxford University Press, 1992), pp. 388 ff.

25. Wald, 'Social Change and Political Response', p. 248.

26. Smith, *Civic Ideals*, p. 218.

27. Wald, 'Social Change and Political Response, p. 144.

28. Smith, *Civic Ideals*, pp. 209–12; Wald, 'Social Change and Political Response', p. 204.

29. Marty, 'North America', pp. 403, 152.

30. Donald C. Swift, *Religion and the American Experience* (New York: M.E. Sharpe, 1998), p. 150.

31. Ibid., pp. 216ff., also Marty, 'North America', p. 410.

32. Hunter, *Culture Wars*, pp. 90–1.

33. Clinton Rossiter (ed.), *Federalist Papers* (Denver, CO: Mentor Books, 1999), 35, 10.

34. Cf. Robert N. Bellah *et al.*, *Habits of the Heart* (New York: Harper and Row, 1985).

35. Matthew Spalding, *A Sacred Union of Citizens* (New York: Rowman and Littlefield, 1996), Farewell Address, p. 183.

36. Ibid.

37. Cf. Wood, *Creation of the American Republic*, pp. 118, 421.

38. Tocqueville, *Democracy in America*, vol. 2 (New York: Vintage Books, 1990), p. 99.

39. Ibid., p. 318.

40. Ibid.

41. Ibid., p. 141.

42. James Madison, *Federalist*, 10 (New York: Mentor, 1961), p. 79.

43. Ibid., p. 81.

44. Ibid., p. 84.

45. 'Memorial and Remonstrance', 1785, in Marvin Meyers (ed.), *James Madison* (New York: Bobbs-Merrill Co.), p. 9.

46. Ibid., p. 11.

47. Ibid.

48. Cf. Wald, 'Social Change and Political Response', p. 262.

49. Seven of the thirteen colonies had established churches, and even after independence states like New Hampshire, Connecticut and Massachusetts did not relinquish their religious establishments until 1818, 1819 and 1833 respectively. Marty, 'North America', p. 390. Many early state constitutions required religious tests for holding office. Some specifically barred Jews and Catholics from office. Eight states barred atheists from office until 1880. As late as 1912, New Hampshire voters refused to delete 'Christian' from requirements for office holders. Cf. Swift, *Religion and the American Experience*, p. 13, and Dunn, *Religion in American Politics*, p. xv.

50. Ibid., p. 7.

51. Hunter, *Culture Wars*, p. 267.
52. Ibid.
53. Cited in Stephen L. Carter, *The Culture of Disbelief* (New York: Doubleday, 1993), p. 110.
54. Hunter, *Culture Wars*, p. 268.
55. Carter, *Culture of Disbelief*, p. 114.
56. Ibid., p. 115.
57. Cf. note 6 above.
58. James Reichley, 'Religion and the Constitution', in Charles W. Dunn (ed.), *Religion in American Politics* (Washington, DC: Congressional Quarterly Press, 1989), p. 7.
59. Hunter, *Culture Wars*, p. 269.
60. Thomas B. Edsall, *Washington Post*, 22 August 1999, p. B01. Since the end of the 1980s, public opinion polls mirror the division between religious modernists and fundamentalists. The religious orthodox and cultural conservatives tend to favour accommodation, while progressives especially in secularist and Jewish communities, tend towards strict separatism. To cite some examples: asked whether strict separation of Church and state ought to be enforced, 87 per cent of academics, 85 per cent of mainline ministers and 92 per cent of liberal rabbis agreed, while only 48 per cent of conservative ministers, 28 per cent of conservative priests and 72 per cent of Orthodox rabbis disagreed. Regarding government support for the public display of religious symbols, 91 per cent of Evangelicals and 85 per cent of conservative Catholics were in favour, but amongst secularists, media elites and academics it was 68 per cent, 58 per cent and 37 per cent respectively. Cf. Hunter, *Culture Wars*, pp. 263, 264.
61. Hunter, *Culture Wars*, p. 305.
62. *Washington Post*, Saturday, 21 August 1999.
63. Cf. Carter, *Culture of Disbelief*.
64. James Bryce, *The American Commonwealth*, vol. 2 (Indianapolis, IN: Liberty Fund, 1995), p. 1396.
65. Ibid., p. 1397.
66. Ibid.

3

Religion and Politics in the United States

CORWIN SMIDT, LYMAN KELLSTEDT, JOHN GREEN
AND JAMES GUTH

Over the past two centuries, astute observers have noted the uniqueness of religion in American society. The first thing to catch Tocqueville's attention upon his arrival in the United States early in the nineteenth century was the religious character of the nation. Nor was he alone. Prominent European visitors throughout the nineteenth century almost invariably remarked about the religious nature of the American people. Even today, the religious beliefs and practices of the American people are truly unique when compared to other Western industrial societies.

Not only has the religious character of the nation been unique, but religion has played an important role in American politics since the beginning of the republic. This chapter addresses the issue of why religious factors are able to play such an important role in American politics. First, this chapter places the study of religion and politics within the broader framework of the theses of modernization and secularization that have long held a central position within modern social science thought. Second, it identifies those features of the American political system that work to enable religion to play a major role in shaping the nature of American politics. And, third, the chapter provides empirical data that reveal how religion is tied to political mobilization in American politics, particularly with regard to the role that the Christian Right played in the 1996 election.

SECULARIZATION AND MODERNIZATION THEORY

Given certain social scientific frameworks of understanding, it may seem strange or even inappropriate to address the role religion plays within American politics. Few organizing concepts have occupied a more central position in modern social science than the notion of secularization, the idea that religion is a vestige of pre-modern culture that is destined to decline in importance and, perhaps, disappear altogether in an age of science and reason.[1] According to such a framework of analysis, it is axiomatic that any 'impact' that religion may have in American politics is either spurious in nature (i.e., a function of some other underlying factor) or simply a remnant of some outmoded, and disappearing, facet of social life.

Secularization theory itself is rooted in broader understandings of the notion of modernization, generally understood as a process of social change rooted in economic growth driven by technological developments that induce change across various domains of society. Modernization theory, when applied to political development, generally equates such development with the progressive Westernization and secularization of society, with secularization being regarded as a *sine qua non* for modernization.[2] Thus, theorists of political development have frequently contended that, 'political development includes, as one of its basic processes, the secularization of polities, the progressive exclusion of religion from the political system'.[3]

However, there is relatively little evidence to support secularization theory (at least if it is defined in terms of the disappearance of religious beliefs) in the United States. Compared to patterns evident in many other Western industrialized states, Americans continue to exhibit a high level of religiosity.[4] Moreover, church membership and church attendance in the United States have remained relatively stable over the last 50 years. For example, 41 per cent of Americans in 1939 reported attending church in the last seven days, while 40 per cent reported doing so in 1990. It is true that Mainline Protestant denominations in the United States have experienced a significant and much-publicized decline in membership and support, but those losses have been balanced, to a large degree, by increases in the membership of Evangelical Protestant denominations. There is evidence that many American 'baby boomers' who dropped out of organized religion in the 1960s are beginning to search for new spiritual homes, whether in the relatively vibrant Evangelical denominations, in cults, in Asian religions, or in New Age spirituality.[5] Such patterns of relative stability are evident in Table 3.1.

How is it, then, that religion continues to exhibit so much vitality in the United States generally and plays such an important role in American politics specifically? While the answer to the former question moves well beyond the scope of this paper, several contributing factors will be identified below, and the answer to the latter question also will be addressed more fully below. Obviously, for religion to play a continuing important role in American politics, there must be some presence of religious vitality evident within at least certain segments of American society. However, even the presence of such religious vitality does not, in and of itself, guarantee that religion would play an important role in American politics. Other factors must be present as well. Consequently, it is the presence of certain distinctive features within the American political system, coupled with

Table 3.1:
Religious patterns in the United States over time, %

Year	Church membership	Church attendance
1990	X	40
1984	68	40
1978	X	41
1977	70	41
1967	X	43
1965	73	X
1957	X	47
1952	72	X
1950	X	39
1939	X	41

Sources: *Emerging Trends*, published by the Princeton Religious Research Center, Vol. 6, No.10, December (1984); 'American: Land of the Faithful', *Public Perspective*, Nov./Dec. (1990), p. 96.

unique developments in American society, that have enabled religion to play an important role in American politics.

CHARACTERISTICS OF THE AMERICAN POLITICAL SYSTEM

Several distinctive features of the American political system have contributed to the ability of religious forces within American society to play a major role in American politics. These features should be viewed primarily as necessary, though not sufficient, conditions for religion to play a major political role in American life. In other words, their presence enables religion to play such a role, but they do not guarantee that religion will inevitably be a major determinative factor continually shaping and influencing American politics.

Disestablishment and Religious Liberty

Historically, the European idea of the proper relationship between Church and state has been that of the employment of a state Church. The idea undergirding the practice was that established churches were to reflect, as well as foster, the unity of the people. Established churches provided the state with some important benefits, while established churches, in exchange received certain social and economic benefits.

The First Amendment to the United States Constitution, however, prohibits Congress from establishing a state Church, while at the same time it protects the free exercise of religion. This proscription has had profound implications for the institutional forms of religion found in the United States. While the free exercise of religion is protected in general, there is no protection for any particular religious organization.

Several consequences flow from this proscription. Certainly, many religious institutions have had to be active proselytizers in order to survive. Existing in a 'free-market' system, religious institutions had to become 'innovators' in order to meet the changing religious demands of the people. With innovations have come, in part, multiple religious denominational structures, worship styles, doctrinal positions and 'religious specialization'. Different religious institutions appeal to, and direct their efforts at, different segments of the market and capture different market shares. The consequence has been that religious life is less uniform, but more embedded, within American life than in those European countries that chose to employ established churches.

As a result, religion in American public life does not typically express the culture of American society as a whole. Rather, it tends to be more the particular expression of its varied subcultures. Accordingly, it is better understood as 'the vital expression' of different social groups, as religion constitutes 'a fundamental category of identity and association' within American life.[6]

Federalism

In contrast to unitary forms of government, the American constitution also divides the power granted to governmental institutions between different levels of government. Federalism provides multiple arenas and contexts within which political forces can seek to foster or resist legislative change. Failure to obtain one's legislative goals at one level of government (e.g., the national level) does not preclude success at a different level (e.g., the state level), while success in some lower, more local arena of government may encourage efforts to secure such results at some higher level of government.

One important consequence of this constitutional provision is that the decentralization of certain political powers provides the more numerous, but generally smaller and more localized, religious bodies that have emerged as a result of disestablishment (and through immigration as discussed below) greater opportunities and abilities to shape legislative provisions. In the United States, local governmental units continue to have political significance and important levels of autonomy with regard to a variety of issues about which many Americans care deeply. As a result, there frequently is a powerful incentive for political mobilization at the local level.

Religious groups that are small in absolute numbers (at least relative to the population size of the nation as a whole) and concentrated in only a few states or locales are likely by themselves to have little ability to shape legislation nationally. But, such a group may well be able to have some impact on legislation drafted at a state or local level of government. Thus, federalism provides religious groups, despite their limited size and possible geographical concentration, with multiple arenas within which they may experience the opportunity and ability to shape legislative provisions.

The Two-Party System

While the American constitution does not specifically provide for a two-party system, its electoral laws foster the emergence of such a partisan arrangement. Several important consequences flow from the single-member, 'winner-take-all' arrangements of American electoral laws. First, highly distinctive, religiously based parties are very unlikely to be competitive in electoral contests. Since proportional representation does not operate, there is little incentive, at least in the long run, for such religiously based parties to compete in elections. Whereas religiously based parties have emerged, competed, governed and continue to exist within many European political systems (e.g., the Christian Democratic parties), they have never been major players within the American party system.

Nevertheless, while American electoral laws tend to 'discourage' the formations of *religious political parties*, they do serve to enhance the political power of religious groups. Since electoral office is won simply by securing the most votes, any group that can provide a political party with a margin of victory is highly prized. Thus, political parties may well court religious groups in efforts to secure their support.

As the mobilization of a group's voters in support of the party is highly valued by party leaders, political activists within the group seek to extract certain pledges from the party in exchange for their support and/or efforts at politically mobilizing the group in support of the party. Given only two major political parties, the mobilization of a particular group on behalf of one party simultaneously works to the disadvantage of the opposing party. As a result, a political party may make clear overtures to such a group to secure their allegiance, promising certain legislative efforts or programmes, should they be elected to office.

Nevertheless, given the two-party system, religious groups, if they seek to be active in politics, are effectively limited in their partisan choices. Different religious groups can thereby come to *support different parties* (e.g., either the Democratic or Republican Party) on the basis of taking differing religious positions with regard to the same specific political issue under debate. At the same time, with only two parties, different religious groups can also come to *support the same party* for different religious reasons on the basis of different political issues that may be differentially salient to such religious groups.

'Weak' Political Parties

Finally, despite this two-party system, American elections are more 'candidate centred' than those in most other political systems. Many democratic systems are 'party centred', meaning that parties, not candidates, are the dynamic element in a campaign. In 'party-centred' systems, parties control nearly all the resources candidates desire and most of the sanctions they fear. In the American system, however, parties offer only some of the resources that candidates desire and control few, if any, sanctions they seek to avoid. Voters, not parties, generally choose the party's candidate for the general election in political primaries. Candidates receive only a small proportion of the financial resources needed for the election campaign from the party. As a result, candidates must raise the vast majority of their funds from individuals and organized groups. Candidates who win the general election campaign have relatively few sanctions to fear from the party once in office. All these features of the American electoral system work to create a set of incentives that link candidates and legislators more closely to their local constituency and supporters than to the national party.

CHARACTERISTICS OF AMERICA'S SOCIAL SYSTEM

While the above features of the American political system help to facilitate the influence religion can play in shaping American politics, they do not guarantee that religion will play such an influence. Obviously, even with such features present in the American political system, religion must be vital to sizable segments of the population before it can come to play some role in shaping the political attitudes and behaviour of citizens within a democratic republic. What, then, has contributed to the continuing existence of religious vitality in the American setting? Here we wish to identify several important ingredients. While this listing may not be inclusive of all such ingredients, it does capture those that have been most important in sustaining religious vitality in the United States.

Immigration

The United States has long been a pluralistic society, as it is overwhelmingly a nation of immigrants. Wave after wave of immigrants have arrived on its shores. Whereas many of these initial waves brought a variety of Protestants (and some Catholics) from Western Europe, subsequent waves in the late nineteenth century brought larger numbers of Catholics and Jews from central and southern Europe, and more recent waves have brought Hispanic Catholics, Asian Buddhists, Muslims, and others from various parts of the world. Differences in nationalities, native language, religious beliefs, cultural practices and personal values expanded immensely through these waves of immigration. Such diversity, particularly in its earlier waves, generated political conflicts and prompted considerable efforts, particularly at the state and local level, to legislate certain patterns of behavioural conformity (e.g., the prohibition of alcohol consumption, Sunday closing laws, mandatory English language instruction in the public schools).

Among every major immigrant group, it has been the parish, the congregation, the shul or the mosque that has served as the place where, after immigrating, people with similar backgrounds regroup. Accordingly, the church (or synagogue or mosque) has become the central institution among almost every major immigrant group. It was the church that frequently served as the vehicle by which ethnic-group allegiance was organized, and the clergy of such churches saw their responsibilities not only in terms of maintaining the religious faith of their parishioners, but in terms of preserving the ethnoculture of the community as well.[7]

In fact, churches helped to define and establish ethnic identity in America. Through immigration, the nature of the 'other' changed, and so too, not surprisingly, did the 'we'. Consequently, the nature of ethnic association in and around the church often broadened beyond what they had experienced in their more narrowly circumscribed society from which they departed.[8]

While the geographic and linguistic boundaries might be broadened, the religious boundaries frequently could become more narrow.[9] In fact, one's particular ethnic associations were determined in large part by the immigrant's specific religious tradition, as religion could serve as an important source of intra-ethnic group differences. For example, Dutch Calvinists and Dutch Catholics did not interact socially or form broader national associations. Dutch Calvinists and Dutch Catholics established separate institutions because they each wanted to establish religious (i.e., Christian) institutions as they each understood them, not because they each desired to establish some ethnic institutions *per se*.

The process of migration and resettlement not only altered the relationship between faith and ethnic identity through its redefinition of the boundaries of peoplehood (who was and was not to be included within the ethnic group), but such migration and resettlement tended to intensify religious reflection and commitment as well.[10] The acts of uprooting, migration and repeated resettlement sparked an 'intense interest in the religious meaning of their break with the past' as well as a 'preoccupation with the ethnical dimension of (their) faith'.[11]

Thus, religious beliefs tended to set the parameters on the new patterns of belonging that were forged after the immigrants arrived in the United States, and the process of migration and resettlement intensified the religious experience and expression of immigrants. Together, these factors helped to root religion socially and embed religious life within a variety of local social institutions that may not have necessarily functioned primarily as religious institutions, but did so secondarily (e.g., schools, ethnic associations, neighbourhood businesses, grange societies). Thus, religion was deeply rooted socially within the different ethnic subcultures that spawned through wave after wave of immigrant groups arriving on the shore of American soil.

Religious Individualism

However, these social patterns with regard to religion were somewhat later coupled with religious perspectives that valued individualized understandings of one's faith. In the American setting, democratic values have meshed over time with religious understandings to foster and forge a highly individualistic stance towards religion. Ever since the Second Great Awakening (which occurred roughly from 1803 to 1840), the dominant theology within American Protestantism (historically the dominant religious expression) has been Arminian in nature, with its emphasis upon free will, grace and unlimited hope for the conversion of all people. Thus, Arminian theology converged with values dominant within American society (e.g., those placed on personal freedom and achievement). This convergence has created what has been called the 'great tradition of the American churches', a tradition that has emphasized religious freedom, a denominational conception of the church and the voluntary basis of involvement in congregational life and activities.[12]

Various features of American religious life flow from this voluntary basis of religious involvement. Religious faith becomes more personal in nature, something freely accepted or rejected. Thus, it is not surprising that the overwhelming majority of Americans hold to strongly individualistic views on religion. Following the birth control encyclical issue by Pope Paul VI in 1968, large numbers of Catholics decided to make their own judgements on the matter and to abide by them rather than the Church. In 1987, over 80 per cent of Americans agreed with the statement 'An individual should arrive at his or her own religious beliefs independent of any churches or synagogues,'[13] while more than three-quarters of all Americans (specifically, 78 per cent; as well as 70 per cent of all churchgoers) stated that one could be a 'good' Christian or Jew without attending church or synagogue.[14]

Nevertheless, this voluntary nature of religion in the United States has also, ironically, enhanced religion's vulnerability to social influence in the American context. Though religion is voluntary, a person's religious faith can be heavily shaped by the values and identities of the social groups to which one belongs, as religious energies are largely channelled within preexisting social and cultural lines. In fact, one can argue that much of the religious vitality evident in the United States is attributable to its deep social roots. Historically, social class, ethnicity, race and region have constituted the social bases of America's faith communities.[15] And, existing denominational structures in the United States have benefited greatly from these close ties between the social and religious elements of life, as such interconnectedness has provided strong communal resources for developing and sustaining religious loyalties.

But what happens when these communal links begin to weaken and dissipate? Rising levels of education, growing opportunities for socioeconomic mobility, increasing levels of geographical mobility, growing exposure to alternative values through the diffusion of media images and messages have all helped to weaken ascriptively based group identities in the American setting. And, with this weakening of ascriptively based loyalties, the individual is further freed to engage in autonomous decision-making, thereby releasing religion, in large part, from some of its historic social moorings. As a result, believers in the United States today confront a situation quite different from previous generations. As believers are less and less bound to some inherited faith, they find themselves increasingly in a position of not only being able to 'shop around' for different religious alternatives, but being able to 'pick and choose' almost idiosyncratically among different religious beliefs, practices and traditions.

How has this loosening of religion from its historic social moorings affected religious belonging in America? Though several consequences can be identified,[16] only two will be noted here. First, given that ascriptive loyalties are playing less of a role in shaping religious communities today, religious adherence is now being forged along new communal and ideological lines. As a result, American religious pluralism is expanding in nature. Second, within existing religious traditions, there is a growing diversity in perspectives among members, as 'differences in modes of meaning and belonging within the religious communities are becoming more pronounced'.[17]

Accordingly, the switching of denominational affiliation among Americans today is 'increasingly motivated by moral culture instead of socioeconomic status',[18] as such switching is decreasingly likely to mirror upward social mobility and increasingly tied to finding church bodies that reflect one's particular religious perspective. Thus, while religious traditions may be becoming more diverse in terms of the religious perspectives held by those within that tradition, particular congregations within that same tradition may be, at the same time, becoming much more homogeneous in terms of the religious perspectives articulated by those within the congregation. With the decline of neighbourhood churches and the increasing ease of mobility, believers are more willing to travel miles to associate with a congregation of believers who adhere to the same doctrinal beliefs as they do, who favour a similar style of worship as they do, and who hold the same expectations with regard to religious commitment as they do. Thus, while the voluntary nature of religion in American life is leading to increased heterogeneity within religious traditions, there may actually be less diversity of religious perspective within particular congregations of that tradition today than was true in the past.

Churches as 'Social Precincts'

Finally, other developments within American social life have led to the weakening of the historic basis of party organizational activity within the United States and have led to the emergence of the church congregation as a highly attractive vehicle by which to mobilize voters to the polls. Historically, parties have depended upon grassroots, precinct, organizational activity grounded in the local community. However, with the decline of ethnic neighbourhoods and the emergence of residences in suburbia that have largely become 'bedroom communities', in which neighbours do not necessarily know who lives in the houses several doors down, there has been a weakening of local communal ties. As a result of this weakening of social ties based on geographical residence, the local precinct has become a more artificial creation than a reflection of some natural communal entity, thereby further weakening the organizational basis of American political parties.

In response, some political activists have come to view church congregations today as natural 'social precincts' of voters. Church congregational life remains one of the few vestiges of American social life that tends to cut across other lines of social cleavage, frequently economic in nature, that may divide Americans politically (e.g., along occupational lines, social status, gender, etc.). Given that most Americans express some religious affiliation, that approximately 40 per cent of all Americans report attending church weekly (see Table 3.1 above), and that local congregations tend to be relatively homogeneous in terms of their religious (and possibly political) perspectives, it is no wonder that political activists have viewed church congregations as natural 'hunting grounds' for particular kinds of voters, socially embedded, with distinct networks of social communication.

ILLUSTRATION: THE CHRISTIAN RIGHT[19]

The second part of this chapter turns to an analysis of how certain of these features of American social and political life come into play when one examines the role of the Christian Right in American politics. More specifically, this portion of the chapter examines the role of the Christian Right in utilizing church-based mobilization techniques as a means to accomplish their political agenda. As we shall see, using churches as a context within which politically to mobilize different segments of the American electorate is relatively common, not just among Christian Right activists, but among political activists advancing other political agendas as well. While such endeavours are also worthy of more careful analysis (e.g., the role of African-American churches in politically mobilizing its congregants), the remainder of this chapter will focus primarily upon the efforts of the Christian Right only. Although this more narrow focus captures a major component of church-based mobilization today, the reader must remember throughout the discussion that follows that the Christian Right is not alone in its efforts to utilize the church as 'a social precinct'.

While Christian Right groups have often argued among themselves as to what constitutes the most promising target audiences and the best means for activating those audiences, their electoral campaigns have, nevertheless, reached many religious people and have influenced recent national elections. They have continually experimented with church-based mobilization techniques. The pioneer organizations, such as Jerry Falwell's Moral Majority, stressed church-based techniques, especially pastoral mobilization. Clergy were the key to electoral action: they were to encourage parishioners to register, inform them where candidates stood on vital issues, and provide them with clear guidance on how to vote. As Jerry Falwell told fundamentalist clergy in 1980, 'What can you do from the pulpit? You can register people to vote. You can explain the issues to them. And you can endorse candidates, right there in church on Sunday morning.'[20]

By the late 1980s, however, Christian Right leaders and political analysts alike had concluded that this approach was relatively ineffective. Not only did most clergy shun overt electioneering, but many parishioners chose not to follow their lead, sometimes resenting the 'politicizing' of the church.[21] As a result, second-generation Christian Right groups, such as the Christian Coalition and the Family Research Council, preferred to contact religious voters without implicating clergy in professionally distasteful or 'risky' activity. The new electoral strategies emphasized the role of committed laity, who would take the lead in both church-based and more conventional tactics. Recognizing that churches were still a 'happy hunting ground' for religious conservatives, active laity within the church would place 'voter guides' inside their churches (or on cars in church parking lots) on the Sunday before the election, or employ standard political tactics used by many other interest groups (e.g., contacting voters directly through phone calls, fax messages, personal visits, or e-mail) – thereby taking advantage of the natural networks of communication among church people. Despite the clear shift in emphasis from church-based to conventional tactics, and from clergy to laity as key actors, in 1996 one could still find the Christian Right organization using each approach, singly or in combination.[22]

To assess this religious interest group mobilization in the 1996 national elections, we use data from a post-election component (N=2392) of a survey of Americans conducted by the Survey Research Center at the University of Akron and funded by the Pew Charitable Trusts. These respondents were part of a two-wave study of potential voters, interviewed first during the summer of 1996 and then immediately after the election. We address three key questions:

1. Which religious communities were most heavily targeted by interest group mobilization efforts in 1996?
2. Which mobilization techniques reached the largest audience?
3. Did Christian Right groups achieve their objectives, increasing the vote for conservative and Republican candidates and enhancing turnout among religious conservatives?

Religious Tradition and Theological Location

To simplify the inquiry, we have limited our analysis to the four major Christian traditions in the United States, namely, Evangelical Protestants, Mainline Protestants, Black Protestants and white Roman Catholics (excluding Black and Hispanic Catholics). These religious communities encompass the great majority of voters and almost all the targeted populations for both the massive Christian Right mobilization and the smaller counter-mobilization by liberal religious groups.[23] These four traditions have historically also constituted the critical religious building blocs for party coalitions. For most of the twentieth century, Evangelical Protestants have been a major component of the Democratic electorate, joined by most Roman Catholics and, since the New Deal, by most Black Protestants. Mainline Protestants, on the other hand, represented the religious core of the GOP,[24] or as the old adage had it, the 'Republican Party at prayer'.

In contemporary politics, however, these historic alignments are being reconfigured in complex ways. First, there has been some realignment of the traditions themselves. Evangelicals, who have been growing in numbers and are upwardly mobile and ideologically conservative, have become the biggest religious constituency of the GOP in recent national elections, joined by more Catholics than ever before. Conversely, the Mainline Protestant community has not only shrunk in size, but some remaining members have also drifted away from their ancestral Republican home, shaking an old religious foundation of party politics.[25] At the same time that religious traditions are en route from one partisan loyalty to another, vital cross-cutting changes are occurring *within* these same traditions. According to James Davison Hunter's vivid depiction, religious communities are being reshaped politically by 'culture wars', heated divisions over abortion, gay rights and other social issues. Mainline Protestants, Roman Catholics and even Evangelicals are dividing into competing factions, with the orthodox aligning with the Republicans, and progressives with the Democrats.[26]

We can use the insights from both perspectives on religion's changing partisan role to pinpoint the targets of interest group mobilization. To classify voters for analysis, we first placed them in a religious tradition based on denominational affiliation, and second, assigned them a theological location (we will use the terms 'orthodox', 'centrist' and 'modernist') within each tradition. Although the details of the procedure need not concern us here, we can summarize the traits of the three theological groups in each tradition: the orthodox are most committed to classic doctrinal formulations, tend to affiliate with traditional religious movements within the church and are quite active in religious life. Centrists are less orthodox on the historic theological tenets of their tradition, tend not to adopt movement affiliations, and are somewhat less active in personal and corporate religious activities. Finally, modernists reject orthodox theological formulations or even adopt heterodox beliefs, often identify with liberal religious movements and, typically (though not always), exhibit lower levels of religious involvement. However, it is important to remember that the theological location of respondents within each tradition is determined primarily by issues central to that tradition. Consequently, comparisons of theological groups should be made primarily within traditions, while those across traditions should be made with great caution. For example, by any comparable measure, Evangelical 'modernists' are probably a good bit more orthodox theologically and organizationally active than their Mainline Protestant or Catholic counterparts. Finally, as the number of Black Protestants in the post-election survey is relatively small (N=180), and as this tradition shows little evidence of theological polarization at this time, Black Protestants were not divided into theological groups.

To determine the extent of religious interest group mobilization in 1996, we asked potential voters five questions:

1. Did you discuss the election with friends at your place of worship?
2. Was information on parties and candidates made available in your place of worship before the election?
3. Were you contacted by a religious group, like the Christian Coalition or the Interfaith Alliance?
4. Did the clergy at your place of worship speak out this year on candidates and elections?
5. Did the clergy or other leaders at your place of worship urge you to vote in a particular way?

Although these questions do not cover all possible kinds of communications, they do include most of the major techniques used. In analysing the results, we have counted respondents who did not know, could not remember, or refused to say whether they have been contacted as 'no contact'. Despite this conservative approach, we find that many Americans were the targets of political communication by religious interest groups and activists.

What, then, was the shape of religious mobilization during the 1996 elections? Which people were most often the recipients of such contacts? And what techniques were most widely used – at least as perceived by potential voters? In Table 3.2, we can see that only a minority in the mass public received any single form of religious contact: almost one in five discussed the election with a friend in church, 15 per cent said that voter guides were available in their place of worship, about one in eight was contacted directly by a religious interest group and a similar number heard a discussion of the election by the clergy, but only 7 per cent reported that their pastor actually endorsed a candidate.

However, these levels increase among people with some minimal level of religious commitment, though the particular forms of contact varied substantially by religious tradition (and by theological location within each). Political discussion with friends in church was the most common contact in the mass public, and Evangelicals engaged most often in such conversations, followed closely by Black and Mainline Protestants. Catholics, on the other hand, seldom talked about the election with friends in church. Why this is so is not clear. Perhaps Catholic worship services and religious activities lack the 'free time' and 'free space' associated with the schedules of most Evangelical, Mainline and Black Protestant churches (e.g., adult Sunday school hours, coffees between Sunday school and church, post-service meals, midweek prayer meetings, choir practice and so on) that offer Protestants opportunities for political talk. Or, perhaps, it is the residual effects of the historic lack of emphasis on the role of the laity within Catholic churches, or the larger size of the typical Catholic congregation may simply limit such activity.[27]

Table 3.2:
Religious contact sources by major religious traditions and theological groups, 1996 election, %

Contact	Talk in church	Voter guides	Interest group	Clergy talk	Clergy endorse	At least one
Mass Public	19	15	12	14	7	38
Evangelical Protestant	28	21	18	16	8	49
Orthodox	41	31	26	21	10	64
Centrist	23	12	15	15	9	43
Modernist	11	14	9	10	4	33
Mainline Protestant	24	13	13	12	6	41
Orthodox	39	17	17	15	8	53
Centrists	25	13	15	13	6	44
Modernist	6	10	7	6	4	25
Black Protestant	26	23	4	42	14	56
Roman Catholic	15	18	13	14	14	39
Orthodox	17	24	21	16	19	49
Centrist	15	17	10	16	10	37
Modernist	12	13	7	8	9	28

Political discussion varied by theological location as well, especially among Evangelical and Mainline Protestants, with the orthodox talking the most. About two-fifths of orthodox Evangelicals and Mainliners reported such exchanges, compared to less than a fifth of the orthodox Catholics. In both white Protestants traditions, political discussion declined sharply among centrists and modernists. These differences reflect, in part, the denser social networks of religious traditionalists, who typically have many close friends in the congregation.

If press accounts and scholars have neglected this strategic role of informal personal discussions within congregations, they have often spotlighted the Christian Right's controversial provision of political guidance through 'voter guides' at houses of worship, typically on the Sunday before the election. Such guides have become almost canonical in some churches, having been used by anti-abortion groups as early as the 1970s.[28] In 1996, the Christian Coalition, Focus on the Family and many other national, state and local religious interest groups distributed at least 45 million such guides, primarily in Evangelical and orthodox Mainline congregations, but also in some Black Protestant and Catholic churches as well.[29] These documents were often criticized for their transparent Republican bias, and liberal groups such as the Interfaith Alliance counter-attacked with their own more 'objective' guides, but certainly failed to match the Christian Right performance in distributing such materials.

How extensive was this voter guide campaign? As Table 3.2 shows, fewer Americans had candidate information available in their place of worship than talked with friends there about the election, but the differences are not massive. As expected, the voter guide strategy fared best among orthodox Evangelicals, a third of whom found such materials in church. This number drops off substantially among centrist and modernist Evangelicals, whose experience was quite similar to that of all the Mainline groups. One-quarter of African-American Protestants also said that election guides were available in church, a figure equalled by orthodox Catholics. In all three white Christian traditions, modernists seldom found voting guides available (or perhaps were not in church to notice and pick one up).

Movement organizations also used more conventional electoral techniques, contacting voters individually through phone banks, door-to-door canvassing, mail, fax messages and even e-mail. As Table 3.2 reveals, such efforts contributed almost as many contacts as voter guides, at least among Evangelical and Mainline Protestants. Black Protestants very seldom experienced such contacts, while Catholics were also somewhat less likely to be approached directly than to have voter guides in church. Once again, the orthodox, regardless of religious tradition, were the most likely to receive contacts, while modernists were seldom the target.

Finally, there were still some attempts in 1996 to elicit pastoral guidance for parishioners' political choices. Although the Christian Right's early enthusiasm for clerical leadership had waned by the 1990s, the Christian Voters League and other groups still urged ministers to inform their parishioners about candidates and even let them know how a good Christian should vote. In 1996, however, very few church people reported that their clergy actually urged a vote for specific candidates, but many more heard discussion of candidates from the pulpit. Only orthodox Catholics reported that 'clergy endorsement' exceeded 'clergy discussion' (19 and 16 per cent, respectively). Clerical endorsement of candidates is lower yet among Black Protestants (14 per cent), despite frequent press accounts of such activities in African-American churches, and very few in white Protestant traditions report endorsements.

Although explicit candidate endorsements were rare in 1996, as in previous years, some clergy no doubt did employ more subtle ways of indicating their preferences.[30] As Table 3.2 reveals, significant minorities of church people listened to their minister or priest discussing candidates for office. Not surprisingly, Black Protestants led the way, with over two-fifths recalling such pastoral discourse, confirming the historic political role of the African-American clergy.[31] One-fifth of orthodox Evangelicals also heard pastoral commentary, followed closely by orthodox and centrist Catholics. Once again, the orthodox in each tradition are the most likely to be contacted, but differences among theological groups are not as wide on clerical activity as on other forms of contacting.

What can we conclude about electoral action by religious interest groups in 1996? On the whole, evidence suggests that Christian Right interest groups hit their targets. Certainly, no one technique reached a majority in any religious community, but many individuals were contacted, both through church-based and more conventional campaign tactics. As a rough overall gauge of the extent of contacts, we calculated the proportion in each religious group who received at least one such contact. As the final column in Table 3.2 shows, almost two-fifths of all Americans were contacted in some way, but this number rises to two-thirds of the orthodox Evangelicals, half of the orthodox Mainliners and Catholics, and over two-fifths of the Evangelical and Mainline centrists. Although more Black Protestants reported some contact than members of any other tradition (56 per cent), much of this is accounted for by pastoral action. On the whole, orthodox Evangelicals have a considerable edge over their Catholic and Mainline brethren, and to a lesser extent, over Black Protestants. While not all the communications received by religious people were laden with clear ideo-logical and partisan messages, the majority no doubt had a conservative and Republican colouration.

The importance of religious contacts should be put in broader perspective. In an era when party organizations have either atrophied or found it difficult to locate and activate sympathetic voters, religious interest groups are an important new force, an exemplar of the 'new politics' of ideological organizations. Such groups have become significant electoral competitors (and often adjuncts) to party committees, candidate organizations and other traditional interest groups. Although we can not elaborate here, the religious contacting shown in Table 3.2 compares quite favourably with voters' contacts by party organizations (32 per cent of the public), political candidates (30 per cent) and business and labour groups (19 per cent). And, among orthodox Christians, especially Evangelicals, religious contacts often equalled or outnumbered secular ones. Obviously, religious interest groups constitute a crucial new set of intermediaries linking the public to the electoral process.

However, before we conclude that religious mobilization worked to any advantage in the 1996 campaign, we need to take into account other factors related to the frequency of contacting, as the orthodox in all three major traditions are more likely to be contacted *and* more likely to vote and vote Republican (data not shown). Such turnout and Republican partisanship may result less from religious contacting, however, than from the strong connection between orthodox theology, conservative ideology and Republican partisanship. Thus, religious interest groups may be 'preaching to the choir', seeking to influence or mobilize those who would inevitably vote and pull the correct lever anyway.

Preliminary indications from the 2000 election suggest that voters reported only slightly fewer religious contacts than in 1996.[32] Voter guides appeared to be less evident, in part, because of their reduced availability in Mainline Protestant and Roman Catholic churches. But, such guides seemingly were as evident in Evangelical Protestant churches in 2000 as they were in 1996. Moreover, it appears that liberal clergy, both Black Protestant and Mainline Protestant, were just as vocal in the 2000 election as they had been in previous years, if not more so.

Any full assessment of the impact of religious group activity requires that we control for the effects of theological, political and demographic variables. To present a strong – and easily interpretable – test, we ran a multiple classification analysis (MCA) on the effects of theological location and types of contacts on electoral choice and turnout in the three major traditions. We included party identification, ideology, gender, age, family income and education level as covariates (control variables), as each has a strong influence over vote choice and/or turnout. First, party identification has long been the most potent way of explaining voters' choice: Republicans vote Republican, and Democrats favour Democrats. Political ideology also has been found to help explain the vote, even when partisanship is taken into account, with liberals liking Democratic candidates, and conservatives choosing Republicans. Much has been made of the 'gender gap' in recent years, with women exhibiting a greater preference than men for the Democratic ticket. And, finally, age, income and education may also have effects on electoral choice.[33]

Our primary concern, however, is not with replicating the findings of earlier voting research, but with isolating the impact of theological orientation and religious interest group activities. Table 3.3 reports the effects of each theological and contact variable statistically adjusted for the effects of party identification, ideology, age, gender, education and income, as well as for the other variables shown in the table. If, under these very stringent conditions, we still discover differences among those contacted, we can say that religious interest groups had some impact.

What do we find? First, even with the controls, religious communities still vary in partisan preferences: thus, their distinct voting choices are not simply the result of party identification, ideology, socioeconomic status – or even differential mobilization by religious interest groups. Evangelicals vote Republican more often than Mainline Protestants, who in turn favour the GOP more often than Catholics. In all three religious traditions, GOP voting tends to decline from orthodox to modernist, although that effect is most striking with regard to presidential voting in 1996. Among Evangelicals and Catholics, turnout is significantly different among theological groups, with the orthodox more likely to vote than other subgroups, but among Mainliners, the orthodox and modernists are closely matched. Thus, even with the imposition of extensive political and demographic controls, religious tradition and theological location retain a significant influence over electoral choice.

Second, religious mobilization effects also persist, but vary in predictable ways by religious tradition and type of contact. Talking with friends in church has a fairly strong net effect, producing a significantly higher GOP House vote among Evangelicals, a larger turnout in all three traditions, and more Republican vote for both House and president among Catholics. On the other hand, the availability of voter guides seems much less efficacious. Although voter guides have a slightly pro-Republican effect on the presidential vote among Catholics, in most instances those reporting the availability of voter guides are

Table 3.3:
Electoral impact of religious contacts, multivariate analysis, 1996 election

	Evangelical			Mainline			Catholic		
	House	Dole	Voted	House	Dole	Voted	House	Dole	Voted
All	75%	65%	54%	60%	56%	60%	53%	46%	55%
			Religious group						
Orthodox	76*	71*	61*	60*	63*	66*	55*	50*	61*
Centrist	73	66	48	62	56	56	54	43	54
Modernist	71	52	51	53	50	68	45	43	46
			Religious contacts						
Church talk									
Yes	78*	65	66*	60	56	68*	59*	52*	64*
No	73	66	49	59	56	58	51	45	54
Voter guides									
Yes	75	61*	51	53	60	61	54	53*	54
No	75	67	55	61	55	60	52	45	55
Interest group									
Yes	80*	79*	66*	61	64*	52	53	39	62*
No	73	61	51	59	55	62	52	48	55
Clergy action									
Yes	71	53*	52	60	45	68*	56	47	51
No	76	69	54	59	58	59	52	46	56
Summary									
Contacted	78*	65	58*	62*	56	61	54*	46	60*
No contact	70	65	50	58	56	60	51	47	52
N=	(265)	(315)	(590)	(200)	(234)	(391)	(192)	(228)	(416)

The numbers represent the mean Republican vote for the House of Representatives and president, and the percentage of those voting, adjusted for the effects of party identification, ideological identification, gender, age, income and education.
* Significant at $p > 10$.

actually *less* likely to report a choice of the GOP House or presidential candidate, although only on the Evangelical presidential vote are the differences statistically significant.

Although direct religious interest group contact is not the most frequent type of communication, it has the strongest effects among Evangelicals, certainly the key target of such efforts, adding 7 per cent to the House GOP vote, 18 per cent to the Dole tally, and 15 per cent to turnout among those contacted. The impact of contacts, among Mainline and Catholic parishioners is mixed, however, producing a stronger Dole vote (9 per cent higher) among the former, and higher turnout among the latter (7 per cent). On the whole, then, direct contact appears to have considerable impact – but only in certain religious contexts.

Clergy activity, however, appears to be relatively ineffectual. When everything is taken into account, most of the differences are statistically insignificant and sometimes run in the opposite direction from those expected.

Another way to summarize the impact of religious contacting is to look once again at the differences between those who received at least one such communication and those who did not. The final section of Table 3.3 provides this information, once again with all controls in effect. Being contacted increases the Republican House vote in all three traditions and increases turnout among Evangelicals and Catholics. Only on the presidential vote do we find no significant net effects. Overall, however, these findings are quite impressive, supporting arguments for the political efficacy of interest group activity. Clearly, religious interest group contacting is often effective among the Christian Right's primary target constituency, Evangelical Protestants, but in some other religious locations as well. And, the techniques vary in effectiveness. Conventional interest group tactics, such as direct contact with voters, seem more effective than some of the church-based techniques, such as the much debated provision of voter guides and pastoral action. Both seem ineffective in the short run and may even be counterproductive in some circumstances. However, one church-based tactic clearly works: informal influences from church discussion partners has considerable impact, especially among Evangelicals, who engage in much political discussion in church, and among Catholics, who are less likely to do so.

Among Black Protestants, all the patterns are much simpler: the controls for party identification, ideology, income and the other variables eliminate much of the tendency of those contacted to vote more Republican in House races. This suggests that contacts by Christian Right groups in the African-American community are aimed at the minority already leaning toward the GOP; such contacts have little effect on partisan choices among other Black Protestants. One clear effect does survive: Black Protestants receiving any form of contact are more likely to vote (53 per cent versus 31 per cent after all controls). This finding confirms the irony noted above, that some Christian Right contacting may have had the undesired result of bringing more Democrats to the polls!

We must issue one final caveat: our analysis here may understate the long-run impact of religious interest group activity, especially with respect to the church-based activities. We suspect, for example, that the growing strength of Republican identification among Evangelicals results in part from a decade or more of insistent Christian Right blandishments to vote for Republican candidates, conveyed through a variety of mechanisms. Most of these long-term and 'indirect' effects would be captured in 1996 by the controls for party or ideology in our statistical analysis, not by the contacting items. Yet, at least indirectly, such political socialization substantially bolsters the Christian Right's long-term achievements.

CONCLUSION

While efforts have been made to insure the separation of Church and state within the American political system, it is impossible to prevent religious forces from potentially affecting American politics. This is true for several reasons. First, it is impossible to prevent religious people, as long as they are eligible to vote, from exercising their franchise should they seek to be politically engaged. It would be undemocratic and unconstitutional to do so.

Second, the American political system possesses several characteristics which, when coupled with its social composition and heritage, enable religious groups to be relatively efficacious in accomplishing their political goals. On the political side of the equation, there exists the First Amendment that, while disestablishing religion, protects the free exercise of religion. There is also the federal system of government, the separation of powers, the committee system in Congress, the two-party system with weak political parties and candidate-driven elections. On the social side of the equation, there exists the continuing flow of immigration into the United States, the individualistic ethos (including religious individualism), and, with the erosion of neighbourhood communities, the creation of 'communities' outside of specifically confined geographical spaces. While certain of these characteristics do not simply enhance the political influence of religious groups specifically, but rather of all social groups generally, it is the confluence of these various factors which contributes to some of the uniqueness by which religious groups can play a significant role in American politics.

Third, it becomes nearly impossible to 'root out' religious influences in democratic life because religion is multifaceted and deeply embedded within everyday life. Religion has a belief dimension (believing), an associational dimension (belonging) and a 'consequence' dimension (behaving). Even when one prevents churches as institutions from engaging in political activities, religion can still play a role politically because the bulk of one's social friends and/or neighbours may be associated with the particular congregation with which one worships, most of one's political discussion partners may be associated with some religious group or tradition, or the media sources from which one gathers political information may be religious in nature.

And, finally, there are both religious and secular political elites who wish to capitalize on such religious beliefs, patterns of religious belonging and religiously based patterns of behaviour as a basis for mobilizing people politically and securing electoral and political victories. Churches constitute one of the major places where like-minded people physically meet together. It is this characteristic that makes religious people the target of political mobilization.

NOTES

1. Jeffrey Hadden, 'Desacralizing Secularization Theory', in Jeffrey Hadden and Anson Shupe (eds), *Secularization and Fundamentalism Reconsidered: Religion and the Political Order*, Vol. 3 (New York: Paragon House, 1989), p. 3. Of course, different scholars advance different interpretations of the nature of secularization. In fact, three different notions of secularization have been advanced: (1) secularization as a decline of religiosity, (2) secularization as the adaptation of religion to modernization, and (3) secularization as the restriction of the range of influence of religion. In addition to these three dimensions, this process of secularization can be studied

at different levels, the individual level, the institutional or organizational level and the societal level. Obviously, the level at which the process of secularization is studied is tied to the particular notion of secularization that is advanced.

2. John Esposito, *The Islamic Threat: Myth or Reality* (New York: Oxford University Press, 1995).
3. Donald Smith, 'Introduction', in Donald Smith (ed.), *Religion and Political Modernization* (New Haven, CT: Yale University Press, 1974), p. 4.
4. See, for example, *Public Perspective,* April/May (1995), p. 25.
5. Wade Clark Roof, *A Generation of Seekers: Spiritual Journeys of the Baby Boom Generation* (New York: HarperCollins, 1993); Dean Hoge, Benton Johnson and Don Luidens, *Vanishing Boundaries: The Religion of Mainline Protestant Baby Boomers* (Louisville, KY: Westminister/ John Knox Press, 1994).
6. R. Stephen Warner, 'Work in Progress toward a New Paradigm for the Sociological Study of Religion in the United States', *American Journal of Sociology*, 98 (1993), pp. 1044–93.
7. Harry Stout, 'Ethnicity: The Vital Center of Religion in America', *Ethnicity*, 2 (1975), pp. 204–24; Robert Harney, 'Religion and Ethnocultural Communities', *Polyphony*, 1 (1978), pp. 1–10.
8. Harney, 'Religion and Ethnocultural Communities', p. 5.
9. Timothy Smith, 'Religion and Ethnicity in America', *American Historical Review*, 83 (1978), p. 1168.
10. Ibid., p. 1183.
11. Ibid., pp. 1174–5.
12. Wade Clark Roof and William McKinney, *American Mainline Religion: Its Changing Shape and Future* (New Brunswick, NJ: Rutgers University Press, 1987), p. 43. Even Roman Catholicism has been shaped by this cultural context. As historian Jay Dolan has noted, American Catholicism tends to become de facto congregational in style, and recent studies by D'Antonio, Davidson, Hoge and Wallace reveal a majority of Catholics favouring horizontal authority relations within the church. See, Jay Dolan, *The American Catholic Experience* (Garden City, NY: Doubleday and Company, 1985), and William D'Antonio, James Davidson, Dean Hoge and Ruth Wallace, *Laity: American & Catholic* (Kansas City, MO: Sheed & Ward, 1996).
13. Andrew Greeley, *The Catholic Myth: The Behavior and Beliefs of American Catholics* (New York: Schribner's, 1990).
14. Roof and McKinney, *American Mainline Religion*, p. 56.
15. Ibid., pp. 64–5.
16. Ibid., pp. 68–70. Among some of the other consequences associated with this loosening of religion from its historic social moorings are that: (1) the family plays a reduced role in the transmission of religious values and identities; and (2) old differences between denominations have blurred, while religious alignments along new ideological lines have intensified.
17. Ibid., p. 70.
18. Warner, 'Work in Progress toward a New Paradigm for the Sociological Study of Religion in the United States', p. 1076.
19. The discussion in this section is drawn heavily from our chapter 'Thunder on the Right? Religious Interest Group Mobilization in the 1996 Election', in Allan Cigler and Burdett Loomis (eds), *Interest Group Politics*, 5th edn (Washington, DC: CQ Press, 1998), pp. 169–92.
20. Quoted in James Guth, 'The Politics of the Christian Right', in Allan Cigler and Burdett Loomis (eds), *Interest Group Politics* (Washington, DC: CQ Press, 1983), p. 73.
21. James Guth, 'The Bully Pulpit: Southern Baptist Clergy and Political Activism, 1980–92', in John Green, James Guth, Corwin Smidt and Lyman Kellstedt (eds), *Religion and the Culture Wars: Dispatches from the Front* (Lanham, MD: Rowman & Littlefield, 1997), pp. 146–7.
22. See, for example, Mark Rozell and Clyde Wilcox (eds), *God at the Grassroots: The Christian Right in the 1996 Elections* (Lanham, MD: Rowman & Littlefield, 1997).
23. For a discussion of the concept of religious traditions, see John Green *et al.*, *Religion and the Culture Wars*, chapters 10, 13–14.
24. The Republican Party is frequently referred to as the GOP in American politics. GOP stands for the 'Grand Old Party'.
25. Geoffrey Layman, 'Religion and Political Behavior in the United States', *Public Opinion Quarterly*, 61 (1997), pp. 288–316.
26. James Davison Hunter, *Culture Wars: The Struggle to Define America* (New York: Basic Books, 1991). James Davison Hunter, *Before the Shooting Starts: Searching for Democracy in America's Culture War* (New York: Free Press, 1994).

27. See, for example, Sidney Verba, Kay Schlozman and Henry Brady, *Voice and Equality: Civic Volunteerism in American Politics* (Cambridge, MA: Harvard University Press, 1995).

28. Marjoire Hershey and Darrell West, 'Single-Issue Politics: Prolife Groups and the 1980 Senate Campaign', in Allan Cigler and Burdett Loomis (eds), *Interest Group Politics* (Washington, DC: CQ Press, 1983), pp. 1–59.

29. R. Scott Appleby, 'Catholics and the Christian Right', in Corwin Smidt and James Penning (eds), *Sojourners in the Wilderness: The Christian Right in Comparative Perspective* (Lanham, MD: Rowman & Littlefield, 1997), pp. 93–113; Allison Calhoun-Brown, 'Still Seeing in Black and White: Racial Challenges for the Christian Right', ibid., pp. 115–37.

30. See the discussion and analysis of political involvement of clergy in James Guth, John Green, Corwin Smidt, Lyman Kellstedt and Margaret Poloma, *The Bully Pulpit: The Politics of Protestant Clergy* (Lawrence, KS: University of Kansas Press, 1997).

31. See, for example, C. Eric Lincoln and Lawrence Mamiya, *The Black Church in African-American Experience* (Durham, NC: Duke University Press, 1990).

32. James Guth, John Green, Corwin Smidt and Lyman Kellstedt, 'Partisan Religion: Analysing the 2000 Election,' *Christian Century*, 118 (21–8 March 2000), pp. 18–20.

33. For a discussion of how these factors affect vote choice and turnout, see Warren Miller and J. Merrill Shanks, *The New American Voter* (Cambridge, MA: Harvard University Press, 1995), and Roy Teixeira, *The Disappearing American Voter* (Washington, DC: Brookings Institution, 1992).

4

Religion and *Laïcité* in a Jacobin Republic: The Case of France

WILLIAM SAFRAN

INTRODUCTION: FROM STATE RELIGION TO *LAÏCITÉ*

A major characteristic of French republican ideology has been *laïcité*, or secularity. The notion that the state should be independent of, and separated from, religion goes back to the early days of the French Revolution, when church property was confiscated, the Christian calendar was replaced by a revolutionary one, and Christianity itself was replaced by a 'religion of reason'. Indeed, *laïcité* was to become one of the fundamental elements of Jacobin doctrine. With their commitment to the idea that a proper democracy implied the sovereignty of the people, the Jacobins insisted that there be no intermediaries between the individual and the state, and hence rejected all mediating institutions, such as provinces, ethnic communities, trade unions and churches. The principle of separation of Church and state was an elementary ingredient of French republican thinking from the very beginning, and even antedated the Revolution. Hostility to the Catholic Church marked the thinking of a number of Enlightenment intellectuals; to Voltaire, for example, religion was incompatible with reason and progress. To be sure, he directed his anti-religious feelings especially to the Catholic Church; because that Church was identified with absolute monarchy, with the Inquisition, and with other manifestations of intolerance, he called for the removal of its influence from public life.

The Declaration of the Rights of Man and Citizen of 1789 made a reference to 'the Supreme Being'; but it also stipulated (Article 10) that 'no one should be disturbed on account of his opinions, even religious, provided that their manifestation does not derange the public order established by law'. It further provided (Article 11) that 'the free expression of thought and opinion is one of the most precious rights of man: thus every citizen may freely speak, write, and print, subject to accountability for abuse of this freedom in the cases determined by law'. In 1790 the Civil Constitution of the Clergy, while not formally separating the Church from the state, forced the clergy to swear allegiance to the civil authorities. The formal separation between Church and state was decreed by the Directory in 1795; subsequently, however, the formal relationship between the two experienced reversals or reinterpretations. The Concordat of 1801, concluded between Napoleon and the Holy See, re-established the Roman Catholic Church as the state religion. The Charter of 1814 reaffirmed this position (and was followed by a law forbidding work on Sundays), but the freedom of other religions was guaranteed. The Charter of 1830, while not 'separating' religion and state, reaffirmed the special position of the Catholic religion as one 'professed by the majority of the French people' and provided that its clergy, as well as that of other Christian religions, receive governmental financial support.[1]

The progression toward the equality of religions, the impartiality of the state, and the principle of *laïcité* made the greatest strides during the Third Republic. It was institutionalized in public policy with the enactment of the Ferry primary education laws of 1882, which instituted a national system of public schools that were to be 'free, obligatory, and neutral', with a uniform curriculum from which religion was deliberately absent. *Laïcité* was further promoted with the transfer to mayors of the obligation to keep civil registers in which religion could not be mentioned and the stipulation that any religious marriage be preceded by a civil marriage. Furthermore, the administration of local public policy, such as health and social welfare, was put under secular control. Finally, although the law of 1901 recognized freedom of association and facilitated the establishment of anticlerical organizations, one of its provisions (Article 14), by requiring prior government authorization, made it very difficult for religious associations (notably Catholic ones) to form and to teach.

Throughout the Third Republic, *laïcité* (as well as the republican form of government itself) was subjected to challenges, which culminated in the Dreyfus Affair. Dreyfus, a Jew, was not the only target of the monarchists and the Catholic establishment, who aimed also at Protestants, Freemasons, socialists and a variety of republicans. However, the Jews were considered to be the most convenient target group because more French people could unite against them. There had been some hope that the issuing in 1891 of the papal encyclical *Rerum Novarum* would make the French Church more accepting of republicanism, but that hope was vain.[2] As a result, all connection of the state with religion was severed in 1905, and churches were henceforth to be private corporations. Furthermore, only civil marriages were officially recognized.

Catholicism was reinstitutionalized under the Vichy state, a regime that was heavily supported by many devout Catholics and most of the Church hierarchy. After Liberation in 1944, a tripartite government coalition of Communists, Socialists and the Christian Democrats was put in place, which committed itself fully to republicanism. The inclusion of the Christian Democrats (at that time represented by the Mouvement Républicain Populaire – MRP) had become possible because many Catholics had become 'republicanized', and some of their leaders had been active in the Resistance.

The constitution of the Fourth Republic (Preamble) affirmed the inalienable rights of every human being 'without distinction of race, religion, or belief' and the duty of the state to provide 'free, secular, public education on all levels', and (in Article 1) characterized France as 'a republic, indivisible, secular [laïque], democratic and social'. The constitution of the Fifth Republic (Article 2) recapitulates these principles. In practice, the principle of laïcité had already been modified, or moderated, during the Fourth Republic with the passage of the Barangé law of 1951, which provided that financial aid be given to families with children of school age regardless of whether the latter attended public or private schools. A further modification took place with the enactment of the Debré laws of 1959, under which government subsidies were to be given to parochial schools that contracted to follow a state curriculum.

These adjustments were minor, and did not have a significant effect on French political culture as reflected in decision-making institutions, public policy expectations and the party system. A number of political parties, notably the Radical, Socialist and Communist parties, have been outspokenly anticlerical, a feature that has also marked certain left-wing interest groups, such as the Confédération Générale du Travail (CGT), one of the country's major trade unions. Knowledge of the Bible is minimal among the public at large as well as among the intellectual elite. This situation seems incongruous, given the importance of Catholicism in French political and cultural development, and the fact that the Battle of Poitiers in 732 (in which Charles Martel repulsed the Muslims) and the exploits of Joan of Arc have been important milestones in the shaping of French national identity. Roman Catholic cathedrals, many of which began to be built in the twelfth and thirteenth centuries, grace almost every sizable town. In short, Roman Catholicism, which once embraced the overwhelming majority of inhabitants of the Hexagon, had been so important that the country was once considered 'the eldest daughter of the Church'.

The numerical dominance of Catholics should not obscure the fact that France has always had a significant number of members of other religions. Their fate has been uneven. Henry IV tried to deal with the Protestant presence by issuing the Edict of Nantes which, in 1588, provided for religious toleration. But that edict was revoked by Louis XIV in 1685 and, as a consequence, many Protestants (Huguenots) left the country. Jews had a more precarious existence. Although they could trace their presence on French soil to the days of Julius Caesar, they had become subject to periodic pogroms and expulsions, in particular during the Middle Ages. Just before the Revolution, most of them lived in Alsace and Lorraine and the area around Bordeaux, while only a small number were settled in Paris. But for the most part they were not fully integrated into French life, and they lived, as members of the 'nation juive', in relative communal isolation. The French Revolution granted the Jews full civil and political rights, after they had agreed to become 'decommunalized'. As Count Stanislas de Clermont-Tonnerre put it in a speech before the Revolutionary

Assembly in 1789, the Jews should be given full rights as individuals, but no rights at all as members of 'a Jewish nation'.[3]

The population of France is overwhelmingly Catholic, at least in numerical terms; nevertheless, Catholicism has been losing ground. In a poll conducted in 1986, 81 per cent of French labelled themselves as Catholics, but this categoric identification had no precise religious content. In a 1994 poll, 67 per cent referred to themselves as Catholics (compared to 2 per cent who labelled themselves Protestants, 1 per cent as Jewish, 2 per cent as Muslim, and 23 per cent as without religion); but only 10 per cent of the population were practising, and 44 per cent never prayed. The majority of Catholics did not believe in original sin; 83 per cent were guided by their own consciences rather than by the Church's positions in the important decisions of their lives; a slight majority believed in the supernatural, and a somewhat larger majority (61 per cent) believed in a god.[4] In a more recent poll, only 24 per cent referred to themselves as convinced believers, 24 per cent as believers by tradition, and 17 per cent as 'uncertain believers'; and only 29 per cent professed a certain belief in a god. In the same poll, 23 per cent of regularly practising Catholics believed that their church intervened too much in political life (against 35 per cent non-practising Catholics) and 35 per cent thought that their church intervened too much in questions of sexual morality.[5] While many French Catholics have a high regard for the present Pope, they disapprove of (and ignore) his position on contraception, abortion, euthanasia and women becoming priests.[6] In a book by prominent specialists on religion and politics it is argued that although most of the French are still nominally Catholic, this has little to do with church attendance – about half of the respondents who label themselves as Catholics seldom go to church – or with Catholic theological or social doctrines. The churches and cathedrals are increasingly less places of worship than they are tourist attractions.[7]

One of the problems relating to the study of the behaviour and attitudes of French men and French women who adhere to a religious categoric group is that such adherence may not have much theological significance. This is true in particular of a highly secularized society such as the French, where a significant majority of Jews, Muslims and Catholics identify as such primarily in a 'cultural' sense and choose their practices accordingly.[8] In 1952, 12 per cent declared themselves to be without any religion; in 1977, 15 per cent; and in 1993, 16 per cent. Religion, and in particular Catholicism, had become largely a matter for the older generation; thus, 82 per cent of those over 65 declared themselves to be Catholics (at least nominally); but only 68 per cent of the under 25 age group did so; and only 63 per cent of *cadres supérieurs* (upper-echelon managers and technical supervisors) and members of intellectual professions of all ages.[9]

A large proportion of Catholics believe that religion and politics should be clearly demarcated. According to a poll, 43 per cent of regularly practising Catholics thought that the Church should be involved in politics; and that only a minority of French citizens (including practising Catholics) are willing to adhere to a specifically Catholic social message. The gulf between (nominal or other) Catholicism and politics is also illustrated by another statistic: on the eve of the legislative elections of 1978, only 36 per cent of regularly practising Catholics, and 20 per cent of occasionally practising, approved a declaration of the Catholic bishops (made in September 1977) about the incompatibility between Christianity and Marxism.[10]

In sum, the majority of French citizens are de-Christianized; for about 80 per cent of the population that still labels itself Christian, such a designation tends in most cases to be reflected in little more than basic rites of passage (such as baptism, marriage, or funeral mass). According to surveys, the (still wide-spread) belief in a god is not necessarily associated with formal membership in a church or even acceptance of a specific church doctrine or position.[11] Impatience with organized religion has affected the Catholic Church in particular, which is reproached for having made common cause too often with oppressive regimes.[12] One indicator of the weakening of Catholicism in the political arena is the decline of the importance of Catholic parties – a development reflected in the gradual replacement of the Mouvement Républicain Populaire (MRP) from a major electoral force in the Fourth Republic by the present Force Démocrate, which can count on the support of no more than about 5 per cent of the electorate.[13] Another is the scission of the major part of the Christian-Democratic trade union, the Confédération Française des Travailleurs Chrétiens (CFTC), and the reorganization of that part into a more or less 'deconfessionalized' successor union, the Confédération Française Démocratique de Travail (CFDT).

Nevertheless, in many respects France remains an essentially Catholic country. The majority of French citizens has always been Catholic; Catholic institutions form an important element of French philanthropy (to the limited extent that it exists); Catholic farmers have a separate association, the Jeunesse Agricole Chrétienne; and to some devout Catholics, the watering down of old-fashioned Catholicism, the vernacularization of prayer, and the tendencies to ecumenism are disturbing enough to lead them to support Marcel Lefèbvre and his 'traditional' Catholics.

Catholicism must now coexist not only with anti-religious elements but also with a variety of non-Catholic religions, notably Islam, Protestantism and Judaism. Yet despite the increasingly secular and pluralistic nature of French society, Catholicism is so clearly woven into the fabric of French history and culture that most other religions appear somehow foreign and do not fit comfortably into the French context. Therefore, despite official commitments to liberty and equality, if not to 'multiculturalism', problems arise with respect to accommodating to non-Catholic, or at any rate non-Christian, concerns.

In most instances, Catholic dominance has been manifested in a secularized form and has had little to do with theology, and for that reason it has not disturbed the lives of those who are not practising Catholics. Among the secularized vestiges of Roman Catholicism are the public holidays, which, with the exception of Bastille Day (14 July) and Labour Day (1 May), are church festivals. This includes Sundays: under the country's 'blue laws', factories, libraries, schools, universities and shops other than small family enterprises are closed, and no newspapers are published. Mail carriers distribute postal calendars that list not only official school holidays but also saints' days. Traditionally, the names parents were permitted to give to their newborn children had to be taken from a list that was largely comprised of the calendar of saints – at least until the mid-1960s, when that list began to be enlarged and liberalized.[14]

Religion has been injected periodically into the public debate and in arguments about public policy, not primarily because of these vestiges of Catholicism, but rather because of the fact that despite the official commitment to *laïcité* the state has continued to be involved in religion in one way or another. At present, it is difficult to imagine that clergy would be called upon to open or close parliamentary sessions with invocations or benedictions. Yet in principle, all major religions enjoy a degree of official legitimation and support, which is reflected in a number of public policies:

1. the maintenance of houses of worship by the state or by local governments, as part of the physical patrimony of France. This includes not only churches but selected synagogues as well;

2. the payment, by national or subnational public authorities, of Catholic, Protestant, Jewish and Islamic chaplains in the army, in prisons and in hospitals;

3. a special social security system for clergy;

4. tax exemptions granted to religious institutions;

5. government subsidies provided to non-profit religious associations that pursue educational or humanitarian tasks in the public interest;

6. the subvention of parochial schools (discussed below);

7. the provision of a special period (traditionally, Wednesday afternoons) for catechism in elementary school schedules, on a voluntary basis;

8. the assignment of national and communal properties specifically to one or another religious group; and

9. the allocation of television time for broadcasts of one or another religious programme, broadcasts which are in part subsidized by the state.

Furthermore, since 1828 there has been a special regime for Guyane, a French possession in South America, under which Catholicism has been recognized as the sole official religion; and the '*régime concordataire*' with Alsace and with Moselle (Lorraine), dating to 1918, under which houses of worship and clergy of Catholics, Protestants (Lutherans) and Jews are supported with public funds.[15]

Religion was reintroduced recently in another way: in early 1998, a law passed five years earlier to eliminate the monopoly of municipal authorities in funerals was finally put into effect. Henceforth, funeral services may be conducted by the private sector, an innovation that will undoubtedly result in the legitimation by the state of religious rituals at funerals.[16]

RELIGIOUS MINORITIES: BACKGROUNDS, POSITIONS AND PUBLIC ATTITUDES

The Protestants

In a formal and legal sense, as we have seen, the French state does not discriminate against any particular religion; to the extent that it deals with religion at all, it does so on an equal basis. In this regard, the Protestants have been in the best position. They are Christian; they are rooted in the countryside and constitute an unquestioned 'indigenous' element; and they have a relatively underdeveloped community consciousness. For all these reasons, their concerns have not much disturbed the collective image that the French have of their society. From the Edict of Tolerance of 1787 (which reversed the repeal of the Edict of Nantes) and the French Revolution (which gave them equal rights) onward, the Protestants, more than members of any other religion, have represented individual freedom, the ethic of achievement, a progressive republicanism, and the values associated with that ideology, including socialism, pluralism, gender equality (more than 15 per cent of pastors are women), a more tolerant approach to birth control and opposition to autocracy. The Protestants' tolerance and pluralism explain why, in proportion to their population, they were more active in the Resistance during the Vichy regime, and did more to save the lives of Jews, than did their Catholic fellow citizens. Protestants have included a large number of cabinet ministers (most of them Socialist), among them Gaston Defferre, Jean-Pierre Cot, Louis Mexandeau, Pierre Joxe, Michel Rocard and Lionel Jospin.[17] It is perhaps no accident that when Rocard was leader of the Parti Socialiste Unifié (PSU), that leftist formation developed a policy of multiculturalism, which included a greater openness to 'the right to be different' with respect to religious traditions as well as ethnocultural ones. If Protestantism has declined, it is in part because of its success – the prominence of Protestants in big business, the higher civil service, and national politics – and because the 'Protestant ethic' is now accepted by an increasing number of Catholics and has come to be equated with a modern republic that is at once productivist and socially responsible.

The Jews

The position of the Jews in French society and the French state has been a matter of controversy for many centuries. The achievement of civil and political equality referred to above had not completely resolved the 'Jewish question', because there was lingering doubt about the full commitment of Jews to the republic and the Napoleonic empire. At the Grand Sanhedrin, an assembly of Jewish notables convoked between 1806 and 1808, Napoleon had posed a number of questions relating to the readiness of the Jews to behave like 'normal' French citizens: would they pledge full allegiance to the French state and accept its political values? Would they serve in the military? Would they cease to regard themselves as a separate nation within the French nation? Would they obey France's civil laws without question? The answers were affirmative; as a diaspora people, Jews had come to accept the Talmudic principle that 'the laws of the state in which you live shall be your laws' (*dina de-malkhuta dina*). Henceforth Jews were no longer regarded as members of a distinct community but rather as adherents on an individual and voluntary basis to the *culte israélite*, presumably in the same way that other French citizens adhered to the different Christian denominations.

The appointment of rabbis, the maintenance of synagogues, ritual and other religious matters were to be regulated by a 'Consistory' (*Consistoire*), which was under the authority of the state. The civil and political rights that Jews acquired were (after a hiatus during the Restoration) gradually extended during the Third Republic, only to be challenged during the Dreyfus Affair and set aside during the Vichy period. By the end of the nineteenth century most of the Jews had been fully integrated into the French political community, and their Judaism was gradually eclipsed by the secular religion of the state.[18] (The more traditional Jews, for whom being Jewish was a primary identity, were for the most part recent immigrants from Eastern Europe.)[19] The assimilation of the Jews progressed to such an extent that they were identified with the Third Republic more strongly than were members of most other religions, and the typical educated Jew was so exclusively French that (like Raymond Aron), he could refer to himself as a *juif déjudaïsé*.[20] His Jewish identification was not so much an existential matter as a matter of descent; he was not a Jew (*Juif*), but rather a 'Frenchman of Israelite origins' (*un Français d'origine israélite*). It is instructive to note that there is no parallel characterization for Christians: one never speaks of a *Français d'origine catholique*. Existential Catholicism is a constituent element of authentic Frenchness, whereas Jews, despite their presence in the country for two millennia, are not really regarded as French by many. This Jewish identitive development was not profoundly reversed even during the Dreyfus Affair, which had called into question the Frenchness and the loyalty of Jews. If Jews regarded themselves primarily as Jews, it was as a reaction to others.[21] This view was prominently expressed by Jean-Paul Sartre, who believed (at least until the 1960s) that Jewish self-identification was accentuated, if not created, as a reaction to anti-Semitism.[22]

In 1939, when World War II broke out, Jews went to the front as Frenchmen, but three years later, following France's capitulation and the establishment of the fascist French state at Vichy, Jews were deported to the death camps as Jews.[23] This exemplifies an inconsistency: Jews are sometimes ignored as a separate categoric group, and at other times clearly differentiated from other French people.[24] An instance of the former has to do with Resistance and victimization. The important and very specific Jewish contribution to the Resistance was never acknowledged officially; in the postwar purges, no French person was punished for having collaborated with the Nazis in the 'Final Solution', at least until the trials of Paul Touvier in 1994 and of Maurice Papon in 1998 (the latter a high Vichy official in Bordeaux who subsequently became a cabinet member in the Fifth Republic) for crimes against humanity. Furthermore, for many years – in fact, until the end of the 1980s – memorial plaques at sites of former concentration camps in France where Jews were held *because they were Jews* and whence they were sent to their deaths made reference to 'Resistance fighters' but not to Jews. An instance of the latter is illustrated by the rue Copernic episode. In 1980, during a Jewish festival, a bomb had been planted outside a synagogue on that street. The bomb did not kill Jewish worshippers emerging from the synagogue, as intended, because it went off prematurely; instead, it killed four passersby. Prime Minister Raymond Barre condemned the act, which 'was aimed at Jews but killed innocent people'.[25] This remark may have been a slip of the tongue; but in its evocation of existential Jewish collective guilt it reminded people of the speech made by General de Gaulle in 1967 in which he referred to the Jews as 'an elite people, sure of itself, and domineering' and as a people 'provoking ill will' on the part of a Christendom that had been basically sympathetic to them. Alluding to 'the wandering Jew', he accused the Jews of using vast amounts of 'money, influence, and propaganda' worldwide and of 'lacking modesty.'[26] Another instance of singling out Jews was the so-called *fichier juif*. In the early 1990s it was revealed that files on 140,000 Jews in Paris that had been prepared by the Vichy state were still preserved in the archives of the Paris police prefecture, and there followed a public debate about the reasons for that preservation.[27]

The Jews began to respond to these events increasingly not as individual members of a religion but as members of an ethnic community. The 're-ethnification' of French Jews, which has begun to make headway since the end of the 1960s, can be attributed to a variety of factors:

1. The arrival of tens of thousands of Jewish *pieds noirs* from North Africa between 1957 and 1964. They were regarded as French 'repatriates', since they had been made citizens *en masse* in the 1870s by law (the Crémieux decree). Although growing up almost completely within the French culture and language, they were imbued with an ethnic collective consciousness rather than with Jacobin ideology, and by their presence on the mainland helped to 'infect' the thinking of Ashkenazi Jews.

2. The contagion of Bretons, Basques, Catalans, and other ethnoregional minorities, who had become increasingly vocal about articulating their cultural particularisms.[28]

3. The establishment of the State of Israel, which provided Jews with a degree

of collective pride; and the perceived threat to that country's existence in 1967 and thereafter.

4. The reaction to anti-Semitic speeches and/or anti-Israel policies by national politicians, including de Gaulle, Pompidou and Giscard d'Estaing. At a Jewish 'fair' that took place in the Paris area in 1980, a mock election took place in which the audience was asked to vote for or against the reelection of Giscard as president in 1981, more than 98 per cent cast 'no' votes.

This new ethnic identity was reflected not only in a selective 'rejudaization' of Jews but also in the increasingly open articulation of specifically Jewish political concerns, notably regarding Israel. As the notion of Jewish 'community' eclipsed that of Jews as individual members of a mere religious sect, the Consistory was eclipsed in importance by non-cultic organizations, notably the Conseil Représentatif des Institutions Juives de France (CRIF).[29] To many Jacobin critics, this Jewish assertiveness was a manifestation of communal lobbying, which was regarded as 'un-French' and led to charges of 'dual loyalty', especially in view of the fact that Jewish lobbying was most often connected with a pro-Israel position, which went against the government's pro-Arab policies.[30] The government, however, responded in a more measured, and generally more positive, tone: its original hostility to the notion of ethnoreligious subcommunities in France gradually gave way to an acknowledgement (however grudging) of the 'Jewish community'.[31]

Such a relatively tolerant view was particularly marked in the case of President Chirac. This seemed paradoxical, since as a Gaullist he could hardly hope for massive support from Jewish voters (to the extent that a 'Jewish vote' existed at all), who had traditionally shown a preference for left-wing parties.[32] Yet Chirac was the first president who dissociated himself from the Gaullist mythology that there was no continuity between the Vichy state and the French republic by acknowledging that it was the French, rather than the Germans alone, who had committed crimes against the Jews.

That public gesture was welcomed by Jews, especially in view of growing tendencies by 'revisionist' historians and hatemongers to question the historicity of the Holocaust. In part in order to fight them, Parliament had enacted several laws that made incitement to religious, racial and ethnic hatred a felony. The most recent measure of this kind is the Gayssot law, enacted in 1990, which makes the public denial of the Holocaust a punishable offence. These laws are anti-Jacobin in the sense that, in criminalizing group defamation, they acknowledge the reality of the rights of groups, including religious ones. A number of prominent persons have already been prosecuted for violating the Gayssot law, including Jean-Marie Le Pen, Roger Garaudy and other disseminators of anti-Semitic and revisionist theses.

The government's sensitivity to Jews was illustrated in May 1990, when a Jewish cemetery in Carpentras was desecrated. This event sparked a mass demonstration of solidarity with Jews in which the president, a number of cabinet ministers and politicians of several parties participated. It is unclear whether this was merely a ritualistic exercise (reflecting a belief in a Jewish vote) or the expression of a guilty conscience for the anti-Jewish attitudes of many Frenchmen, including much of the Christian leadership. The sensitivity of the public authorities is closely linked (either as cause or effect) to that of the Catholic establishment. At an official 'ceremony of repentance' in September 1997, in front of a memorial in Drancy (a suburb of Paris that had served as a staging area for the deportation of Jews to Auschwitz), a Catholic archbishop, speaking on behalf of the French Church, apologized to the Jews for the silence of the Catholic Church leadership in the face of Vichy anti-Semitic legislation.[33]

To be sure, this sensitivity applies to Jews as members of a sister religion rather than as members of an ethnic subcommunity. At the same time, the role that Israel has played in the religious consciousness of most Jews is increasingly appreciated. Moreover, the frequently voiced claim of Cardinal Lustiger, the archbishop of Paris who was of Jewish origin and had converted to Catholicism, that he is still a Jew has not been disavowed by the Catholic establishment – a fact that suggests the acceptance of the thesis that Jewishness is not merely defined in terms of religion. In any case, this Christian sensitivity was signalled in the open criticism by Albert Decourtray, the late archbishop of Lyons and the primate of France, of the Pope's invitation to Kurt Waldheim, the ex-Nazi president of Austria. Until his death, Cardinal Decourtray did a great deal to make Muslims welcome and to mediate between them and French Catholics, so that the extreme-right National Front referred to him as 'the Arabs' bishop'.[34] Religious tolerance, pluralism and ecumenism are also reflected in the fact that, increasingly, Catholic priests make their premises available for Muslim prayers and in the growing collaboration among Christians, Jews and Muslims in certain matters, such as issuing common appeals in the fight against racism.

The Muslims

The number of Muslims in France is estimated at between four and five million, which makes the Islamic religion second only to Roman Catholicism. Yet Muslims have had some difficulty gaining acceptance among the public at large and gaining full legitimation on the part of the state. Hostility to Islam is sometimes rationalized by the argument that Islam is more than a religion in that it makes no distinction between religious belief and adherence to codes of quotidian social behaviour; and that its value system runs counter to such republican features as democracy, pluralism, secularism, individual liberty, gender equality and the supremacy of civil law.[35] It is also argued that Islam is a 'foreign' religion because many mosques and Koranic schools are subsidized by Saudi Arabia and Algeria and that a number of Muslim countries have been sending 'reliable' imams to function in France.[36] According to official sources, 40 per cent of the approximately 500 imams in France in 1994 were Moroccan, 25 per cent Algerian, and 13 per cent Turkish.[37] Conversely, there are those who argue that Islam, like other religions in France, is capable of becoming Western-ized and republicanized; and once it has evolved in that direction, it will be treated like the other religions by society at large. In the opinion of some observers, this process will take time; after all, they argue, it took Christians and Jews more than a century to accommodate themselves to the supremacy of the republican state.[38] In the eyes of many others, Islam in France has already evolved sufficiently, so that that religion is now increasingly accepted as being a part of the French scene.

This perception seems to be shared in growing measure by the general public. According to a public opinion survey, 95 per cent believe that it is possible to be fully integrated into French society and still practise Islam in private; 66 per cent do not believe that the more integrated one is to French society, the less Muslim one is; 72 per cent do not believe that Muslims should benefit from special status for marriage and divorce; 72 per cent agree that French secularism allows any religion to express its faith; and 78 per cent, that laws must apply equally to all citizens.[39] This is indicative of a significant *francisation* and republicanization of Muslims in France. According to an opinion survey taken shortly after the terrorist attack on the World Trade Center in New York, religious observance among French Muslims has been going up, but the degree of their integration into French society has risen as well, because Islam is increasingly accepted by French society at large. The survey shows, for example, that in 2001, 22 per cent of French citizens thought of Muslims as fanatics (compared to 37 per cent in 1994). At the same time, an ever larger number of Muslims appreciate the political culture of *laïcité*, because it allows all religions to express themselves. Curiously, French citizens close to the left are more accepting of the building of mosques than those on the right. Many of the latter cite a number of happenings to call in question the meaning of such polls.[40] They refer to the Islamic head-scarf or *foulard*; to the influence of foreign imams; to periodic pronouncements of Muslim clergy that emphasize the supremacy of *sharia* law; and to inter-mittent support of Algerian fundamentalists and terrorists by Muslims residing in France. These critics also emphasize the belief that, because of perceptions of relative deprivation, the Muslim community has become more permeable to the thesis of Islamic extremists (illustrated by growing support within the Hexagon of Algerian terrorist networks – and the efforts of the Ministry of the Interior to dismantle them).[41] These confusing images have led to an ambivalent position on the part of the non-Muslim majority. On the one hand, most French citizens are committed to the notion of equal rights for all religions, including Islam; on the other hand, more than half the population would not welcome the election of a mayor of Muslim origin.[42]

The overwhelming majority of Muslims in France are neither dogmatic fundamentalists nor terrorists; on the contrary, they have become so republican-ized and secularized that in their behaviour and political attitudes they can be distinguished only with difficulty from other French citizens. According to a poll of 1989, fewer than 16 per cent of the Muslims went regularly to Friday mosque.[43] According to a poll conducted in 1994, only 27 per cent of Muslims in France described themselves as observant; however, 60 per cent observed Ramadan, and large numbers celebrated Id al-Kebir, the feast of sacrifice, during which lambs are slaughtered in public ceremonies. The one rite of Islam that is observed almost universally is male circumcision. This ritual minimalism has led Charles Pasqua (minister of the interior in the mid 1980s and the mid 1990s) and others to warn against tarring all Muslims with the brush of fundamentalism (*intégrisme*); he has insisted that Islam be treated not as a foreign religion but a French one, and hoped that the proper institutions would be created to facilitate that development.

Enlightened politicians argue that Islam should be treated like other religions in France. They favour granting municipal permits for the building of Friday mosques on the same basis as for the construction of churches and synagogues; and in Alsace and Lorraine (Department of Moselle), they favour giving to Islam the same kind of official legitimation (including government subsidies for clergy) already possessed by the Catholic, Lutheran, Reformed, Eastern Orthodox and Jewish religions. There are about 1,000 mosques in France (364 of them in Paris), many of which are served by imams of the foreign nationalities as mentioned above. Their number is likely to grow (despite opposition from the extreme-right National Front), especially in large cities where Muslims account for a sizable proportion of the electorate. In addition, there are more than 1,200 prayer rooms and nearly 900 Islamic voluntary associations. Furthermore, there are numerous Muslim bookstores, and markets that sell meat prepared according to Islamic dietary prescriptions.[44]

In practice, the French authorities have not yet decided how to take official cognizance of the Islamic reality.[45] One step forward was taken by the Ministry of the Interior (headed by Pierre Joxe, a Socialist) in 1990 when it set up the Conseil de Réflexion sur l'Islam en France (CORIF), an organization of Muslims whose primary purpose has been the promotion of a Westernized Islam. This organization collaborates (and competes) with the Conseil des Imams, which was created in 1999 to bring together 29 imams representing 80 Islamic houses of worship. Since the September 2001 terrorist attack on New York, Muslims have been under intensified pressure to unite into a representative 'peak' organization – a Conseil Français du Culte Musulman, which would be in effect liaison with the government.[46] Eventually, Muslim-sponsored private schools (which today hardly exist in France), would have to be subsidized, as are Catholic and Jewish-sponsored schools today; however, given the negative image of 'fundamentalist' Islam, this might meet considerable public resistance. This image is fed by, among other things, selected positions of spokesmen of fundamentalist Islam. The job of countering that negative image has rested on the shoulders of (or has been appropriated by) Dalil Boubakeur, the rector of the Great Mosque in Paris. He has often spoken of a specifically 'French' Islam and has acted as the interlocutor between the Muslim community and the French national government, made many declarations of loyalty to the republic, and maintained contacts with all major political parties. In order to demonstrate his ecumenism, he has been an active member of the Fraternity of Abraham (an organization embracing Christians, Jews and moderate Muslims), and has even participated in celebrations of the 50th anniversary of the founding of the State of Israel.

Moderation, however, is difficult in some cases. One of the issues was the *fatwa* against Salman Rushdie, the 'dissident' Muslim writer of *The Satanic Verses*, a book considered to be anti-Islamic. Boubakeur protested vehemently against the visit of Rushdie in France and his appearance on a public television network. Whether this position was necessary is a matter of controversy, for most Muslims did not get involved in this matter, and did not respond to pressures to obey the *fatwa*. Moreover, the moderation of most Muslims in France was demonstrated by the fact that they tried hard not to take sides in the conflict between Iraq and the West. During the Gulf war, 54 per cent of French Muslims felt close neither to Iraq nor to the Western allies, and 56 per cent had a negative opinion of Saddam Hussein.[47]

The ambiguous image of French Muslims is reflected in ambivalent positions on the part of the government. While worrying about the uncertain commitment of French Muslims to the republican system, and periodically apprehending terrorists, it has been pursuing an unqualified pro-Arab, and therefore pro-Islamic, foreign policy position (in part for commercial reasons) and has subsidized the Institut du Monde Arabe, an Arab-Muslim cultural centre in Paris. Occasionally, pro-Arab politicians (e.g., Claude Cheysson, who served as a Socialist foreign minister, Jean-Pierre Chevènement, a leftist nationalist who occupied several cabinet posts and was a founder of the Franco-Iraqi Friendship League) argue that the Arab leaders and regimes they support are 'secular' ones, but such an argument is patently disingenuous.

An example of the complicated involvement of the state in matters pertaining to Islam was the publication of a best-selling book critical of that religion.[48] In that book, author Jean-Claude Barreau, a secularist who became a convert to Catholicism and subsequently a specialist on Islam and was appointed to the Office of International Migrations, argued that Islam was an obstacle to democratic development.[49] Barreau was dismissed from his post, although it was not clear for what reason. CORIF (see above) criticized Barreau for contravening the spirit of the Constitution, while the Ligue des Droits de L'Homme (an organization normally devoted to promoting freedom of expression) excoriated Barreau for attacking freedom of religion.[50]

Often, meanwhile, 'Islam is tolerated as long as it is hidden', as an Alsatian bishop once put it.[51] The reference is to the decision of Islamic authorities in an Alsatian mining town to refrain from amplifying calls to prayer from the minaret of the local mosque 'so as not to drown out the hourly peals of their Catholic neighbours'. Opposition to Islam is sometimes expressed in terms, not of opposition to the practice of that religion as such, but to its concrete manifestations, especially if these tend to impinge upon the physical aspect of a locality. This explains why municipal authorities often find ways of withholding permits for the construction of mosques. A particularly interesting case was a referendum held in a small mining town in northwestern France (Libercourt, in Pas-de-Calais) on the question of forbidding the construction of minarets higher than the local mining cottages or slag heaps. Although supported by 83.5 per cent of the voters, the referendum (initiated by the Communist mayor) was of no juridical value, because, apart from violating the principle of freedom of religion, the French constitution makes no room for local referenda.[52]

THE REPUBLIC, EDUCATION AND RELIGION

In modern states, school systems have been the principal arenas for preparation for the labour market, elite recruitment and socialization. From the mid-nineteenth century on, the inculcation of republican citizenship had implied a strictly secular education; but this approach was challenged by many who could not imagine the omission of instruction in a religion with which French collective consciousness had traditionally been identified. By means of piece-meal legislation, districts and departments were obligated to provide elementary instruction for all, but such instruction remained for the most part the responsibility of the churches. The Falloux law of 1850, which required all communes with more than eight hundred inhabitants to maintain primary schools for girls and boys, also confirmed the freedom of instruction by permitting the existence of church schools, but on condition that these be funded privately. The importance of such schools diminished considerably after the enactment of the Ferry laws, which provided for publicly funded schools. That school system proved to be a highly successful instrument of national integration, in the sense that it transformed immigrants as well as members of indigenous ethnoregional minorities, who spoke their own languages, into culturally more or less undifferentiated French citizens.

This, however, was not to be the end of the matter, for many French citizens wished to retain a choice of schools for their children. As France modernized and urbanized, private schools were regarded by many as reactionary, to the extent that their curricula included Breton, Alsatian, Basque and other minority subject matter that was equated with 'backward' cultures and with a Catholicism that was regarded as having antirepublican tendencies. Because of their close identification with republicanism, most left-wing political parties became staunch defenders of the public schools and were little inclined to support any official subsidization of private schools.

Since the end of World War II, however, private schools were preferred to public schools by many parents, including secular ones. By the 1970s, about 15–20 per cent of primary- and secondary-school children were enrolled in private (mostly Catholic) schools. That figure does not imply that an equivalent percentage of the French were religious. Rather, it reflected the fact that many parents were dissatisfied with urban public schools, which were often over-crowded and beset with problems of discipline and violence and where standards of instruction were being lowered. In contrast, private schools had smaller classes and devoted greater attention to individual students. Most private schools were not particularly religious in nature; that included many nominally Catholic schools, where teachers were for the most part not practising Catholics. In fact, in some of the 'parochial' schools little if any religion has been taught.[53]

In response to that development, the Debré law was enacted in 1959, which involved the government more closely in the functioning of parochial schools. Under that law, parochial schools that wished neither to become integrated into the public-school system nor to be left to their own financial devices were given two other options: they could sign a contract with the state under which the latter would participate in the remuneration of teachers if they adhered to the qualifications established by the state; alternatively, the state would pay the teachers' salaries and contribute as well to the cost of the general functioning of the school, if the schools in question included state-approved courses in its instructional curriculum.

This situation did not sit very well with the Communist and Socialist parties. This was true of several of the trade unions as well. The Fédération de l'Education Nationale (FEN), the largest union of teachers, was ideologically so committed to *laïcité* that it opposed government support of private (paro-chial) schools in principle. Among other powerful organizations promoting *laïcité* was the Comité National d'Action Laïque (CNAL), which, in concert with the leftist parties (Parti Socialiste [PS], Parti Communiste Français [PCF], and Mouvement des Radicaux de Gauche [MRG]) demanded a 'resecular-ization' of public instruction, a demand that was incorporated in the Common Programme of the Left (1972). All these organizations exerted pressure on the Socialist government of Pierre Mauroy, whose minister of education, Alain Savary, in 1983 introduced a bill designed to 'integrate' the private schools into the national public-school system. The bill was intended to put into legislative form the Socialists' election campaign platform, embodied in Mitterrand's *110 Propositions pour la France*, which called for the creation of a 'large, unified public education service'.[54] Given the continuing decline in religious observance, the government thought that it was on safe ground; indeed, the bill passed the National Assembly in 1984.

The bill provoked an unexpected public reaction; there were massive demonstrations by more than a million people in Paris and elsewhere, mobilized largely by the political right and centre. They objected to the bill primarily because it threatened freedom of choice of parents of schoolchildren. Many of the protesters were not practising Catholics; as pointed out above, they had been opting for private schools for reasons that had nothing to do with religion. Moreover, the legislation was in conflict with another principle that had been embraced by the Socialist government – that of encouraging the maintenance and public support of ethnocultural and linguistic pluralism, more specifically the Breton, Catalan, Basque and Occitan cultures, most of which were heavily infused with Catholicism.[55] In any case, the enactment of the bill was shelved by the government. Finally, there were those who were less inspired by right-wing ideology than by opposition to excessive *étatisme*, of which the centralized school system was a major symbol.[56]

The shelving of the Savary bill was not the end of the controversy over education. The government's position remained ambiguous, because it was buffeted on both sides. The FEN, a major supporter of the government, maintained its commitment to anticlericalism and to a *laïciste* monopoly in education; however, that association was racked by internal conflicts and in the early 1990s lost more than half its 500,000 members to a rival teachers' union (the Syndicat National Unitaire des Instituteurs, Professeurs d'École et de Professeurs de Collège [SNUipp]), which was even more anticlericalist and was resolutely opposed to any public support for parochial schools.[57] Conversely, the CFDT, one of the three largest trade-union confederations, retained considerable Catholic sensitivities even after it broke away in the mid 1960s from the CFTC, its 'mother' organization.

Although the Socialist government continued to favour laic public education as a matter of principle, it could not ignore the fact that a large portion of the public opposed an excessive skimping on private schools. It was also confronted with a decision of the Council of State (Conseil d'État, the highest court of administrative appeals) in 1991, which forced the government to grant those schools more than 1.8 billion francs in back pay in order to bring support up to the level of the public schools.[58] In partial response to this decision, Jack Lang, the Socialist minister of education at the time, made an agreement with Father Max Cloupet, the newly appointed head of the Association of Catholic Education, to assure parity between public and private schools (a position that met with hostility on the part of hard-nosed secularists). The agreement contained an important condition: that the recipient schools provide the same kind of educational background and the same state examinations for teachers in both systems as the public schools. The Catholic establishment, however, opposed this condition, and the agreement was withdrawn.[59]

In the past decade, the controversy over the place of religion in education seemed to lose its sharp edge. Due in part to the declining impact of Catholicism in recent years, secularists had arrived at a greater tolerance toward religion. Towards the end of the 1980s, public-school authorities and teachers were prepared to accept a '*laïcité ouverte*', which meant on the one hand, a greater permissiveness, albeit selective, towards religious symbols, and on the other, a willingness to have religion dealt with in public schools as an academic subject.[60] This change corresponded to an evolution of attitudes among the general public. Because of the effective operationalization of *laïcité* in the public schools, the vast majority of French have grown up without any knowledge of religion. This lacuna was considered to be undesirable, in view of the fact that so many global conflicts were related to religious causes. In the mid- and late 1980s, school authorities as well as teachers' unions (including the very *laïciste* FEN), held discussions on the matter and agreed that schools should teach the history of religions. They recognized that religious input to certain public-policy questions (e.g., relating to the interruption of pregnancy, cloning and other matters of medical ethics) could be valuable; and that the study of religion (in particular comparative religion) as an academic subject was a legitimate element of a public educational curriculum.[61] In a 1988 poll, two out of three respondents were favourably disposed to courses on the history of religions in the public schools, while 14 per cent opposed them on the grounds that they were incompatible with the principle of *laïcité*, and 19 per cent opposed them on the grounds that they would lead to religious indoctrination.[62]

Such openness had its limits; it did not imply any increase in readiness to compromise in favour of parochial schools as such, that is, to go much beyond the Falloux law of 1850, which permitted the existence of Church schools, but on condition that they be funded largely from private sources, with no more than 10 per cent of the budget coming from government sources. In 1994, when François Bayrou (minister of education in the right-of-centre government of Edouard Balladur) wanted to reform that law in order to permit local authorities to finance private schools to a greater extent, there was a large public demonstration in the name of *laïcité*, and the Constitutional Council (Conseil Constitutionnel, the body charged with ruling on the constitutionality of pending legislation) ruled partially against this reform.

The place of religion in education became a much more serious matter of controversy when the issue was not Catholicism, but non-Christian religions, in particular Islam. Tolerance and pluralism implied treating schoolchildren of all religions equally within school premises, provided that they show themselves to be receptive to the national republican curriculum. This principle began to be severely tested when, in 1989, three Muslim schoolgirls showed up in a public junior high school (*collège*) in Creil, a small town in the Paris region, wearing an Islamic veil or headscarf (*foulard*).

The principal of the school reacted by demanding of the three girls that they not wear the headscarf to class, or else not to come to school. They were excluded from class for a few days, and then returned to class without the headscarf. Subsequently they came back with the headscarf, and were suspended for several weeks. The government and the Socialist party leadership adopted a flexible position, and the minister of education temporized, bucking the matter back to local school authorities: he suggested that the school principal reason with the parents and try to convince them to tell their daughters not to wear the headscarf to class; but if the principal failed in his attempt at dialogue, to let the girls come to class anyway. SOS-Racisme, an anti-racist 'rainbow coalition' (formed in the early 1980s with the encouragement of the Socialist government), and various immigrant and human rights associations argued that the girls not be excluded under any conditions, as long as they accepted the regular school curriculum. This tolerant position was defended by a number of public figures (including

Danielle Mitterrand, the wife of the president) in the name of freedom of expression as well as the newly developing tolerance towards cultural pluralism, or 'the right to be different' ('*droit à la différence*').[63]

Within the Socialist party, the dominant position was an absolute ban on the headscarf, in the interest of both *laïcité* and the rights of women. France-Plus (an organization of young Beurs[64] who fought for integration) agreed, demanding that the girls cease wearing the headscarf to class and adhere to the norms of the *école laïque*.[65] Within the conservative camp, specifically the Gaullist party (Rassemblement pour la République – RPR) and the liberal-centrist coalition (Union pour la Démocratie Française – UDF) there was division; the more 'liberal' politicians opposed the wearing of the headscarf in the name of separation of religion and state, while more traditional conservatives, who were generally more tolerant toward Catholic symbols, raised questions about Muslim ones, arguing that Islam was 'un-French' because, unlike Christianity and Judaism, it did not distinguish between religious practice and political values; and they used the controversy to demand a debate on immigration.[66] The problem was left in abeyance; meanwhile, about 700 girls in France had begun to wear the headscarf, but this did not become a public issue because the majority of local school authorities appeared to let them get away with it. The government was faced with a dilemma: on the one hand, it had to maintain the principle of *laïcité*, on the other hand, it could not be too hostile to symbols of Islam, lest Muslims overreact by establishing Islamic schools and claiming government support in the name of equal treatment.[67]

The Council of State, to which the case was sent, adopted a differentiated attitude; in 1992, it issued a general directive that reflected a degree of tolerance: it argued that the wearing of religious symbols, including the Islamic headscarf, was not by itself incompatible with *laïcité* in a public school, as long as it did not constitute pressure, provocation, or proselytism and did not disrupt the process of instruction. It left the interpretation to school authorities, some of which suspended Muslim girls wearing headscarves, while others turned a blind eye to them. In a circular issued by Education minister François Bayrou (himself belonging to the Centre des Démocrates Sociaux [CDS], the 'Catholic' component of the UDF) in September 1994, he refined that directive of the Council of State by stipulating that the religious symbols must be 'discreet' and not 'ostentatious'.

The question of ostentatious religious symbols presented itself in a related case in 1996, when a Catholic *lycée* in Paris was used as a venue for the administration of a state examination for the baccalauréat in philosophy. Under the terms of the Debré law, the state has a right to demand of parochial schools subsidized by it under contract that they make their premises available for state examinations. The particular hall in the lycée, however, was equipped with crucifixes, and noises came from adjacent classrooms in which courses on the catechism were being taught. These phenomena led to complaints by several students, who were permitted to take their examinations in another room. The parochial school authorities rejected subsequent public criticisms by arguing that noises from the adjacent classrooms had been sufficiently muffled; that the state has not objected when Jewish students showed up for exams wearing skullcaps, and that it has not demanded that soldiers remove their uniforms when they present themselves for exams.[68]

The problem of Jewish particularity came up repeatedly with respect to the school calendar and, more specifically, school examinations, which sometimes take place on Saturdays, the Jewish sabbath, or on other Jewish holy days. A circular letter in 1989 made it possible for the school calendar to be planned around the major religious festivals, taking into account all denominations, including those of Muslims and Armenians. When confronted by the demands of Jewish students for leaves of absence on Saturdays, however, a statutory order on 18 February 1991 on pupils' rights and duties strictly recalled the principle of obligatory school attendance. The Central Consistory and two Jewish associations responded by lodging an appeal to the Council of State. The controversy was particularly divisive within the Jewish population itself, with the *laïque* movements forcefully opposing community orientations as defined by the Chief Rabbi of France.

Ultimately, it was the Public Affairs Tribunal of Nice that mediated in the conflict, on the one hand recalling existing principles, and on the other discouraging any rigidity in their application. In 1993, a Jewish (senior) secondary-school student in Nice was expelled for repeated absences from his Saturday lessons. The Nice tribunal ruled in favour of the school, which led to an appeal before the Council of State in 1995. The council rejected the appeal insofar as it was attempting to win a general leave of absence for Jewish pupils on the Sabbath. At the same time, the council stopped short of confirming school attendance as being absolutely obligatory: it held that pupils who request leave could be authorized not to attend, as long as those absences are 'not in contradiction with the tasks inherent in their studies and that they do not disrupt public order within the establishment'.[69] It decided that a law passed in 1991, which mandated school attendance, 'cannot legally be used to prevent an individual student from being authorized to be absent from school for religious worship or the celebration of a religious holiday'.[70] This decision led to a spirited polemic between those who welcomed the decision in the name of liberty and equality of religious groups and those for whom the decision represented an attack on *laïcité*. Moreover, the *laïciste* critics argued that if such permissiveness were extended to all religions in the name of fairness, the national school system would be disrupted.

The issue of a level playing field for members of minority religions was raised by Chief Rabbi Joseph Sitruk in connection with a matter that had to do not with education but with elections. In the spring of 1994, Rabbi Sitruk complained about the fact that the second round of cantonal elections were scheduled for Passover; he argued that orthodox Jews might be violating religious prescriptions by voting and suggested that they abstain from voting. In this as in other respects, the chief rabbi acted as 'intermediary' or 'intercessor' (*shtadlan*), a position accorded to him under the Consistory system established by Napoleon (see below). In this instance, however, he was accused of having gone too far. He was charged with religious interference in the political process, with the result that Sitruk reconsidered his call.[71] After all, French elections at all levels normally take place on Sunday, which is the Christian day of rest.

THE STATE, THE CHURCH AND THE POPE

The image of France as a de-Christianized country is subjected to a severe challenge when it comes to relations with the Pope. In 1904, in the wake of the Dreyfus Affair, and just before the 'disestablishment' of religion, France's relationship with the Vatican had deteriorated to such an extent that diplomatic relations were broken. These relations were re-established in 1920/21; however, in order to maintain its image as a secular state, France had to deal with the Vatican with the utmost care.[72]

This was a particularly sensitive matter, in view of the cordial relations the Vatican had maintained with the Vichy regime. Such relations were made easier under Pope John Paul II, who embodied a new official Catholic attitude of tolerance, ecumenism and republicanism. This evolution explains the official visit of President Chirac to the Vatican in January 1996. Chirac's reference during that visit to France as 'the eldest daughter of the Church' had led to vehement criticisms by secular French personalities; and Chirac had to use the occasion of the Pope's visit to France in September 1996 (his fifth visit), to rectify the statement by welcoming the Pope 'in the name of republican and secular France'. Nevertheless, the Pope's visit aroused a great deal of hostility on the part of anticlerical forces.[73] In some eyes, that papal visit was a more or less normal diplomatic one; in the opinion of others, it was a purely private affair with which the public authorities should have had as little to do as possible. Many among these critics argued that ordinary protocol perhaps required that the Pope (as the head of a sovereign state) be welcomed by the president and bid farewell by the prime minister; but that it did not require the expenditure of public funds – estimated at about 18 million francs – connected with the visit to three cities.[74]

The Pope's visit coincided with the observance of the 1500th anniversary of the baptism (13 April 496) of Clovis, a Merovingian tribal chief who, in the fifth century, became the first King of France. The event was commemorated by Pope John Paul II at a mass in Reims, where Clovis was baptized. A state committee headed by Prime Minister Alain Juppé had been formed to oversee the celebrations. But the day the official celebration took place, 22 September, happens to be 'Republic Day' in France, and the event was not regarded as a coincidence by adamant secularists.[75] In their eyes, the celebration was a wrong and inappropriate element of the mythology of France: wrong, because Clovis was a barbarian who was baptized for reasons other than religious; and inappropriate, because France is a republic.[76] These conflicting views – they were reflected in an opinion survey according to which 40 per cent of the respondents were in favour of a national celebration and 40 per cent were opposed[77] – were emblematic of the religious–secular divide that persists in France, and the Church had to be sensitive to this fact. In his welcoming speech to John Paul II, Mgr. Gérard Defois, the archbishop of Reims, while not denying the laic and republican character of the country, argued that although 'it is not the Church that made France, one cannot deny that France was also the political choice of individuals who were believers and sometimes saints'.[78]

The reaction to a subsequent papal visit to France, which took place in August 1997 in connection with the twelfth global Catholic youth festival, was more complex. This festival was a major public and media event, which was reflected in mass rallies in Paris.[79] There was some discussion of whether the engagement of thousands of police officers for the event was a violation of the principle of separation of Church and state; but most observers were in agreement the use of police was for the purpose of public order rather than a manifestation of official support of the Pope's visit or of an endorsement of Catholicism. Moreover, it was pointed out that many of the more than 250,000 young people who showed up seemed to welcome the event not because they were religious – in fact, fewer than 4 per cent of those under 35 went to mass more than once a month – but because the Pope offered an alternative message to that brought by the various political ideologies. During this visit, both the Pope and the government acted in a conciliatory manner. The Pope apologized for the St Bartholomew's massacre of Protestants – it had taken place on 24 August 1572, during the wars of religion – which he regarded as contrary to the teachings of the Gospel, and called for a reconciliation between Catholics and Protestants. For his part, Chirac affirmed France's principle of separation of Church and state, and Prime Minister Jospin called for guarding *laïcité*.

CURRENT PROBLEMS AND UNSETTLED QUESTIONS

France's commitment to *laïcité* is manifested by numerous symbols of a 'civic religion': a Panthéon (where great men and women of the Republic are entombed), a hagiography (depicting the achievements of the Republic), a liturgy (including the Marseillaise), statues, saints (military and other heroes after whom streets are named) and myths.[80] Unfortunately, some of these myths, so carefully constructed by de Gaulle after Liberation – e.g., France's liberation by its own efforts, the importance of the Resistance, and the notion that there was no continuity between the Vichy state and the Republic – have been undermined by young historians who have had no skeletons in their closets; and the myths were almost entirely dismantled during the Papon trial.

There is no doubt, however, that there is continuity in France's republican ideology, and that *laïcité*, under whatever interpretation, is a major element of

it. Pierre Brechon, a prominent political scientist, distinguishes among several
types of *laïcité* in France:

1. *laïcité de combat*: an ideological approach identified with the Left, which,
   since the nineteenth century, regards Catholicism as an arch-enemy of
   republicanism and views all religions as standing in the way of progress and
   democracy and believes that these goals can be secured only by a '*laïcité pur
   et dur*': an uncompromising commitment to secularity as a matter of policy
   and personal behaviour;
2. *laïcité de fait*: growing secularism and indifference to religion as a consequence of modernization; and
3. *laïcité institutionnelle*: the state's neutrality with respect to religions, as
   manifested in constitutional texts, legal provisions, public policies and the
   public-school system.[81]

All of these versions have contributed to a state of affairs where organized
religion is a largely private matter, and as such is no longer a factor in the social
and political behaviour of citizens.

One of the problems has to do with the precise demarcation of private and
public. The fact that state funerals (in the form of requiem masses) of Presidents
de Gaulle, Pompidou and even Mitterrand (a Socialist) took place in Notre
Dame Cathedral in Paris, suggests that the church has been transformed into a
quasi-official venue for state funeral observances – when a secular place might
have been more appropriate.[82] It is often argued that, in an era of secularized
Catholicism, Notre Dame and other cathedrals should be regarded, not as
religious edifices, but as part of the physical, cultural and architectural heritage
of France and as manifestations of the 'Frenchness' of the national community
viewed historically. It is true that under Jacobin doctrine, membership in that
community is defined in purely political terms, so that Protestants, Jews, Eastern
Orthodox and Muslims are as much part of that community as Roman
Catholics. It is doubtful, however, whether the majority of the French are quite
ready to accept physical symbols of religions other than Christian as authentic
parts of the French landscape. The label given to certain houses of worship as
components of the 'constructed patrimony' (*patrimoine bâti*) of the country,
under which the French subsumed public property whose upkeep is the
responsibility of the government authorities, does not apply exclusively to
churches.[83] But since this label applies essentially to buildings built many years
ago, and certainly before the massive influx of Muslims, it can hardly be expected
to be used for mosques.[84]

The criterion of tradition and 'anterior rights' has affected the debate over
the distinction between public and private physical space and between the secular
and the religious domain, especially on local levels. A case in point is the
celebration of country harvest festivals, during which the processions often take
on a quasi-religious character; another case is the use of church bells – not

primarily to call the faithful to prayer (as do Muslim muezzins from minarets) but to announce weddings or deaths in the village. But, what if the country festival is more 'folkloric' than religious; and what if church bells are sounded to alert the villages to the fact that a fire has broken out? The answer given by public authorities depends on a number of criteria: the extent to which processions or the sound of church bells disturb the public order; or the 'public' character of the church in question.[85] Over the past century, the Council of State has taken a fairly flexible position, and has tended to delegate responsibility in such matters to mayors, whose decisions have sometimes involved legal sophisms.

Another problem is whether the neutrality of the state with respect to religion should apply indiscriminately to all faiths. Since religion impinges upon secular political matters, such as republican values and civil and criminal jurisdiction, there have been growing concerns about more recently emerging cults and sects. These concerns have been reflected in parliamentary inquiries about Mormonism, which condones polygyny; the Horus sect, which has been accused of murder; and Scientology, which has been subjected to criminal prosecution because of the allegedly questionable psychological and financial methods it has used to recruit and retain its adherents. Obviously, such concerns exist with respect to Islam: charges that faithful adherents to that religion cannot be genuinely French because of its anti-democratic and anti-pluralistic orientations. But given the diversity of its membership with regard to observance and the fact that it is the second largest religion in France, its progressive legitimation can hardly be stopped, despite arguments, articulated especially by the French political Right, that the Muslims cannot be easily 'Gallicized' because their religious and political values are incompatible with the 'Judeo-Christian civilization' (*sic*) on which France has been based, values that, *inter alia*, include pluralism and *laïcité*.[86]

Still another problem relates to the connection between ethnocultural and religious diversity. That connection is taken more or less for granted when it comes to Bretons and Basques, whose ethnic particularism tends to be more readily accepted perhaps because these ethnic groups are indigenous and Catholic; conversely, the majority has been reluctant to think of the Jews in ethnocultural terms or, conversely, to think of Muslims in purely religious terms. The connection between religion and ethnicity became a subject of debate during the initial era of Socialist rule (1981–86) under the Mitterrand presidency, when the government officially embraced a policy of cultural pluralism, and when the 'right to be different' (*droit à la différence*) was considered to be a major expression of equality, liberty and diversity, if not of *laïcité*. From the end of the 1980s on, however, economic difficulties as well as the pressing needs of 'national integration' led to a renewed underemphasis of such a right.

Precisely what role religion will play in the future is uncertain; it is reasonable to suggest, however, that it will be influenced by three developments: decentralization, pluralism and the growth of 'participatory democracy'. As the regions gain increasing power, those with strongly implanted Catholic traditions (e.g., Brittany and Corsica) are likely to see the development of subnational cultures significantly informed by those traditions. To the extent that pluralism implies both a growing autonomy of 'civil society' and an assertion of the market, it will make for greater competition between the state and religious organizations, especially with respect to the media – as illustrated by the growth of regional TV channels and private radio stations in which religious programmes are presented. Another aspect of pluralism is the increasing use of private endowments of cultural and educational institutions (often of a religious nature), endowments that are publicly recognized for tax purposes.[87] Still another feature of pluralism is the growing multiformity *within* each religious group. 'Participatory democracy' is reflected, inter alia, in the form of parent–teacher associations divided along anticlerical and clerical lines, whose input is sometimes crucial in a school's decision on whether, and in what form, discussions of religion become part of the curriculum.[88]

To some observers, these developments tend to be conducive to the weakening of the role of the state in guarding the principle of separation of religion and state and to add to the periodic worries of the French about their national unity. Such worries appear to be groundless, for, at this writing, religious identities are too diverse, weak and unthreatening to undermine the stability of the French political community or the principle of *laïcité* on which it is based.

NOTES

1. Claude Durand-Prinborgne, *La laïcité* (Paris: Dalloz, 1996), pp. 19–20.
2. See David Thomson, *Democracy in France since 1870* (London: Oxford Univesity Press, 1969), pp. 139–42.
3. In Clermont-Tonnerre's words, 'Il faut refuser tout aux Juifs comme nation et accorder tout aux Juifs comme individus …; il faut qu'ils ne fassent dans l'Etat ni un corps politique, ni un Ordre; il faut qu'ils soient individuellement citoyens.'
4. Jean-Paul Guetny, 'Les Français sont-ils religieux?', *L'Etat de la France*, 95–96 (Paris: La Découverte, 1994), pp. 202–5.
5. CSA/LeMonde, 6–7 September 1996, reported in *Le Monde, Dossiers et Documents*, no. 249, December 1996.
6. Poll conducted at the end of 1999. See 'Les Français jugent l'action de Jean Paul II', *Le Monde, Dossiers et Documents*, no. 285, March 2000, p. 7. Note that in 2000, only 44 per cent of Catholic couples married in church (compared to 78 per cent in 1965); and that in 2000, 40 per cent of births were out of wedlock (compared to 6 per cent in 1967). Gérard Mermet, *Francoscopie 2001* (Paris: Larousse, 2000), pp. 132–3.
7. Guy Michelat, Julien Potel, Jacques Sutter, Jacques Maître, *Les Français sont-ils encore Catholiques?* (Paris: Le Cerf, 1991).
8. See Rochdy Alili, 'La question de l'Islam de France', *L'Etat de la France*, 94–95 (Paris: La Découverte, 1994), pp. 37–40.
9. Hughes Portelli, 'L'évolution politique des catholiques', SOFRES, *L'Etat de l'opinion* (Paris: Seuil, 1994), p. 181.
10. Ibid., pp. 186–7. SOFRES, February 1993.
11. According to a *Figaro* poll (December 1997), 59 per cent of French believe in God and 26 per cent pray often. Cited in Michelat *et al.*, *Les Français sont-ils encore catholiques?*
12. See René Rémond, *Le christianisme en accusation* (Paris: Desclée De Brouwer, 2000).

13. Religion still correlates with right-wing voting, but it is not the only – and perhaps not the decisive – factor.

14. During Epiphany, most French men, women and children (whether Catholic or not) eat special round flat cakes (*galettes du roi*); and throughout the year, one may buy several different kinds of pastry with 'religious' names, not necessarily flattering, e.g., *une religieuse* (a nun, a frosted cream puff) or *un pet de nonne* (a 'nun's fart', a kind of fritter).

15. Pierre Brechon, 'Le rôle de l'Etat face à la diversité des groupes religieux', *Cahiers de Meylan* (1992/3), pp. 31–6; and 'Clovis, l'église, et la République', *Le Monde* (special issue), 19 September 1996, p. iii.

16. Acacio Pereira, 'Le deuil s'accompagne de nouvelles cérémonies funéraires', *Le Monde*, 11–12 January 1998, p. 7.

17. See 'La grande revanche des protestants', *Le Point*, 27 January 1996, pp. 72–9. One Protestant (François Guizot, 1847) was president at the end of the 'July Monarchy'; another (Gaston Doumergue, 1924) during the Third Republic.

18. See Pierre Birnbaum, *Les Fous de la République: Histoire politique des Juifs d'Etat de Gambetta à Vichy* (Paris: Fayard, 1992).

19. See Dominique Schnapper, *Juifs et israélites* (Paris: Gallimard, 1980). The division between the assimilated israélites, labelled by Pierre Birnbaum '*Juifs d'Etat*', and the more traditional *juifs*, is reminiscent of the two kinds of Catholic clergy at the time of the Revolution; those who accepted the Civil Constitution of the Clergy issued in 1789 and swore an oath to the new regime, and the traditional (and monarchist) 'non-juror' priests. On this point, see Hervieu-Léger, 'The Past in the Present: Redefining Laïcité in Multicultural France', in Peter L. Berger (ed.), *The Limits of Social Cohesion: Conflict and Mediation in Pluralist Societies*, report to the Club of Rome (Boulder, CO: Westview Press, 1998), p. 42.

20. Raymond Aron, *Mémoires* (Paris: Julliard, 1983), p. 500.

21. See Chantal Benayoun *et al.*, *Les juifs dans le regard de l'autre* (Toulouse: Presses Universitaires du Mirail, 1988).

22. The most widespread articulation of that view is found in Jean-Paul Sartre, *Réflexions sur la question juive* (Paris: Gallimard, 1954).

23. Pierre Birnbaum, 'Grégoire, Dreyfus, Drancy, et Copernic: Les juifs au coeur de l'histoire de France', in Pierre Nora (ed.), *Les Lieux de mémoire, III. Les France 1* (Paris: Gallimard, 1992), pp. 561–613.

24. See André Harris and Alain de Sédouy, *Juifs & Français* (Paris: Grasset, 1979).

25. Henry H. Weinberg, *The Myth of the Jew in France, 1967–1982* (Oakville, NY, London: Mosaic Press, 1987), pp. 77–82.

26. William Safran, 'The Dreyfus Affair, Political Consciousness, and the Jews: A Centennial Retrospective', *Contemporary French Civilization*, 19: 1 (Winter–Spring 1995).

27. See Laurent Greilsamer, 'L'INSEE utilisait jusqu'en 1987 un répertoire national d'identification intégrant la mention de "juif indigène"', *Le Monde*, 15 November 1991, p. 12; and same author, 'De la transparence au double mensonge', *Le Monde*, 17 December 1991, p. 18.

28. See William Safran, 'The French State and Ethnic Minority Cultures: Policy Dimensions and Problems', in J.R. Rudolph, Jr, and R.J. Thompson (eds), *Ethnoterritorial Politics, Policy, and the Western World* (Boulder, CO and London: Westview Press, 1989), pp. 115–57.

29. Dominique de Montvalon, 'Les juifs de France en 1994', *Le Point*, 16 June 1994, pp. 16–21.

30. William Safran, 'France and her Jews: From "Culte israélite" to "lobby juif"', *Tocqueville Review*, 5: 1 (Spring/Summer, 1983), 101–35.

31. 'Jewish Community praised', *News From France*, 17 March 1997, p. 1. At the same time, the traditional Jacobin view of French Jewry is officially maintained. Note that the Jewish museum opened in Paris under national government auspices is called, not *Musée juif*, but *Musée d'art et d'histoire du Judaïsme*.

32. On Jewish voting see Chantal Benayoun, *Les juifs et la politique: Enquête sur les élections législatives de 1978 à Toulouse* (Paris: Editions du CNRS, 1984), esp. pp. 135–57; and Sylvie Strudel, *Votes juifs: Itinéraires migratoires religieux et politiques* (Paris: Presses de la Fondation Nationale des Sciences Politiques, 1996), esp. parts 4 and 5.

33. 'La déclaration de repentance' de l'Eglise de France', *Le Monde*, 1 October 1997, p. 19.

34. Decourtray was a member of the Académie Française; and after his death, Lustiger succeeded him – in part because of the efforts of Chirac (who was then still the mayor of Paris). This did not necessarily reflect a particularly 'discriminative' approach to Catholics; for Jacob Kaplan,

who had for many years been the chief rabbi of France, had been a member of the Académie as well.

35. Claude Imbert, 'L'Islam et la République', *Le Point*, 2 March 1996, p. 7; and Philippe Aziz, 'Les intégristes sapent la République', same issue, pp. 40–7.
36. Jean-Loup Reverier, 'Islam: La deuxième religion de France', *Le Point*, 6 March 1989, pp. 26–7.
37. *News From France*, 7 October 1994, p. 5.
38. Rémy Leveau and Dominique Schnapper, 'Religion et politique: Juifs et musulmans maghrébins en France', in Rémy Leveau and Gilles Kepel (eds), *Les Musulmans dans la société française* (Paris: Presses de la Fondation Nationale des Sciences Politiques, 1988), pp. 99–102.
39. IFOP–*Le Monde*, cited in *News From France*, 3 March 1994, p. 4.
40. IFOP poll, 22–8 September 2001, cited by Xavier Ternisien, 'Plus pratiquants, les muselmans de France sont aussi mieux intégrés', *Le Monde*, 5 October 2001.
41. Henri Tincq, 'L'islam de France se radicalise', *Le Monde*, 12 August 1994.
42. 'Islam in France', *News From France*, 3 March 1995, p. 4.
43. Brechon, 'Le retour de la laïcité', *Cahiers de Meylan*, 1 (1992), pp. 9-13. According to another source ('Des lieux de culte nombreux et diverse, à l'image de la communauté', *Le Monde*, 27 June 2001, p. 11), the figure is 10 per cent.
44. *News From France*, 7 October 1994, p. 5.
45. Rochdy Alili, 'La question de l'Islam de France'.
46. Xavier Ternisien, 'Pressés par les attentats, les musulmans se préparent à élire leurs représentants', *Le Monde*, 13 October 2001.
47. IFOP poll, January 1991, reported by Henri Tincq, 'L'incertitude et la peur dominent chez les musulmans français', *Le Monde*, 30 January 1991.
48. Jean-Claude Barreau, *De l'Islam en général et du monde moderne en particulier* (Paris: Editions Pré-aux-Clercs, 1991).
49. It is interesting to compare the thinking of Barreau to that of Roger Garaudy, Abbé Pierre and other public figures whose religious evolutions made them intolerant toward religions they had come to dislike, in this instance Judaism.
50. Jacques Duquesne, 'L'Islam ne pardonne pas', *Le Point*, 16 November 1991, p. 73. See also Brechon, 'Le rôle de l'État', p. 36.
51. Tom Mashberg, 'The New Mosque's Minaret Is Silent, But It Has Much to Say to France', *New York Times*, 29 November 1990.
52. *Le Point*, 6 May 1991, p. 6.
53. Most of the teachers in nominally Catholic schools are laypersons; a considerable number of them, in fact, are *laïque* if not agnostic, and relatively little of the curriculum is religious. Pierre Brechon, 'Le retour de la laïcité', p. 7.
54. Hervieu-Léger, 'The Past in the Present', p. 51.
55. See Safran, 'The French State and Minority Cultures', pp. 115–57.
56. Hervieu-Léger, 'The Past in the Present', p. 53.
57. William Safran, *The French Polity*, 5th edn (New York: Longman, 1998), p. 159.
58. Nathaniel Herzberg, 'La République fait la paix avec l'école catholique', *Libération*, 15 June 1992, p. 24.
59. Hervieu-Léger, 'The Past in the Present', p. 54.
60. Jean Bauberot, 'Le débat sur la laïcité', *Regards sur l'Actualité*, nos 209–10 (March–April 1995), pp. 51–62.
61. Ibid., pp. 61–2.
62. Ibid., pp. 58–9. According to a poll (*Le Monde de l'Education*, July–August 1991, cited in Brechon, 'Le retour de la laïcité', p. 7), that kind of interest corresponded to a certain intellectual interest in religion outside the school system, which is not confined to Catholicism; it included the writings of Martin Marty, Emmanuel Lévinas and a number of Islamic scholars.
63. See Henri Giordan, *Démocratie culturelle et droit à la différence*, rapport au ministre de la culture (Paris: Documentation Française, 1982).
64. The designation 'Beur' refers to French individuals of Arab origin.
65. Brechon, 'Le retour de la laïcité', pp. 9–13.
66. Ibid.
67. Christian Ruby, 'Le foulard et la laïcité', *L'État de la France*, 95–96 (Paris: La Découverte, 1995), p. 206.
68. Eric Pelletier, 'Des crucifix ont perturbé l'épreuve de philo', *Le Figaro*, 21 June 1996, p. 30.

69. Hervieu-Léger, 'The Past in the Present', pp. 63–4.
70. *New York Times,* 14 April 1995.
71. Henri Tincq, 'Les crispations du judaïsme français,' *Le Monde*, 19 March 1994, p. 1.
72. Charlemagne's visit to the Holy See in 800 was the last such visit by a French chief of state until the twentieth century. The visit of René Coty, the last president of the Fourth Republic, took place in May 1957, and that of President de Gaulle in June 1959.
73. One manifestation of that hostility was a bomb placed in a church on the Pope's itinerary; another, in response to the Pope's appeal for donations to help pay for his visit, was the sending of thousands of envelopes containing condoms.
74. Christian Makarian, 'Ce que pèsent les Catholiques de France', *Le Point*, 14 September 1996, p. 74.
75. Mary Dejevsky, 'Historians battle over Clovis, first French king', *The Independent* (London), 24 April 1996.
76. In fact, Clovis's positive image as a nation-builder turned out to be far behind that of Charlemagne and Jules Ferry. 'Clovis, L'Eglise, et la République', *Le Monde* (special issue, 19 September 1996), p. iv.
77. Survey sponsored by *Le Monde*, cited by Jean Bauberot, 'La laïcité comme "pact laïque"', paper read at meeting of the Association Française de Science Politique, Rennes, 28 September–1 October 1999, p. 4.
78. Henri Tincq, 'L'héritage chrétien fait partie de notre patrimoine national', *Le Monde*, 17 September 1996, p. 13.
79. 'Jean Paul II, un pape très médiatisé', *Le Monde*, Television-Radio-Multimedia, 11–17 August 1997, pp. 2–4.
80. Hervieu-Léger, 'The Past in the Present', p. 61.
81. Brechon, 'Le retour de la laïcité', pp. 2–13.
82. Mitterrand's purely religious private funeral in January 1996 took place in Jarnac, a provincial village. In this connection, it should be noted that the body of Pierre Mendès-France, a Fourth Republic prime minister, lay in state in the National Assembly; and that at the burial of Georges Clémenceau, no religious rites whatsoever were performed. For a debate on this issue, see Emile Poulat, 'Une affaire d'Etat: Le Président, la République, et Dieu', *Esprit*, no. 221 (May 1996), 151–61.
83. There are a handful of exceptions: the old synagogues of Carpentras and Cavaillon have been declared historic buildings and as such are maintained with public funds.
84. See Henri Tincq, 'La "séparation", une bénédiction pour les minorités religieuses', *Le Monde*, 'Clovis, L'Eglise, et la République' (special issue, 19 September 1996).
85. Specifically, a church constructed before the separation of state and religion has a more public character than one built afterwards. See Durand-Prinborgne, *Laïcité*, pp. 90–4.
86. This theme is expressed by the ultraconservative Club de l'Horloge in *L'Identité de la France* (Paris: Albin Michel, 1985), p. 205. Curiously, this characterization of French civilization is used primarily in questioning the 'Frenchness' of Muslims rather than in affirming that of Jews.
87. Jean Bauberot, *Histoire de la laïcité française* (Paris: Presses Universitaires de France, 2000), p. 117.
88. See Martine Barthelemy, 'La logique d'ouverture de l'école publique, élément de fragilisation de la laïcité française?', paper read at meeting of Association Française de Science Politique, Rennes, 28 September–1 October 1999, pp. 9–15.

5

The Significance of Religion in British Politics

JOSEPHINE E. SQUIRES

INTRODUCTION AND HISTORICAL BACKGROUND

Contrary to the common perception of the United Kingdom as a secular society, the seat of modern democracy in which politics and religion do not generally mix,[1] the history and politics of Britain have been influenced by religious cleavages for the past four centuries. The cleavages that existed in the seventeenth century were markedly different from those of more recent emergence. In spite of this, a thread of unity across time runs through them. Religious groups have all promoted their respective claims as to which particular brand of moral conscience should guide policy and the law of the land.

Prior to Henry VIII's Anglicanization of the majority of British Catholic churches and cathedrals, with the exception of a relatively small group of Jews, the inhabitants of the British Isles were followers of the Roman Church. Since the meaning of conscience was linked intimately with the teachings of the Church, those few elites who influenced government of the Kingdom were, for the most part, guided by their Catholic religion. Jews were ineligible for positions which would allow them to exert some aspect of political or moral influence on society and were more or less relegated to trading and money lending, occupations that were seen as less than virtuous and not to be practised by any God-fearing Christian. At this time, English, Scottish, Welsh and Irish societies could hardly have been labelled 'secular' as the influence of the Roman Catholic Church and the papal mandate were all-important to political decision-making. As it was bestowed by God, the Divine Right of Kings to rule over their people could only be usurped by the even higher religious authority of the Pope.

It was not until Henry VIII's schism with the Church of Rome in the sixteenth century, his renunciation of papal authority, and his installation of the Church of England as the one official church of the land, that the Catholic–Anglican cleavage emerged. Efforts were made to prohibit the conducting of any non-

Anglican services and the Act for the Uniformity of Common Prayer required that 'all Persons, having no lawful or reasonable Excuse to be absent, are required to resort to their Parish Church'.[2] After the Glorious Revolution[3] in 1688, the state led by the Church of England became more accepting of 'moderate dissenters', such as Presbyterians. The Toleration Act of 1689 granted limited privileges to non-Anglican Trinitarian Protestants and abolished several Elizabethan acts that were designed to ensure uniformity in the Protestant Church. This legislation, while it provided certain freedom of worship, did not excuse any person wishing to hold public office from taking an oath of loyalty to the Monarch and to the English Church, while firmly renouncing the authority of the Pope. No congregation, Anglican or nonconformist, was allowed to meet without first having been certified by the Bishop of the Diocese or the Archdeacon of the Archdeaconry within whose province the congregation fell. After the Act of Toleration, although it was no longer a crime to be a nonconformist, it was considered by some Justices of the Peace to be an omission of conscience.[4]

The Toleration Act of 1689 allowed certain freedoms to those Protestant churches that proclaimed the trinity, but few concessions were made for nonconformist Protestants. In fact, the Blasphemy Act (1698) provided punishments, including imprisonment, and in some circumstances death, for anti-Trinitarians. Although the Toleration Act was broadened in 1779, it was not until 1813, with the Unitarian Relief Act, also known as the Trinity Act, that these groups became emancipated. In 1828 the Test and Corporation Act, through which all those occupying public office, regardless of their religious affiliation, had to take the oath of non-injury to the Church of England, was repealed. At this point, all nonconformist Protestants were allowed most of the freedoms that had hitherto been allowed only to Anglican Protestants.

Although the Catholic Relief Act of 1778 repealed the harshest of anti-Catholic laws, the Union of Great Britain with Ireland in 1800 resuscitated the Anglo-Catholic question in an acute form. At this point Roman Catholics were still ineligible for election to the Westminster Parliament. However, in spite of opposition from the Crown and from many Tories, legislation was passed making it lawful for a Catholic to vote for Members of Parliament, to be elected a Peer and to become a Member of Parliament in either House. However, certain offices, such as that of Justice, Regent of the United Kingdom, Lord High Chancellor, Lord Keeper or Lord Commissioner of the Great Seal, were still reserved for Anglicans. Moreover, a Roman Catholic could not occupy the position of Lord Lieutenant of Ireland or High Commissioner to the General Assembly of the Church of England. Those Catholics who did take on any public office did so under the condition that they swear that they would 'never exercise any Privilege to which I am or may become entitled to disturb or weaken the Protestant Religion or *Protestant Government* in the United Kingdom' (emphasis added).[5]

Until 1830, Jews in Britain were unemancipated. In 1845, a statute was established that permitted Jews to vote and to hold municipal office. However, this group was still prevented from election to Parliament because of the oath that was required professing Christian beliefs. It was not until 1858 that a measure was taken modifying the oath for Jewish members.[6] The Public Oaths Act of 1866 provided further security for Jews.[7]

In 1868, Benjamin Disraeli became Britain's first Prime Minister of Jewish ancestry. His grandfather, a Sephardic Jew from Spain, had quarrelled with the synagogue officials and had his children baptized as Christians. Had it not been for this event, Disraeli's political career would not have developed, much less encountered such success. Although he served two terms as Tory prime minister, it is said that his Jewish ancestry, upon which he proudly insisted, inspired some mistrust, even among his followers.[8]

CHRISTIANITY AND BRITISH WORKING-CLASS POLITICS

The effects of industrialization on mid-nineteenth-century British workers were brutal. Among those who protested working-class conditions were clergymen Charles Kingsley and John Ludlow. They saw workers as victims of an exploitive and uncaring social system and churches as complacent bystanders insensitive to the drudgery and hopelessness of working-class lives.[9] Early experiments on the part of Anglican socialists were directed towards forming producer cooperatives. This aim was not achieved. However, their ideas heavily influence Labour politics. Leaders of the movement were convinced that Christianity and socialism were linked inextricably. 'Socialism without Christianity, on the one hand, is as the feathers without the bird, however skillfully the stuffer may dress them. Christianity, on the other hand ... becomes in its turn chilly and helpless when stripped of its social influences.'[10] Trade unions grew out of the necessity for workers to be protected from the harsh conditions imposed on them by unregulated industrialization.[11] At that time, the religious preference of the union members was non-Anglican, with strong support for the Wesleyan Methodist Church.

BRITISH SUFFRAGETTES AND RELIGION

Early in the twentieth century, suffragettes attempted to shock British churches out of their complacency towards women's positions in social and political life. The Women's Social and Political Union (WSPU) accused the Church of England of having aided and abetted government in robbing women of their political rights. The group insisted that it was the duty of the Church to insist on moral and political reform and to assist women in claiming political rights. The women vowed to provide the Church with constant reminders of its duties until it complied with their demands. This promise was kept through constant harassment and even violence. Some suffragettes protested by boycotting their churches while others resorted to more drastic means. Nine different disruptions of services occurred at Westminster Abbey.[12] Bombs were planted in church sanctuaries, including one which was found in St Paul's Cathedral near the Bishop's throne. Suffragette attacks were not limited to Anglican churches. Roman Catholic and Wesleyan churches were also set ablaze. The WSPU was prompt in claiming responsibility for these violent acts. 'Like official preachers these suffragettes claimed, in a very public manner, what they believed were religious truths. In so doing, they transgressed the gender norms which required women to be spiritual, but to keep quiet.'[13] By the time women were granted the vote in 1918, many male clerics had become war casualties. The issues taken up by the suffragettes then extended beyond the franchise to advocacy for women's ordination.

REGIONAL DIFFERENCES

Scotland

The role of the Presbyterian Church is important in the Scottish Nationalist Movement. Presbyterian ministers have largely defined its moral content. Scotland's union with England was unusual in that law, education and *religion*, the key institutions in civil society in Scotland, were kept intact. Turner claims that it is not language but, rather, religion in the form of Presbyterianism that kept Scottish nationalism alive.[14] If we are to agree with Turner, then the recent success of Scottish nationalists in achieving an autonomous Scottish Assembly, which was inaugurated in 2000, is proof of religion as an important player in Scottish and British politics.

Wales

Many Welsh people, particularly in the northern part of that country, are Anglicans, members of the Church in Wales. In the past, this group has tended to be supportive of Conservative politics, in spite of the large, established, Labour group in the rest of Wales. Aside from the Anglican group, the Welsh have also developed a large nonconformist religious group. Until recently, perhaps the principal manner by which the Welsh distinguished among themselves was based on whether a person was 'Church' or 'Chapel'.

In the early twentieth century, during a period of continuous antagonism between coal owners and miners, many of the newcomers to Wales were nonconformists who had a close association with the developing socialist cause. Keir Hardie's ethical approach to social and economic problems influenced the socialist cause in Wales and was accepted by most progressive religious affiliations. However, when the Communist Party of Britain was formed in the 1920s, an anti-religious alignment formed and Christianity and the communist version of socialism diverged. The Labour Party's brand of socialism, however, has retained a very strong influence in Wales, particularly among nonconformists.

Northern Ireland

If asked to identify a single area in the United Kingdom where religion has had, and continues to have, a drastic impact on society and politics, many people would propose Northern Ireland. Since King James I of England and VI of Scotland 'planted' English and Scottish settlers in Ireland's northern counties in the Ulster Plantation of 1607, usurping the Irish Roman Catholic landowners, the conflict in Northern Ireland has endured to the present day, at times simmering and at times raging. Throughout the conflict, although political and economic factors were always at stake, the principal cause of contention has been held up as religion. There was a cleavage not only between Roman Catholics and Protestants as a general category, but also between Roman Catholics and different Protestant denominations.

Of late, the most radical proponent of Unionism is the strongly anti-Catholic Presbyterian minister and Member of Parliament Ian Paisley, who constantly reminds his followers of their sacred separation from the Catholic Irish. In the public marches by the Orange Order, the Royal Black Institution and the Apprentice Boys of Derry, marchers wear their Order regalia and march behind the Union Jack and banners with pictures of William of Orange and biblical themes. The motto of the original Ulster Volunteer Force (UVF), a civilian 'commando' organization formed at the beginning of the twentieth century, was 'For God and Ulster'.

Social segregation of Catholics and Protestants still exists, entrenched though it may be, but this is due to the reliance on historical memory as a guide for present and future actions. Although religion played a large role earlier in the England–Ireland conflict, I argue that it has now become a scapegoat, an easy label, while the true reasons for the current conflict, which are more difficult to explain or justify, are, to a large extent, neglected.

POST-WORLD WAR II DEVELOPMENTS

The 'Established' Anglican Church in the Post-World War II Years

The Church of England claims to be committed to working towards the goal of full unity within the Christian Church and is already in communion with other churches both at home and abroad. These include some of the old Catholic churches in the Philippines and southeast Asia, the Evangelical Lutheran Churches of Finland, Norway, Iceland, Estonia, Lithuania, and the Church of

Sweden. In the Meissen Agreement in 1992, and the Reuilly Common Statement in 1999, the Church of England committed itself to working together for full visible unity with, respectively, the Reformed, Lutheran and United Churches in Germany and the French Lutheran and Reformed Churches. On a national level, the Fetter Lane Agreement of 1996 made a formal commitment between the Church of England and the Moravian Church in the United Kingdom. The Church of England also is in full ecumenical discussions with the Methodist Church and is holding conversations with the United Reformed Church and the Baptist Union. The Anglican–Roman Catholic Committee sustains relations with the Roman Catholic Church.

Church attendance is generally down in the United Kingdom and has slowly dropped over the past 50 years. In some areas, only 2 per cent of the population attend services with any regularity. Recent cooperation between different denominations and churches could well be the result of a practical need to sustain religious life before it is even further eroded, particularly since the Church of England, although still an influence on social and political life in the United Kingdom, is facing opposition from other faiths, especially those based on non-Christian ideas.

Postcolonialism and the Impact of non-Judeo-Christian Religions

Because of World War II casualties, postwar Britain experienced a shortage of labour. Around the same time, largely because of the Labour Party's accession to power and the advent of a burgeoning welfare state, the British working class met with unprecedented opportunities for improving its standards of living and education. This meant that certain jobs became socially undesirable. Requiring little skill, training or linguistic proficiency, these occupations attracted immigrants from member-countries of the dwindling British Empire. Since Britain, in contrast to many other colonizers, readily bestowed British nationality on citizens of its colonies, immigration, from a bureaucratic perspective, was relatively simple.

Many of the former colonies were experiencing overpopulation, high unemployment, poverty, communal troubles and even natural disasters. These factors all encouraged emigration, even when workers were aware that they almost always would be offered low-paying, menial jobs.[15] Such was the case with immigrants from the Indian subcontinent, formerly the jewel in the crown of the British Empire. From 1955 to 1960 it is estimated that 50,000 South Asians came to Britain, mainly from India and Pakistan. They brought their religious practices, mostly Muslim or Hindu, with them.

Although most Indian immigrants are of the Hindu religion, many of the immigrants from the Punjab area of India are Muslim, like their Pakistani neighbours. Punjabi Sikh immigrants comprise the second largest Indian religious group in post-World War II Britain. Sikhism is an offshoot of Hinduism that has developed into a completely separate religion. When Pakistan split in 1971,

Bangladeshis were added to the list of South Asian immigrants to Britain. This group is mainly Muslim. In any case, South Asian immigrants often are categorized collectively in spite of their religious, and subsequently cultural, differences that are often quite considerable.

In great part due to their tradition of family and community cooperation coupled with hard work, many South Asian immigrants have achieved notable success in commerce. In some cases, those who have achieved financial success have chosen to direct their 'postmaterial' efforts towards achieving religion-related political rights for themselves and the rest of their respective religious groups. Not all Asian immigrants have undergone the rags-to-riches experience though, and there are many who have not been able to rise out of a squalid, isolated Indo-Pakistani underclass. Asians from East Africa form another immigrant sector, quite different from those of the other groups. Refugees from black-African rule, they are mostly financially well-positioned white-collar workers or professionals.[16]

The Asian minority group is scattered throughout Britain, mainly in the larger cities, and constitutes the largest minority group in the United Kingdom. Populations in cities such as Coventry and Bradford, which were made up almost exclusively of Christians together with a very small number of Jews 50 years ago, now include tens of thousands of south Asians. Increasingly, political demands are made by non-Christian south Asians with the goal of incorporating some of their social and religious customs into the British constitution and way of life. As succinctly expressed by one Muslim:

> The laws of this country were made before Muslim peoples arrived, you see. Now they must adapt to us. Others must respect our faith. We are law abiding. But we are not calm. The government must stop sleeping, it must pay attention to us. In a truly Islamic society there is no separation between state and religion, you see.[17]

Another large immigrant group is comprised of Caribbean immigrants, largely from Jamaica, who also brought with them religious practices quite different from those traditional to Britons. Christianity was brought to the Caribbean islands by British missionaries during the nineteenth century. In this area, Christian activity was tinted with the slave–master mentality that made no secret of its stereotypical perceptions of blacks. It was the missionaries' insistence on the heathenness of the slave, and on his/her laziness, infidelity, dishonesty and lasciviousness, that prompted their evangelism.[18]

Ironically, it was because of this evangelistic influence that many of the 1950s–60s Jamaican immigrants felt that England was their spiritual homeland where they would find not only material advantages but also a warm welcome. They were disappointed. In general, Caribbean Christians experienced rejection, isolation and racism. This encouraged them to set up their own organizations that, collectively, became known as the Black Church.

Although many Jamaican immigrants are Christian, their practice of

Christianity is far removed from the traditional Eurocentric focus of Christianity and very distinct from Anglicanism. The prevailing religion among Caribbean immigrants is Pentecostalism, which places great emphasis on the power of the Holy Spirit. While some Caribbeans have felt that in order to become accepted they must Anglicanize their religion, others have insisted in keeping the traditional 'black spirituality'.

The other important black group, claimed by some to be religious in nature and by others purely political, is the Rastafarian organization. With the exception of this latter group, black religious groups in Britain have been somewhat less politically active than the Muslims. Nevertheless, some of their members are attempting to influence political decision-making.

Islamic Influences on British Policies

The first major disjunction between Islam and Christianity occurred during the time of the Crusades between the ninth and eleventh centuries. Crusaders saw themselves as warriors of Christ conducting a just war against followers of a false prophet. It has been argued that that series of conflicts was not exclusively over religion but over identity politics. Maintaining Europe separate from the growing Islamic world, not only in terms of religion, but politically, economically and geographically, was the purpose of the Crusades. Following this argument, religion, standing alone, could well be considered to have been a scapegoat.[19]

The separation of Church and state is a Western idea that is rejected by Muslims and even seen by them as sacrilegious. Rather than suffering persecution by affiliates of the political status quo, as Jesus did, Mohammed was, as Bouchat points out, a respected religious, political and military leader.[20] Over the past 20 years, political and even militant Muslim groups have emerged in Britain. In 1989, the Party of Islam was formed with the express intent of promoting the political interests of Muslim immigrants and their families. Some saw this as being in direct response to the uproar over the publication of Salman Rushdie's *The Satanic Verses*. However, leaders of the party insist that their movement had been growing in strength over a number of years and the book was only 'the last straw'. The essentially political aim of the Deobandi sect, the second largest Muslim group in Britain, is to have Muslim law accepted by the British Parliament.

Considerable social and political tension exists between Islamic groups and non-Muslims in Britain. Prior liberal immigration policies are frequently blamed for allowing Britain to be flooded with a million citizens who 'take religion, quite literally, with deadly seriousness'.[21] 'Muslim' has become a word of abuse and Islamophobia appears to be the aversion of the day. In 1996, the Runnymede Trust appointed an 18-member commission to investigate the phenomenon. Results of the study showed that across all sections of British society there was a pervasive hatred of Islam. While the British Action Committee on Islamic

Affairs welcomed the report, Dr Ghayassudin Siddiqui, a Muslim leader, called it an 'exercise in futility' and insisted that Muslims are 'tired of nice words' and demand some action.[22]

High on the list of changes that the Islamic Party wishes to see is the abolishment of interest on loans. Interest, they claim, is responsible for fuelling inflation, child abuse, alcoholism, gambling and prostitution. The party insists that all other religions descending from Abraham should follow their example and insist that laws be made to establish a system free of interest, following God's prohibition of interest.

Hinduism and British Politics

Hindus, while less militant than Muslims, are no less concerned about promoting their group political rights and religious freedoms. They are concerned about laws such as 'Sunday closing', which is based on the Christian Sabbath. Areas such as Southall in London, whose population is heavily Asian, have spawned many local political activists, including those from various sects of Hinduism. An occasional non-Hindu British politician, including the Labour Minister of Parliament Syd Bidwell, has portrayed himself as a Hindu Minister of Parliament. However, it has been pointed out that politicians' identities are often linked to self-interest. Bidwell has also presented himself as a Muslim Minister of Parliament and a Christian Minister of Parliament.[23]

Gerd Bauman, in discussing Hinduism in Britain, claims that the British have placed a convenient label onto a group of people who, in fact, are comprised of many different sects. On the one hand, Bauman claims that this is a good thing, because it embodies the acceptance of 'other' and the 'welcoming' aspects of Hinduism. On the other hand, it leads to the false notion that the Hindu religion is related to ethnicity.[24]

Immigrant Christian Groups

Often referred to as fundamentalists of one shade or another, immigrant Christian groups include Pentecostals and Seventh Day Adventists. In response to rejection by the traditional Protestant churches, including non-Anglican denominations, Pentecostals in Britain have tended towards isolationism. Diane Austin Broos discusses the importance of Pentecostalism in Jamaica and its influence on politics.[25] Pentecostalism is also the religion of preference among Jamaicans and other blacks in Great Britain. However, a large and increasingly politically influential group of blacks are Seventh Day Adventists.

Caribbeans in the United Kingdom immigrated from different islands, each with its distinct cultural mores. In Britain, when faced with unacceptance, obstacles and frank racism, they were gradually able to discard their differences and form a united group. It was from this union in the face of adversity that the politically activist group the West Indian Unity Association was formed.

Bauman claims that this cross-island unity in face of conflict was accentuated politically by the first post-World War II race riots in Britain, the Notting Hill riots of 1958.[26] This has been explained in the following way: 'The hate of injustice among West Indian people is common to all the islands. At the end of the day, it's the black man that's in trouble. Island doesn't matter now. Blackness and being black means more.'[27]

Though cultural cleavages have faded among Afro-Caribbeans in Britain, the same cannot be said for religious cleavages. There is a marked split between the evangelical Christians and those who are not Christian and an even more pronounced split between Rastafarians and non-Rastafarians.

Rastafarians

The very definition of Rastafarianism[28] is difficult to pinpoint, as some black British see the movement as purely political, devoted to fighting capitalism and the exploitation of blacks, while others see it as a religion. In any case, as Bauman notes, the movement contains political, religious, cultural and musical elements. The group has frequently been accused of racism and thuggery.

The Rastafarian movement emerged in the urban areas of Jamaica after Marcus Garvey's ill-fated Negro Improvement Association, which sought to return all blacks of the world to what he considered their rightful birthplace, Africa. Garvey's organization claimed to run on strictly secular lines. However, he also founded an American-based African Orthodox Church. Shortly before his death, he was reputed to have prophesied: 'Look to Africa when a Black shall be crowned, for the day of deliverance is near.' Jamaican blacks thought of this promise when Haile Selassie was crowned Emperor. Drawing on biblical Old Testament scriptures, they incited blacks to return to Africa, 'The Blacks' Zion'. Members of the group grew beards and twisted their hair into long braids in imitation of Zulu warriors and preached black superiority and hatred of white society.

Until the late 1960s, few Jamaican immigrants in Britain identified with Rastafarianism. Then, encouraged by the Black Power movement in the United States and the growing popularity, worldwide, of the Rasta organization, young Jamaicans established the London branch of the movement. Cashmore claims that the Rastas should not be underestimated or dismissed as having 'a chip on their shoulders'. He claims that by attempting, in hostile and violent ways, to sever their ties with the white world they are inflicting a significant wound on British society, including other immigrant communities.[29] In some cases, Rastafarians have been successful in influencing the British government's policies. One of the areas in which they have been most successful is the prison system. Several reports have claimed that the numbers of black inmates being introduced to the prison system far exceeded their proportion in the general population. West Indians, many of them Rastafarians, form the largest black group in British prisons.[30]

Religious and dietary needs have long been recognized in the British prison system. However, it is customary for all prisoners to have short hair. Rastafarians claim that their religion requires them to wear dreadlocks and that a requirement to cut them would constitute disregard for religious freedom. In 1976, the Home Office issued a circular claiming that Rastafarianism was not a religion. As a result, it explained: 'It follows that no facilities such as access by visiting "ministers", holding of services, provision of devotional books from public funds or acceptance of periodicals will be afforded. It has been confirmed with the resident priest of the [Ethiopian Orthodox] church that long hair is not a requirement and governors may, therefore, require their hair to be cut.' This policy proved to be disastrous and was replaced by an overall prison policy on Rastafarians.[31] Further reforms in the prison system, which are intended to better the lot of ethnic and religious minorities, have been proposed by the Commission on the Future of Multi-Ethnic Britain, chaired by Bhikhu Parekh.[32]

While there still exists some debate as to whether or not Rastafarianism is a true religion, clearly the British government is treating it as such. Furthermore, it is by presenting themselves as a religious group that Rastafarians have been able to make their political demands heard.

RELIGIOUS DIFFERENCES AND THE BRITISH POST-WORLD WAR II EDUCATIONAL SYSTEM

Although the Church of England, together with the Church of Scotland, is the established church in the United Kingdom, its hegemonic role is now almost extinct. One of the remaining influential roles of the Church of England is through its impact on education. The 4,774 Church of England schools make up 20 per cent of state schools in England. The Church also maintains a link with independent schools with a Church of England foundation. At present, about 1,000 of the 1,300 independent preparatory and secondary schools in the United Kingdom have a Church of England ethos. The schools' officers work closely with the British government's Department of Education and Skills, as well as with a variety of professional and educational institutions and representatives of other denominations and faiths.[33] Twenty-five per cent of all primary schools and 6 per cent of all state secondary schools are Church of England schools. Moreover, 18 per cent of all primary and 5 per cent of all secondary pupils in England attend these schools. The government refers to them as 'the jewel in the state sector crown'.[34]

There are two varieties of Church of England school: voluntary-aided and voluntary-controlled. In the former, the majority of governors are appointed by the Church and teachers are employed by the governing body. Fifteen per cent of the costs of maintenance and repairs, as well as capital projects, is raised by the governors and religious education in the schools has a distinct Anglican flavour. Voluntary schools' boards of governors are partially appointed by the

Church, but there is no Church majority on their boards. Teachers are employed by the local education authority, which also funds repairs and capital projects. Religious education follows the local agreed syllabus. However, the worship, usually confined to a short prayer session during morning assembly, is Anglican. The Church of England Board of Education fully supports current legislation that maintains that daily collective worship is the right of every child and should be part of every child's educational experience. This law accommodates, at least in theory, other denominations and faiths.

The House of Lords, in spite of recent changes eliminating hereditary peers from participating in political decision-making, is still a forum for debate, and it so happens that 26 Church of England bishops are in the Lords' chamber. These bishops are neither hereditary nor life peers and must step down at the age of 70. However, it would be difficult completely to deny their influence on policy decisions and legislation, even in light of the diminished influence of the House of Lords. While it is impossible to predict the future of the bishops, given the Labour government's plans to reform the House of Lords, for now it might be said safely that the Anglican faith carries more weight in British government than other religious organizations. While the law maintains that 'other' faiths be accommodated, this point is hotly debated by subscribers to non-Christian religions.

In spite of the million and a half Muslims in Britain, up to half of whom are of school age, there is no voluntary-aided Muslim school. Sahib Mustaqim Bleher, a German who converted to Islam in the late 1960s, and who is the spokesman for the Muslim parents of Batley, claims that the Batley city council practised apartheid by concentrating Muslims in certain schools and then denying them *halal* meat and the right to worship according to their religion. He also claims that the council is guilty of discrimination by not supporting the application from the local Islamic girls' school for voluntary-aided status.[35] Moreover, Christians and Jews are given a state-funded right to religious education, while Muslims are not. The Association of Muslim Schools claims that the government 'wishes to maintain a Judeo-Christian monopoly in controlling the minds of youth in the state education system'.

BLASPHEMY LAWS

One of the characteristics of English law that seems incongruent with a democratic secular society, and of increasing salience over the past 50 years, is the existence of the Law of Blasphemy. The law, which has rarely been implemented in recent years, is especially relevant to new immigrants of different religious convictions.

The origin of the offence of blasphemy lies in ecclesiastical law, and traditionally was dealt with by the Star Chamber and the Court of High Commission, both components of the Ecclesiastical Courts. With the dissolution of these courts and the abolition of the common law writ *de Haeretico Comburendo*[36] in the seventeenth century, the Court of the King's Bench declared blasphemy a common law offence, punishable by common law practices.[37]

The blasphemy law was incorporated into common law precisely to protect the Church of England, as the official state church, bearing the authority of the monarch, from 'seditious calumny'. In effect it was meant to protect the monarchy, and its god-given right to rule, from dissident factions.[38]

Christianity was held to be part of the law of England and, therefore, to speak against Christianity was seen as subversion of the law. Common law courts were able to prosecute any attack on the official church, the Church of England, as an attack on the state. However, attacks on religions other than the state recognized one were not subject to the law of blasphemy.[39] When blasphemy laws were first introduced, any criticism of the fundamental ideals and beliefs of Christianity was sufficient to warrant criminal prosecution.[40]

Initially, it was the content of the publication or statement that made it punishable, not the way in which it was made public. However, over time the justification for punishment came to rest more on the prevention of social disorder than on offence to God. The nature of the attack became more significant than its content. The modern offence, as expressed in the 1917 clause of 'vilification or irreverence' was taken as part of the blasphemy laws and had become entrenched in modern law by the early 1920s. The modern offence, then, no longer protects the institutions of the established church but, rather, protects the sensitivities of believing Christians. As mentioned, the law rarely has been evoked in recent times. In fact, in 1949, the offence was declared 'dead'.[41] Nevertheless, in 1977, when media standards campaigner Mary Whitehouse brought a suit against *Gay News* magazine for publishing a poem that portrayed Jesus Christ as a homosexual love object, she evoked the Law of Blasphemy.[42] Although between 1922 and 1979 there were no successful prosecutions for blasphemy in England, in 1979 in *Whitehouse* vs. *Lemon*, the House of Lords confirmed the continued existence of blasphemous libel laws. In contrast to this, the religious sensitivities of non-Christians are not protected by law. In response to the publication of *The Satanic Verses*, the case made against Salman Rushdie for his offence against Islamic law was dismissed by the British court system. Clearly, this unevenness of interpretation of the law does not sit well with many non-Christians in the United Kingdom.

PARTIES, VOTING PATTERNS AND RELIGIONS

Prior to World War I, the British party structure was based, to a large extent, on religious affiliation.[43] Anglicans tended to support the Tory Party with its conservative values while, generally speaking, nonconformists gave their votes to the Whig/Liberal Party. Although religiosity in the United Kingdom, with the possible exception of Northern Ireland,[44] has dropped very significantly during the past 50 years, most members of the Anglican elite retain their allegiance to the Conservative Party. Census-based analysis of religion and voting from 1918 to 1970 and for each major party show that the majority of heavily Anglican constituencies chose Conservatives. Also, in highly religious areas the Labour Party tended to do badly. The Liberals of this time period showed varying relations with religion and no clear pattern was seen. The correlation between religion and party affiliation rose between the wars, but dropped to a low level in the 1950s.[45]

However, since the demise of the Liberal Party and the rise of the Labour Party, the relationship between political and religious cleavages is not as clearly defined. Again, the probable explanation for this is that people are generally less religious in all aspects of their lives, including the political aspect. Crewe claims that the Irish tend to vote for the Labour Party while Jews vote for Conservatives or Liberal Democrats.[46] Over time, Jewish voting patterns have changed. During the mid to late nineteenth century, Jews generally received more support from, and were more supportive of, the Tory Party. However, from the foundation of the Labour Party in the 1920s, British Jews supported it. This support remained fairly constant until, during the Thatcher era, a *rapprochement* occurred between the Jews and the Conservative Party.

One population group that has been distinguished since the 1990s is immigrants, in particular, those who are Muslim, Hindu, or nonconformist Christian. When they become citizens, they tend to support the Labour Party.[47] Overall, between 1974 and 1997, four out of five Black and Asian votes were for Labour.[48] In the case of Muslims and Rastafarians, the voting pattern could be explained by their religious views on capitalism. However, it is not clear whether support for Labour emanates from their religious views or from their socioeconomic class condition. In all probability, both factors are involved. However, of late, with the advent of New Labour, many ethnic and religious minorities have denounced the movement of the Labour Party towards the centre, claiming that the party now tends to represent middle-class values and materialism, rather than the interests of the downtrodden and ethnic minorities, as was traditionally the case.[49]

Regardless of their position within the political spectrum, it appears that one of the most passionate appeals from within minority religions is to members of their own groups. There is an urging of religious minorities to become more active in politics and to run for political office on all levels. It is only through representation by those who empathize with their problems that they feel they will make any political progress. Even within the traditional political structure this plea does not fall altogether on deaf ears. The Royal Commission on the Reform of the House of Lords argued that, should an elected second chamber be instituted, a situation of which the Commission is not supportive, all people 'should be able to feel that there is a voice in Parliament for the different aspects of their personalities, whether regional, vocational, ethnic, professional cultural or religious, expressed by a person or persons with whom they can identify'.[50] Another development regarding the House of Lords is that the number of life peers from ethnic and religious minority groups tripled between 1997 and 2000.[51]

POLITICAL INTERESTS AND LABELS

At the dawn of the twenty-first century, a number of religious cleavages exist in the United Kingdom, some long-standing and others recently developed. When it is considered beneficial, politically and economically, diverse religious groups, while insisting on maintaining religious differentiation, are willing to find some other common thread of identity that, in the interest of political pragmatism, identify them as a single group.

An example of religious and even racial identity being subsumed to one overarching identifier is to be found among certain Asian and black British groups in Britain even though that identifier may not, in scientific terms, be valid. Among political activists of radically anti-racist convictions, the idea has emerged that 'all citizens disadvantaged on the basis of their dominant ethnic-cum-cultural [and religious] classification form a single community united under the term "Black" as its political colour'.[52] This manner of self-identification has been adopted notably by socialist and feminist groups who perceive that they stand a better chance of influencing policy as a united group, even if this means relinquishing to some extent other identities, including those which pertain to religion.

Perhaps the most remarkable instance of surrendering religious identities to acceptance of commonalities that provide more optimistic alternatives for society's future is to be observed in Northern Ireland. In the recent poll questioning Roman Catholics and Protestants about their commitment to the peace agreement and to a referendum which would decide Northern Ireland's future, 75 per cent of the participants were in favour of letting their religious differences fade into secondary positions in the effort to achieve peace. This also gives credence to my claim that religion has been used as a scapegoat in the 'Troubles' of Northern Ireland and that, for several decades, rather than being the main source of conflict it has been an easy, if inaccurate label with which to explain the situation, as well as a tool used by the few whose interests lie in maintaining the conflict.

CONCLUSIONS

Whether religion is considered to be a problem for a democratic society, as Karl Marx argued, or is emphasized as a positive force in establishing social ties through collective beliefs and practices, according to Emile Durkheim, it would be difficult to deny its infusion into the apparently secular British democracy.

Tillich's claim concerning the inescapable relationship between religion and secular life, in which religion is 'grasped by an ultimate concern' such as nationalism and communism, and today one might add ethnic and racial movements, appears to be well founded. Tillich proposes that certain political beliefs are tantamount to 'secular faiths' and may be embraced with a fervour equal to that commanded by theistic religions. I would add that certain religious beliefs are often affiliated with secular movements, perhaps because of the close association between religious and 'everyday' practices. Moreover, in some cases, religion is seen as the underlying motivation for political action, when the true reason is more obscure. These observations are deserving of closer examination

Since the only faith in England to be protected is the Anglican faith, it could be argued that, *de jure*, all other religious groups suffer discrimination. Nevertheless, it appears that, *de facto*, most minority religions in Britain are as well protected as they are in the United States and other Western countries. However, many Britons would not agree with the latter statement, particularly immigrant former-colonials.

The large-scale South Asian and Caribbean immigration to Britain, bringing some religious practices that are far removed from traditional Judeo-Christianity and, in some cases, seen as inseparable from political life, has had considerable impact on British society and politics. It remains to be seen whether this will 'prove almost as great [an impact on the social order] as that precipitated by the arrival of William of Normandy in 1066'[53] or whether immigrant religions and the political and cultural mores that accompany them will gradually become just one more point of contention set within a relatively stable traditional British society.

In terms of contemporary general elections in the United Kingdom, it would be difficult to identify one in which religion has become more directly involved than that of 1997. In contrast to the European Continent, where Christian democracy has been a constant in many post-World War II elections and governments, in Britain, religion has kept a relatively informal back-seat position. It appears that this situation may have been changed, to some extent, by Tony Blair's open espousal of Christianity, together with anxiety over apparent societal decay and the growth of single-issue activism in relation to questions of moral choice.[54]

The recent involvement of religious groups in politics is not limited to Christians. The need to combat social problems and injustices has driven the involvement of Muslims in elections. Those who promote a Muslim parliament claim that there can be no separation between Church and state and that, in spite of the fact that Muslims have generally voted Labour, Muslims should now consider boycotting elections and unite behind a political group dedicated entirely to Muslim concerns. Less extreme, and perhaps more pragmatic, Muslim groups advocate greater Muslim involvement with established political structures. In this way, it is hoped that Muslims will overcome their marginalization by established political parties and stand a better chance of having their needs met.[55]

Among the most recent recommendations of the Commission on the Future of Multi-Ethnic Britain[56] are the following:

> Legislation should be introduced prohibiting direct and indirect discrimination on grounds of religion or belief ... [and] ... A commission on the role of religion in the public life of a multi-faith society should be set up to make recommendations on legal and constitutional matters.[57]

At present, then, there is a clearly discernible attempt, on the part of religious minorities, to assert their differences, in terms of both social and political needs.

In certain instances and during specific periods in history, religion could hardly have been dismissed as a key player in British politics. However, its influence and its specific content are dynamic and ever changing. It would be difficult, perhaps impossible, to justify any claim that religion no longer influences policy and is, therefore, a relic in the political arena. In certain cases, notably those connected with the Muslim faith and centred around questions of blasphemy, religion may be a true player, a primary instigator of political demands. In others, such as the 'Troubles' of Northern Ireland, it has become a scapegoat. Clearly, if issues are couched in 'religious belief' terms that grasp the emotions and psychological identity much more readily than mundane, material expressions, organizers of political movements are more likely to gain support. If only for this reason it is likely that religion will remain an important tool for political manipulators.

In late twentieth-century Britain, where regular church-going has declined, in spite of the presence of an official Church both in England (Anglican) and in Scotland (Presbyterian), contentious issues between Christians and non-Christians are frequently presented as purely religious. I contend that the real issues revolve around the much more overarching concerns of identity. Groups wish to retain their uniqueness and separate identities and one of the simplest and easiest to point out differences is that of religion. Once again, as was the case during the Crusades, religion often is seen as the single salient identifying factor, although it is not by any means the only factor, to separate groups.

NOTES

1. This perception is less likely to be found among practising, religious non-Christians, frequently to be found among post-World War II immigrant groups.
2. From 'An Act to retain the Queen Majesty's subjects in their due Obedience', a statute made in the twenty-third year of the reign of Queen Elizabeth I.
3. Also known as the 1688 Revolution, the Glorious Revolution was a coup in which James II was deposed and replaced by his daughter Mary II and her husband William III. This revolution is considered to be the basis for parliamentary supremacy over the Crown.
4. J.F. MacLear gives a detailed account of this in *Church and State in the Modern Age* (Oxford: Oxford University Press, 1995), p. 10.
5. From the statutes of the United Kingdom of Great Britain and Ireland (1829) 10, 50, London.
6. '[T]henceforth, any Person confessing the Jewish Religion, in taking the said Oath may omit the Words "and I make this declaration upon the true faith of a Christian"', from *A Collection of*

the Public General Statutes, passed in the Twenty-First and Twenty-Second Years of the Reign of Her Majesty Queen Victoria (London, 1858), p. 259.

7. MacLear, *Church and State*, p. 192.
8. *Encyclopaedia Britannica*, 15th edn (Chicago, IL: Encyclopaedia Britannica, 1990), p. 899.
9. MacLear, *Church and State*.
10. John M.F. Ludlow, *The Christian Socialist: A Journal of Association* (London: London Working Men's Association, 1850), pp. 1–2.
11. See Leonard Freedman's *Politics and Policy in Britain* (New York, Longman, 1996).
12. The War on Churches', reported in different issues of *Suffragette*, 1913–1914.
13. J.R. De Vries, 'Challenging Traditions: Denominational Feminism in Britain, 1910–1920', in Billie Melman (ed.), *Borderlines: Genders and Identities in War and Peace, 1870–1930* (London: Routledge, 1998).
14. B.S. Turner, 'Marginal Politics, Cultural Identity and the Clergy in Scotland', *International Journal of Sociology and Social Policy*, 1, 1 (1981), pp. 89–113.
15. Venetia Newall, 'A Muslim Christmas Celebration in London', *Journal of American Folklore*, 102, 404 (1989), pp. 186–94.
16. *The Economist*, 28 October 1989.
17. Quoted as spoken by the administrator of a Bradford Mosque in David Caute's article, 'The Holy War', *The New Statesman and Society*, 2, 52 (June 1989).
18. Valentina Alexander 'A Mouse in a Jungle: The Black Christian Woman's Experience in the Church and Society in Britain', in Delia Jarret-Macauley (ed.), *Reconstructing Womanhood, Reconstructing Feminism: Writings on Black Women* (London: Routledge, 1996).
19. Roger Ballard in *Desh Pardesh: The South Asian Presence in Britain* (London: Hurst, 1984), pp. 1–5, maintains that separatist views between whites and south Asians in the UK are still based on some of the same reasons.
20. C.J. Bouchat, 'The Religion Factor After 25 Years', *Journal of Psychology*, 107, 1 (1981), pp. 7–10.
21. Yasmin Alibhai, quoting the words of Peregrine Worsthorne 'Satanic Betrayals', *New Statesman and Society*, 2, 38 (1989).
22. F. Nahdi, 'No More Muslim Apartheid', *New Statesman*, 10, 477 (1996).
23. *The Gazette*, 26 September 1986.
24. G. Bauman, *Contesting Culture: Discourses of Identity in Multi-Ethnic London* (Cambridge: Cambridge University Press, 1996).
25. D.J. Austin Broos gives a good account of religion and politics in Jamaica in 'Politics and the Redeemer: State and Religion as Ways of Being in Jamaica', *New West Indian Guide*, 70, 1 and 2 (1996).
26. Bauman, *Contesting Culture*.
27. This is taken from a report by T. Yabsley on research interviews conducted among people of West Indian/Caribbean origin in Britain, 1990.
28. Rastafarian is derived from the name of the Ethiopian Emperor, Ras Tafari.
29. E. Cashmore, 'More than a Version: A Study of Reality Creation', *British Journal of Sociology*, 30, 3 (1979), pp. 307–32.
30. Among those who make this claim is M. Kettle, 'The Racial Numbers Game in Our Prisons', *New Society*, 61, 1037 (1981), pp. 535–7.
31. Ibid.
32. *The Future of Multi-Ethnic Britain: The Parekh Report* (London: Profile Books, 2000).
33. This is described in more detail in 'The Church of England as an Educator', *About the Church of England*, published by the Church of England on its web-site www.cofe.anglican.org/about/educator.html.
34. Ibid.
35. *Times Educational Supplement*, 2 September 1989.
36. The Latin phrase *de Haeretico Comburendo* is translated to 'Burning of Heretics'. Throughout Europe, those suspected of heresy, that is of holding beliefs contrary to church dogma, were burned at the stake. The burning of Joan of Arc in fifteenth-century France is a well-known example of the enforcement of this law.
37. See the Trial of Sir Charles Sedley (1663) 1 Sid 168, cited in W.S. Holdsworth, *A History of English Law*, 7th edn, vol 8 (London: Methuen, Sweet and Maxwell, 1972).
38. J. Kramer, 'Letter from Europe', *New Yorker*, 66, 48 (January 1991).

39. See, for example, *R.* vs. *Gathercole* (1838).
40. The Blasphemy Act (1698) made it an offence for anyone in or having professed Christianity (in the Church of England's interpretation) to deny its truth.
41. See Lord Denning, 'Freedom Under the Law', Hamlin lectures, 1st series, London, 1949.
42. Kramer, *Letter from Europe.*
43. L.B. Brown, 'The Religious Factor after 25 Years', *Journal of Psychology*, 107 (1981), pp. 7–10.
44. Some polls indicate that the vast majority of the Northern Irish rarely attend church.
45. William M. Miller, 'The Religious Alignment at English Elections between 1918 and 1970', *Journal of Political Studies*, 25, 2 (June 1977), pp. 227–51.
46. See I. Crewe, 'The Black, Brown and Green Votes', *New Society*, 48, 862 (1979), pp. 76–8.
47. Ibid.
48. *The Parekh Report.*
49. Ibid.
50. Ibid.
51. Ibid.
52. Bauman, *Contesting Culture*, p. 161.
53. Ballard, *Desh Pardesh.*
54. See Caroline Daniel's article 'Which Way Will God be Voting?', *New Statesman*, February 1997.
55. Ibid.
56. The Commission on the Future of Multi-Ethnic Britain was established in January 1998 by the Runnymede Trust, an independent think-tank dedicated to the cause of promoting racial justice in Britain. The recommendations to which references are made appear in the 2000 report.
57. *The Parekh Report.*

6

Religion, National Identity and the Conflict in Northern Ireland

ADRIAN GUELKE

Northern Ireland is a subordinate part of a much larger political entity, the United Kingdom, which stands out as a prime example of a successful secular, constitutional democracy. The prominent role that religious differences play in the politics of Northern Ireland therefore stands in sharp contrast to the rest of the country. This contrast is mirrored in social differences between Northern Ireland and the rest of the United Kingdom, such as the very much higher level of church attendance among all denominations in Northern Ireland. The province's geographical separation from the mainland of the United Kingdom and its history of effective political autonomy for 50 years following the partition of Ireland in 1920 provide part of the explanation for the limited influence that practices in the rest of the United Kingdom have had on Northern Ireland. But because the Northern Irish problem has tended to be viewed in the context of a much longer history of conflict between Britain and Ireland, the religious dimension to the province's political difficulties has tended to be subsumed under the question of clashing national identities.

Thus, at the start of Northern Ireland's recent troubles, which are usually dated from 5 October 1968, when clashes between the police and civil rights marchers in Londonderry/Derry attracted the attention of the world to the existence of the Northern Ireland problem, it was still common for those writing about the conflict to portray it as a clash between British imperialism and Irish nationalism. However, with the passage of time, this characterization of the conflict became less and less credible because of the evident lack of enthusiasm of the political establishments in Britain and the Republic of Ireland to support either of the protagonists in Northern Ireland. This was most obvious in the attempt of the British and Irish governments to put pressure on the parties in Northern Ireland to cooperate through provisions of the Anglo-Irish Agreement of November 1985, which envisaged devolved institutions in Northern Ireland replacing the process of consultation between the governments under the

Agreement. By the time of the publication in 1990 of John Whyte's magisterial study of the literature on the conflict, he was able to conclude that internal interpretations of the conflict predominated. Admittedly, Whyte's classification of the theories at first sight might seem perverse in that he included under the heading of internal conflict interpretations, studies, such as my own, that placed special emphasis on the role of international factors in sustaining the conflict.[1]

THE DOMINANCE OF RELIGIOUS LABELLING

The justification for Whyte's approach was that the more recent studies of the internationalization of the conflict in contrast to the literature before the start of the troubles did not deny that the principal protagonists in the conflict were the two communities in Northern Ireland. What is more these communities were almost invariably identified in religious terms, i.e. as Protestants and Catholics rather than Unionists and nationalists, while the terms Loyalist and Republican were applied to the most militant elements in each community. Jonathan Tonge puts the point as follows:

> Labelling by religious denomination remains the most convenient method of identifying the division between the communities. The terms Catholic and Protestant are preferred to nationalist and Unionist or republican or loyalist as they embrace the vast majority of the people and are less problematic than other labels.[2]

In particular, surveys asking people to identify themselves politically or which ask them what constitutional option they prefer have tended to produce a wide range of different answers depending on the precise framing of the questions and the timing of the survey. There is often a difficulty of separating people's preferences in the medium term from their aspirations in the long run. Thus, many people who would identify themselves as 'nationalists' would not necessarily give a united Ireland as their preferred option. The obvious explanation for this apparent contradiction is that they do not regard the option of a united Ireland as feasible at present and are willing to accept some other option in order for there to be a settlement. By a somewhat similar process, whether people identify themselves as Unionists or nationalists does not necessarily correspond with how the party they support would identify itself.

An advantage of the terms Protestant and Catholic is that they convey much more effectively than any political label the sense of people's involuntary membership of a group. In Northern Ireland, one is born a Protestant or a Catholic. That is strongly reinforced by the extent of segregation between the two communities, with the vast majority of the urban population living in streets overwhelmingly if not entirely drawn from one community, especially in working-class areas, and going to state schools in the case of Protestants and Catholic schools in the case of Catholics, with fewer than 2 per cent of children attending integrated schools. Admittedly, religious affiliation might seem like political affiliation ultimately to be the choice of the individual, since it depends on belief. However, given the way that society is structured in Northern Ireland, in practice, the capacity of an individual to change religion or to disavow membership of one or other community is limited, as the common use of the notions of Protestant atheists and Catholic atheists underlines.

When Richard Rose carried out a survey in 1968 on the eve of Northern Ireland's troubles, 99 per cent of his sample identified themselves as Catholics or members of Protestant denominations.[3] One effect of the troubles has been to increase the numbers of people who refuse to identify their religion or give the answer none. The response to the question on religion in the 1991 census is given below.

Table 6.1:
Religion as percentage of population

Protestant	50.6
Catholic	38.4
None	3.7
Not stated	7.3

Source: Northern Ireland Census 1991.

The breakdown among Protestant denominations was as follows:

Table 6.2:
Protestant denomination as percentage of population

Presbyterian	21
Church of Ireland	18
Methodist	4
Baptist	1
Congregationalist	1
Free Presbyterian	1
Others	4

Source: Northern Ireland Census 1991.

The census figures can be compared with those of the large British attitude survey in Northern Ireland in 1990. In the case of the survey an even larger number of respondents declined to answer the question on religion. By cross-tabulating the answers on the religious question with those on political party affiliation, the extent of polarization between the two communities is evident. The results are given below.

What is evident from Table 6.3 is that the number of Protestant nationalists is virtually insignificant. In fact, not a single respondent out of a survey of over two thousand identified himself or herself as both a Protestant and a supporter of either of the two nationalist parties, the Social Democratic and Labour Party (SDLP) and Sinn Fein. There are also very few Catholic Unionists. Only one respondent identified himself or herself as both a Catholic and a supporter of the more moderate of the two Unionist parties, the Ulster Unionist Party (UUP). One might surmise that in the case of individuals from a Protestant background who identify with a nationalist party or people from a Catholic background who identify with a Unionist party, there is a tendency not to call themselves Protestant or Catholic. The extent of sectarian political polarization is also partly mitigated by the existence of parties that cross the sectarian line, such as the Alliance Party and the Workers Party. Support for such parties in the 1990 survey amounted to 11 per cent of the total.

Table 6.3:
Religious affiliation and political party identification, %

	Catholic	Protestant	None/other/no reply
TOTAL	36	49	15
Alliance	33	42	25
Democratic Unionist	0	85	15
Ulster Unionist	1	87	12
Sinn Fein	88	0	12
SDLP*	98	0	2
Workers Party	44	24	32
None/other/no reply	46	34	20

*Social Democratic and Labour Party.
Source: Northern Ireland Attitude Survey 1990.

But despite extensive use of the categories of Protestant and Catholic to map Northern Ireland's deep divide by assessing the attitudes of the two communities in different fields and despite widespread recognition among political analysts of the utility of the categories, there remains paradoxically very strong resistance to the proposition that religion plays an important role in the conflict, except as a marker of conflicting national identities. This is all the more surprising considering that Marxist explanations have tended to fall into discredit. Their loss of influence was only partly due to external factors, such as the collapse of communism in Eastern Europe. It was also because of changes in Northern Ireland's economic circumstances. These undercut the economic factors that Marxists highlighted as causes of the conflict. In particular, the notion that Protestant antipathy towards a united Ireland was based on the economic privileges Protestants enjoyed relative to Catholics in Northern Ireland was difficult to sustain in the face of vigorous efforts by the British government to tackle the issue of Catholic social and economic disadvantage and increasing concern among Protestants that they had become the victims of discrimination.

An argument more sympathetic to Northern Ireland's large Protestant working class was that partition reflected the divergence in the economic interests of different parts of Ireland, with the industrialized north-east of the island having little in common in terms of economic interests with the much more rural south. However, the argument that it is the Republic's economic backwardness that repels Northern Protestants has been undermined by the Republic's economic miracle of the 1990s that has seen GDP per capita incomes in the Republic overtake those of the United Kingdom. The structure of the argument put forward in relation to both sets of factors is similar. If economic privilege of Protestants or the poverty of the Republic was so important in sustaining Protestant opposition to a united Ireland, then why did the change in economic circumstances produce no change in Protestant attitudes? Implicit in the structure of the argument is that what needs explaining is why attitudes in Northern Ireland have been so resistant to change and the conflict so intractable. (A similar structure of argument has been advanced to deny that religious trends have exercised an influence on the course of the conflict.)

What is worth emphasizing at this point is that the peace process and its culmination in a political settlement at the very least complicates this line of argument. What needs to be explained, it would seem, is no longer the intractability of the conflict, but rather what made the Good Friday Agreement possible. That casts the cumulative efforts of successive British governments to create conditions of greater equality in Northern Ireland and the change in the Republic of Ireland's economic fortunes in a very different light as factors that may have contributed to the ending of the conflict. Of course, it can reasonably be argued that it is too early to conclude that the conflict is over and it may yet turn out that the current peace process will be seen simply as an interlude in the conflict, made possible by temporary paramilitary truces. That represents the pessimistic pole of opinion about current prospects. Its optimistic counterpart is that the Good Friday Agreement is a final settlement of the Northern Ireland problem. As will be seen, religious explanations of the conflict/problem tend to gravitate to the pessimistic pole of interpretation of the prospects. The approach taken by Steve Bruce in his 1986 book, *God Save Ulster*, provides an example:

> What has correctly been understood by both republicans and loyalists, but overlooked by analysts and successive Westminster governments is that there is no Northern Ireland 'problem'. The word 'problem' suggests that there is a 'solution': some outcome which will please almost everybody more than it displeases almost everybody. Conflict is a more accurate term for Protestant/Catholic relationships in Northern Ireland. Conflicts have outcomes, not solutions. Somebody wins and somebody loses.[4]

One reason for the strength of opposition to religious interpretations of the Northern Ireland problem/conflict is that they tend to the conclusion that nothing can or should be done to promote a political settlement on the grounds that the differences at the heart of the conflict are not amenable to compromise.

THREE RELIGIOUS INTERPRETATIONS OF THE CONFLICT

In the next section of this chapter, I intend to examine the arguments of three analysts who advance the case that religion is an important factor in the conflict and then to examine McGarry and O'Leary's critique of religious interpretations of the Northern Ireland problem.[5] A seminal contribution to debate on the role of religion in the conflict is Frank Wright's 1973 article 'Protestant Ideology and Politics in Ulster'.[6] This is a complex piece that has strongly influenced two of the other main writers in this field, John Hickey and Steve Bruce, though their analysis is by no means as sophisticated as that of Wright.[7] The writings of Bruce form McGarry and O'Leary's main target; Bruce's over-statement of the influence of Paisley on Unionist politics and misuse of evidence provide an all too easy basis for McGarry and O'Leary's refutation of religious interpretations.

Wright's article examines the role of Protestant ideology in relations between the two communities in the north-east of Ireland in a variety of political circumstances. His purpose is to assess the prospects for, and the limits of, cooperation across the sectarian divide. In the process he identifies sharp differences within the Protestant community over these issues, examining in particular the role that class has played in shaping different responses in different sections of the Protestant community. He sets out his approach as follows:

> In an obvious sense, beliefs held by Protestants which maximize their idea of the hostility which Catholics and Catholicism hold toward them, generate emotive hostility towards Catholics. But that is only one implication of such beliefs. Knowledge (even false knowledge) is open to alternative implications. An exaggerated Protestant sense of Catholic hostility tends to militate against co-operation with the Catholics for any purpose. But it does not do so absolutely.[8]

Wright employs the political career of William Johnston during the nineteenth century to illustrate his theme of conditional cooperation.

> Those Protestants who, like Johnston, see periods of harmony and inter-religious co-operation as interludes between periods of defending Protestant religious and political beliefs against Catholics and Catholicism are generally those who see the Roman Catholic community as a monolithic and authoritarian structure, implacably hostile to Protestants and Protestantism. We describe as 'extreme' Protestants who hold this type of perspective on the nature of Catholics/Catholicism.[9]

Wright draws a contrast between 'extreme' and 'liberal' Protestants on the basis of whether they perceive Catholicism as monolithic or not. He argued that 'extreme' Protestants had 'an essentially religio-political conception of the nature of Ulster politics, which sees the conflict in terms of the battle between two religious systems carried on in the field of politics'.[10] He identified a number of factors that affected the susceptibility of different groups of Protestants to this ideological perspective:

1. exposure to the socialization processes of evangelical religion or Loyalism;
2. experience of intense periods of unleashed antagonism between the different communities (living through a period of 'troubles');
3. location in a geographical situation in which any hostile act by the other community would be particularly devastating (isolated Protestant in predominantly Catholic border area);
4. location in an occupation, socioeconomic class, in which the threat from the other community appeared considerable (e.g., membership of an occupation monopolized by Protestants, known to be a grievance to Catholics).[11]

Under (1) Wright examined the role played by socialization by evangelical religious institutions and by the Orange Order. He made much of their influence in urban working-class Protestant neighbourhoods and argued that this influence provided the context of the operation of (2) and (4).

A difficulty for Wright's argument was relatively low church attendance among working-class Protestants, notwithstanding the number of religious institutions in their midst. On this point he quoted the Rev. Martin Smyth, a leading Orangeman, that the Protestants of the Shankill (a low-income Protestant neighbourhood in Belfast) were 'Bible lovers even if not Bible readers'.[12] Membership of the Orange Order provided an alternative basis for socialization into 'extreme' Protestant ideology. One out of three Protestant adult males in Northern Ireland was a member of the Orange Order at the peak of its influence and its influence was strongest in working-class communities. The primary purpose of the Orange Order is political: expressing loyalty to the British Crown, but crucial to the Order is that the Crown is Protestant by law. A candidate being initiated into the Orange Order is read the Qualifications. These require the candidate, *inter alia*, to:

> love, uphold and defend the Protestant religion, and sincerely desire and endeavour to propagate its doctrines and precepts; he should strenuously oppose the fatal errors and doctrines of the Church of Rome, and scrupulously avoid countenancing (by his presence or otherwise) any act or ceremony of Popish worship; he should, by all lawful means, resist the ascendancy of that Church, its encroachments and the extension of its power, ever abstaining from all uncharitable words, actions or sentiments towards his Roman Catholic brethren.[13]

At the time it was published Wright's article provided a basis for explaining the political rise of the Rev. Ian Paisley and his Democratic Unionist Party (initially named the Protestant Unionist Party). In particular he demonstrated how socioeconomic and politico-religious issues fused into a generalized hostility among working-class Protestants both to Catholics and to the reformist Unionist administrations of the late 1960s and early 1970s. Wright's account was also an explanation of the decline of the Northern Ireland Labour Party, which before the troubles had managed to a small degree to bridge the sectarian divide in Belfast. That became much more difficult in the context of demands for greater equality of the civil rights movement. The great value of his argument was that it helped to explain why Paisley's appeal went far beyond the members of his small religious denomination, the Free Presbyterians, despite the fundamentalist terms in which it was couched.

The historical roots of Paisley's fundamentalism can be traced back to the Calvinism of the lowland Scots who settled in the north-east of Ireland during the course of the seventeenth century as a result of the Elizabethan conquest and Jacobean plantation.[14] They formed a component both of the official plantation that followed the flight of the earls in 1607 and of private ventures of the period. The English authorities took advantage of the departure of the area's traditional landowners to acquire land for settlement in what are now the counties of Armagh, Cavan, Donegal, Fermanagh, Londonderry and Tyrone. (Two of these, Cavan and Donegal, now form part of the Republic of Ireland.) The lands confiscated from the chiefs were given to companies who in return for the title to the land undertook to colonize the land with settlers from England and Scotland. But a much larger movement of population took place from Scotland to what are now the counties of Antrim and Down as a result of land purchases unconnected with the government. This migration was facilitated by the short sea passage between Scotland and the north-east of Ireland, a mere 19 miles apart at its narrowest point. Anglicans tended to predominate among those who came to Northern Ireland as part of the official plantations; Presbyterians among the private migrants. In fact, the authorities were scarcely less hostile towards Presbyterian settlers than they were to the Catholic native population.

Nevertheless, the broad coincidence between British settler and Protestant and Irish native and Catholic has sustained an enduring settler–native interpretation of the conflict in Northern Ireland. An example is the work of Pamela Clayton.[15] Part of the appeal of this perspective is that it lends itself readily to the portrayal of the problem of Northern Ireland as one of colonialism, underpinning the Republican movement's view of its campaign of violence against British rule as an anti-colonial struggle. Lending verisimilitude to this perspective has been the persistence of features of the seventeenth-century settlement over subsequent centuries. Donald Harman Akenson graphically illustrates the point:

> Through my reading over the years, I have found a very simple way to predict where the Catholics were in any given area of colonized Ulster from the mid-seventeenth century onward. How high above sea level is any given piece of land and what is the height above sea level of the nearest town? If the difference is more than fifty meters, one is usually dealing with Catholic-held

farmland, if less, it is usually Protestant. In Ulster, land quality declines radically as one rises above sea level: excessive moisture prevails, the growing season is shorter, and in any case, cultivating mountainous land is difficult. So, in the planted portions of Ulster, a pattern emerged, locale by locale, whereby the native Irish, embittered but unbowed, lived on the heights and looked down on the fertile valleys possessed by the Scottish and English invaders.[16]

Hickey's book *Religion and the Northern Ireland Problem* was published in 1984. It was written in the aftermath of the hunger strikes by Republican prisoners in 1980 and 1981, after a decade of direct rule from London and in the light of the failure of the power-sharing experiment of 1974. It was a low point in relations between the two communities, although the level of violence had fallen from the levels it had reached in the mid 1970s. Hickey concluded his book:

> All attempts at negotiation and compromise have foundered on the rock of the Protestant fear of being absorbed into the Republic of Ireland and lack of trust in any assurances that this will not happen. Protestant leaders who have attempted negotiation and compromise have rapidly found themselves without an effective following. On the basis of the available evidence one can say that the peace and harmony, mentioned earlier, will not come to Northern Ireland until Protestants here cease to regard Roman Catholics as agents of the Irish Republic and as representatives of a Church that will not respect their integrity as fellow Christians. Only when this happens will the Protestants consent to share their society on equal terms with the Catholics.[17]

Hickey left open the possibility that the religious beliefs of the two communities might evolve in such a way as to assist in keeping Northern Ireland intact and to avoid the destructive polarization evident when he wrote his book. Like Wright, Hickey emphasized the existence of different views within the Protestant community. However, his actual analysis of the role of religion in the conflict was not particularly profound. His method was to demonstrate the weakness of other, especially Marxist, interpretations of the conflict. He also provided information underscoring the importance of religion in everyday life in Northern Ireland. (This will be dealt with below in the context of McGarry and O'Leary's critique of religious explanations.)

Steve Bruce's book *God Save Ulster* was published in 1986. It was sub-titled *The Religion and Politics of Paisleyism*. As such the book has considerable merit, though it owes a great deal to the argument sketched in Wright's article discussing the rise of Paisleyism. Of course, by the time Bruce wrote his book, there was much more material to draw on to demonstrate the thesis that Wright had advanced. In particular, the electoral success of the Democratic Unionist Party (DUP) had put it in a position by the early 1980s to challenge the Ulster Unionist Party (UUP) as the province's leading party. Bruce's argued explanations of Unionism in terms of adherence to British nationalism were inadequate as Unionist adherence to Britain was not reciprocated on the British mainland. He therefore rejected the notion of the conflict as a clash between British and Irish nationalisms or as a clash between people having a British national identity and those with an Irish national identity, where there was a large measure of coincidence between religious belief and sense of national identity. He argued that Protestantism was crucial to Unionists' sense of their identity. In particular, he contended that Loyalism depended on its religious base and that 'beyond evangelical Protestantism, no secure identity is available'.[18]

Yet just before making this strong claim for the role of religious belief in underpinning the divide, Bruce described the Protestant community in terms that fit better the notion of religion as the marker for a group distinctive in other ways than simply religious belief.

> The first step towards understanding the political behaviour of Protestants of Northern Ireland is to see them as an 'ethnic group'. They see themselves as the outcome of shared historical experiences and as the embodiment of a culture of a distinctive kind, with its shared traditions, values, beliefs, life-style, and symbols. They expect the bearers of this culture to be granted certain rights and privileges. In particular, they feel they have a right to see their values and cultural symbols displayed in the operations of the state; the Union Jack flying on government buildings and 'On Her Majesty's Service' printed on official envelopes, for example.[19]

In fact, Bruce's emphasis on the role of religion had a strongly polemical aspect to it. He used it to underscore his denunciation of British policy as misguidedly directed towards the unachievable objective of political accommo-dation between the two communities. In his 1994 book, *The Edge of the Union*, Bruce concludes that the British government's attempts through the Anglo-Irish Agreement to satisfy the conflicting political aspirations of Unionists and nationalists had been futile. He argues that the government would be better advised to pick a side, the Unionist one since Unionists constituted a majority of the population.[20]

CRITICISM OF RELIGIOUS INTERPRETATIONS

McGarry and O'Leary devote a chapter of their 1995 analysis of different explanations of the Northern Ireland conflict, *Explaining Northern Ireland*, to a critique of religious interpretations of the conflict. In 'Warring Gods?', they also usefully review (and, where necessary, update) evidence commonly advanced in support of religious interpretations of the conflict. For example, they include data on the high level of religiosity in Northern Ireland as measured by church attendance compared to other societies in Western Europe. In particular, they quote survey evidence from 1989 that over half the adult population attended church once or more a week, though this was down from a figure of two-thirds in 1968. This provides the basis for a familiar line of argument. 'The fact is', argue McGarry and O'Leary, 'conflict started, escalated, and has continued while these levels have been declining.'[21] Trends in other indicators, such as divorce and children born out of wedlock, as McGarry and O'Leary point out, give further support to the proposition that Northern Ireland is gradually becoming a more secular society. McGarry and O'Leary also discuss endogamy (the very low level of mixed marriages in Northern Ireland) and the segregated nature of the education system. They dismiss the notion that they play a fundamental role in the conflict or, in particular, that greatly increased levels of integrated education would make a significant contribution to the resolution of the conflict.

In arguing the case against religious interpretations of the conflict, they make the following points:

1. '[T]here is no noticeable correlation between these areas most affected by the conflict and the intensity of the religious convictions of the inhabitants.'
2. 'Relations between the churches were improving when conflict erupted in the late 1960s.' This is a reference to the influence of the second Vatican Council.
3. '[P]olitical activists seek to avoid religious labels. No minority party or paramilitary group describes itself religiously.'
4. 'The key macro-policy of nationalist politicians and militants is an agreed or united Ireland which would transcend sectarianism, rather than the construction of a Catholic state.'
5. '[Unionist politicians] address themselves to secular issues, calling for a strengthening of the Union and for stronger security policies. They do not call for a Protestant theocracy.'
6. 'Protestants' desire to maintain the Union cannot be reduced to their religion, as Great Britain is increasingly less Protestant.'[22]

One might add to these points the conflict that arose between the Catholic Church and the Republican movement during the course of the hunger strikes by Republican prisoners in 1981. McGarry and O'Leary cite survey evidence to show that neither Protestants nor Catholics in Northern Ireland perceive religion as the primary cause of the conflict. They summarize their position as follows:

> Interpretations of Northern Ireland which emphasise the primacy of religion err by ignoring the multiple nature of the divisions between the two communities, and by understating the evidence which shows that the national conflict has greater salience. Protestants and Catholics are divided by religion by definition, but they are also divided by differences in economic and political power, by historical experience, and, most intensely, by national political identity. The thesis that religious motivations are not primary for either nationalists or unionists, or for republican or loyalist paramilitaries, is on our judgement convincing. Religion is the key ethnic marker, facilitating

the residential, marital and educational segregation which helps reproduce the two ethnic/national communities. Because religion is the key marker its importance is exaggerated. It is an analytical mistake to endow the boundary-marker with more significance than the fact that it is a boundary.[23]

But while McGarry and O'Leary's insistence on the primacy of national identity as a source of division in Northern Ireland constitutes an effective refutation of the most simple-minded versions of the religious interpretation of the conflict, their treatment of religion as simply a boundary-marker is not persuasive. In the first place, they tend to ignore or gloss over evidence of the extent to which religious belief has infused and coloured the conflict over national identities. In particular, they make no mention of the widespread use of Catholic religious imagery during the course of the hunger strikes by Republican prisoners in 1980 and 1981, notably the portrayal of the suffering of the hunger-strikers as akin to that of Christ.[24] In the case of the Loyalist paramilitaries, they ignore the admittedly minority of instances where evangelical influence has been to the fore.[25] In the second place, a number of their arguments has been undermined by the achievement of the Good Friday Agreement (on 10 April 1998) and the differing responses of the two communities to the Agreement. Given McGarry and O'Leary's commitment to such a settlement and their belief that it was achievable, this is somewhat ironic.

THE IMPLICATIONS OF THE GOOD FRIDAY AGREEMENT

Of course, the implications of the Good Friday Agreement for interpretations of the Northern Ireland problem depend on a reading of its significance. Reference has already been made to a spectrum of views on the Agreement from regarding it as a transitional step to seeing it as a final settlement. That spectrum presupposes the survival of the Agreement. A further perspective might be that it is a short-lived arrangement destined, like previous British initiatives, to fail. Such a perspective itself encapsulates a range of possibilities depending on the source of failure, from a lack of commitment by the Republican movement to the Agreement to breakdown due to loss of confidence in its provisions among a majority of Unionists. A view of the Agreement as short-lived presents little problem for established interpretations directed to answering the questions why the conflict continues and why the Northern Ireland problem is so intractable. By contrast, a view of the Agreement as a resolution of the problem begs the question of what has changed since 1974 when a similar Agreement (Sunningdale) foundered on the rock of Unionist grassroots opposition in the form of a general strike by Protestant workers.

Factors in the greater acceptability of the Good Friday Agreement to Unionists include the following: elements in the Agreement to reassure Unionists such as changes in the constitution of the Republic of Ireland and the establishment of a British-Irish Council that were not present in 1974; demographic change which has weakened Unionist bargaining power; war-weariness and the promise of peace held out by the truce among the main paramilitary groups; and Unionist recognition of the strong position of the Blair government. But whether these factors are sufficient to explain the change between 1974 and 1998 seems doubtful, putting the spotlight on wider changes that have taken place in Northern Ireland society under direct rule since 1974. (It is worth pointing out in this context that although the troubles continued up to the paramilitary cease-fires of 1994, there was a substantial decline in the level of political violence in the conflict after 1976.) It is for example plausible that the equality agenda pursued under direct rule played a part in helping to erode Protestant opposition to power-sharing by reducing what Protestants stood to lose under arrangements enshrining the principle of equality of opportunity for members of the two communities.

Similarly, it seems plausible that both secularization and an evolution of attitudes within the main churches also contributed to changing the climate of opinion in the Protestant community, a change making it possible for leading Protestant clergymen to declare their support publicly for the Agreement during the referendum campaign. Admittedly, the clergy were by no means united on the issue and in some of the evangelical churches, strong opposition was expressed to the Agreement, encapsulated in the catch-phrase – 'It's a sin to vote yes'. The referendum campaign highlighted deep divisions among Protestants over the Agreement that the large 71 per cent 'yes' vote tended to mask, since Catholics constituting over 40 per cent of the electorate were nearly unanimous in their support for the Agreement. A clearer picture of the divide emerged from the results of the elections to the Northern Ireland Assembly on 25 June 1998. The results are set out in Table 6.4.

Table 6.4:
Northern Ireland Assembly elections, 25 June 1998

	Seats	Percentage of first preferences
Ulster Unionist Party	28	21.28
Social Democratic and Labour Party	24	21.99
Democratic Unionist Party	20	18.03
Sinn Fein	18	17.65
Alliance	6	6.50
UK Unionist Party	5	4.52
Progressive Unionist Party	2	2.55
Northern Ireland Women's Coalition	2	1.61
Independent Unionist candidates	3	

Sources: *Irish Times*, 27 and 29 June 1998 and Nicholas Whyte's internet site on the elections.

The pro-Agreement Unionist parties (the Ulster Unionist Party and the Progressive Unionist Party) won 30 seats in the Assembly, while the anti-Agreement Unionists (the Democratic Unionist Party, the UK Unionist Party and the three independent Unionists) secured 28 seats. A complicating factor was that three of the successful Ulster Unionist Party candidates campaigned against the Agreement in the referendum campaign and their commitment to their party's position on the Agreement was weak from the outset. However, they did not defect from their party in the initial voting on the election of a First Minister, thereby enabling the UUP leader, David Trimble, to be elected, since the vote required the support of a majority of Unionist members.

This brings us back to Frank Wright's distinction in his 1973 article between 'extreme' and 'liberal' Protestants. One might quibble with his use of the term 'liberal' to describe the more moderate group of Protestants, but otherwise his categorization provides a useful basis for discussing the divide within Protestantism over the Good Friday Agreement. The religious dimension appears secondary to political and constitutional issues in the context of charac-terizing Unionist or Protestant attitudes as a whole. But it is more difficult to deny the significance of the religious dimension in relation to the articulation of the views of 'extreme' Protestants, since religiously grounded anti-Catholic rhetoric is so much more central in the expression of their political position. McGarry and O'Leary might well retort that even so political and constitutional issues enjoy primacy for 'extreme' Protestants and they could cite as evidence for that, the content of the DUP's communication for the referendum urging a 'no' vote, which made perfunctory reference to the religious dimension in its use of the phrase 'For God and Ulster'.

It is important that the case for assigning importance to religion should not be overstated. In particular, opposition to the Agreement could readily be justified in wholly secular terms and it is reasonable to suggest that the greatest threat to the Agreement is that Unionists will become disillusioned with the Agreement on political and security grounds, particularly if there is further violence from fringe Republican paramilitary groups and/or if the Provisional Irish Republican Army were to resist pressure to continue the process of decom-missioning. But what the religious dimension arguably does provide is a strong core to opposition to any form of political accommodation with Catholics within the Protestant community. This is perhaps best illustrated by the issue of marches by the Orange Order.

The issue of an Orange Order parade from Drumcree church down the Garvaghy Road (at the heart of a Catholic residential neighbourhood) to Porta-down has been a source of major contention since 1995, the year of the first Drumcree crisis. The crisis was resolved that year when residents were persuaded by the authorities to agree to the march taking place. However, the triumphalist behaviour of the marchers, including the striking of a medal to mark the occasion and the formation of a radical pro-march group within the Orange Order called 'The Spirit of Drumcree', ensured that the residents were unwilling to give their consent to the march in subsequent years. In 1996, the police initially banned the march. However, they reversed their decision as a result of growing disorder over the issue across Northern Ireland and the massing of Orangemen at Drumcree and forced the march through. In 1997, the newly elected Labour government followed the same course of action. This was on the advice of the Chief Constable of the Royal Ulster Constabulary that this represented the lesser evil in the view of the threat of life-threatening Loyalist violence if the march did not take place. The decision followed unsuccessful attempts at mediation between the Orange Order and the Garvaghy Road residents. The police again used force to clear the road for the marchers, to chants of 'no cease-fire' from the residents.

Despite this outcome, the Provisional IRA renewed its cease-fire on 20 July, shortly after the climax of the marching season on 12 July. By 1998 a Parades Commission had been endowed with legal powers to make binding decisions on contentious marches, though there remained scope for the Chief Constable to appeal against the decision of the Commission in exceptional circumstances. The Parades Commission ruled against the Orange Order being allowed to march down the Garvaghy Road in 1998, though this was balanced by a decision to allow the Orange Order to march along the Ormeau Road, a contentious route in Belfast. Massing of Orangemen occurred once again along with widespread rioting in Protestant areas, contributing to pressure on the government to find the means to reverse the decision of the Parades Commission. The position of the Ulster Unionist Party was that the Orangemen should be allowed to march, despite the stance of the Orange Order against the Good Friday Agreement during the referendum campaign. However, the UUP First Minister, David Trimble, made it clear that his preference was for a negotiated solution which would not damage relations between the two communities or threaten the survival of the Good Friday Agreement. For those opposed to the Agreement, the crisis presented a golden opportunity to destroy it before the north-south bodies for cooperation with the Irish Republic had been established.

The government underlined its commitment to enforce the Parade Commission's ruling by sending extra troops to Northern Ireland to assist in blocking the path of the Orangemen. With nightly clashes between massing Orangemen and the security forces, violence on a large scale seemed in prospect on Monday 13 July, the public holiday for the main Orange Order parades. In the event, the deaths of three Catholic children in a sectarian arson attack in Ballymoney on 12 July averted further conflict. The massing of Orangemen at Drumcree was abruptly called off. Senior figures in the Orange Order denounced the violence that had accompanied the build-up of tension during the previous week. A chasm opened up between militants who accused Orange leaders of treachery and members of the Order who regarded the violence of the militants as bringing disgrace on the Order. The Church of Ireland authorities abruptly ended their tacit acquiescence in the behaviour of the militants, demanding that they leave church property. This included the church's fields where the Orangemen had massed in successive Drumcree crises. (The Orange Order parade down the Ormeau Road on 13 July went off peacefully, with the residents holding a silent black flag protest along the route in memory of the children killed in Ballymoney.)

The resolution of Drumcree strengthened the position of pro-Agreement Unionists, but once again highlighted divisions among Protestants and in doing so focused attention on the role that religious fundamentalism played in the attitude of the militants. For example, *The Irish Times* carried a telling description of the books and pamphlets on sale at 'The Spirit of Drumcree' stand at Scarva on 14 July 1998. Scarva is where the most senior of the loyal orders, the Royal Black Perceptory, stages an annual mock battle in celebration of the Protestant victories of 1690. The titles of the books and pamphlets are sufficient to convey their character: 'The Day Rome Burned a Baby', 'Murder in the Vatican', 'Maria Monk – Awful Disclosures of Convent Life'. Available by order for those interested were 'The Borgia Pope', 'Horrible Lives of the Popes' and 'Convent Horror'.[26] McGarry and O'Leary acknowledge the existence of what they describe as 'Cathophobic views'. Indeed, they provide numerous examples themselves in 'Warring Gods?'.[27] However, they treat such expressions of sectarian hatred as a by-product of the violent conflict that has taken place over the constitutional issue, rather than, as Wright does, an autonomous source of hostility towards political accommodation with Catholics. However, in the light of nationalist acceptance in the Good Friday Agreement of the principle of consent, which entails that the constitutional status of Northern Ireland cannot be changed without the consent of a majority of the people of the province, it has become more difficult to account for the strength of opposition to the Agreement from a section of Protestant opinion without reference to the religious dimension. The issue of Drumcree has continued to be a source of tensions between the communities in the month of July, though in 1999, 2000 and 2001, it did not lead to violence on as large a scale as it had in either 1996 or 1998.

CATHOLICS AND THE SOUTH

Catholic intolerance towards the people of other faiths, including Protestants, as well as towards non-believers, has less commonly been seen as one of the causes of the conflict in Northern Ireland. However, a case can be made that it has played a part in the framing of the conflict. Correspondingly, it can be argued that the weakening of the power of the Catholic Church in the Republic of Ireland during the 1990s has played a significant role in easing Ulster Protestant fears of the Republic's intentions towards them. A fact often cited by Ulster Protestants in explaining their hostility towards the concept of a united Ireland has been the fate of the Protestant minority in the South after the partition of Ireland in the 1920s. In particular, at the time of partition Protestants constituted

10 per cent of the population of the Irish Free State. By the time of the 1991 census that figure had fallen to 3 per cent. The decline is attributable to a number of factors, including emigration, a low birth-rate and absorption into the majority population as a result of intermarriage, a process accelerated by the Catholic Church's absolute insistence that the offspring of mixed marriages be brought up as Catholics. One of the causes of emigration in the 1920s was the intimidation of Protestant landowners by the Irish Republican Army during the course of the War of Independence. However, over time, in sharp contrast to the position of the Catholic minority in Northern Ireland, the small Protestant minority shed its pre-partition ethnic identity so that only religious practice now separates this minority from the rest of the population. Further, despite discrimination against Protestants in the early decades of the new state, the minority's position has been and remains a relatively privileged one in social and economic terms.

The very special place of the Catholic Church in Irish society owes a great deal to historical circumstance, in particular, as John Coakley points out,

> to the fact that the institutional Catholic church in Ireland up to the nineteenth century was not a major landowner, was not linked with the old regime, and was neutral or sympathetic on the issues of democratisation and nationalism, rather than being suspicious or hostile, as in continental Europe.[28]

In the second half of the nineteenth century there was a devotional revolution in Irish society, with attendance rates at the weekly mass approaching 100 per cent among the Catholic population. The fidelity of Irish society to the church was reflected in the total absence of an anticlerical tradition in Ireland and the lateness and relative weakness of secularizing tendencies.

The Irish constitution of 1937 declared in Article 44 that 'the State recognises the special position of the Holy Catholic Apostolic and Roman Church as the guardian of the Faith professed by the great majority of the citizens'.[29] It went on to acknowledge the existence of other religions and, initially, this, rather than the privileged position it accorded to the Catholic Church, was what provoked controversy, though the campaign for the constitution to be amended to recognize Catholicism as the one and only true church was ultimately unsuccessful. After the start of the troubles in Northern Ireland in the late 1960s, the Irish government recognized that Article 44 presented an obstacle not just to Protestant acceptance of the case for a united Ireland but to that for any Irish dimension to the settlement of the conflict. A referendum was held which removed the special position of the church from the constitution.

However, the power of the forces of Catholic conservatism was demonstrated during the 1980s. In 1983, an amendment to the constitution prohibiting the legalization of abortion was passed by a more than two-thirds majority in a referendum, while in 1986, a proposed amendment to remove the constitutional prohibition on the legalization of divorce was defeated by almost as large a majority. The results of the two referenda were a defeat for the government in power and in both cases a strongly expressed plea from the Irish prime minister, Garret FitzGerald, that the adoption of a conservative Catholic stance on the issue in question would alienate Northern Protestants, failed to shift opinion. For their part, Northern Protestants said nothing to encourage the view that they might be less hostile to the concept of a united Ireland if a more liberal stance was adopted on these issues in the Republic. The reaction of the Catholic minority in Northern Ireland to these debates was muted and characterized by an unwillingness to be seen to be taking sides.

Events in the 1990s provoked a liberal reaction to the referenda of the 1980s. In particular, the highly contentious 'X' case arose in 1992. An outcry was caused when the Attorney-General sought and obtained a High Court injunction prohibiting a 14-year-old rape victim from travelling to Britain for the purposes of obtaining an abortion. The Attorney-General argued that he had been obliged to take this action because of the pro-life amendment to the constitution. However, on appeal the Supreme Court overturned the injunction on the grounds of a threat to life arising from the prospective mother's threat to commit suicide if she was not permitted to terminate the pregnancy. Pro-life groups were infuriated by this judgment and sought without success to amend the constitution by referendum to close this loophole. At the same time amendments were passed by referendum guaranteeing the right to travel and to receive information about birth control. In 1993 the law restricting the sale of contraceptives in the Republic was amended and there was also a liberalization of the law in relation to homosexuality. At the same time, a series of scandals undermined the authority of the church. A pattern of the sexual abuse of children by members of the clergy came to light, as did affairs of leading members of the church hierarchy. Public trust in the Church fell. Despite this, the level of attendance at church by Catholics in both parts of Ireland remains high by comparison with other countries in Europe.

CONCLUSION

Let me sum up the argument of this chapter. For a minority of Protestants in Northern Ireland, religion is more important than simply a boundary marker between Unionists and nationalists. Their opposition to Catholicism is based on more than just hostility to the nationalist project of a united Ireland, but has a religious basis. These Protestants provide a core of opposition to political accommodation in Northern Ireland. The growth of more liberal attitudes in the main churches has reduced the influence of such religious fundamentalists, so that on their own they are likely to prove unable to perpetuate the conflict. To wreck the Agreement they need a cause capable of securing support from a wider constituency. However, such a cause does currently exist in the form of the unwillingness of the main paramilitary organizations on both sides of the sectarian divide to go beyond the partial cease-fires they declared in 1994 (and in the case of the Provisional IRA renewed in July 1997).

In an attempt to force the Provisional IRA to start the process of decommissioning its arsenal of weapons, the Ulster Unionist Party refused during 1998 and much of 1999 to agree to the formation of the Executive and thus to the establishment of the other institutions envisaged under the Good Friday Agreement, including cross-border bodies. However, this tactic failed to shift the Provisional IRA. In November 1999, the Ulster Unionist Party agreed to the formation of the Executive prior to a start to decommissioning, but on the understanding that it would follow soon after the establishment of devolved government and the setting up of the cross-border bodies. The Ulster Unionist Party leader, David Trimble, ran into strong opposition from a minority within his party to his dropping of decommissioning as a precondition for the formation of the Executive. His position was made even more difficult in January 2000 as a result of the failure of the Republican movement to reciprocate the Unionist concession. The Agreement itself requires all the political parties to use any influence they may have to achieve the decommissioning of all para-military arms within two years of the May referenda in Northern Ireland and the Republic endorsing the Agreement.

To prevent Trimble's enforced resignation, the Secretary of State for Northern Ireland, Peter Mandelson, suspended the operation of the institutions on 11 February 2000. Even so, Trimble subsequently only narrowly survived a challenge to his leadership of the party, in which leading figures in the Orange Order played a prominent part. A major factor in the failure of the Republican movement to take any step to reassure Unionists as to the durability of the Provisional IRA's cease-fire appears to have been the fear that such a step would precipitate a split within the organization. However, the suspension of the operation of the Good Friday Agreement by the British government, though bitterly denounced at the time by Republicans, prompted movement on the issue of arms by the Provisional IRA. In May 2000, it agreed to the inspection of a number of its arms dumps by prominent international political figures. This gesture – and the promise that it would put its arms beyond use in the context of the full implementation of the Good Friday Agreement – proved sufficient for the restoration of devolved government.

However, the future of the Agreement seems far from assured. On 21 September 2000 the candidate of the Democratic Unionist Party, Rev. William McCrea, a Free Presbyterian minister and gospel-singer, won a by-election in the Westminster constituency of South Antrim, a seat previously held by the Ulster Unionist Party with a large majority. On 7 June 2001 voters in Northern Ireland went to the polls to elect 18 members of the Westminster Parliament in the British general election. Voting for local councils in Northern Ireland took place on the same day. In the two sets of elections the more centrist parties lost ground to their more militant counterparts on both sides of the religious divide. The outcome of the voting for the Westminster Parliament is set out in Table 6.5.

Table 6.5:
Results of UK general election of 7 June 2001 in constituencies in Northern Ireland

Party	%	+/– 1997	Seats	Net +/– 1997
Ulster Unionist	26.8	–5.9	6	–4
Democratic Unionist	22.5	+8.9	5	+3
Sinn Fein	21.7	+5.6	4	+2
SDLP	21.0	–3.1	3	0
Other	8.0	–5.5	0	–1

Source: BBC Northern Ireland, June 2001.

At the start of the election campaign, the First Minister, David Trimble, announced that he would resign at the end of June 2001 if the Provisional IRA failed to initiate the decommissioning of its weapons. In short he was demanding that the IRA go beyond the step it had taken of permitting the inspection of some of its arms dumps by international figures. In the absence of a response from the Republican movement Trimble duly resigned. The atmosphere of crisis this engendered was partially ameliorated by the recognition that his resignation would be the prelude to a period of prolonged negotiations among the parties, including the British and Irish governments. However, a common assumption was that at the end of this process the Good Friday Agreement could not survive the continuing refusal of the IRA to establish a mechanism to put its arms totally and verifiably beyond use. Opinion differed on whether the IRA could be persuaded to take such a step, as a result either of a deal over other issues, including policing and demilitarization, or of the threat of the exclusion of Sinn Fein from the Executive or a combination of such factors. In the event, external pressures, particularly as a consequence of the attack on the United States of America on 11 September 2001, helped to persuade the Provisional IRA to initiate decommissioning in October 2001. The restoration of the full workings of the Good Friday Agreement followed. However, Protestant opinion is still sharply divided and it remains to be seen if the Good Friday Agreement will finally take root and make possible the evolution of attitudes that might marginalize both Protestant religious fundamentalism and physical force Republicanism.

NOTES

1. John Whyte, *Interpreting Northern Ireland* (Oxford: Clarendon Press, 1990), pp. 194–205.
2. Jonathan Tonge, *Northern Ireland: Conflict and Change* (London: Prentice Hall Europe, 1998), p. 81.
3. Richard Rose, *Governing without Consensus* (London: Faber, 1971), p. 248.
4. Steve Bruce, *God Save Ulster: The Religion and Politics of Paisleyism* (Oxford: Clarendon Press, 1986), p. 268.
5. John McGarry and Brendan O'Leary, *Explaining Northern Ireland: Broken Images* (Oxford: Blackwell, 1995).

6. Frank Wright, 'Protestant Ideology and Politics in Ulster', *European Journal of Sociology*, XIV (1973), pp. 213–80.
7. John Hickey, *Religion and the Northern Ireland Problem* (Dublin: Gill and Macmillan, 1984). For Bruce, see note 4 above.
8. Wright, *Protestant Ideology*, p. 213.
9. Ibid., p. 216.
10. Ibid., p. 223.
11. Ibid., p. 244.
12. Ibid., p. 245.
13. 'Qualifications of an Orangeman', in Michael W. Dewar, *Why Orangeism?* (Belfast: Grand Orange Lodge of Ireland, 1959), p. 23.
14. See the chapters on 'The Elizabethan Conquest' and 'The Plantation of Ulster', in Jonathan Bardon, *A History of Ulster* (Belfast: The Blackstaff Press, 1992), pp. 75–147.
15. See, for example, Pamela Clayton, 'Religion, Ethnicity and Colonialism as Explanations of the Northern Ireland Conflict', in David Miller (ed.), *Rethinking Northern Ireland: Culture, Ideology and Colonialism* (London and New York: Longman, 1998), pp. 40–54.
16. Donald Harman Akenson, *God's Peoples: Covenant and Land in South Africa, Israel and Ulster* (Ithaca, NY and London: Cornell University Press, 1992), pp. 110–11.
17. Hickey, *Religion and Northern Ireland Problem*, p. 126.
18. Bruce, *God Save Ulster*, p. 258.
19. Ibid., pp. 257–8.
20. Steve Bruce, *The Edge of the Union: The Ulster Loyalist Political Vision* (Oxford: Oxford University Press, 1994), pp. 152–3.
21. McGarry and O'Leary, *Explaining Northern Ireland*, p. 189.
22. Ibid., pp. 189–99.
23. Ibid., pp. 211–12.
24. See, for example, the photograph of a hunger-strike wall mural in Charles Messenger, *Northern Ireland: The Troubles* (Twickenham, Middlesex: Hamlyn, 1985), p. 174.
25. See, for example, Martin Dillon, *God and the Gun: The Church and Irish Terrorism* (London: Orion, 1997), especially the chapter, 'Walking with Christ?', on the Loyalist paramilitary leader, Billy Wright.
26. Patsy McGarry, 'Drumcree Spirit evaporates leaving Paisley behind', *The Irish Times*, 18 July 1998.
27. McGarry and O'Leary, *Explaining Northern Ireland*, pp. 182–5.
28. John Coakley, 'Society and Political Culture', in John Coakley and Michael Gallagher (eds), *Politics in the Republic of Ireland* (London and New York: Routledge, 1999), p. 41.
29. Quoted in Michael Gallagher, 'The Changing Constitution', in Coakley and Gallagher (eds), *Politics in the Republic of Ireland*, p. 77.

7

Church and State after Transition to Democracy: The Case of Spain

VÍCTOR URRUTIA ABAIGAR

BACKGROUND

In Spain, relations between religion and politics, characterized in previous centuries by mutual tensions and distrust, have gone through major changes during the last decades. These changes have been led by two processes that have had a profound social impact: the *process of secularization* initiated during the 1960s, and the *process of political transition to democracy* since the late 1970s onwards. The logical evolution of both processes has contributed to a 'redirection' of mutual relations among religious institutions (especially Roman Catholic ones), the state and civil society. Such 'redirection', which is based on a different type of social leadership of religion, obliges the analyst to review not only theories about religion, especially the secularization theory, but also those approaches related to the evolution of democracy in contemporary society.[1]

These changes have pointed to the need for a rethinking of those perspectives that, either from the myth of secularization[2] or from the so-called 'death of god', foresaw the disappearance of religion and its institutional bodies, notably churches. In the same way, this new situation arouses a renewed interest in the role of organized religion as a social factor that spreads with different intensity across collective life and has political repercussions.

We should not be surprised, then, that most analysis on religion in Spain begins by questioning the theory of secularization and, consequently, pays more attention to the role of religion in a re-established project of modernity.[3] According to this approach, the significance of religion transcends the discursive-ideological and has an impact on the roles played by religion in the whole civil society. This impact has a special relevance in a country that, some time ago, underwent all the social and political transitions – including the religious one – towards modernity, but that had not been able to complete the process in a satisfactory manner.

The Process of Secularization

One must take for granted the process of secularization as a far-reaching social process, whose origin can be found in the Enlightenment, and that currently shows some ambiguous profiles. However, it has completed the split between official churches and modern states and governments, and as a result, stands for the autonomy of the political community (state) *vis-à-vis* the religious one (Church). This process, which in theory is usually embedded in wider social processes – such as modernization – or confused with them, offers a number of analytical perspectives.[4] My approach departs from the quantification of religious practices as a way of showing the impact the process of secularization has had in contemporary Spanish society.[5]

As we can see in Table 7.1, religious self-identification of Spanish citizens, defined by the extent of Sunday practices (weekly attendance to mass), presents a progressive change that can be understood as a two-way shift of attitudes: a loss of religious practice in favour of either a non-practice attitude or non-belief.

Table 7.1:
Religious auto-identification of Spanish citizens (1965–89), %

Year	Catholics		Non-believers and indifferents	Other religion
	Practising	Non-practising		
1965	83	15	2	–
1970	87	9	2	1
1975	74	14	2	0.2
1980	72	23	5	–
1985	65	30	4	1
1989	53	19	26	2

Notes: The tables may not add up to exactly 100 per cent since the numbers are rounded off.
Source: R. Diaz Salazar and S. Giner (eds), *Religión y Sociedad en España* (Madrid: CIS, 1993).

If we take age as a discriminatory variable, the result also follows this overall tendency despite some deviation for the youngest generation (15–17 years old) in Table 7.2.

These data pose some interesting questions that not only unveil in part the ambiguity of secularization but also the vagueness of the quantitative variables used to measure the religious phenomenon.

Some studies allude to this point[6] and agree that *indifference* and *unbelief* cannot be considered equally. If new indicators are introduced to grasp the religious experience, one detects a growing trend towards an 'inward' religiosity, which is not institutional and which appears more often among the young; 'what seemingly happens in fact – more among the youngest generations than among the adults – is that those who consider themselves as not being religious show a rate of belief, and also of prayer and meditation [that is] not to be despised'.[7] In

Table 7.2:
Religious auto-identification by age in 1989, %

	Total	15–17	18–21	22–25	26–35	36–45	40–60	61+
Very good Catholic	3.4	1.3	0.8	1.4	2.0	1.9	5.0	7.7
Practising Catholic	23.9	19.1	12.9	12.3	13.2	21.0	35.0	38.2
Not very practising Catholic	25.9	31.2	23.2	23.7	23.9	29.9	26.8	24.2
Non-practising Catholic	19.4	16.9	19.5	23.7	23.7	21.2	17.6	13.8
Indifferent	20.7	25.7	34.0	29.7	28.0	17.8	12.2	12.3
Atheist	5.4	5.3	8.6	8.1	7.7	6.2	2.6	2.3
Other religion	0.8	0.3	0.4	0.8	1.1	1.4	0.3	0.7
Dnk/Dna	0.5	0.3	0.5	0.3	0.3	0.5	0.4	0.8
(N=)		241	385	378	760	657	882	711

Note: The tables may not add up to exactly 100 per cent since the numbers are rounded off.

Sources: R. Diaz Salazar and S. Giner (eds), *Religión y Sociedad en España* (Madrid: CIS, 1993), and P. Gonzáles Blasco and J. González Anleo, *Religión y Sociedad en España do los 90* (Madrid: SM, 1992).

the view of some observers, this re-direction of religion, where other aspects such as the 'fragmentation of the Catholic doctrinal coherence' also meet, would reveal a 'de-institutionalization' of religion, the 'going out' from the 'ecclesiastic' dogma towards the world of para-religious beliefs, eclectic and diffuse mysticism, and 'religion à la carte'.[8]

In this context, we can think of some hypotheses related to the social or political culture that some of these religious trends generate:

1. The effect of what we could call 'flight from the world', and therefore an indifference to, or rejection of, politics in favour of 'individualistic' trends in contemporary culture.

2. The effect of counter-offensive or defensive neo-fundamentalism against anything that means pluralism or tolerance because these are originators of the religious loss. Later on, we will come back to this point as it has a potential force for social mobilization linked to conservative political ideologies.

3. The effect of the transference of religious feeling to the so-called 'sacred secularities'[9] or 'intermediate transcendence'[10] – in other words, the substitution of the great referents of traditional religions by new ones with a secular character, such as mother country, nature and sports. Some nationalisms, mainly in the Basque Country, assume this role when they elevate to the status of the sacred those myths, legends, or personages that one may die or kill for. Land, nation, or language are conceived also as sacred domains, i.e., as essences that have a wide effect on people's consciences and to which citizens must adapt for the sake of some collective rights taken in their whole purity from their origins in the tribal group.

To sum up, the loss of religious beliefs and the decline of religious practices appear as a historical factor of the Spanish modern society. In accordance with Western culture, with the progressive autonomy of the relations between the state and churches and with the deeply rooted Spanish Catholic tradition, recorded changes disclose a secularization rate that could be assessed as stable. It can even be assessed as a rate 'of (religious) sense recomposition from the spiritual stocks available in the religious and cultural larder of society, where meanings are at present many-sided and a social re-legitimation of the religious scenario can be carried out'.[11] This process implies a dispersion towards non-institutional fields, which is characteristic of a diffuse religiosity.

The Process of Political Transition to Democracy

The political role of the Catholic Church in the process of transition to democracy has been pointed out by a number of analysts, always in highly positive and favourable terms.[12] Stimulated by the renewing winds of the Second Vatican Council, the Spanish Catholic Church managed progressively to change its course since 1965. During the 1970s, the ecclesiastical associative web turned into a 'freedom zone' that facilitated the reemergence of labour unions, the rise of the citizens' movements, and, in short, contributed to the reconstruction of political parties. Many labour and political leaders of the democratic period were formed in the specialized groups of Catholic Action (JOC, HOAC, VOJ),[13] and their places sheltered the clandestine anti-Franco movement in many parts of the country. The Catholic Church had matured with the overall society and had gone into a new culture, more democratic and more sensitive to the social and political problems of the country. This change was more evident in the urban areas, among the working classes and among the young.

The social change within the Church was manifested in its 'civil society' as well as its hierarchy. The election of Monsignor Tarancón (1972) and his successor, Monsignor Diaz Merchán (1981), both of a progressive frame of mind, as presidents of the Spanish Episcopal Conference not only facilitated most of the hierarchy's relations with the ecclesiastic organizations, which at that time were open to social and political changes, but also fostered a rapprochement of Spanish society toward the world at large, which was already perceiving democratic changes.[14]

In short, during the process of democratic consolidation the Catholic hierarchy managed to move away strategically from attempts to influence the masses and handed the leading role in matters of sociopolitical concerns over to the political parties and civil associations.[15] This attitude entailed a confrontation with Pope John Paul II, who agreed neither with the role given to the Catholic Church in the new Constitution nor with the handing over of ecclesiastic leadership to the emerging democratic political forces.

This ecclesiastic position showed that the most influential institution in Spanish society, which was also the one with the strongest presence in its associative web, had a capacity of adaptation to the new cultural and political reality for the sake of a social understanding expected since the civil war.

THE DEMOCRATIC PERIOD

The development of democracy progressively introduced new political and cultural patterns into Spanish society. With regard to religion, and particularly to the Catholic feeling of the population, a significant change of course took place not only in the institutional relations between the churches and the state, but also in the stance taken up by the hierarchy and the Catholic faithful.

Throughout this period, the adoption of a framework of constitutional democracy was accompanied by a 'normalization' of state relations with all religions, including the minority ones. Popular Catholic religious culture adapted itself to an increasingly secular society; religious attitudes began to lose the previous radicalism that had characterized citizens' political (electoral) positions; and a religious-civil pluralism increasingly took shape in tune with developed Western societies' cultural tendencies.

A New Non-Confessional State: The Church–State Relationship

The adoption of the 1978 Constitution was a decisive step in the differentiation between the state's political powers and the religious ones, which is a structural trend widely accepted in the modern world. Not taking into account the reluctance felt by leftist groups in Parliament because of Article 16, 'the wise move of the [new] Constitution was to avoid the State's defining itself on religious issues or interfering with a certain belief defining the public domain'.[16]

The groundwork for the rupture was prepared by the turn given in the last years of the Franco regime by the Hierarchy, which understood 'the spirit of new times' in Spanish society and the direction taken by the coming political change to which many believing Christian members had contributed during the 1960s and 1970s. This development was a significant step on the long path towards a new political culture that affected not only the 'manners' of public institutions but also the population as a whole: it can be referred to as the consolidation of a non-confessional state in the conscience of citizens. Because the configuration of a non-confessional state is a historically new phenomenon in Spain, this consolidation must be interpreted as a strategy for change in the medium and long term. This is why, not only from a normative point of view but also from a sociological one, this 'new constitutional consideration' of religion implies a progressive social assimilation process, which does not lack reservations and contradictions.[17] It requires, as does any transformation affecting a nation's cultural roots, a change of mentality at different levels. Therefore, the consolidation of the non-confessional state must be understood as an uncompleted maturing process, which required a profound internalization of the religious spheres of the Catholic Church as well as minority cults and their demarcation from the state administration. Many of the conflicts that occurred in the last decades (including during both UCD and PSOE governments) are due to this kind of adjustment effort that in several instances has rebounded in a reemergence of the conflict between deep secularism (anti-clericalism) and 'fundamentalist' cultures that live inside people and organizations.[18]

It is not possible here exhaustively to assess the developments of the Agreements with the Holy See, which, signed immediately after the approval of the Constitution,[19] 'broke up' relations with the state (Basic Agreements of 1976; Agreements involving the ministries of Legal Affairs, Economic Affairs, Education and Cultural Affairs and relating to religious attendance in the armed forces and the military service of clergymen and members of religious orders, all of them in 1979) and which have been the subject of extensive rules (Laws, Decrees, Ministerial Orders, etc.) capable of clarifying and normalizing the relationship between the Catholic Church and the state during these years. This legal network has meant a strengthening of the legal, social and economic positions of the Catholic Church in Spanish society despite the critics and complaints that the hierarchy has repeatedly voiced.

A highly significant event in the culmination of this new Constitutional model based on religious freedom and non-confessionality, is the signature, in 1992, of the agreements of cooperation among the state and the Federation of Evangelical Religious Entities of Spain (FEDERE), the Federation of Israelite Communities of Spain, and the Islamic Commission of Spain, which are, all of them, entities representing religions that are noticeably socially rooted. These churches or religious entities represent a significant minority of Spanish society. They include more than a million people distributed throughout the country and grouped into 570 organizations of different types, as shown in Tables 7.3 and 7.4.

These legal-normative agreements not only make the aconfessional character of the state, declared in Article 16.3 of the Constitution, evident, but also have had as a main objective the attainment of a 'real and effective' religious freedom under conditions of equality for the whole Spanish population.

All this has a double effect. On the one hand, consideration has been given to the noticeably 'rooted' minorities, Protestants, Jews, and Muslims, as equal to the majority (Catholics). On the other hand, there is a commitment to respect each group's peculiarities and special requirements of each belief to the extent allowed by the principles of equality among all the citizens and of the state's confessional neutrality. The Agreements mean a departure from the historical tradition of the religious intolerance of the last five centuries, and a revival of the earlier pattern of religious pluralism, under which the communities of various religions had lived together in Spain peacefully and fruitfully for long periods of time. The consequences of these legal steps have their related social effect in terms of associative growth and the expansion of cult places of all the religious minorities that have followed a parallel and ascendant process with democracy's development (Tables 7.5 and 7.6).

Table 7.3:
Non-Catholic religious entities in Spain (entities and number of cult locations)

	Entities		Places for cult	
Confessions	N	%	N	%
1. Churches & Evangelical entities	744	83	1.638	61.4
Charismatic	89	9.8	113	4.2
Brothers Assemblies	120	13.3	143	5.3
Baptists	213	23.6	247	9.2
Pentecost	64	7.1	259	9.7
Presbyterian	36	4	58	2.1
Philadelphia Evangelic Church	1	0.1	613	22.9
Christ Church	9	1	19	0.7
Salvation Army	1	0.1	9	0.3
Anglicans	17	1.9	26	0.9
Inter-denominational churches and entities	60	6.6	13	0.4
Churches of pastoral attention to foreigners	25	2.8	9	0.3
Other evangelical churches	106	11.7	53	1.9
Adventists	3	0.3	76	2.8
2. Other Christian confessions	10	1.1	29	1
3. Orthodox	5	0.5	5	0.2
4. Islam	99	11	45	1.7
5. Judaism	15	1.6	15	0.5
6. Buddhism	13	1.4	13	0.4
7. Hinduism	3	0.3		
8. Other churches and confessions with Christian references	2	0.2	903	33.7
Church of the Last Days	1	0.1	30	1.1
Jehovah's Witnesses	1	0.1	873	32.6
9. Other confessions and entities	8	0.8	24	1
TOTAL ENTITIES	899		2,672	100

Source: Ministry of Justice. Table prepared by the author.

The Catholic Church and the Autonomous Cultural Identities

With the structuring of the autonomous state 'new relations' are emerging among the diocesan churches and their corresponding subnational authorities – provincial, municipal or autonomous. These relations must not be understood in the sense given to the confluence or split of political powers between the state and the Church, but as a domain for administrative and informal relations, which offer an important frame for analysis.

In the first place, we must consider the role played by local churches in the recovering of regional collective identities, especially where nationalist require-ments pose some problems, such as the Basque Country and Catalonia. The controversy emerged in the summer of 1995 because of the designation of Monsignor Blazquez as bishop of Bilbao, or the continuous leadership of the bishop of San Sebastián, Monsignor Setién, which are indicators not only of symbolic significance but also of the real power held by the ecclesiastic hierarchy in the Basque Country. One must also note the fact that in these two communities two Christian Democratic parties have been ruling for a long time (PNV in the community of the Basque Country and Unió in Catalonia) and that their ideological proximity has strong electoral correspondence among the clergy. All this contributes to the maintenance of quite fluid relations between the ecclesiastic hierarchies and the autonomous governments.

Table 7.4:
Federations with agreements of cooperation with the state by their religious orientation

Federations with agreements of cooperation with the state	Churches or federated communities	Churches or federated communities as per cent of their own religion
Federation of Evangelical Religious Entities of Spain – FEREDE	488	64.5
Federation of Israelite Communities of Spain	11	73.3
Islamic Commission of Spain	71	71.7

Source: Ministry of Justice.

Almost the same can be said about other Autonomous Communities, such as Castilla-León and Galicia. They find in the roots of history and culture valuable sources for recovering a collective identity which is to be built as a factor for political action (regardless of the ideological orientation of the government in power). Second, there is another phenomenon that presents some ambiguity but that can be considered significant because of its influence in some economic sectors – especially tourism – that are highly important for regional and local economies. This is the case of the Pilgrims Road to Santiago de Compostela in which the Xacobeo celebration and its international promotional campaign are included; or the cultural-tourist phenomenon of the exhibitions about 'Ages of Man' in the Castilian Cathedrals;[20] or the religious festivals of Easter in Andalusia and other regions of the country.

Formal attempts by local churches of adjustment to the reality of sub-national autonomy are still timid, and the political effects of such adjustment are still uncertain in view of future relationships between the Catholic Church and the state. Nonetheless, the celebration of the Tarragona Council (1994) and its repercussions in the probable creation of the Episcopal Conference in Catalonia has not gone unnoticed by the Vatican which, in accordance with this autonomous Spanish reality, appointed in 1995 a new nuncio (Monsignor Lajos Kada) with a wide experience in federal affairs after his stay in Germany.[21]

Table 7.5:
Expansion of non-Catholic religious entities

Confessions	<79	80–97	Total	Faithful*	%
1. Evangelic churches and entities	222	522	744	500,000	43
2. Other Christian confessions	1	9	10		
3. Orthodox	3	2	5	5,000	0.5
4. Islam	5	94	99	400,000	34
5. Judaism	11	4	15	30,000	2.5
6. Buddhism	0	13	13	60,000	5
7.Hinduism	1	2	3	10,000	1
8.Other Christian churches	2	–	2	120,000	10
9. Other confessions and entities	4	4	8	50,000	4
TOTAL	249	650	899	1,175,000	100

Source: Ministry of Justice. Prepared by the author.
*Approximate Data.

Table 7.6:
Evolution of non-Catholic entities and cult places

Registration year	Number of entities	%	Number of places for cult	%
Before 1970	108	12	120	5
1970–74	97	11	271	10
1975–79	44	5	322	12
1980–84	121	13	298	11
1985–89	143	16	518	19
1990–94	244	27	740	28
1995–97	142	16	403	15
TOTAL	899	100	2,672	100

Source: Ministry of Justice. Prepared by the author.

Vote and Religious Stance

Electoral analysis is one of the most commonly used to demonstrate how the political side of religious change has taken place in Spain. As J.R. Montero[22] put it, in the same way as many other Western countries, 'also in Spain religion is associated with electoral preferences'. It is a relevant element, but certainly not determinant. It seems to be clearly proved that 'religion's role has separated itself from the traditional confrontations between clerical and anticlerical people' which had characterized past times converting religion in a suitable arm for political confrontation. As Table 7.7 shows, the variable 'religiosity' appears to be shared between the two majority parties, having suffered an important change since 1979.

This change generates 'some perplexity' among analysts[23] who, after the description of the electoral data in Tables 7.7 and 7.8 ask, which explanation can be given to the fact that with the religious politics of Socialist governments, which has provoked constant tensions with the Catholic hierarchy, the Catholic electorate of the PSOE has remained equal, and has even relatively increased its number in the elections of 1993. Apart from different interpretations – such as 'the socialist capacity to develop catch-all strategies' (Montero) or 'the ruralization of the socialist vote' (Nasarre) – all data agree that the influence of the religious factor on electoral behaviour is extremely low.

This change in electoral culture, which we may consider irreversible, corroborates the structural change that involves the secularization process, and which from an institutional point of view is seen as a split between the spheres and powers of politics and the spheres and politics of religion.

Table 7.7:
Vote in general elections (1979, 1982 and 1993) by religiosity levels

RELIGIOSITY	PCE/IU	PSOE	UCD/CDS	AP-CD/PP	TOTAL	N
		Vote in 1979				
Very good Catholic	1	11	51	6	14	511
Practising Catholic	2	13	42	4	12	1,737
Little practising	5	52	31	3	15	1,217
Non-practising	10	32	15	1	18	965
Indifferent	15	29	7	1	24	522
Atheist	23	16	1	–	32	262
		Vote in 1982				
Very good Catholic	2	29	10	34	21	333
Practising Catholic	1	33	10	39	13	1,083
Little practising	2	57	6	21	11	1,070
Non-practising	3	67	2	11	15	826
Indifferent	11	66	–	2	20	455
Atheist	26	47	–	12	6	168
		Vote in 1993				
Very good Catholic	1	31	1	46	8	80
Practising Catholic	3	34	2	34	8	377
Little practising	6	40	2	23	11	342
Non-practising	11	36	2	27	12	348
Indifferent	17	33	2	10	14	145
Atheist	28	24	–	4	20	50

Note: The 'Does not answer' has been excluded for the percentages' base. It is probable that rows do not add up to 100 as other voted parties have not been included.
Source: J.R. Montero, 'Religión y elecciones en España, *Claves*, 62 (1996), pp. 26–37. (per cent horizontals).

Table 7.8:
Religious composition of the PSOE's and PP's electorates (1977–93)

	Practising Catholic		Non-practising Catholic		Indifferent or atheist	
Year	PSOE	AP/PP	PSOE	AP/PP	PSOE	AP/PP
1977	19	79	55	17	23	3
1979	25	63	53	33	21	3
1982	24	62	57	37	19	1
1986	21	54	58	38	20	5
1989	24	62	59	35	16	3
1993	32	51	55	43	13	5

Source: E. Nasarre, 'Religion y voto en la España de los Noventa', *Nueva Revista*, 41 (Madrid, 1995), pp. 94–103.

Between Religious Privatization and Civil Society

Among some students of the secularization phenomenon there has been an agreement on the hypothesis of an increasing reductionism of religion to the 'sphere of privacy', as a sign of loss of its historic leadership which would end in its social isolation. In other words, religion would come back to the 'sacristy' in a way that would make it invisible to society.[24]

The appearance in the 'political arena' of new religious groups or the request for their support on certain issues from the political domain, introduces some questions about the former approach. That approach, which marks a shift of religion from the public domain to the private one, with its subsequent social irrelevance, ignores the fact that the world of privacy is decisive for social behaviours in public life.[25]

What is interesting about this question is to determine whether there is a new process of de-privatization of religion in Spain; how the paths of convergence between the old and new religions in civil society are built; how the religious experience is publicly projected; and what kind of social orientation develops – whether it is a neo-conservative or a progressive one. Facing this question in our environment, once any anticlerical temptation (which historically has characterized a good part of the lay intellectuals) has been overcome, would require going inside an objective analysis of the Catholic Church as a complex organization. This would be tantamount to grasping not only its underlying theological perspectives of the Church but also the shape that its public 'appearances' (collective as well as individual) take in civil society.

It is not possible now to face such a project seriously, but we can point out some highly significant aspects linked to the appearance of new associative phenomena, in which religious attitudes (particularly those of the Catholic Church) have a great influence. There has been a gradual recomposition of the Spanish associative network once the country's legal-political structures have been consolidated.[26] I will point to three main tendencies:

1. The traditionalist one. It represents the attempt to 'recover the lost way' of the ecclesiastical (Catholic) public presence in every field (education, social welfare, etc.), but above all to recover the 'exclusivity of the ethic message'. Leaders of the Church would like to see (and work for) a 'turning back' in the agreements between the state and the Catholic Church. They accuse Socialist (PSOE) governments of being directly responsible for the 'de-Christianization' of Spanish society, and of favouring 'hedonism' and a 'liberal permissiveness' that underlie this approach. Traditionalists are represented by an important part of the Catholic ecclesiastical hierarchy as well as fundamentalist and 'conservative' Catholics.

2. The neo-conservative one. Here we find those Catholics (and other religious believers) who accept the ethic of pluralism; who do not seek a dogmatic imposition of their religious principles; who are open to close collaboration between public and religious institutions; and who belong to political parties of Christian democratic, Christian socialist, and/or nationalist traditions.

3. The critical one. This approach is represented by a great part of those Christians coming from the anti-Franco struggle. They are often linked to trade unions, leftist parties and groups (Marxist or not); are connected, at different stages, with social movements and civic associations; and, as an overall trend, maintain a critical position regarding the Catholic hierarchy. Many of them have suffered a lack of understanding from the parties on the left as well as a loss of ideological referents in an environment of crisis affecting these parties and the concept of political militancy itself.[27]

It is important to stress the relevance of two facts that, from this de-privatizing perspective, not only have a clear relationship to the two last tendencies, but also reveal the transforming power of religion. The first one is the growth of voluntary associations and social movements in Spanish civil society. As I have written elsewhere, 'we are witnessing a reconstruction of primary networks or associative webs on which a whole political culture is based; this is the politics of community',[28] which precisely finds among the religious groups one of its main engines.[29]

The second phenomenon is the change of course of civic militants participating in these associative/volunteer webs. The crisis of political parties and the critique of politics as a whole have diverted the attention of many of these militants towards organizations with a humanitarian or welfare character. The emergence of NGOs, Free Time Clubs, pacifist groups,[30] associations against social exclusion, groups cooperating with the Third World, and so on, many of which have been stimulated by the Catholic Church, are a good indicator of this 'change of course', which, in fact, has deeper social roots. This organizational development has an ideological ambiguity which is peculiar to every emerging social phenomenon. What is meant is a turning away from the structural militancy of the 1970s to the humanitarian and welfare militancy of the 1990s. There is, however, no doubt that this ambiguity harbours the strong possibility that new generations will seek to involve themselves more directly in political action.

NOTES

1. One symptom of this worry about the search for new perspectives for the analysis of the religion–politics relationship is the recent publication of some works such as: A. de Miguel, *Política y Religión en la España actual en AA.VV., La influencia de la religión en la sociedad española* (Madrid: Libertarias/Prodhufi, 1994); J.M. Mardones, 'Religión y Política', *Leviatán*, 59 (1995), pp. 15–26; Reyes Mate, 'Religión y Política: Por un nuevo planteamiento', *Iglesia Viva*, 178/179, Valencia (1995), pp. 429–49. From a wider perspective of religion and society we can point to R. Diaz Salazar and S. Giner (eds), *Religión y Sociedad en España* (Madrid: CIS, 1993), and *Formas modernas de religión* (Madrid: Alianza, 1994); P. Gonzalez Blasco and J. Gonzalez Anleo, *Religión y Sociedad en España*, 90 (Madrid: SM, 1992); A. Tornos and R. Aparicio, *¿Quién es creyente en España hoy?* (Madrid: PPC, 1995).
2. J. Estruch, 'El mito de la secularización', in Salazar and Giner (eds), *Formas modernas de religión*, chap. 11, pp. 266–80.
3. J. Casanova José, 'El "revival" político de lo religioso', in R. Dias Salazar and S. Giner (eds), *Formas modernas de la religión* (1994), chap. 10.
4. V. Pérez Díaz, *Iglesia y religión en España in El retorno de la sociedad civil* (Madrid: Instituto de Estudios Económicos, 1987), pp. 442–73. Re-edit in *La primacía de la sociedad civil* (Madrid: Alianza, 1993), chap. 3, pp. 145–225. J. Estruch, 'El mito de la secularización', in Salazar and Giner (eds), *Formas modernas de religión*, chap. 11, pp. 266–80. J. Casanova, 'El cristianismo en la esfera pública de la sociedad civil', *Iglesia Viva*, 178/179, Valencia (1995), pp. 395–411.
5. For the Spanish case, see P. González Blasco and J. González Anleo, *Religión y Sociedad en España*, and F. Andrés Orizo, *Sistema de valores en la España de los 90* (Madrid: CIS, 1996). For a comparative analysis see R. Inglehart and J. Diez Nicolas (eds), *Tendencias mundiales de cambio en los valores sociales y políticos* (Madrid: Fundesco, 1995).
6. Miguel, *Política y Religión*; Tornos and Aparicio, *¿Quién es creyenti?*; J.M. Mardones, *¿A dónde va la religión? Cristianismo y religiosidad en nuestro tiempo* (Santander: Sal Terae, 1996); Andrés Orizo, *Sistema de valores*.
7. Andrés Orizo, *Sistema de valores*.
8. Mardones, 'Religión y Política'; A. Moncada, *Religión a la carta* (Madrid: Espasa, 1996).
9. E. Gil Calvo, 'Religiones laicas de salvación', in Dias Salazar and Giner, *Formas Modernas*, pp. 172–87.
10. T. Luckmann, 'Religion and the Social Conditions of Modern Consciousness', *II Congreso Mundial Vasco: Filosofía, Etica y Religión*, Vitoria (1988), pp. 405–16; V. Urrutia, 'Religiones de suplencia', *Iglesia Viva*, 146, Valencia (1990), pp. 177–87.
11. F. Andrés Orizo, *Sistema de Valores*.
12. Pérez Díaz, *Iglesia y religión*; R. Díaz Salazar, *El capital simbólico* (Madrid: HOAC, 1988); Diaz Salazar and Giner, *Religión y sociedad en España*; J. Pérez Vilariño, 'El futuro de la religión en España', *Papers*, 47, Barcelona (1995), pp. 9–29; A. Brassloff, *Religion and Politics in Spain: The Spanish Church in Transition, 1962–1996* (London: Macmillan, 1998).
13. JOC: Juventud Obrera Católica/Catholic Workers' Youth; HOAC: Hermandad Obrera de Acción Católica/Catholic Action Workers' Guild; VOJ: Vanguardia Obrera Juvenil/Young Workers' Vanguard.
14. During this period 1972–81 the most significant events of the Transition took place: Carrero Blanco's assassination 1973; Franco's death 1975; the first legislative elections 1977; the constitutional referendum 1978; the signature of the Agreements between the Holy See and the state; municipal elections and statutory elections in the Basque Country and Catalonia 1979; the General Act of Religious Liberty 1980; the Law of Divorce 1981; and the electoral victory of the PSOE 1982.
15. The Catholic hierarchy declared its support of Catholics' freedom of vote. It did not explicitly support the Christian-Democratic Party, which obtained marginal electoral results.
16. See A. Motilla de la Calle, 'Relaciones Iglesia-Estado en España', *Anuario de la Fac. de Derecho de Alcalá de Henares, cours 1991–92*, 1, Alcalá (1992), pp. 91–107. Reference is made to section 3 of article 16, which provides that 'no confession will have a State nature' and that 'the public authorities shall take the religious beliefs of Spanish society into account and shall in consequence maintain appropiate co-operation with the Catholic Church and the other confessions'.
17. Garcia Morillo, 'Un tributo a la Historia: la libertad religiosa en la España de hoy', in *Cuadernos*

Constitucionales de la Cátedra Fadrique Furió Cerial, 9/10, Univ. de Valencia (1995), pp. 115–35, discusses some of these reservations, which have to do with the sociological/historical understanding of religious freedom and the effects that our past of confessional state has on the present.

18. Some declarations between the years 1985 and 1990, as characterized by the very tense relations between the socialist governments and the EEC Spanish Episcopal Conference, give us a clear idea of the situation. F. Sebastian, Secretary of the EEC, stated that 'there exists a state of siege and almost attack from the dominating secularism against the Church, against Christian culture, and against the religious faith itself' open letter to I. Ellacuría, 22 December 1985. Assessment of Martin Toval to the EEC document called 'On public morality': 'aberrant and antidemocratic', *El País*, 22 November 1990. Also very clarifying are J.L. Martin Descalzo's words:

> this previous document, in some commentators and politicians' opinion, [reflects] the split between Church and State. But, does it mean that the State would only bear a dumb Church? Whether the State likes it or not, the Church, as long as it carries out its duty, will say these painful truths. ... [And], why would a State that prides itself of being democratic not be able to exist side by side with a dialoguing Church? In Spain, we lack any self-critical capacity, above all when it is about issues related to the Church, because anticlericalism seems to be one constituent element of the national soul. But someone should start daring to take that document without prejudice and to look at oneself in it as if it were a mirror. (*ABC*, 25 November 1990)

19. The Basic Agreement was signed in 1976, i.e., before the Constitution, and this haste probably reflected the Socialists' partial abstention and the Communist vote against.

20. The exhibits of 'The Ages of Man' have attracted to the various provincial capitals of Castile Burgos, Valladolid, León, Salamanca, Soria, Palencia more than three million visitors between 1988 and 1999. This figure gives us an idea of the cultural and economic impact of this Foundation, which is wholly organized by the bishops of Castile-León.

21. In this context, we should also mention the conflicts created by COPE Radio Station, whose main partner is the European Union CEE. The informative and opinion strategy held by this station with Basque Country politics and specially with Basque nationalism, forced a split with the Bilbao bishopric, which acquired the property of the station Radio Popular of Bilbao and made it independent from the Madrid management. Similar conflicts took place during 1996 in Catalonia evolving into an open confrontation between a number of bishops and COPE's management, who harassed the CiU political line. J. Sánchez, previously Secretary of the CEE, in his intervention, 'The Contribution of the Church to 20th century's society in Club Siglo XXI', recognized that 'the Spanish Church has never meditated about this reality the autonomic one' and that 'is a subject to be taken up in the new century and millennium', March 1996.

22. J.R. Montero, 'Iglesia, secularización y comportamiento político en España', REIS, 34 (1986), pp. 131–59; and 'Religión y elecciones en España', *Claves*, 62 (1996), pp. 26–37.

23. See E. Nasarre, 'Religión y voto en la España de los Noventa', *Nueva Revista*, 41, Madrid (1995), pp. 94-103.

24. T. Luckmann, *La religión invisible* (Salamanca: Sígueme, 1973).

25. J.M. Mardones, 'La desprivatización del catolicismo en los años ochenta', *Sistema*, 83 (1990), pp. 123–36; R. Díaz Salazar, 'La privatización del hecho religioso: ¿Realidad sociológica o falacia ideológica?', *Euroizquierda y Cristianismo* (Madrid: Fundación F. Ebert/Instituto Fe y Secularidad, 1991), pp. 107–46.

26. It is important to point out the vast organizational structure of the Catholic Church:

Order, religious communities and associations	15,548
Dioceses	67
Bishops	113
Priests	19,516
Parishes	22,500
Nuns	56,008
Friars	13,500

Source: Conference 1993 and Director General of Religious Affairs, *Guía de entidades religiosas de España. Iglesias, confesiones y comunidades minoritarias* (Madrid: Ministerio de Justicia, 1998). Prepared by the author.

27. CPS, Cristianos por el socialismo, '17 años de compromiso a través de 38 documentos', *Dialogo*,

14–15 (Barcelona: Secretariado, 1989); R. Díaz Salazar, 'Sociología socialista de la Iglesia. El futuro de la política religiosa del PSOE', *Pastoral Misionera*, 165, Madrid (1989), pp. 46–70, J.M. Mardones, *¿A dónde va la religión?*

28. V. Urrutia, 'Transformaciones y persistencia de los movimientos sociales urbanos', *Política y Sociedad*, 10, UCM, Madrid (1992), pp. 49-56.
29. D. Casado, *Organizaciones voluntarias en España* (Madrid: Hacer, 1992).
30. Aguirre, R., Mardones, J.M. and Urrutia, *La Iglesia Vasca* (Madrid: Ministerio de Justicia, Unpublished Document). J. Vitoria, *La presencia pública de los cristianos en la sociedad* (Madrid: HOAC, 1995); *Cuadernos* (1995), 22; I. Zubero 'Violencia y religión en el Pais Vasco', *Iglesia Viva*, 187 (1997), Valencia, pp. 83–8.

8

Poland's Transition to a Democratic Republic: The Taming of the Sacred?

RAY TARAS

Distinguishing the sacred from the profane is a time-honoured philosophical activity. It is also one that political practitioners have often emphasized in many different societies. American anthropologist Ruth Benedict remarked that:

> The striking fact about [the] plain distinction between the religious and the non-religious in actual ethnographic recording is that it needs so little recasting in its transfer from one society to another. No matter into how exotic a society the traveler has wandered, he still finds the distinction made and in comparatively familiar terms.[1]

The dichotomy between what is Caesar's and what is God's is, then, almost universally accepted.

Transitions from Communism in the 1990s provided laboratory conditions for testing many different hypotheses. Two that relate to the distinction between the secular and the sacred will be examined in this chapter. First, the ideological character of the Communist regime posited an atheistic and materialist consciousness in society. When Communism collapsed, we would expect that the antithesis of such an ideology would exert a crucial influence in shaping the new order. Put another way, during the transition political space opened up for the sacred–religious values, religious institutions and religious leaders. They shaped the construction of the new political order. Second, even if rehabilitation of the sacred took place in the early stage of political transition, the distinction between the religious and the non-religious was maintained under the new system of constitutional democracy. It is such a fundamental distinction in any society that we would be surprised to find it gone.

Ideally, testing these two seemingly contradictory propositions should involve cross-national inquiry. The significance and reliability of the findings would be enhanced by comparative research. This chapter focuses on only one country, Poland, but arguably it is the most illuminating case to apply these hypotheses.

CATHOLICISM IN POLAND: HISTORICAL BACKGROUND

In 1847, Count Zygmunt Krasinski, one of Poland's great Romantic poets (though less celebrated in the West than are Adam Mickiewicz and Juliusz Slowacki), mused in a personal letter: 'the real reason for the existence of Poland is to realize on earth the kingdom of heaven, to merge politics and religion, to found the future Church of humanity and to show the whole world that sovereignty does not reside in a king or in a people but only in the nation.'[2] Only a few decades earlier, Mickiewicz had compared partitioned Poland to Christ suffering on the cross to redeem humanity. Krasinski's messianic vision of Poland was, in turn, as the founder of the kingdom of heaven on earth. In one way or another, these interrelated conceptions of the nation's destiny have preoccupied its spiritual and even secular leaders from the time of King Mieszko I, who converted to Christianity in 966.

When Poland broke from Communism in 1989, an important historical debate was revived: has the country always been an ethnically and religiously homogeneous country (as the common perception in the West would have it), or has it also experienced being a multinational state reflecting religious diversity? Evidence furnished by historians is contradictory. For the first four centuries under the Piast dynasty, Poland consisted largely of related tribes. But, in 1370, a Polish–Lithuanian Union was created that transformed the ethnically homogeneous state of the Piast dynasty into a multinational one under the new Jagiellonian kings. The Union's expansive borders stretched from the Baltic Sea in the north to the Black Sea in the south. Within this country, most Lithuanians were Catholic, like the Poles, but large Ukrainian and Belorussian groups (Slavs, like the Poles) were incorporated into this mini-empire and belonged predominantly to the Eastern Orthodox faith.

The adage that being Polish meant being Catholic, then, was already an oversimplification of the ethnic and religious makeup of Poland in medieval times. Even equating an ethnic Pole with a Catholic was imprecise. During the Reformation of the sixteenth century, Protestantism was given legal recognition (in 1555) and religious toleration and equality were proclaimed (in 1573). Even if accounting for a small proportion of citizens, Lutherans and Calvinists had an important presence in some urban areas. Even further undermining the myth that to be Polish was to be Catholic was the presence of about 80 per cent of the world's Jews in the country at this time. One writer observed how 'in no other country than ancient Israel, have Jews lived continuously for as many centuries, in as large numbers, and with as much autonomy as in Poland'.[3]

Not surprisingly, during his 1997 pilgrimage to Poland, Pope John Paul II celebrated the culture that Catholic and Jewish Poles had helped forge over centuries. The leader of the world's Catholics stressed how Polishness was not an attribute solely of Catholic Poles. The Pope urged the latter group to put an end to the attitude common in the interwar years that Jews were 'among us' but not 'of us'. Even though the country's current Jewish population numbers less than 20,000, John Paul II's universalist message signified that if Poland was to construct the kingdom of heaven on earth, it had to be ecumenical.

To be sure, this approach departs from a more proprietary attitude traditionally taken towards the nation by the Catholic Church. In the mid-fifteenth century, Poland's role in Europe was widely seen in terms of an *antemurale christianitatis* – the easternmost bulwark of Roman Catholicism. It was regarded as a nation lying on the fault line of Western and Eastern civilizations, under constant threat of becoming absorbed by the non-Catholic East. Over the next centuries, a Polish manifest destiny was elaborated to encompass secular political values founded on this perspective in addition to religious ones. In this view, the country represented the outpost of *European* civilization generally. To its east, the culture of Rus, Byzantinium, Asia began. The philosophy that evolved to explain this destiny was called Sarmatianism (from an ancient Slavic tribe that came to dominate neighbouring peoples). It assigned a special mission to Poland as a shield protecting Christianity – and Europe – from pagans and barbarians.

Both religious and secular versions of the *antemurale* myth have been stressed in Polish historiography. One of the best illustrations of the myth was the Ukrainian Cossack revolt against Polish rule in 1648, which initiated 'The Deluge' – in quick succession Poland was at war with Tatars, Turks, Russians and Swedes. In 1655, the Swedish army, having swiftly overrun most of the country, could not overcome the last-ditch defence of the Częstochowa monastery. The successful Polish resistance was attributed to the intercession of the Blessed Virgin whose icon, the Black Madonna, was (and is) kept there. She had remembered that Poland was the *antemurale christianitatis*.

An even more vivid example of Poland's historic mission as defender of Western Christian civilization came in 1683 when King Jan Sobieski defeated the Turkish armies outside of Vienna, thereby saving Europe from Islam. The Catholic Church where he prayed before the battle still stands in the Vienna Woods. Clearly, in these formative years of Poland's history the sacred largely defined the nation, its mission, and its political uniqueness.

Based on this historical overview a few generalizations about Church–state relations are in order. Stein Rokkan's model of political cleavages called attention to the interrelationship between the Catholic Church and nationalism in certain European states. 'The Catholic Church played a major role in the development of peripheral nationalism in some of the territories of Counter-reformation Europe' such as Poland, he asserted.[4] The underpinning reason for this was the centrality of the Church in the struggle against foreign domination. In the same vein, David Martin pointed to 'the accretion of further roles' by the Church with the 'attainment of national independence'.[5] This might suggest that the Church historically competed with the state for political influence. However, because of the absence of a strong state for most of its history, a Church–state conflict in Poland is in reality either ahistorical, or atypical of the conflicts that went on in Western European countries.

SACRALIZING THE SECULAR UNDER COMMUNISM

There is little doubt that the Catholic Church in Poland has always performed a multiplicity of functions. Whether during the partitions, under German occupation in World War II, or in the Communist period, it served as a galvanizing force of national resistance and constituted the principal institutional opposition to alien rule. The Church was also concerned with political socialization as well as with many practical religious rituals at the parish, family and individual levels. The author of a study of religion in Poland summarized these many functions:

> the Church's unique role in contemporary Polish politics intertwined moral and political authority with national, historical and cultural traditions and with the current demands and expectations of national survival. As long as there exists a sovereign Poland the Church can and will promote the nation's interests.[6]

While scholarly research on Polish Catholicism usually focuses on the political aims of the ecclesiastical hierarchy, postwar Polish Catholic thinkers were a politically diverse and provocative lot that deserves special attention. These included Stefan Kisielewski, Boleslaw Piasecki and Janusz Zablocki. Catholic ideological apparatuses like Znak ('Sign'), Pax ('Peace') and Wiez ('Link') – discussed below – were also intriguing theoretically and controversial politically. In his monograph, Norbert Zmijewski reported that even prior to the Polish October of 1956 Kazimierz Klosak (a popularizer of Thomism in Poland) recommended dialogue with Marxists. He focused on their common epistemologies and metaphysics while ignoring differences concerning beliefs. Zmijewski persuasively contended that, 'confrontation between Thomism and Marxism in the early years of the Communist regime in Poland demonstrated, to both participants, that scientific arguments either for God's existence or for Communist society had little sense'.[7]

Catholic intellectuals also questioned free-market capitalism and its ideological offshoot, humanitarian liberalism. One article inveighed that 'Liberalism is harmful to society; it exaggerates the value of freedom, breaks up the bonds of society, destroys the authority of the state and threatens to unleash destructive social forces.' This anti-liberal critique appeared not in *Trybuna Ludu* (the Communist party's organ) but in *Tygodnik Powszechny* (the Catholic weekly).[8]

Catholic organizations differed in their political strategies under Communism. While the authoritarian regime condemned the practice of religion and even arrested the Catholic Primate in 1953, some religious freedom was countenanced and certain Catholic groups favoured. Pax was the sinister pro-regime, totalitarian-inclined group headed by Piasecki from which future prime minister Tadeusz Mazowiecki was expelled in 1955. Znak was an independent Catholic group that in some ways served as an early prototype of political dissidence. But its occasional *Realpolitik* made it look cynical when contrasted with the humanist socialism of a Pax splinter group, Wiez. The utopian personalism of the more liberal faction of Wiez, led by Mazowiecki, made it a unique intellectual community in a region still emerging from high Stalinism. Moreover, the impact of the protracted Catholic–Marxist dialogue of those years still has resonance in today's Poland where questioning of capitalist materialism and the threat to national identity posed by entry into Europe has carried on.

From the outset, Communist authorities were cautious in attacking the privileged position of Catholicism. Even when Cardinal Stefan Wyszynski was placed under house arrest in 1953 (the subject of a recent film called *Prymas Tysiacalecie* [The Primate of a Thousand Years], over time, as the Catholic–Marxist dialogue showed, 'the sharpness of the Communists' determination to annihilate religion might have dulled and fraternization and compromise might have grown from a tactic to a condition'.[9] This was a pattern that extended to other Soviet-bloc countries 'because the costs to the Communist authorities in foreign policy, internal popular discontent, and ideological embarrassment outweighed any need to liquidate the "religious problem" through precipitate means'.[10]

It was apparent that in a zero-sum game with the political authorities, the Church was gaining ground. Moreover, it appeared that the Church did not have to compromise its fundamental principles to gain advantage: 'Communism has rendered the Church the signal service of sparing it the necessity of undertaking the difficult task of coming to terms with the modern world that has been thrust upon the Churches of the West.'[11]

Curiously, the influence of Catholic intellectuals on self-doubting Communist leaders may have been greater than on the doctrinally unbending, self-confident ecclesiastical hierarchy. Conservative theologian Cardinal Ratzinger acknowledged this fact: 'Paradoxically (or not so paradoxically) the faith seems to be more securely rooted in Eastern Europe, where it is officially persecuted. Doctrinally we have scarcely any problems with the Catholicism of these regions.'[12]

Under Communism, determined Catholic leaders regularly called into question the precept of rendering Caesar his due. One of the most prominent Catholic writers of the period, Jerzy Turowicz, wrote in the aftermath of martial law in 1985:

> The Church in its concern for the true good of man cannot confine itself to proclaiming its doctrine and communicating it to the faithful. It also has the right and the duty to react to events and situations, to judge and condemn injustice and violence, to stand up for the offended and oppressed, to call for justice and respect for human dignity and human rights, in particular man's right to be a subject, to be able to forge his own destiny. The Church will never give up this critical function with respect to secular society, because it is of the very essence of its mission in the world. In the exercise of this function, the Church has the right and the duty to express its opinion about the problems of political life, to issue requests, to protest or even condemn or denounce.[13]

This redrawing – and apparent negation – of the boundary between the city of God and the city of man was a long way from the traditional approach of Catholics to politics which, paradoxically, Communists could grudgingly accept: 'the "entry into politics" of a believer takes place via a rejection of politics as defined by the government. More accurately, such a move will involve a subordination of politics to a higher, spiritual and moral register'.[14] With bitter irony, the official Communist response to Turowicz's seminal article inveighed: 'Isn't this counter to the teachings of the Gospel?'

Partly for strategic reasons, partly in order to make virtue out of necessity, Communist authorities gradually expanded the political space the Church could operate within. Under Edward Gierek in the second half of the 1970s, meetings between the Communist Party head and the Catholic Primate and other members of the Episcopate became routine. Catholicism's strength was reinforced through a tactical alliance with the lay opposition and, most importantly, the election of a Polish pope in 1978. Table 8.1 encapsulates other achievements that the Church recorded in developing political space for itself and its allies. Even after martial law was imposed the Church was treated as a partner of the Communist state. In June 1983, just before the second papal visit, Adam Lopatka, minister of religious affairs, asserted that the authorities 'no longer held the opinion that the Church should keep out of politics as long as it was in keeping with the constitution and respected the international interests of Poland'.[15] In the same week, a Communist Party publication designed for party activists acknowledged that 'Polish Communists are aware of the mass nature and the millennial tradition of Catholicism in Poland.'[16] In the 1980s, the secular leaders of Britain, France, or Germany would not have conceded as much autonomy and influence to a religious institution in their countries as the Communist authorities did to the Catholic Church in Poland. But, the different approaches owed much to the different forms the sacred took in these societies. Thus, a Communist-approved author pointed to the existence 'in Poland of a *people's* Catholicism which differs from the French variety by its emotional coloring, its forms of service and the imagery that it utilizes'.[17] In other words, the political reality in Poland required that the Communist government engage the vigorous Church, secure in its popular appeal, in a dialogue.

On the other hand, we should not underestimate the intellectual weight of Catholicism that was brought to bear against the Communist regime. French writer Patrick Michel observed how 'in Poland a popular type of religiosity, in the sense that it was strongly associated with religious and national values, has given place, owing to special historical circumstances, to a more selective and intellectualized type of religion'.[18] One of the areas that best illuminate this facet of Polish Catholicism is the dialogue it carried out with Marxist theorists.

After three decades of Communist rule, Communist rulers realized that combating the sacred was counterproductive.[19] As Michel concluded:

In the Polish situation, when the government attacked the Church and sought to compromise it or force it to compromise, it merely helped the Church to gain in influence. Its only hope would have been to claim to incorporate the Church, and that was the one thing its own ideology forbade it to do.[20]

Table 8.1:
The influence of the Catholic Church under the Communist regime

Issue	Poland	Czechoslovakia	Hungary
Religious identity facilitating identification with the nation	A	C	C
Hegemony of Catholic Church over religion	A	A	A
Existence of a legal Catholic press independent of the state	A	C	C
Existence of a legal Catholic university independent of the state	A	C	C
Existence of lay groups promoting a Catholic ethos	A	A	B
Existence of Catholic youth groups independent of the state	A	C	C
Criticism of government by Church leaders	A	B	C
Official Episcopate statements on social and economic issues	A	C	C
Organization of Church-sponsored cultural events	A	C	C
Existence of clandestine Catholic press	B	C	C
Access by Catholic groups to the mass media	A	C	C
Reference to the Church by opposition groups	A	B	C

A = Strong, B = Moderate, C = Weak
Source: Adapted from Patrick Michel, *Politics and Religion in Eastern Europe* (Cambridge: Polity Press, 1991), Table 3, p. 26.

Communist construction of a secular, let alone atheist state had faltered. Leading dissident Adam Michnik wrote in the 1970s that 'the People's Republic of Poland is not a democratic, secular state. It is a totalitarian state subject to a particular ideology. For it to be secularized and laicized, it is essential that its totalitarian structure should be abolished.'[21] Although Michnik imputed a religious nature to totalitarian ideology which thereby impeded the founding of a secular state, it may well be that Communist ideologues were inadvertently using Catholic teachings as a model for conducting political socialization work. In the process, they sacralized Marxism despite Marx's strictures against doing so.

In the early years of his pontificate, John Paul II developed a programme of spiritual resistance for the Communist world. The fifteen-month Solidarity period cemented the political influence of the Church over the opposition movement. An example was the Solidarity programme adopted at the union's first congress in September 1981, which made explicit reference to Christian values. Paradoxically, the martial law regime's dispensing with Solidarity left the Church in a stronger position:

Because of the linkage between national feelings and Catholicism, the powerful ecclesiastical structures, the specific place of priests in society, the rapprochement in the 1970s between the lay opposition and the Church, the latter remained the privileged vehicle for the faith and religious expression, and the sole legal structure around which the initiatives of civil society could be taken after December 13.[22]

Shortly before the democratic breakthrough in Poland, Georges Mink claimed, 'The Church has moved closer to the nation, the nation has not been absorbed by the Church.'[23] The two assertions are mutually exclusive. The more debatable of the two is, surprisingly, that the nation had not been absorbed by the Church. By the late 1980s, with the consumer boom of the mid 1970s a distant memory, the Communist leadership held in scorn, and the political opposition seen as amateurish and incompetent, Poles trusted no other institution as much as the Catholic Church, as numerous surveys confirmed. Under Cardinal Jozef Glemp, the new Primate, the Church exuded triumphalism even before there had been a triumph. It had successfully encroached on secular space and had ensured itself a captive following. All that was left was for it to be entrusted to broker the transition from Communism. The April 1989 roundtable agreement conferred that role on it. Absurdly claiming political impartiality, Church leaders welcomed the charge and proceeded to ensure that, first, Solidarity was 'sacralized' and that, second, its candidates won the June 1989 elections which, according to the terms of the roundtable agreement, were to be non-competitive. The first freely elected representatives of the nation were quickly corralled by the Church.

THE CHURCH TRIUMPHANT? SACRALIZATION OF POLITICS IN THE 1990S

The potential for conflict between a state seeking to democratize politics and a Church striving to maintain and extend its political influence was heightened with the semi-free elections held in summer 1989. Mirella Eberts summarized the Church's vision of its place in the democratic republic:

the powerful and privileged position of the Church has posed an important dilemma for the democratization process in Poland. Not unlike the PZPR [former Communist party] hierarchy in the past, the Church has been attempting to secure a leading role in Polish society, both in public and private spheres. With the fall of the Communist order, the Church immediately sought to obtain the widest possible influence over the emerging democratic institutions and the policy-making process. It has aimed to ensure that its positions on religious education, abortion and birth control, among others, become firmly entrenched in the new democracy.[24]

The Church's effort to consolidate its role in democratic Poland originates with its actions during the 1989 elections. Officially, it appealed for national accord in the contest between the Communist Party and Solidarity. In practice, it made parish halls available to Solidarity candidates throughout the country. Church presses produced most of their campaign leaflets. Parish priests helped organize meetings with voters and exhorted voting for the opposition in their Sunday sermons. That year's Corpus Christi processions included a political message to vote for Solidarity. In short, the Church used every means at its disposal – the pulpit, its printing facilities, its meeting rooms, its many voluntary workers, above all its good name – to persuade citizens to vote against all Communist candidates. The nexus between Church and Solidarity was re-established, then, and it would remain in place throughout the 1990s. Frances Millard described how 'religious ritual appeared to become an accepted dimension of public life. Priests and bishops acquired a quasi-obligatory presence at state and local political functions.'[25] Public servants felt obliged to make the pilgrimage to the Czestochowa monastery where the Black Madonna icon was kept.

Not only was the Church seeking to commandeer the new democracy to suit its institutional interests, it was also suffering from an internal democratic deficit as well. Millard summarized: 'As a centralized, hierarchical institution, the Episcopate found it difficult to adapt to the challenges of the new post-Communist freedoms.'[26] Its support for controversial ideas like a constitutional status for itself, an advantageous Concordat with the state (see below), restitution of ecclesiastical property, compulsory religious instruction in school, and Christian values in broadcasting, together with its bitter opposition to abortion, divorce and sex education, quickly provoked a backlash against it. The general wealth of the Church in Poland – indeed its sheer opulence as seen in a spate of grand Church buildings constructed in poor parishes in the 1990s – is at odds with the hardships suffered by many of the faithful during shock therapy and after. Nonetheless, new-found political parties of the early 1990s believed that they could succeed in electoral politics by having the backing of the Church.

CLERICAL POLITICAL PARTIES

The first years after the democratic breakthrough marked a return to narrow national and religious loyalties reflected in the emergence of a new party system. One author noted how 'The new parties in Polish politics are Catholic, nationalistic, and right wing. They claim for themselves a continuity of resistance against Communism, and they reject dissident intellectuals as left wing and cosmopolitan, elitist and alienated.'[27] These parties attacked secular liberal groups at the centre of the political continuum. But they succeeded only in weakening the entire non-Communist camp, leading to parliamentary and presidential victories for the secular reformed Communists.[28] The right's mistaken belief that a pro-Church policy was inevitably an electoral winner, combined with its split into a traditionalist orientation stressing family, God and the nation (which often took a populist form) and a neo-liberal approach stressing economic individualism and free market (associated with urban professional groups), kept secular parties entrenched in the legislative or executive branches of government for most of the 1990s.

Attempts to exploit the religious-secular cleavage were in part justified. One study concluded that in Poland and other post-Communist states in Europe religiosity was of the 'greatest relevance to voting choices' while cleavages based on socioeconomic class were only a 'weak source of partisanship'.[29] Likening party cleavages in Eastern Europe to those found in Western Europe, another cross-national study described how 'There was a clerical versus anti-clerical cleavage in Catholic countries like France and Italy, or Lithuania and Poland, often expressed in disputes about schooling, abortion, or divorce.'[30] Hubert Tworzecki's analysis of electoral results convinced him that 'religiosity (operationalized as the frequency of Church attendance) is of major importance as a predictor of support for the rightist tendency'. For example, a region's religiosity was a strong predictor of AWS support in 1997.[31] Writing about the same election, Krzysztof Jasiewicz suggested that 'if at the end of the twentieth century in Poland we want to guess how someone voted in recent elections or will vote in the next ones, we have to ask him not about his occupation, education level, or paycheck, but how often he recites the rosary'.[32] The same author's preliminary analysis of the October 2000 presidential election also pointed to the continued salience of religiosity as a variable affecting voting.[33]

A caveat is in order: the right versus left division does not correspond perfectly to a Church versus secular statist one. Rather, Tomasz Zarycki contends that even though 'the main issues defining the Left–Right conflict are clearly associated with the Church-state conflict over the scope of each other's influence in public life', this is the *effect* of the alliance between the Church and Polish traditionalists.[34] Thus, abortion was depicted as a danger for the Polish nation rather than a contravention of Catholic teachings.[35]

In the 1990s, political parties of both right and left splintered frequently, entered into different *electoral pacts* with other groups, and changed names. Once in the Sejm (or legislature), their elected members joined forces to form *parliamentary clubs*. Let us look at only one political grouping – the one that began with closest ties to the Church. The Christian National Union (ZChN) ran in the 1991 parliamentary elections under the label Catholic Electoral Action (WAK). For the 1993 parliamentary elections, the Catholic alliance was called 'Fatherland'. For the 1995 presidential elections, the ZChN formed part of the Alliance for Poland. And for the 1997 legislative elections and the 2000 presidential ones, the party became part of the Solidarity coalition calling itself Solidarity Electoral Action (AWS). By the 2001 parliamentary elections, the Catholic camp was hopelessly divided as the parties of the centre and right splintered.

An illuminating case of the futility of the Catholic right to make headway in political institutions was the candidature of a Catholic-supported woman for the presidency in 1995. The highly respected president of the Polish National Bank, Hanna Gronkiewicz-Waltz, seemed at one time poised (according to polls measuring voting intentions) to eliminate Lech Wałeşa as the candidate of the right-of-centre bloc against Alexander Kwasniewski, leader of the reformed Communist Party (SLD). The most plausible explanation of her shooting star candidacy was that she was taken hostage by the Catholic Church and its party, the ZChN, as the election campaign progressed. According to a contributor to the Catholic journal *Wiez*, Gronkiewicz-Waltz initially had strong popular support due to her perceived professionalism at the National Bank. But the Church forced her to become 'an ostentatious Catholic' during the campaign, spotlighting her religiosity and family values.[36] This boomeranged on her candidacy. Moreover, Walesa already had impeccable credentials as a devout Catholic and, coupled with growing societal distaste for the Church's involvement in politics, her programme emphasizing Catholicism rather than professional expertise was her undoing. She received barely 3 per cent of the votes in the first round of the elections in November 1995, indicating repudiation of a highly qualified candidate if she or he became too closely associated with the Church. In the 2000 presidential elections the Catholic right faired even worse with 70 per cent of the votes going to candidates who had been officials in the Communist era. The party system proved elusive to the Catholic establishment. Two-term president Kwasniewski explained the hostility to the Church: 'We are not going to have a theocratic state in the middle of Europe at the end of the twentieth century.'[37]

SOCIETAL VALUES

One measure of the hold of religion on citizens is the values and attitudes that they espouse. The most remarkable phenomenon emerging from surveys carried out in Poland over the past ten years, for example, is the attitudinal shift that transformed the Church from the most trusted institution in the country to the one with most unwanted influence in politics.

An attitudinal survey carried out in autumn 1994 found that 71 per cent of respondents asserted that the Church had too much influence in public life. The Church ranked behind both the army and the police in terms of trustworthiness: from 90 per cent confidence levels in the Church before Communism's fall, only about 50 per cent of respondents expressed trust in the Church by 1994. Miroslawa Grabowska found that non-religious people most often accused the Church of having too much political influence. Conversely, 'three-quarters of fervent believers and over one-half of regularly-practicing Catholics have no reservations about the presence of religion and the Church in public life'.[38]

The authors of a major comparative study, called the World Values Survey, came away with the perception of a more religious Poland. They noted how 'Almost all of the socialist or ex-socialist societies are characterized by (1) survival values, and (2) a strong emphasis on state authority, rather than traditional authority. Poland is a striking exception, distinguished from the other socialist societies by her strong traditional-religious values.'[39] While it shared survival values with other countries which had per capita GDP of under $4,000, along with Ireland, Poland was described as a

> hyper-Catholic society manifesting relatively traditional cultural values across a wide range of areas. Not only in religion, but also in politics, gender roles, sexual norms and family values, their values are far more traditional than those generally found in industrial societies.[40]

The conclusions drawn about Poland by the authors of this study are challenged by survey data compiled by Polish social scientists. Their data reveal a much less religious Poland than depicted by outside scholars. Poles provided a much more inclusive, civic rather than exclusionary, ethno-religious under-standing of citizenship. Whereas sharply drawn ethnic boundaries and their enforcement would reflect a less open attitude to minorities, inclusiveness would suggest tolerance and liberalism. In an autumn 1994 survey, respondents were asked who, in their view, was Polish. The leading answers were someone who speaks Polish (cited by 96 per cent of respondents), whose citizenship is Polish (92 per cent), whose parents were Polish (82 per cent), or who lives in Poland (80 per cent). Surprisingly, not much more than one-half of the sample (57 per cent) said that a Pole was someone who was Catholic.[41] These answers on national identity indicate a considerably more liberal orientation than those warning of a narrow Polish nationalism founded on religious devotion.[42]

Was the Catholic Church losing believers as well as overall respect in Poland at the turn of the century? One survey research institute found that Poles' religiosity, measured in terms of self-expressions of faith, attendance at Mass and at other Catholic ceremonies, was virtually unchanged in 1999 compared to 1986. It added that practising Catholics were more likely than the non-religious to develop civic values important to a democracy.[43] But in a survey of Poles' assessment of public institutions carried out in March 2000, only 57 per cent gave a favourable evaluation of the Church and 26 per cent a negative one. That put the Church behind such 'institutions' as firefighters, the postal service, the media, and even the national sports lottery.[44] Experience of democracy seemed to be eroding Poles' earlier unquestioning respect for the authority of the Church.

THE CHURCH IN THE POLICY PROCESS

The Church's intervention in the policy process has at times boomeranged. Its stand on abortion triggered the first backlash against it.[45] After the Communist regime's liberal abortion-on-demand policy, the highly restrictive law passed under the Solidarity government was arguably the first evidence indicating that the public would not reject everything done by the Communists or accept everything carried out by Church-backed Solidarity. The abortion controversy gave rise to the perception of a meddling and misguided Church that it has never fully overcome since.

The Church was also held responsible for depriving women of rights they had obtained in the Communist system. Whereas Marxism made the economic liberation of women a high priority, Catholicism stressed the unique role women have to play as mothers and the nucleus of the family. If the Communist system imposed a double burden on women – as indispensable participants in the labour market and as homemakers – the Church took a more one-sided view, seeing women as givers of life, raising children to be practising Catholics and serving as the heart of the family.[46]

Some Church leaders did not conceal their glee that economic factors, such as high unemployment rates, succeeded in changing women's roles in line with Catholic teachings. Because they account for a greater proportion of believers, women face greater moral agonizing than men when deciding whether to conform fully with Catholic teachings. If they internalized Catholic values, they might be inclined to reject some of the emancipatory, secular, modern ideas commonplace in Western countries today, and politically correct ones under Communism also.

Many Poles were disappointed in the leadership of Cardinal Glemp, viewed as too conservative and certainly no Cardinal Stefan Wyszynski, the Catholic Primate who had struggled valiantly against the Stalinist authorities in the 1950s. They were upset at the ineptness Glemp showed in the early 1990s, first in dealing with the controversial plan to build a Carmelite convent close to Auschwitz, which he eventually agreed to abandon. Then he was slow to condemn some notorious anti-Semitic remarks made by Father Henryk Jankowski, Wałeşa's confessor. In 2001, the Primate was quick to express regret for the role Poles played in the massacre of over a thousand Jews in July 1941 in the village of Jedwabne, an event brought to the world's attention by historian Jan Gross's book *Neighbors*.[47] Many considered that he subsequently mishandled the Church's commemoration ceremony, holding it on a holy day in the Jewish calendar when Jews could not participate. Glemp's generally nationalistic views also proved embarrassing to Polish political leaders engaged in accession talks with the European Union. The Primate was aware that EU membership would make Poland a more secular society as it would then have to conform to the *acquis communitaire*, a body of laws that were the same for all member-states, whether Protestant, Catholic, or Greek Orthodox.

To be sure, extensive research carried out by Lena Kolarska-Bobinska on the Polish clergy's attitudes towards European integration found generally positive views, especially concerning the advantages Poland would obtain in social, economic and political spheres. By contrast, priests were more anxious about the negative impact of EU membership on moral and religious values in the country and on the future of the Polish family.[48]

During much of the 1990s, parliament focused on writing a new constitution to replace the much-amended 1953 document. Apart from controversy over the balance of power between executive and legislative branches of government, lawmakers were divided over the Church's insistence that it receive official recognition of its special role in Polish society and, conversely, that the idea of a secular state be constitutionally rejected. Some Church leaders even wanted a constitutional ban on abortion, demanded a specific clause on the protection of human life from conception until birth, and pressed for a provision making marriage possible only between members of the opposite sex.

The very preamble to the constitution proved contentious. There was disagreement whether it was the Polish nation or all citizens of Poland that were the subjects of the document, and whether the special role of Catholicism in the country should be explicitly mentioned (as was the case in the Irish constitution). The constitution finally adopted in May 1997 compromised on both these subjects. It incorporated references to both the Christian heritage of the Polish nation and to all Polish citizens, as well as to God as the source of 'truth, justice, goodness, and beauty' and to universal values that were the source of these ideas for non-believers.

The agreement reached between the Polish state and the Vatican, termed the Concordat, was even more controversial. The term itself was used rarely by the Vatican. The 1925 Concordat brought even Pilsudski into conflict with the Church since it allowed the Church to make property claims going back to the nineteenth century. The Second (interwar) Republic did not act impartially: it was generous in deciding claims brought by the Catholic Church and stingy involving those of the Orthodox Church. The Concordat signed in July 1993 between President Wałeşa and Pope John Paul II also seemed to privilege the Catholic Church. Its opponents alleged that many of its provisions violated the European Union treaty.

The agreement consisted of 29 articles over 14 pages, and it began with the assertion that 'The Catholic religion is practiced by the majority of the Polish population.'[49] A similar clause in the constitution of the Second Republic was more provocative since, at the time, Poland had several sizeable ethnic and religious minorities. The first article asserted that 'the State and Catholic Church are, each in its own domain, independent and autonomous'. An explicit reference to separation of Church and state was left out. The Concordat expressed an intention 'to eliminate all forms of intolerance and discrimination based on religion'. But, Catholic education in schools was formalized. Church marriages were to have the same legal status as civil ones, though the Concordat did not make any changes to divorce laws.

The most controversial aspect of the agreement was Article 22, a cryptic clause dealing with restitution of Church property. A special Church–state commission was to make legal changes such that 'The new regulation will take into account the needs of the Church given its mission and the practice hitherto of Church life in Poland.' Added to this was Article 27: 'Matters requiring new or additional treatment will be regulated by new agreements or understandings.' In this way, Sejm approval of the Concordat would provide a carte blanche for future changes. As one writer put it: 'Today anyone who naively believes that Church-state conflict was invented by Communists and with their demise this chapter is closed forever is making a major and possibly in the future costly mistake.'[50] The agreement was signed while the Sejm was dissolved, raising further questions about the Church's respect for democracy.

When the coalition government composed of the reformed Communist parties of workers (SLD) and peasants (PSL) took office in autumn 1993, it was careful not to antagonize Pope John Paul II and Cardinal Glemp on the question of Concordat ratification. The fact that the mainstay of the PSL constituency – the peasantry – was largely Catholic and conservative on social issues forced the PSL, in particular, to tread carefully. The Pope's visit to Poland in June 1997 created new momentum for adopting the Concordat but it was after the victory of the AWS coalition a few months later that parliament ratified the Concordat. President Kwasniewski signed the legislation in January 1998.

CONCLUSION

Harvard economist Jeffrey Sachs was one of the first to draw a comparison between Poland's and Spain's economic development after 1950. Both countries had similar economic conditions then: comparable population size, a large agricultural sector, part of peripheral regions of Europe lagging behind in modernization and, of course, Catholic. But 'Spain shot ahead of Poland in the next thirty-five years. Spain started to catch up with the rest of Western Europe, while Poland fell farther behind.'[51] Sachs identified economic integration with Europe as the key factor behind Spain's success but it is possible to add the existence of greater secular space in Spain and of broader space for the sacred in Poland as additional factors producing differential rates of development.

Neo-liberal economist Jan Winiecki made a strong case for treating Catholicism as a fetter on economic growth:

> Catholicism has once again shown itself as a historical factor making pro-capitalist changes harder. Its communalism, pressure to subordinate the interests of the individual to those of the community, its dislike of the creation and use of wealth by the individual, were an important binding agent of dislike of the 'new'.[52]

The clash between Church and the democratic republic can be extended to include the collision between Church and the capitalist order.

Do contemporary religious–state relations in Poland help strengthen its new democracy? Alfred Stepan sets forth four types of 'twin tolerations' in a democratic system:

1. a secular state that is friendly to religion;

2. a non-secular state that is friendly to democracy;

3. sociologically spontaneous secularism where religion has become a not very important factor in political life; and

4. a secularism that is very unfriendly to religion, producing an unstable pattern of religious-state relations.[53]

From our preceding account, we are confident in locating Poland somewhere between the first two types. Even with the strong recent electoral support for political leaders committed to secularization of public life, it seems premature to categorize Poland as a fully secular state. But even if there is much about it that remains non-secular (including a vocal minority of right-wing Catholic nationalists), the quasi-constitutional status of the Church does not give it any policy prerogatives directly affecting citizens. Nor can the Church do much about the political and even religious pluralism that is a hallmark of every country in or seeking entry to the EU.

Distinguishing betwen sacred and secular space is not all that different from the late Communist era, then. It is questionable whether the autonomous space belonging to the Church today is significantly greater than that it vaunted two decades ago. Today few question the democratic system's capacity to remain untouched by any upturns or downturns in Church–state relations.

NOTES

1. Ruth Benedict, 'Religion', in Franz Boas (ed.), *General Anthropology* (New York: D.C. Heath, 1938), pp. 628–9.
2. Quoted by Andrzej Walicki, *Philosophy and Romantic Nationalism: The Case of Poland* (Oxford: Clarendon Press, 1982), p. 289.
3. Earl Vinecour, *Polish Jews: The Final Chapter* (New York: New York University Press, 1977), p. 1.
4. Stein Rokkan, Angus Campbell, Per Torsvik and Henry Valen, *Citizens, Elections, Parties: Approaches to the Comparative Study of Development* (New York: McKay, 1970), p. 128.
5. David Martin, *A General Theory of Secularization* (Oxford: Oxford University Press, 1975), p. 55.
6. Bogdan Szajkowski, *Next to God Poland: Politics and Religion in Contemporary Poland* (London: Frances Pinter, 1983), p. 226. See also R.C. Monticone, *The Catholic Church in Communist Poland 1945–1985* (New York: Columbia University Press, 1986).
7. Norbert Zmijewski, *The Catholic–Marxist Ideological Dialogue in Poland, 1945–1980* (Aldershot: Dartmouth Publishing Company, 1991), p. 24.
8. Quoted by Zmijewski, *The Catholic–Marxist Ideological Dialogue in Poland, 1945–1980*, p. 42.
9. Nathaniel Davis, *A Long Walk to Church: A Contemporary History of Russian Orthodoxy* (Boulder, CO: Westview Press, 1995), p. xxi.
10. Davis, *A Long Walk to Church*, p. 6.
11. Patrick Michel, *Politics and Religion in Eastern Europe* (Cambridge: Polity Press, 1991), p. 196.
12. Cardinal Ratzinger (in collaboration with Vittorio Messori), *Entretiens sur la foi* (Paris: Fayard, 1985), p. 234.
13. Jerzy Turowicz, 'Kosciol i polityka', *Tygodnik powszechny*, 12 (1865), 24 March 1985.
14. Michel, *Politics and Religion in Eastern Europe*, p. 103.

15. Adam Lopatka, *Polityka*, 4 June 1983.
16. Zycie Partii, 8 June 1982. Quoted by Michel, *Politics and Religion in Eastern Europe*, p. 47.
17. Dionyzy Tanalski, *Katolicyzm – ewolucja ideologii* (Warsaw: PWN, 1978), p. 168.
18. Michel, *Politics and Religion in Eastern Europe*, p. 27.
19. This lesson had been learned much earlier. Prior to the Bolshevik revolution, Lenin had calculated that Communists had more to gain by desisting from attacks on Russian Orthodoxy than by making an enemy of it.
20. Michel, *Politics and Religion in Eastern Europe*, p. 190.
21. Adam Michnik, *The Church, the Left: A Dialogue* (Chicago, IL: University of Chicago Press, 1990), p. 124. The monograph first appeared in Polish in 1977.
22. Patrick Michel and Georges Mink, *Mort d'un prêtre – l'affaire Popieluszko: Analyse d'une logique normalisatrice* (Paris: Fayard, 1985), p. 35.
23. Georges Mink, lecture, 'Ecole des hautes etudes en sciences sociales', 16 March 1987. Quoted by Michel, *Politics and Religion in Eastern Europe*, p. 171.
24. Mirella W. Eberts, 'The Roman Catholic Church and Democracy in Poland', *Europe-Asia Studies*, 50, 5 (July 1998), pp. 817–18. PZPR stands for Polska Zjednoczona Partia Polityczna, or Polish United Workers' Party.
25. Frances Millard, *Polish Politics and Society* (London: Routledge, 1999), p. 125.
26. Millard, *Polish Politics and Society*, p. 124. For other problems that the Church encountered in a democratic system, see Tadeusz Szawiel, 'Kosciol polski–spojrzenie z zewnatrz', *Civitas*, 3 (1999), pp. 134–6.
27. Irena Grudzinska Gross, 'Post-Communist Resentment, or the Rewriting of Polish History', *East European Politics and Societies*, 6, 2 (Spring 1992), p. 147.
28. See Andrzej Walicki, 'Totalitarianism and Detotalitarization: The Case of Poland', *Review of Politics*, 58, 3 (Summer 1996), pp. 526–7.
29. Stephen Whitefield and Geoffrey Evans, 'Electoral Politics in Eastern Europe: Social and Ideological Influences on Partisanship in Post-Communist Societies', in John Higley, Jacek Pakulski and Wlodzimierz Wesolowski (eds), *Post-Communist Elites and Democracy in Eastern Europe* (London: Macmillan, 1998), pp. 238–9.
30. Stephen White, Bill Miller, Ase Grodeland and Sarah Oates, 'Religion and Political Action in Post-Communist Europe', *Political Studies*, 48, 4 (September 2000), p. 687.
31. Hubert Tworzecki, 'Learning to Choose: Electoral Politics in East-Central Europe', unpublished manuscript (July 2000), pp. 173, 305.
32. Krzysztof Jasiewicz, 'Portfel czy rozaniec? Ekonomiczne i aksjologiczne determinantly zachowan wyborczych', in Radoslaw Markowski (ed.), *Wybory parlamentarne 1997: system partyjny, postawy polityczne, zachowania wyborcze* (Warsaw: Friedrich Ebert Stiftung, 1999), p. 167.
33. During the electoral campaign, the strongest attack on Kwasniewski's record was a film clip showing him encouraging an aide to kneel down and kiss the ground in a mocking imitation of the Pope. Poles were offended by Kwasniewski's religious irreverence. Even though his support fell by up to 10 per cent, Kwasniewski nevertheless handily won the presidency in the first round with 54 per cent of the vote.
34. Tomasz Zarycki, 'Politics in the Periphery: Political Cleavages in Poland Interpreted in their Historical and International Context', *Europe-Asia Studies*, 52, 5 (July 2000), p. 862.
35. On this see Anna Sosnkowska, 'Tu, tam–pomieszanie', *Studia Socjologiczne*, 4 (1997), pp. 61–86.
36. Zbigniew Nosowski, 'Katharsis? Kosciol a wybory prezydenckie', *Wiez*, 447 (January 1996), p. 67.
37. Survey results and Kwasniewski's statement are taken from Tom Hundley, 'Catholic Church Losing Clout in Poland', *Chicago Tribune*, 13 November 1994.
38. Miroslawa Grabowska, 'Boskie i cesarskie: religijnosc oraz stosunki miedzy panstwew a Kosciolem a postawy i zachowania polityczne', in Markowski, *Wybory parlamentarne 1997*, p. 181.
39. Ronald Inglehart, Miguel Basanez and Alejandro Moreno, *Human Values and Beliefs: A Cross Cultural Sourcebook* (Ann Arbor, MI: University of Michigan Press, 1997), p. 27.
40. Inglehart *et al.*, *Human Values and Beliefs*, pp. 30–1.
41. Centrum Badania Opinii Spolecznej, 'Komunikat' (Autumn 1994).
42. On the other hand, an affliction often associated with Poles, a stubborn anti-Semitism that does not go away, puts into question society's real commitment to tolerance.

154 THE SECULAR AND THE SACRED

43. Centrum Badania Opinii Spolecznej, 'Religyjnosc Polakow w III RP' (March 1999). See www.cbos.pl/cbos_pl.htm
44. Pracownia Badan Spolecznych, 'Instytucje i urzedy w Polsce, czerwiec 2000'. The survey was carried out in March 2000. See www.pbssopot.com.pl/wyniki_instytucje062000.html.
45. On this, see Eberts, 'The Church and Democracy in Poland', pp. 823–6.
46. For an intellectual attempt to reconcile Catholicism and feminism in Poland, see *Wiez*, 8 (1992), 1, 6 (1993), 12 (1994), 3, 6 (1996), 2, 6 (1997), 2, 5 (1998). See also Jaroslaw Gowin, *Kosciol po komunizmie* (Krakow: Znak, 1995), pp. 229–77. For the thesis that the two cannot be reconciled, see Tomasz Wozniak, 'Katolicy modernisci wobec problemu emancypacji kobiet', *Studia Socjologiczne*, 3 (2000), pp. 93–109.
47. Jan Tomasz Gross, *Neighbors: The Destruction of the Jewish Community in Jedwabne, Poland* (Princeton, NJ: Princeton University Press, 2001).
48. Lena Kolarska-Bobinska, Jacek Kucharczyk, Beata Roguska and Elzbieta Firlit, 'Duchowienstwo polskie wobec perspektywy integracji europejskiej', in Kolarska-Bobinska (ed.), *Polska Eurodebata* (Warsaw: Instytut Spraw Publicznych, 1999), p. 108.
49. 'The Polish Concordat of 1993', in J. Gruca, *Spor o konkordat* (Warsaw: Adam, 1994), article 1.
50. Stanislaw Podemski, 'Zadowoleni i niespokojni', *Polityka*, 32 (7 August 1993).
51. Jeffrey Sachs, *Poland's Jump to the Market Economy* (Cambridge, MA: MIT Press, 1994), p. 25.
52. Jan Winiecki, 'The Reasons for Electoral Defeat Lie in Non-Economic Factors', in Winiecki (ed.), *Five Years After June: The Polish Transformation, 1989–1994* (London: The Centre for Research into Communist Economies, 1996), p. 87.
53. Alfred Stepan, 'Religion, Democracy, and the "Twin Tolerations"', *Journal of Democracy*, 11, 4 (October 2000), p. 42.

9

Greece: A Problematic Secular State

ADAMANTIA POLLIS[1]

HISTORICAL BACKGROUND

The spread and consolidation of the modern nation-state in principle symbo-lized the replacement of earlier ideational systems by secularism and nationalist ideology. The Enlightenment ontology of secularism in conjunction with national-ism formed a new modern social order. The universalist doctrines of the Enlight-enment were to be implemented within the boundaries of the nation-state. Be it modernization and the 'high culture' argued by Gellner or Anderson's print capital-ism and the imagined community, modern ideology is embodied in nationalism and the nation-state. Concurrently, with secularism, the preeminence of religion and the predominance of religious identity prevalent in the Middle Ages receded as secular ideals became the foundational principles of the modern nation-state. Religion was to be relegated to the private sphere as the Weberian legal-rational regime, underpinned by national identity, became the organizing principle.

The nation-state gradually spread from Western Europe throughout the world and sovereign states became the principal international actors. In the modern era it is the nation that legitimates the sovereign state, a nation which in theory encompasses all those who share a national identity. Loyalty to the nation-state in itself is a secular act that transcends religion as the primary reference group. As nationalism spread, however, in many cases Enlightenment principles faded and nationalism was recast in terms of a 'primordial' ethnic identity thereby constructing an equivalence between national and ethnic identity. Religion, in turn, was frequently incorporated as a central ingredient of ethnonational identity. As a consequence, such nation-states are grounded in a tense coexistence between secularism and religiosity, with multiple permutations in different specific instances. The centrality of religion in ethnonational states is characteristic of Israel and the 'new' states of the former Yugoslavia, among others.

Greece considers itself not only a modern state but, in recent decades, an integral part of Europe, rooted in the European heritage. It proudly proclaims that ancient Athenian democracy was the forerunner of modernity and liberal democracy. Despite these assertions, the Enlightenment and its tenets of modernity, reason and secularism, largely bypassed modern Greece.[2] The national identity that was constructed became coterminous with ethnic identity, in which religion, specifically Eastern Orthodoxy, became an essential ingredient. It should be noted, however, that historically the process of constructing an ethnonational identity was gradual and was not fully consolidated until the Metaxas dictatorship of the 1930s which explicitly set the parameters of 'Greekness', by grounding its 'Third Greek Civilization' in an exclusive ethnic identity.[3] Hence, the modernity project in Greece became equated with the construction of an ethnic nation which was to be embodied in a sovereign state. Later still modernity was equated with modernization, with the drive towards economic development.

At the time of Greek independence in 1829, the Greek nation was conceptualized as a resuscitated Byzantium – a Christianized Ottoman Empire – that would incorporate a multiplicity of religions, cultures and ethnicities. The premises of the Greek nation and of nationalist ideology, which were contested among nationalist ideologues during the eighteenth century, were resolved only gradually. Even as late as the Balkan Wars (1912–13) and immediately after World War I, official Greece defined itself as a territorial nation intent on reclaiming its historic lands. The ethnicity or religion of the people in the territories it coveted was of little significance. A confluence of historical factors in the early 1920s, most importantly, Kemal Atatürk's Turkish nationalist revolution as the Ottoman Empire was collapsing forcefully ended the dream of a reconstituted Byzantium. Greek political thought and policy turned inwards. The Greek nation was gradually reconceptualized and reconstructed in terms of an exclusive ethnicity in which 'Greekness' manifested several indelible attributes. In this gradually reconstituted nation, religion played an increasingly central role.

Even though the twentieth-century construction of an exclusive ethnonational Greek identity legitimating the modern Greek state was relatively recent, religion, more specifically Eastern (Greek) Orthodoxy, was a contentious issue from the outset. Revolutions, on the whole, do not completely transform preexisting societies and cultures, although values and beliefs are frequently recast in a different form and structure. The heritage of Byzantium and the religiously based *millet* system of the Ottoman Empire, persisted in the modern Greek state, with religion gradually becoming a marker of Greek ethnic and national identity. The 'nationalization' of Orthodoxy in turn signified the abandonment of ecumenical Eastern Orthodoxy and the projection of a nationalist Greek Orthodoxy. At the time of the Greek revolution for independence from Ottoman rule, village priests from the Greek mainland were in the forefront of the uprising. Excommunicated by the Patriarch of Constantinople, who opposed the revolution, the newly formed Greek state in 1833 proclaimed the establishment of an autocephalous Church whose secular affairs were to be administered by the state. Relations with the Patriarchate were reestablished in 1850, but the Greek Church remained autocephalous.[4]

Despite the persistent issue of religion, in light of the initial territorially based construction of the Greek nation, which encompassed diverse ethnicities, cultures and religions, Eastern Orthodoxy could have been dissociated from the state and become part of civil society were it not for the power of church institutions in everyday life, the clergy's participation in the revolution and the defeat of the Greek troops in Asia Minor after World War I. The latter led to agonizing reappraisals of the foundations of the Greek nation and intense debates over its future construction.

At the time of the Greek revolution in the early nineteenth century the slogans of the revolutionary movement, as expressed by the Philiki Heteria, vacillated between nationalist doctrines and Orthodoxy; it was ambiguous as to whether or not its goal was to establish an Orthodox religious state. Meanwhile, nationalist intellectuals in the process of constructing an imagined modern Greek nation were contesting whether religion or language was the defining feature of 'Greekness'.[5] Immediately after the formation of an independent Greek state, as the advocates of Enlightenment principles for Greece receded, a hotly debated issue was the demand of Greek state elites that the heir to the Catholic monarch of Greece who was installed by foreign powers, convert to Eastern Orthodoxy. All Greek constitutions from the first in 1844, to those of 1863, 1911, 1927, 1952, 1968, through the most recent one in 1975, in one way or another specify that Greek Orthodoxy is the state religion, although the terminology has shifted from 'established' religion to 'prevailing' religion.

The 1920s and 1930s were a period of fluidity in which multiple intellectual strands contested the conceptual boundaries of the Greek nation. The secularist Greek intellectuals lost out. Historical descent, language, culture and *religion* were triumphant in circumscribing the parameters of the reconstructed Greek ethnonational identity. Those who did not meet all these criteria were not considered authentic Greeks even if they were Greek citizens and even if their ancestors had lived in Greece for centuries; religious minorities, as well as ethnic minorities, were marginalized. The political regimes of the Metaxas dictatorship (1936–40), the post-World War II semi-democracy culminating in the Papadopoulos-Ioannides military rule (1967–74) whose slogan was 'Greece of Christian (Orthodox) Greeks', all espoused an exclusive ethnic identity in which religion was a *sine qua non*.

CHURCH–STATE RELATIONS

Orthodoxy became so deeply embedded in the construction of the modern Greek nation and national identity that the expectations of progressive Greek intellectuals that the post-junta constitution of 1975 would secularize the Greek state did not come to fruition. Nor did the revisions of the constitution in 1985 alter the Church's status. Orthodoxy had become the 'prevailing' religion, instead of the established religion, but in essence, the Church remains a state institution albeit with considerable autonomy. Other European countries have established churches, foremost the Church of England, but as will become apparent, they do not enjoy the privileges which the Greek Church does. In the past decade or so, however, Greek elites, anxious that their country adhere to European principles and be identified as European rather than proclaiming Greek exceptionalism, have rekindled a debate on the role of the Church in the Greek polity.

Throughout most of its modern history, aside from religion as a theology and an element of Greek national identity, a symbiotic relationship has existed between the state and the institutional Church.[6] The Orthodox Church is a legal person incorporated under public law, whereby, although a separate legal entity, it is part of the state administration.[7] The Church is subject to the state's supervision but is entitled to all the rights and privileges of state administrative entities. Furthermore, the salaries and pensions of the Orthodox clergy are paid by the state. The Church's income moreover, is supplemented through additional revenue sources such as its real estate holdings and donations, none of which are subject to taxation. Moreover, the Orthodox clergy is automatically exempt from military service, while those of other religious faiths encounter difficulties.[8]

Ecclesiastical matters, spiritual, dogmatic and clerical are within the domain of the Church. Upward mobility in the Church hierarchy (providing the priest is celibate) depends on the Holy Synod in accordance with canon law, which decides placement and promotion including the selection of the Archbishop. And, in the Church–state symbiotic relationship, each is expected to support the other in their respective domain. The President formally appoints the bishops and archbishop, while the state, including the police, is expected to enforce church decisions. Historically, however, the state has frequently been instrumental in the selection of the Archbishop, a selection based on a judgement of his reliability and loyalty to the regime in power. Archbishop Serapheim, who died in April 1998, in actuality had been appointed in 1974 by General Ioannides, the last dictator of the military junta. The Church is ostensibly subordinate to the state in the political realm and is expected to be a defender of Greek national interests as set forth by the rulers, be they dictators or democrats. Concurrently, however, it exercises considerable political power particularly when it perceives its institutional interests challenged or when state policy is considered detrimental to Orthodoxy. Priests in fact have been known to take militant action. In 1993, they took to the streets when it was proposed that the new Greek identity cards eliminate identification of religious affiliation. Despite pressure from the European Union, the Papandreou government abandoned the proposal.[9] In early 2001, this issue was raised once again. This time, despite massive protests by the clergy and the circulation of a petition by Archbishop Christodoulos opposing this action, the government remained adamant and religious affiliation no longer appears on identity cards. Recently, in 2000, priests demonstrated in opposition to the European Union's Schengen agreement, not on the grounds that it violated privacy, but that it used Satan's symbol 666. Other Church protests will be considered below.

In the last decade or so Church–state relations have periodically been on the political agenda. A debate on this issue had been initiated in the 1980s during Papandreou's rule. When in opposition, Andreas Papandreou had expressed his support for separation of Church and state. Once in power he introduced a bill in 1985 providing for expropriation of monastic properties and leading to the disestablishment of the Church. These efforts were abandoned, however, when the Prime Minister gave in to the Archbishop's vehement opposition.[10] In the course of 1998, several developments portend a confrontation between Church and state. While these in time could lead to the disestablishment of the Church and hence to the secularization of the state, the vehement opposition of the Church, a powerful political force, and of right-wing nationalist groups, make prediction impossible.

In the course of the last few years, the public debate on the role of the Church and Orthodoxy has intensified. The current prime minister, Simitis, has taken cautious steps to distance his government from the Church. One such minor move was its non-involvement in the selection of a new archbishop in 1998. Of far greater symbolic and institutional significance was the recent proposal for a constitutional amendment made by deputies, principally from the ruling socialist party, PASOK, to change the oath of office from a religious one (in the name of the Holy Trinity) to 'in the name of the Greek people and the nation'.[11] This proposed change is somewhat reminiscent of Papandreou's early advocacy of separation of Church and state by differentiating between state and nation arguing that religion was obviously a critical feature of the nation but not of the state. The recently proposed amendment was followed by the signing of a text by many public figures calling for separation of Church and state.[12] The newly elected Archbishop of Greece, revealing his ethnoreligious views, protested vigorously, contending that such a change would be a threat to Greek identity, as is the elimination of religion from identity cards.[13] Agreeing with him were many deputies from the conservative New Democracy party, and a few from the ruling PASOK party.[14] In this confrontation, the government once again backed off. Nevertheless, the symbiotic, mutually reinforcing Church–state relationship is clearly strained and heading for continual clashes. Church–state relations, the nature of the Greek state and the conceptualization of the nation all appear to be under scrutiny.

RELIGIOUS MINORITIES

A multiplicity of domestic policies over nearly a century geared towards homogenizing the population, in conjunction with international developments, such as the exchange of populations and the Holocaust, has resulted in the increasing 'ethnic purity' of Greece. Nevertheless, religious minorities (in

addition to ethnic minorities) remain. Accurate statistics are not available, but
it is estimated that approximately 10 per cent of the population may not be Greek
Orthodox.[15] There are Muslims, Jews, Catholics, a variety of Protestant sects
including Evangelicals, Jehovah's Witnesses, Old Calendrists and others. The
Jews (both Greek Jews pre-dating Christianity and Sephardic Jews who emigrated at the time of the Inquisition) were a large community, particularly in
Salonica. They were devastated by the Holocaust in which 50,000 perished. Only
about 5,000 remain. Although the Jews were officially recognized following
World War I, it should be noted that it was not until 1998 that public recognition
was given to the historical prevalence of Jews in Salonica, and the community's
obliteration during the Holocaust.

Religious minorities in Greece encounter numerous legal and administrative
obstacles in exercising their religious freedom.[16] No non-Orthodox religious
establishment in Greece (except for the Muslims and Jews) has had legal status,
which obviously restricts their ability to practise their religion. Many minority
religions circumvent this non-recognition either by establishing 'cultural' centres
or ignoring their legal limbo. Religious minorities in fact, at the instigation of
the Orthodox Church, have been subject to state surveillance.[17] Increasingly,
however, minority religions are resorting to the European Court of Human
Rights. In January 1999 the Greek government settled out of court a case
brought to the European court by a Jehovah's Witness charging the state with
surveillance.[18] Recently, the Catholic Church in Chanea, Crete, won a judgment
from the European Court of Human Rights which in essence stated that the
Catholic Church had a historical presence in Greece and that *de facto* it did have
legal standing and could own property and sue the state.[19]

Although the legal status of the Catholic Church has been ambiguous, the
legacy of the two recognized religious minorities – the Jews and the Muslims –
conceptually harks back to the *millet* system of the Ottoman Empire. In the case
of the Muslim community (which the Greek government labels as Muslim or
Turkish depending on political expediency) its legal religious rights are guaranteed by the Treaty of Lausanne subsequent to the exchange of populations in
1923 betweeen Greece and Turkey.[20] The Jewish community, as stated earlier, had
received legal recognition in 1920.

Although the Greek constitution recognizes freedom of religious conscience,
minority religions encounter formidable obstacles in practising their religion.
The constitution states that only 'known' religions are authorized to build a
'house of worship', but without stipulating which agency is responsible for
making a definitive determination. As a consequence, the administration and
various courts often issue contradictory rulings, recognizing the Jehovah's
Witnesses in one town for example but not in another. Such a practice has
severely affected the Evangelicals, the Jehovah's Witnesses, and the Mormons.[21]
Furthermore, even when the issue of 'known' religion is resolved, religious
minorities, except the Muslims, are subject to the power of the Orthodox
Church. The latter has had a decisive role in the procedure involved in granting

permits for the establishment of non-Orthodox places of worship. Permission for a building permit must be obtained from the Ministry of Education and Religious Affairs which in turn requests an advisory opinion from the local Orthodox bishop. He ostensibly makes a determination based on his judgement as to whether there are a sufficient number of believers of the faith in question (50 families) in the area.[22]

In recent years, taking advantage of Greece's ratification of the European Convention on Human Rights and Fundamental Freedoms, religious minorities are increasingly resorting to the European Court of Human Rights.[23] Both the number of cases and the specific issues that Greek citizens of non-Orthodox faiths have brought before the European Court of Human Rights, in which they charge Greece with violating their religious freedoms, have increased. On the whole, the plaintiffs win; the judgements are repeatedly against the Greek state. A particularly contentious provision in the constitution prohibits proselytism, behaviour which was criminalized during the Metaxas dictatorship and which remains in the criminal code. While the constitution prohibits *all* proselytism, which in principle includes Greek Orthodoxy, religion is taught in the primary and secondary schools and religious education is the responsibility of the Ministry of Education and Religious Affairs.[24] The prohibition against prose-lytism, until a recent European Court decision, had been implemented forcefully particularly against Evangelicals and Jehovah's Witnesses. Clearly, such action by governmental authorities violates not only religious freedom, but freedom of communication.

Several cases involving proselytism have been brought before the European Court of Human Rights. The first case directly confronting the issue of prose-lytism was the Kokkinakis case in 1993 in which the court questioned whether the actions, for which Kokkinakis was arrested, of this Jehovah's Witness, con-stituted proselytism. The Court voted against Greece but did not rule outright that the prohibition against proselytism violated the European Convention on Human Rights.[25] The Greek government's initial response to this decision was not to arrest persons for proselytism except in the rare cases involving minors. But the constitutional prohibition and the criminal statutes remain unchanged. Recently, in 1998, the European Court dealt with an interesting case of proselytism involving three officers of the Greek air force belonging to the Pentecostal Church found guilty by the Greek court of proselytizing both their subordinates and civilians. The court upheld the government with regard to proselytizing subordinate military personnel because of the hierarchical relationship, but condemned Greece for the conviction with regard to civilians.[26]

Other cases before the European Court have involved the refusal to grant exemption from military service to clergy other than the Greek Orthodox,[27] and penalties imposed on students who, because of their religious beliefs, refuse to participate in celebrations commemorating national holidays.[28] Furthermore, the Court (in Manoussakis, 1996), strongly condemned Greece's refusal to issue building permits to minority religions.[29] Significantly, in June 1997, when the

European Court of Human Rights was about to hold hearings on a case involving criminal charges brought against Jehovah's Witnesses for renting a place to hold religious ceremonies without the requisite permit, Greece dropped the case and issued the building permit.[30] From 1998, as a result of both the European Court decisions and the policy of the recent Greek Minister of Education and Religious Affairs, no impediments have been placed on the issuance of building permits for religious minorities. In 1997 local authorities in Salonica brought charges against 16 Christian congregations for operating without the necessary permit. In line with the government's recent non-enforcement of this administrative regulation, the Salonica District Court at the end of 2000 handed down a decision acquitting the defendants.

An intense debate has been raging in Greece over the issue of conscientious objectors, the overwhelming majority of whom are Jehovah's Witnesses. Until recently, charges were brought against them for their refusal to serve in the armed services and they were sentenced to serve four years in prison. There have been approximately three hundred in prison at any given time. All other West European states provide for alternative service. Finally, in 1997, legislation permitting alternative civilian service under certain conditions was enacted, although the length of time was twice that of military service.[31] Another move towards extending the rights of minorities was a recent action by the Greek Parliament which eliminated a discriminatory provision in the citizenship code. Until January 1999 article 19 of the citizenship code had provided that a Greek citizen who was a member of a minority group could have his/her passport lifted and lose citizenship upon leaving the country on the presumption that he/she had abandoned it. While implemented most frequently against ethnic minorities, it had also been used against religious minorities, in particular Muslim Turks.

GREEK ORTHODOXY – A MARKER OF GREEKNESS

Greece is one of numerous states in the Balkans and in Russia whose legitimacy is grounded in ethnicity. Ethnicity in turn, which defines the nation and sets individual ethnonational identity, is composed of a complex set of criteria, most frequently a presumed historical continuity, language, culture and religion. While ethnicity as a modern phenomenon is constructed under particular historical circumstances, once consolidated it can be a powerful political force. Since religion is a central tenet in Greek ethnonational identity, a person who is not Greek Orthodox is not considered an authentic Greek and can face legal and social barriers. And of course, he/she cannot defend Greek national interests. A recent incident highlights the pervasiveness of this belief. Christos Rozakis, a Deputy Foreign Minister, was attacked in the Vouli (legislature) in December 1996 as being untrustworthy in furthering Greek national interests because of his non-Christian origins (Jewish heritage).[32] He resigned and his resignation was accepted on the pretext of poor health. He is currently a judge in the European Court of Human Rights.[33]

Despite the imbeddedness of Orthodoxy, as stated above, moves towards secularization of the state reemerged in the 1980s. During the first Papandreou government, legislation was enacted which radically reformed Greece's family law by providing for gender equality, legalized abortion and recognized civil marriages.[34] The Orthodox Church opposed all these measures arguing that they contradicted Church doctrine. Of all these measures, the most vociferous opposition was to civil marriage, which led some cynics to contend that the Church's opposition was motivated in large measure by the potential loss of revenue. Papandreou made one of his characteristic compromises with the Church by legalizing both civil and religious marriages.

If a meaningful transformation is to take place in the conceptualization of Greek national identity and Church–state relations, rather than minimal gestures, it is essential to probe the meaning and psychological import of religion in everyday life. On one level, Orthodoxy is pervasive in Greek society and culture, but this statement needs more in-depth probing. As is well known, in addition to the family, education is a principal socializing agent; it transmits to the young the values and ideology of their society and culture. In Greece, the centrality of religion is reflected in the Ministry of Education and Religious Affairs, which is responsible for the religious education of students. Their national identity is thus constructed and they become authentic Greeks, a reference group that is reinforced by institutions, laws and ceremonies.[35] The inextricable intertwining of religion with nationality can be seen in the Greek Council of State's recent decision that the Ministry of Education's proposal to reduce by one hour per week the teaching of religion was unconstitutional.[36]

Overt religious discrimination is rarely apparent. The Rozakis case dramatized what is normally a more subtle process. All upper echelon positions in the public sector – judges in Greece's two high courts, the upper echelons of the military, education, the bureaucracy and cabinet members – are informally restricted to those of the Orthodox faith.[37] Nevertheless, despite these policies, critical for any transformative process to take place is the extent to which Orthodoxy is deeply embedded. Is religion for Greeks a salient reference group and a testimonial of one's faith, or is national/ethnic identity the principal reference group in which religion is one element, an element that could be gradually marginalized?

Although there are no firm data, indirect evidence seems to indicate that religiosity qua religiosity is weak. Despite the centrality of Orthodoxy as a marker of Greekness, Greeks on the whole, by contrast to practising Catholics, are notorious for the absence of theological conformity or spirituality. A fundamentalist neo-Orthodox intellectual movement propounded by Orthodox scholars does exist.[38] Paralleling this is an activist fundamentalist movement spearheaded by the current Archbishop of Greece, in which religion is seen as of the essence of Greekness. Nevertheless, the predominant Greek attitude remains one of conformity to Church rites and rituals but minimal adherence to doctrine and dogma. In part, this can be attributed to Orthodox theology itself, which does not claim to be all knowing since God on earth is represented by man and man is not God. But Orthodoxy as a marker of Greekness is deeply imbedded in the Greeks' conscience. The Church by exploiting the substance of Greek ethnicity, reinforces its political power. It can be argued that the flying of the Greek flag by churches on religious holidays, while proclaiming the unity of religion and nation, symbolizes the primacy of the nation. In this unity, religion cedes primacy to the nation, since Orthodoxy is only one of the markers that sets the parameters of national identity and of the Greek nation. Nevertheless, even in this implicitly diminished role the presumption that all authentic Greeks are Orthodox results in the perception that religious minorities are the 'other' and hence of questionable loyalty and subject to social and economic discrimination.

CONCLUSION

The construction and reconstruction of the Greek nation and of Greekness has undergone several transformations in modern times. As of the present, the consolidated ethnonational state remains largely intact and the secularism of the Greek state is problematic at best. The centrality of the Eastern Orthodox religion as a marker of Greekness, the legal status of the Greek Orthodox Church and its symbiotic relationship with the state, the remaining restrictions on religious freedom for minority religions, all attest to Greece's divergence from the secular principles of the Enlightenment and the basic tenets of most West European states.

For the last decade or so Greece, however, has been experiencing two contradictory trends pulling in opposite directions. On the one hand, developments in the last decade provide evidence that a transformation towards a secular state and a civic nationalism could be under way. On the other, developments as recently as 1998 portend a fierce reaffirmation of nationalist forces proclaiming the exclusivity of the Greek nation and its religious foundations. Nevertheless, the hitherto unchallenged givens of the Greek nation, inclusive of religion, and the nation's embodiment in the state are being contested in a fierce current debate.

The emergence of particularistic ethnic and national constructs is contingent on historical circumstances as is their reconstruction. Recently, both the domestic and international environment of the Greek state and society has altered radically. First, the demography of Greece is rapidly changing. In its entire modern history Greeks have emigrated, mostly for economic reasons, primarily to the United States, Canada and Australia and more recently as 'guest workers' to Germany. In the past few years, for the first time, Greece is becoming a country of immigrants. Relative religious and ethnic homogeneity is giving way to diversity and multiculturalism. Iranians, Iraqis, Kurds, Poles, Georgians and

Albanians, among others, have sought refuge in Greece. The exclusivity of Greek ethnicity in which Eastern Orthodoxy is a central component is becoming increasingly difficult to sustain. Inevitably, it is confronting the challenge of incorporating a religiously and ethnically diverse population into the Greek economy and society. And, while the issue of refugees and migrants is a policy issue for the entire European Union, its implications for an exclusive ethnonational state, such as Greece, are potentially far-reaching.

Until a few decades ago, when about to embark on a trip, Greeks would say 'we are going to Europe' thus revealing their self-perception as being distinct from the Europeans. Recently, membership of European regional organizations, in particular the European Union, the government's efforts to meet the Maastricht agreement criteria for adopting the Euro, in conjunction with the European and secular orientation of a large segment of the political and intellectual elite in Greece, has fuelled a Europeanization of Greece. Once viewed as a vehicle to be exploited by Greece for its economic benefits, conformity to the principles, norms and values of the European Union is becoming essential for Greece's new self-image as a European state.[39]

The judiciary in Greece remains committed to legal positivism which allows for little flexibility in the interpretation of existing law,[40] while the bureaucracy remains rigid. Nevertheless, Greece is gradually accepting European law, and in particular for our purposes, the European Convention on Human Rights and Fundamental Freedoms. Although Greece had re-ratified the Convention after the junta collapsed and although its constitution recognizes the primacy of its provisions, Greece has been slow in implementing some of its principles. In recent years, however, repeated condemnation by the European Court of Human Rights and Greece's reluctant and hesitant acceptance of its decisions condemning Greece for violating the right to freedom of religious practice, is incrementally moving Greece towards a more religiously pluralist society with equal rights for religious minorities. Greece's acceptance of the judgements of the European Court is manifest in a resolution adopted by the Greek cabinet in December 1997. Although more than four years after the Kokkinakis decision, the cabinet stated that the government had informed all competent authorities, including the judiciary, of the decision and states that 'given the direct effect attributed to the Court's judgment, there is no more risk of repetition of the violation found'.[41]

Reaction to the hesitant moves towards secularization and the potential recasting of the parameters of Greek identity has been fierce. Resurgent extreme right-wing nationalism and religious fundamentalism led by the charismatic, populist Archbishop Christodoulos are attempting to mobilize popular support for preserving the conceptual parameters of the Greek nation as currently constituted. Equating the Greek nation with Greek Orthodoxy, the Archbishop's rhetoric evokes a vision of Greece's glorious past as he speaks of Greece's lost homelands (referring to Asia Minor)[42] and issues calls for reclaiming them. Politically ambitious, Christodoulos' ideological goal appears to be to resuscitate the Byzantine Empire with the caveat, however, that it will be an exclusively

Greek nation. Although he was coerced by the government to reluctantly accept the Pope's brief visit in May 2001, bishops and parish priests protested vehemently. His intervention in political matters and his policy pronouncements, particularly in foreign affairs, such as his sermons on Greece's lost lands in Asia Minor and Turkey, and his opposition to membership of the European Union, violate a basic premise of Greek Church–state relations; namely, two separate spheres of competence. The Prime Minister in fact felt compelled to reassert this principle.[43]

In conclusion, it can be argued that, on the one hand, the demographic changes in Greece, and its efforts at European integration in conjunction with the governing elite's commitment to being perceived as 'Western', could have a profound impact on the reconstruction of Greek national identity and the secularization of the Greek state. On the other hand, however, the negative impact of the privatization policies, the increased 'labour flexibility' in a market-oriented economy and the proposed social security and the pension plans, has brought about the marginalization of some and a pervasive sense of insecurity, as the unemployment rate hovers over 10 per cent. As in other countries, the reaction, particularly among the young, may be a turn to fundamentalist religion cloaked in nationalist aspirations, for both personal and national salvation.[44]

NOTES

1. My thanks to Professors Nicos C. Alivizatos of the University of Athens and John O. Iatrides of the Southern Connecticut State University for their invaluable comments on an earlier draft.
2. For an analysis of the 'deviation' of liberal doctrines in modern Greece see Constantine Tsoucalas, 'Enlightened Concepts in the Dark: Power and Freedom, Politics and Society', *Journal of Modern Greek Studies*, 9, 1 (May 1991); for a discussion of the enlightenment in the Balkans see Paschalis Kitromilides, 'The Enlightenment East and West: A Comparative Perspective on the Ideological Origins of the Balkan Political Traditions', *Canadian Review of Studies in Nationalism*, X, 1 (1983); see also Victor Roudometoff 'From Rum Millet to Greek Nation: Enlightenment, Secularization and National Identity in Ottoman Balkan Society, 1453–1821', *Journal of Modern Greek Studies*, 16, 1 (1998).
3. Metaxas discriminated against both ethnic minorities and religious minorities. For example, in order to be a member of the youth organization he established, one had to be an Orthodox Christian. See Jon V. Kofas, *Authoritarianism in Greece: The Metaxas Regime* (New York: Columbia University Press, 1983), pp. 61–2, 89.
4. For a detailed discussion of the relations between the Patriarchate of Constantinople and the Church in Greece see Charles A. Frazee, *The Orthodox Church and Independent Greece, 1821–1852* (Cambridge: Cambridge University Press, 1969).
5. For a discussion of the controversy between religion and language see Elli Skopetea, *The Protypo Vasilieo ke i Megali Idea* (in Greek) (no publisher listed, Athens, 1988).
6. For a discussion of the historical relationship between the Eastern Orthodox churches and the state, regardless of the political regime, see Pedro Ramet (ed.), *Eastern Christianity and Politics in the Twentieth Century* (Durham, NC: Duke University Press, 1988).
7. It is ironic that in Orthodox theology the Church is not considered an institution. It is a transcendent spiritual community of all believers; see Adamantia Pollis, 'Eastern Orthodoxy and Human Rights', *Human Rights Quarterly*, May (1993), p. 343.
8. This is particularly the case with the Old Calendrists who although of Eastern Orthodox faith do not accept the authority of the official Greek Church and moreover adhere to the Justinian calendar.

9. Prime Minister Papandreou's reversal on the ID cards is discussed in Adamantia Pollis, 'Modernity, Civil Society and the Papandreou Legacy', *Journal of the Hellenic Diaspora*, 23, 1 (1997); other religious issues are also discussed in this article.

10. For a discussion of the negotiations between Prime Minister Papandreou and Archbishop Serapheim see Elizabeth Prodromou, 'Democratization and Religious Transformation in Greece: An Underappreciated Theoretical and Empirical Primer', in Paschalis M. Kitromilides and Thanos Veremis (eds), *The Orthodox Church in a Changing World* (Athens: Hellenic Foundation for European and Foreign Policy (ELIAMEP) and Centre for Asia Minor Studies, 1998).

11. Athens News Agency, 2 May 1998.

12. Athens News Agency, 7 May 1998.

13. Recently, in May 2001 Archbishop Christodoulos proclaimed in a church service that Greeks are losing their blessings with the influx of migrants into Greece, *To Nea* (Greek daily), 28 May 2001, p. N15.

14. Athens News Agency, 8 May 1998; also Athens News Agency, 5 May 1998; in a 5 May statement the new Archbishop Christodoulos stated that any effort to separate Orthodoxy from national life would be a blow to national unity and cohesion.

15. This does not take into account the ongoing demographic changes resulting from an influx of legal and illegal immigrants which has resulted in far greater religious pluralism. The figure 10 per cent does include an estimated 5 per cent who are Eastern Orthodox but who do not accept the authority of the official Greek Orthodox Church and who adhere to the Justinian calendar.

16. For a comprehensive legal discussion of the position of religious minorities see Nicos C. Alivizatos, 'The Constitutional Treatment of Religious Minorities in Greece', N. Valticos (ed.), *Mélanges* (Paris: Pedone 2000); see also Adamantia Pollis, 'The State, the Law and Human Rights in Greece', *Human Rights Quarterly*, 9, 4, November (1987).

17. In September 1983 the then Archbishop Serapheim issued an encyclical titled 'Anti-Heresy Campaign', in which he listed numerous religions, including the Protestants, as heretical and commanded the clergy and the military to provide the Holy Synod with information regarding their activities in each parish; cited in Jehovah's Witnesses *Ecclesiastical Truth*, Athens, 1 October 1983.

18. Cited in *International Herald Tribune*, section Kathimerini, an English summary of news that appears in the Greek daily, *Kathimerini*, 23–4 January 1999.

19. Council of Europe, European Court of Human Rights, case of *Canea Catholic Church v. Greece*, Judgment, 16 December 1997 (143/1996/762/963), Strasbourg.

20. This does not mean that there are not a host of discriminatory policies with regard to the Turkish community.

21. For a more detailed discussion of the impediments confronting minority religions see Pollis, 'The State, the Law and Human Rights'; see also Stefanos Stavrou, 'Citizenship and the Protection of Minorities', in Kevin Featherstone and Kostas Infantis (eds), *Greece in a Changing World: Between European Integration and Balkan Disintegration* (Manchester: Manchester University Press, 1996).

22. Pollis, 'The State, the Law and Human Rights'; Alivizatos, 'The Constitutional Treatment', states that as of 1997 no building permit had ever been granted to a religious minority.

23. The European Court of Human Rights deals with a multiplicity of religious issues involving many of the signatories on a variety of issues, including whether religious law takes precedence over state law. For a legalistic review see Stephanos Stavrou, 'Freedom of Religion and Claims for Exemption from Generally Applicable, Neutral Laws: Lessons from Across the Pond?', *European Human Rights Law Journal*, 6 (1997).

24. It should be noted that recently, parents who do not wish their children to attend religious classes can so petition the school, although they confront intense social pressure not to exercise this right while the children are frequently ostracized.

25. Council of Europe, European Court of Human Rights, *Kokkinakis v. Greece*, Judgment, 25 May 1993, Series A No. 260-A.

26. Council of Europe, European Court of Human Rights, case of *Larissis and Others v. Greece*, Judgment, February 1998 (140/1996/759/958-960), Strasbourg.

27. In a case involving two ministers from Jehovah's Witnesses, whom Greece had refused to exempt from military service the Court condemned Greece; Council of Europe, European Court of Human Rights, case of Tsirlis and Kouloumpas, Judgment, 29 May 1997 (54/1996/673/859-860), Strasbourg.

28. Council of Europe, European Court of Human Rights, case of *Valsamis* v. *Greece*, Judgment, 18 December 1996 (74/1995/580/666), Strasbourg.
29. Council of Europe, European Court of Human Rights, case of *Manousakis and Others* v. *Greece*, Judgment, 26 September 1996 (59/1995/565/651), Strasbourg.
30. Council of Europe, European Court of Human Rights, case of *Pentidies and Others* v. *Greece*, Judgment, 9 June 1997 (59/1996/678/868), Strasbourg.
31. For details of this legislation and continued difficulties see Amnesty International, Press Release, 21 November 1997.
32. A delegate from the New Democracy Party raised this issue in the Vouli, pointing out that Rozakis' name is Rosenstein-Rozakis as stated in various official documents. Proceedings of the Vouli, *Government Gazette*, 10 December 1996. It took the Minister of Foreign Affairs 10 days to repudiate this attack saying among other things that religious prejudice was not acceptable.
33. Interestingly he recently authored the introduction to Constantinos Tsitselikos and Dimitrios Christopoulos (eds), *To Mionotiko Phenomeno stin Ellada* (Athens: Kastanioti, 1997), a volume on minorities in Greece.
34. For a detailed discussion of the new family law of 1983, see Adamantia Pollis 'Gender and Social Change in Greece: the Role of Women', in Theodore C. Kariotis (ed.), *The Greek Socialist Experiment* (New York: Pella Publishers, 1992).
35. The presence of priests at all national ceremonies is ubiquitous as it is at most public and private events.
36. For a legal critique of this court decision see N.K. Alivizatos, 'To Thriskftiko ke i Alithia', *To Vima*, 31 May 1998.
37. In 1986, I was conducting interviews of judges at Greece's two high courts – the Council of State and the Supreme Court. I obtained access to their personnel files and I noticed that there was no information solicited on religious affiliation. This surprised me and when I inquired, I was told 'everyone is obviously Greek Orthodox'.
38. Christos Giannaras, *To Kseno stin Trehousa Politiki* (Athens: Kastanioti Publisher, 1989). He is a foremost philosopher of neo-Orthodoxy.
39. Of symbolic significance would have been a change from the religious oath of office to a secular one, signifying increased differentation between state and nation. Unfortunately the government conceeded to the Church and withdrew its own proposal.
40. Greek jurisprudence is German legal positivism. It is interesting that while moves have been made in Germany to modify this legal philosophy, Greece has shown few signs of change.
41. Appendix 18, CM/Del/Dec (97)610, Resolution DH (97) 576, Committee of Ministers, Athens, Greece.
42. These statements were made by the Archbishop in a tour of islands off the east coast of Greece, see *I Kathemerini* (daily Greek newspaper), 24 June 1998.
43. *I Kathimerini*, English section, 7 September 1998; furthermore, the Archibishop's relations with the Patriarchate in Istanbul, which represents ecumenical Orthodoxy are strained.
44. A disturbing development is the emergence of Golden Dawn, a neo-fascist group which has been violently attacking immigrants and presumed 'leftists'. There is considerable speculation in Greece that Archbishop Christodoulos may form an alliance with Golden Dawn.

10

Religion and Collective Identity: The Ethnopolitical Barriers to Democratization in the Balkans

STEVEN MAJSTOROVIC

The demise of the bipolar-Cold War world has brought the issue of ethnic identity and ethnonationalism to centre stage in Eastern Europe over the past decade, and also has sharpened discussion about ethnic minority problems in Western Europe. The breakup of three federal states, the Soviet Union, Czechoslovakia and Yugoslavia expanded to 28 the number of states in the area. More important, only six of these states are relatively ethno-homogeneous (Albania, Armenia, the Czech Republic, Hungary, Poland and Slovenia). The other states must confront ethnopolitical, ethnoterritorial, ethnoreligious and ethnonational issues as a matter of course in the difficult transition to democracy and market economics.[1] Since 80–85 per cent of the world's 190 states are multiethnic, the complexity of ethnocultural relations in Eastern Europe should come as no surprise.[2] In order to consolidate these new states, many of the dominant ethnonational formations have unfurled the banners of religious identity and nationalism, while minority ethnic groups have formulated strategies of resistance, autonomy and even outright secession. In the case of the former Yugoslavia, Slovenia, Croatia, Macedonia and Bosnia-Hercegovina successfully seceded from Yugoslavia, although the Serbs in territorially compact communities within Croatia and ethnically mixed areas within Bosnian-Hercegovina failed in their bloody secession campaigns from 1991 to 1995. This pattern has been repeated in the Serbian province of Kosovo, where the Albanian secessionists were locked in a low-level civil war with the Belgrade authorities until March 1999 when the NATO alliance started bombing Yugoslavia for failing to sign the Rambouillet peace plan dictated by the United States in February 1999.[3] The NATO forces finally forced Slobodan Milošević to sign a new settlement agreement in June 1999 and withdraw his forces from Kosovo, and now it is the Albanians who are the oppressors. In Macedonia, the Kosovo pattern has been repeated as the Albanian minority has demanded more rights and constitutional changes to insure a more inclusive political system. The conflict over these demands finally broke out into armed rebellion as Albanian guerrillas began to wage a military campaign in spring 2000. The European community has desperately tried to maintain control of the situation through diplomacy and shaky cease-fire declarations. The Macedonian majority Slav population considers the Albanian insurgents terrorists, while the Albanian population refers to the fighters as the NLA (National Liberation Army), and these very differing perceptions hinder the construction of political solutions.

Clearly, the glow of 1989 has dimmed and the harsh reality is that questions of ethnicity are perhaps the most difficult barrier to a successful democratic transition. The political cultures of Eastern Europe are not examples of a 'civic culture'[4] in which the norms of individual rights, political pluralism and cultural tolerance have taken root. Plans for economic development as a panacea for conflict have missed the essential point that in Eastern Europe the problem of ethnic conflict requires approaches that are not found in policies based on economic assumptions. Policy solutions are profoundly complicated when political decision-makers face the disturbing reality that '[t]he disconcerting intensity and persistence of ethnopolitical conflicts derives largely from the fact that they are driven by the clash of nonmaterial interests'[5] that often conflate religion and ethnicity.

ETHNICITY, DEMOCRACY AND THE STATE

The sequence of democratic transition in Western Europe and the United States generally followed a pattern in which the development of liberal democracy and individualism preceded the evolution of large-scale capitalist development.[6] On the spectrum of political development, Eastern Europe falls between the West and the underdeveloped states of the South. In the early development literature,[7] the simplistic stress on an economic path to democracy was proven to be shortsighted as the cultural dislocation produced by rapid social and economic change led to corporatist authoritarianism and 'political decay'.[8] The policies of privatization and of generating an entrepreneurial ethic in Eastern Europe are difficult enough tasks.[9] But when the barrier of ethnicity as an organizing principle grounded in ethnoreligious identity is erected, the challenges to free-market evolution and democratic transition become even more daunting. The transition to a market economy in Eastern Europe will probably be somewhat successful over time, although the experience of the Asian Tigers demonstrates that Francis Fukuyama's 'end of history' proclamation minimizes the cultural elements of the historical dialectic.[10] Instead, Fukuyama describes the ascendance of capitalism and gives liberal democracy a supporting role; economic variables are prioritized over cultural and ethnic identities. Most Asian and now Eastern European states, although more or less market oriented, are still not examples of strong liberal democracy and, with few exceptions, exhibit strained ethnocultural relations.[11]

A central characteristic of a secular liberal-democratic state is the primacy of individual identity in both the political and economic sphere. In Eastern Europe, however, the end of the one-party state, the dismantling of the centralized command economy, and the inception of multiparty democratic elections have not succeeded in transforming citizens into people with a notion of political rights that is based on individual identity. In rump Yugoslavia, Croatia, Bosnia-Hercegovina and Macedonia, collective interests rooted in ethnoreligious identity dominate the political systems and constitutional arrangements. The constitutions enshrine many elements of ethnic nationalism instead of civic nationalism. Ethnic minorities are either completely ignored or characterized in a type of constitutional language that subordinates their legal position in relation to the dominant ethnonational group.[12] This state of affairs is not a surprising outcome if one examines the historical experience of ethnonational identity in Eastern Europe.

While Europe was evolving the nation-state system, Eastern Europe, including the Balkans, was dominated by a system of empires that restricted the political options of ethnonational actors. The Austro-Hungarian, Ottoman and Russian empires did not collapse until World War I and then the states and peoples that rose out of the ashes of the war all had memories of medieval golden ages but failed the test of democracy in the interwar years.[13] The experience under the tutelage of empires solidified collective identity and the brief flirtation with democracy between the two world wars quickly decayed into assertion of political control by the most powerful ethnic groups in the new nation-states. When the Communists took control after World War II, the focus on ethnic collectivity was replaced with an emphasis on class collectivity. Thus, when state-directed socialism collapsed in 1989, the nations of Eastern Europe had little if any experience with political and cultural pluralism, norms in Western European and American culture that stress the prioritization of individual rights over collective rights. Exceptions to this pattern were the Czechs, who were somewhat successful with their interwar democratic experiment and the independent Serbian state from 1878 to World War I when its early attempts at parliamentary democracy were cut short in 1914, and then the Serbs, who, along with the Croats, failed in creating a democratic Yugoslavia between the two wars.

Tito's Yugoslavia did recognize cultural pluralism by recognizing the Bosnian Muslims as a constituent Yugoslav nation in 1971. The recognition in a single stroke created a buffer between Serbian and Croatian claims about Muslim identity.[14] But this decision also ethnicized a religious identity and thus precipitated future demands on the political system. A similar but opposite process took place in Macedonia. Bulgarians claimed that language similarities made it clear that the Slavs of Macedonia were essentially ethnic Bulgars. In response, an autocephalous Macedonian Orthodox Church was created in 1967 over the protests of the Serbian Orthodox Church that had dominated Orthodox practices in Macedonia. The Communist Party supported the new independent Macedonian church not from any interest in religion but as a clear indication of the existence of a Macedonian ethnic nation. Much of the discussion in Tito's Yugoslavia revolved around a simultaneous acceptance of a religious pluralism that might foster a greater state allegiance while always evoking the negative aspects of ethnic nationalism.[15] Eventually the ethnicization of a religious group, as in the Bosnian case, and the religious recognition of an ethnic group, as in the Macedonian case, fostered maximal ethnopolitical demands and the irreducibility of ethnonational identity to democratic arrangements in the post-Tito and then post-1989 system. Institutional and political engineering could not overcome cultural inertia.

In the Balkan successor states religion itself should not be reduced to a belief system but is itself a tool of ethnopolitical strategies. Ethnic identity is inextricably intertwined with religious affiliation. The political role usually associated with Eastern Orthodoxy and its close relationship to the state (Caesaro-Papism), and exemplified in ethnoreligious identity in Serbia/ Montenegro (rump Yugoslavia), can also be ascribed to the new Croatian state, the Muslim statelet of Bosnia-Hercegovina, Macedonia, Kosovo and perhaps even a future independent Montenegro with its own future autocephalous Orthodox Church. Thus, any examination of ethnopolitics in the Balkans must address the collective and essentially non-material nature of ethnoreligious identity, and also it must confront the perceptual differences in historical understanding and ethnic identity evolution among and between the ethnonational formations of the former Yugoslavia.

Tito's mission to fashion socialism and class solidarity after World War II failed because Balkan ethnicities in the nineteenth and twentieth centuries, including the Bosnian Muslims and the Macedonians, had already politicized and transformed themselves in reaction to the modern state, and the alienation and dislocation caused by the industrial revolution did not precipitate a bonding along class lines but instead fostered a reaffirmation of ethnonational identity.[16] Dualism also created ethnopolitical conflict in the Yugoslav nation-state. There was a significant ambiguity in the relationship between the state and the various ethnonational groups that comprised the state. The state disseminated a picture of a nation that can transcend and subsume the differences between political allegiance to the state and ethnonational identity. Very few states, however, have succeeded in making the state and nation congruent.[17] This dualism also results in an ideological conflict between the political ideal of the nation-state and the historical reality of the nation.[18] In interwar Yugoslavia the attempt to create congruence between nation and state led to pronouncements that a Yugoslav identity was in the process of creation. These naive assumptions were inspired by oversimplified analyses that emphasized ethnocultural similarities and the inevitable convergence of Croat, Serb and Slovene identity. After World War II, the Communists tried to construct a socialist national identity that transcended ethnicity and religious differences by embarking on endless Yugoslavianism campaigns and by suppressing politicized religious expression. Like the interwar efforts to fashion a common identity, these efforts were also in vain and in fact only precipitated greater identity differentiation.[19]

A recently prominent analysis of the continuing conflicts in the Balkans characterizes the strife as a 'civilizational' struggle among competing religions.[20] Another perspective contends that despite the seemingly ethnoreligious nature of the conflict, the interethnic hostility is essentially the effort of entrepreneurial ethnic elites who have manipulated their ethnic followers into assuming that their physical and cultural survival is threatened.[21] Both of these approaches, however, miss the essential nature of the Balkan conflict. Despite the ethnoreligious and ethnopolitical alignments among the warring actors, the issues in question are matters of ethnonational identity and

> religion is the dominant identity marker [along with language in the case of the Kosovo Albanians] that has been politicized over the centuries in order to mobilize various Balkan ethnic formations in the pursuit of ethnopolitical goals ... [T]he contemporary violence is not simply a matter of elite manipulation but is also rooted in cultural memories that are validated in a continuous process of remembering the past and then applying this past to present circumstances.[22]

It is clear that analysts who present a primordial-religious perspective on ethnonational[23] identity in the Balkans have plenty of empirical data. Social constructivists and instrumentalists, however, can also insist that ethnonational identity is artificial and created in the modern period by ambitious ethnic entrepreneurs who exploit and politicize ethnic differences. It cannot be over-emphasized the degree to which ethnoreligious processes over the centuries have reinforced both real and mythicized events. The experiences of Balkan ethno-religious groups have produced historical memories that limit and constrain the choices that contemporary ethnonational leaders exercise in conflict creation and in peacemaking. The ethnoreligious and historically imposed constraints on both elites and masses is especially relevant in the Serbian and Croatian cases, and somewhat less for the Bosnian Muslims. This combination of both pre-modern, primordial ethnoreligious expressions of ethnic identity and modern politicized elements are both fundamental aspects of the present conflicts and are the central obstacles to the evolution of liberal-democracy in the Balkan successor states.[24]

Today the primary threat to the state system and international stability is not conflict between nation-states but ethnic strife within nation-states.[25] In the case of the former Yugoslavia this conflict seems to be based only on religious and civilizational affiliation. The essence of the conflict is a manifestation of competing ethnopolitical programmes for creating new states in order to insure ethnocultural identity survival against perceived threats. Ethnonational identity is an independent variable whose political expression can be manifested by the conflicts over language, religion and economic inequality.[26] These political expressions, however, are not the essence of ethnicity and of the forces that drive ethnoreligious and ethnopolitical struggles to such intense levels. Ethnicity is a form of shared identity which is self-defined; it is subjective.[27] The intangible nature of this subjective and ascriptive bond implies that language, religion and economics/class are epiphenomenal and that the essential nature of ethno-national identity and its political expression will remain resistant to analyses that depend upon objective categories, like religion, to explain ethnopolitical behaviour and conflict. It is this self-defined nature of ethnonational identity that is at the core of the historically rooted conflicts that plague the Balkans.

The self-defined/subjective orientation is very applicable in examining the character of the ethnonational bonds in the Balkans, and observers of the present strife should never underestimate the emotional and psychological hold that ethnonational identity has on Croats, Bosnian Muslims, Serbs and Kosovo Albanians.[28] In the final analysis, it is not the collection of objective identity markers and historical facts that shapes the ethnic consciousness of the Balkan actors. Instead, it is what these respective people believe are the facts that reinforces the memories and myths that have impact on contemporary cultural behaviour and political decision-making.[29] The Balkan struggles, rooted in religious affiliation, have always been part of a greater political agenda of identity maintenance, mass mobilization and territorial claims.

In a nineteenth-century version of the civilizational thesis, Baron insisted that the great religions have shaped the historical forces that produced modern nationalism.[30] It is religious strife that creates nations, binds peoples and fosters revolutions. He observed that all of the major peoples in Europe belong to a single religious denomination, except for the Germans and Hungarians. The stability and maintenance of ethnic-religious boundaries led Baron to conclude that religion was the driving force behind the various nationalist movements in Europe during the eighteenth and nineteenth centuries. Religion is the foundry within which nationalism in Europe was forged. Thus, religion must be more than just a set of beliefs about life after death or some transcendental world of moral perfection. Religion also has political implications. After all, religion directs how the world should be organized through law, authority and hierarchy. Religious rituals serve an important political function, apart from the spiritual emotion they foster, through a collective reinforcement of the authority of church leaders and the organizations they represent. The recommendations of church leaders can often extend as far as political behaviour and moral codes. The power of religious injunctions is in their moral absolutism and claims to universal validity. This absolutism is a powerful social cement and guide to ethnopolitical behaviour. Talcott Parsons remarked that religion 'is the point of articulation between the cultural system and the social system, where values from the former are embodied in the latter'.[31]

Attempts by state authorities to suppress or destroy the religious organi-zations of ethnonational minorities can be accomplished with the impressive coercive power of the modern state. However, when states deny their multiethnic character and attempt to denationalize or assimilate ethnonational minorities, the result is that ethnic survival is permeated with spiritual significance. Thus, ethnopolitical consciousness is galvanized and the propensity for conflict increases.[32] However, state authorities or conquerors do have options over religious policy and ethnonationalism:

> Military conquerors and separatists alike have recognized the political potency of national churches and their utility in weaning populations from earlier allegiances. Thus, the Germans allowed believers in occupied Byelo- russia to organize a Byelorussian Autocephalous Orthodox church in 1941. And the Ukrainian Autocephalous Orthodox church, [which] was to play an active role in fomenting anti-Russian nationalism in German occupied Ukrainia during World War II. Similarly, Ante Pavelic, pogalvnik [head] of the wartime Independent State of Croatia, established an Autocephalous Croatian Orthodox church in hopes of convincing some [Serbian] Orthodox believers that they were Croats.[33]

In Yugoslavia, the strife between the Bosnian Muslims, Serbs and Croats is within a context in which they speak a language in which the Croat and Serb variants are very similar. Bosnian Muslims, Serbs and Croats can understand each other perhaps more readily than someone from Maine would be under- stood in Texas. But Serbs are Eastern Orthodox, the Bosnian Muslims follow Islam and Croats are Roman Catholic. Moreover, the conflict between Albanians and Serbs in the Serbian province of Kosovo has had a long history of violence. Serbs and Albanians speak very different languages, and in Albania, many Albanians are Eastern Orthodox, although most are Muslim and a few are Roman Catholic.[34] Some analysts have persuasively suggested that the goal of Albanian nationalism is 'Albanianism' and not any particular confessional orientation. But in Kosovo, 99 per cent of the Albanians are Muslims and the interethnic hostility is palpable.[35]

Ramet contends that 'religion was national before it was universal'.[36] The universalist creed that Moses brought to the Jews became a national religion. In the same way, the universalist religious creeds that, according to some, should shape the outlines of the millennial clashes along the tectonic fault lines of colliding civilizational plates have instead, in large part, become ethnonational for Bosnian Muslims, Croats, Serbs, Albanians and Macedonians. The Balkan successor states practice the doctrine of collective rights, or more precisely, the doctrine of ethnoreligious rights. Today these states are still in democratic transition and are characterized by authoritarian practices. Moreover, the nascent expressions and exercises in democracy are limited and only benefit the dominant ethnonational group.[37] In the former Yugoslavia, religious homegenity only exists in Croatia and Slovenia which are overwhelmingly Catholic. The bulk of the former Yugoslavia still exhibits the type of ethnoreligious pluralism that has yet to be adequately institutionalized in democratic arrangements. The most recent area of conflict, western and northwestern Macedonia, has an Albanian

Muslim majority, while the rest of Macedonia has an Eastern Orthodox Slav
majority.

RELIGION AS POLITICS AND MEMORY IN THE BALKANS

During the sixth century, migrating Slavic tribes settled the part of the Balkans
that includes Yugoslavia. These Slavs were independent until the beginning of
the twelfth century when the Croatians yielded to Hungarian sovereignty, while
the Serbs lost their independence at the hands of the Ottoman Turks at the end
of the fourteenth century. The Balkans were then externally ruled by Austria,
Hungary, Italy, or Turkey until the dawn of the twentieth century, although the
Serbs were an exception since after several revolts beginning in 1804 they had
formed an internationally recognized state in 1878.

The South Slavs [38] were distinguished by self-defined variances in custom and
culture,[39] and then further differentiated by the schism in the Christian Church.
Roman Catholicism defined the Croats and Slovenes, while the Serbs were part
of the Byzantine Empire and had formed an independent Serbian Orthodox
Church by the thirteenth century. This East–West schism was solidified when the
Serbs succumbed to Ottoman rule, while the Croats and Slovenes bowed to
Rome and Hungary, and eventually to the Austro-Hungarian Empire.

Under Tsar Dusan, fourteenth-century Serbia had expanded into a medieval
empire that encompassed the Balkans from the Adriatic to western Bulgaria and
much of Albania and areas in northern Greece. The system set up by Dusan
started to erode after his death in 1355 but stability was restored in 1371 when
Prince Lazar came to power.[40] This period of stability ended at Kosovo Polje
(The Field of Blackbirds) on 28 June 1389.[41] The battle between the Serb forces
of Prince Lazar and the Ottoman Turks was at the time perceived as either a
pyrrhic victory for the Turks or indecisive. The titanic nature of a battle in which
Prince Lazar and his son were beheaded, the Turkish Sultan Murad was
disembowelled by the Serbian knight Milos Obilic,[42] and where there were
horrific losses on both sides created an ethnoreligious myth that continues to
shape contemporary Serb ethnic identity, particularly over the issue of Kosovo.[43]

The Serbs also mythicized what they see as their forced exodus from Kosovo
in the late seventeenth century,[44] the subsequent incursion of an Ottoman-
supported population from Albania, and then the triumphant return in 1912.[45]
Despite Ottoman dominance, the events from 1389 to 1912 were politicized and
cast in an ethnoreligious context by the Serbian Orthodox Church [46] and by folk
musicians who regularly told the story in an ever evolving epic poem and passion
play (The Kosovo Cycle).[47] This cultural and anti-Muslim conditioning suggests
that the current tragedy in Kosovo may prove to be even more catastrophic than
the war in Bosnia.

The independent Serbian state which was dissolved to form a multiethnic
and multireligious Yugoslavia also influences the Serb notion of sacrifice and

political martyrdom.[48] The Serbs suffered enormous losses in both world wars and have always chronicled their part in the Allied victories and contrast their efforts to Croat Catholic, Bosnian Muslim and Albanian Muslim collaboration with the Nazis.[49]

Today, the policies of the Catholic Croatian Ustasha state and their Bosnian Muslim allies[50] during World War II are often used by Serbs to stereotype all Croatians and Muslims ethnopolitically and ethnoreligously. During World War II, many Croatian Franciscans joined the Ustasha.[51] The clergy made the decision to privilege Croatian national identity over their confessional role. Similarly, many of the crimes committed against hapless Croats and Bosnian Muslims during the 1991–95 wars were rationalized by some Serbs as a sort of 'Christoslavism' which saw itself under siege by the combined forces of Islam and the Vatican.[52]

Croatians also have a memory of a medieval kingdom, but it is one that voluntarily relinquished its sovereignty in 1102 to Hungary. The Croatian ethnopolitical and ethnoreligious effort has been to present a picture of a con-tinuous Croatian state in existence since 1102 as evidenced by peasant uprisings, a succession of Croatian kings,[53] and advances in Croatian culture and learning which depict Catholic Croatia as a part of a Western European culture that is distinct from the Serbs.[54] However, the idea of a multi-confessional Yugoslavia was first articulated in the nineteenth century by Croatian Bishop Josip Strossmayer and Friar Franjo Racki in an attempt to reconcile Croatian and Serbian differences.[55] But another vision of Croatian identity that was closely tied to the Catholic Church and the Vatican and was led by an ex-seminarist Ante Starcevic became the ideological precursor to the Ustasha. Starcevic and his followers emphasized the high achievements of Western Catholic, Croatian culture, while Serbian culture was depicted as oriental and inferior. Starcevic's ethnopoliticized brand of Catholic Croat ideology was dominant by the early twentieth century.[56]

Croatian ethnoreligious and political identity was heavily reinforced by the failure of the Croatian Republic to secede from Yugoslavia during the 1968–72 Croatian Crisis. The crisis began as a campaign for political and economic liberalization. But the campaign was soon dominated by secessionist elements and by a sympathetic Croatian Catholic Church. In response, Tito brutally purged the Croatian party of liberals and then effected a type of ethnic balance by purging Serbian liberals.[57] These events only served to harden the Croatian view that they were a liberal and Western culture that was besieged by the oriental Serbs. Moreover, during this period Franjo Tudjman, the president of Croatia today, was transformed into a nationalist and began to write revisionist books and essays about the Croatian role in World War II.[58]

When the war in Bosnia began in 1992, there were competing interpretations of Bosnian Muslim identity. Serbs still believe that the Muslims are Islamicized Serbs, while Croats insist these same Slavs were once Catholic Croats. Moreover, many Bosnian Muslims contend that they are descended from a heretic

Manichean sect called the Bogomils.[59] Other Muslims argue that they are really ethnic Turks and only share a Slavic language with the Serbs and Croats.[60] When the Tito regime declared in 1971 that the Bosnian Muslims were an official nationality, their ethnopolitical and religious identity was legitimized in Bosnia-Hercegovina Although many scholars present an idealized version of Bosnian history replete with interethnic harmony and cooperation,[61] there were undeniable ethnoreligious roots to the 1992–95 Bosnian war.[62]

Islamic conversion in Bosnia was a complicated process in which once-Slavic Christians with a distinct Bosnian identity converted in a pragmatic and gradual manner which began during the fifteenth century. With the ebbing of Ottoman supremacy at the end of the nineteenth century the Bosnian Muslims often demonstrated the capacity for compromise as they organized political parties and interest groups that delicately balanced Croat and Serb attempts to capture their loyalty. Many Muslim nationalists romanticize this period of supposed multiethnic tolerance[63] but historical scrutiny reveals a more complicated picture. Developments in medieval Bosnia were intimately connected to ethnopolitics, Serbia, Croatia and the Ottoman Empire. The Ottoman *millet* system identified ethnic groups by religion instead of ethnicity and consequently politicized ethnoreligious identity. Some scholars mistakenly assume that since the Turks used a non-ethnic marker to identify Croats and Serbs only as Christians, a pre-nineteenth-century Croat and Serbian identity did not exist in Bosnia. But Serbians started migrating into Bosnia by the early fifteenth century to escape Ottoman oppression in Kosovo, the Serbian heartland. During the same period, the Franciscan order organized the maintenance of a Croat ethnic presence in the area of western Bosnia known as Hercegovina. In addition, the Austrians offered Serbs land to act as a military *cordon sanitaire* against the Turks, and by the seventeenth century Serbs occupied the Krajina in Croatia and adjacent areas in Bosnia.[64]

In the social system fashioned by the Ottomans, Muslim converts were landowners and freeholders while the majority of peasants, who were taxed heavily and lived as second-class citizens, were Christians.[65] The peasants who lived in this Jim Crow system chafed at the ethnopolitical inequities disguised as religious identification and started to revolt by the nineteenth century, especially the Serbs. Of particular relevance to a contemporary insight into ethnic relations is that as the Ottoman Empire declined and was forced to make concessions to subject populations, it was in Bosnia and Kosovo where local Muslim landlords were the most reactionary and hostile to any adjustments in ethnoreligious rights that might threaten their dominance.[66]

Although Bosnia in 1992 may not have been a hotbed of 'ancient hatreds', the ethnoclass divisions fostered by the Ottoman system were still in evidence and Milošević in Serbia and Tudjman in Croatia, often referred to as architects of the war in Bosnia, easily exploited the ancient ethnoreligious frictions. In order to allocate responsibility, however, one should also examine the rather radical Islamic political views of Bosnian president Alija Izetbegovic's[67] and his reneging on the Lisbon Agreement of 1992 that would have maintained a multiethnic Bosnia.[68]

Today Bosnian and Kosovo Muslim ethnoreligious identity is still in the process of being defined. For the Bosnian Muslims the myths will be built on Sarajevo and Srebrenica, while for the Kosovo Muslims the mass expulsion from Kosovo during the spring of 1999 will be the touchstone of legend and memory as the 1389 battle was for the Serbs. Bosnian Muslim women wearing traditional veils have recently appeared in villages and on the streets of Sarajevo.[69] Moreover, a civilizational aspect has appeared with documented evidence of links to Islamic forces from the Middle East, particularly Iran.[70] Islamic extremists were also observed in Kosovo prior to the 1999 breakout of war.[71] Unfortunately, the Serbs more than the Croats or Muslims are hobbled by a history and identity that suggest an apocalyptic destiny, and perhaps the NATO bombing of Serbia only reinforces this vision of ethnic paranoia combined with a belief in a messianic role, to mount the Christian ramparts against the Islamic hordes.

Curiously, the recently deceased Croatian President Franjo Tudjman decided to re-bury Ustasha soldiers from World War II at the site of the Jasenovac concentration camp that holds the remains of hundreds of thousands of Serbs and thousands of Jews. For the Croats this is a way to close the door on the past, but for Serbs and Jews this is seen in a hostile light.[72] Moreover, Pope John Paul II beatified Croatian Cardinal Aloysius Stepinac in October 1998. Stepinac's actions and relations with the Ustasha during World War II are the focus of sharp criticism by Serbian and Jewish war survivors.[73] In all fairness, although Stepinac was a fervent Croatian nationalist, he did complain repeatedly to Ustasha leader Ante Pavelic about the brutality towards Jews and Serbs. Today the position of religion in Croatia has been depicted as a struggle between ecumenical forces comprised of 'the Catholic Church in Croatia' and a culturally intolerant nationalist outlook exemplified by extremists and the 'Croatian Catholic Church'.[74] It must be noted that Croatia's democratic transition took a positive turn in December 2000 when the party of Tudjman was defeated at the polls by democratically minded reformers. The President of Croatia, Stipe Mesic, has spoken of reconciliation and the return of refugees, and the new government has been active in turning over indicted war criminals to the Hague and in keeping the power of the Catholic Church at arm's length.[75]

Of all the ethnic actors in the Balkans, the Serbs are perhaps the most constrained by a historical vision that may continue to hobble them. They have already mythicized the expulsion of 300,000 Serbians from the Krajina region of Croatia, an event that the United States refrained from labelling ethnic cleansing. The Serbs have also focused on the massacres of Serbs near Srebrenica[76] before the Bosnian Serb army atrocities of July 1995 as new examples for their perceived role as Christian Orthodox martyrs. In a hopeful sign, the Serbian Orthodox Church turned on Slobodan Milošević and sided with the pro-democracy protest movement that saw almost 100 days of continuous protest, sometimes by hundreds of thousands of protestors, in the streets of Belgrade throughout

December 1996 and into March 1997.[77] And in 2000, the Serbian Orthodox Church criticized Milošević's Kosovo aggression and called for a peaceful, multiethnic accord.[78] The Serbian Church has also strongly supported the new president of Yugoslavia, Vojislav Kostunica, whose election victory in October 2000 caused Slobodan Milošević to step down from power soon afterwards. Although the Serbian Church seems to be on the side of democratic forces in Yugoslavia today, it was only a few years ago that the leaders of the church supported the brutal Serbian military offensives in Bosnia. As recently as 1995, the Serbian Church tried to address the low birth-rate of Serbs in Kosovo versus the high Albanian birth-rate. In order to protect the 'Serbian Jerusalem', the Orthodox Church started to bequeath medals on Serbian women with the highest fertility rates.[79]

Continuing events related to ethnopolitical expression in the former Yugoslavia have left open the question of future ethnocultural accord and religious tolerance. In March 1997, a Catholic church in Sarajevo was damaged by an explosion and a few days earlier another Catholic church was the site of a grenade explosion. These events were presumably perpetrated by Muslim extremists who protested Pope John Paul's visit to Sarajevo.[80] An Orthodox Christmas celebration on 7 January 1997 in Sarajevo was the site of a tear gas attack by 'unknown' perpetrators.[81] Also in March 1997 in northeastern Bosnia, a mob of Serbs attacked and burned down several homes that returning Muslims had rebuilt on the Serbian side of the demilitarized zone. Russian Orthodox soldiers watched the attack but did not intervene.[82] More recently, in June 2001, Bosnian Serb police had to use tear gas and water cannons to disperse a mob of Serbian demonstrators intent on preventing the rebuilding of the sixteenth-century Ferhadija mosque near Banja Luka, Bosnia.[83] The mosque was destroyed by Serbian extremists in 1993 in a manner similar to the destruction of the Muslim Ayodhya mosque in India by Hindu extremists in 1992. In both cases, claims were made that the Muslims had built their mosques on non-Muslim holy sites.[84] Some more traditionally Muslim elements in the Bosnian government criticized the expression of Western culture and cracked down on Christmas celebrations in Sarajevo and some Muslim groups have even started to cover up examples of Western art. In Kosovo the ethnic card has turned against the Serbs, and over 120 monasteries and churches, many of them dating back to the twelfth century, have been razed by the now ascendant Kosovo Albanians, and much of the Serbian population has been driven out of the province.[85]

The Balkan cycle of tragedy has inevitably returned to Kosovo, where both Serbians and Albanians have met violent deaths over the past few decades and where the process of ethnonational and international warfare might even further reshape Balkan ethno-geography. Despite the presence of NATO forces, the situation is still quite ominous and the Balkan powder-keg has begun to explode again as the restive Albanian population of Macedonia recently voted for independence in an unofficial election. The actions of the NLA have been supported from Kosovo by the still powerful KLA (Kosovo Liberation Army). Despite the enactment of many cease-fires, mutual 'distrust' could still destabil-ize Macedonia and lead to a civil war which may include the Albanians of Montenegro, Serbia and perhaps even Greece.[86] From the perspective of a civic culture, the Albanians are articulating grievances that in a Western liberal-democratic context would be addressed through routine political debate and peaceful protest. The Albanian pattern of armed rebellion is no different than the Serbian pattern in Croatia during 1991–92. Perhaps the most explosive recent event in Macedonia occurred on 25 June 2001 when American troops 'rescued' several hundred members of the insurgent NLA as they were surrounded by Macedonian troops in the capital city of Skopje. American KFOR forces bussed the Albanian fighters out of the capital, and within hours, a crowd of 5,000 Macedonian Slavs marched through the capital displaying anti-Western slogans.[87] The reaction of the Macedonian Orthodox Church to the Albanian insurgency has been to advocate a military solution by suggesting that 'Macedonia should be liberated of those who threaten our lives and possessions' before any further talks with the Albanian community might commence.[88]

Despite the dissatisfaction of the Albanians, the new millennium has brought some important and hopeful changes to the former Yugoslavia. Since Franjo Tudjman's death in early 2000, the newly elected president of Croatia, Stipe Mesic, has pursued policies that suggest a turn towards democracy and the beginnings of ethnic accord with the Bosnian Muslims and the Serbs. In Sarajevo, Alija Izetbegovic has stepped down as the President of Bosnia and the support among some sectors of the Muslim population for a more Islamic Bosnia has wained. The latest election results from the November 2000 Bosnian election revealed that the Serbian and Croatian nationalist parties had lost much support but still maintained majority support, while a reformist multiethnic party has slowly gained support.[89]

But, most important, Slobodan Milošević has fallen from power as a new president of Yugoslavia. Vojislav Kostunica was elected in late October 2000 and was able to force Milošević to concede defeat only after days of demonstrations and a successful storming of the parliament by hundreds of thousands of Serbs, including thousands of peasants and workers from Serbia's heartland. But Kostunica's moderate and legal constitutional approach, although hailed in the West, may yet reignite Kosovo as the Albanians see their aspirations for inde-pendence erode as the West supports the possibility of a democratic Yugoslavia.

CONCLUSION

If liberal democracy is the goal, then there is a long way to go in the Balkans and much of the rest of Eastern Europe. Scholars have never failed to mention the advantage that the West had in timing. Timing was everything in being the first to industrialize, to democratize, to concretize the ideas of the Enlightenment, and to build viable nation-states. What is generally missed in the whole timing analysis is that in Western Europe the state came into being before ethnonational minorities were politicized. The European state was built on the ruins of centralized monarchical proto-states that had subdued resistant but not politicized ethnicities, at least not politicized and mobilized in the modern sense. Today in Western Europe, ethnic minorities follow routinized political means of expression and organization. They join broad-based political parties, they form interest groups and social movements, and they demand and often receive appreciable levels of cultural and religious autonomy. The violence in Corsica and the Basque area in northern Spain are the exceptions.

In Eastern Europe, ethnonational groups chafed under the rule imposed by foreign emperors well beyond the end of the nineteenth century. These ethnonational formations became politicized and mobilized in the modern sense before modern states were formed. And that reversal in timing has implications that will continue into the next millennium because the state has continued to be a bone of contention that the Western Europeans have managed to avoid for the last 300 years, the devolution of Great Britain notwithstanding. The Hungarians in Vojvodina and Slovakia are watching what may happen in Kosovo and Macedonia, since the international community, led by the United States, decided to breach the barrier of state sovereignty in the Balkans and has now performed a partial about-face by lifting many of the sanctions against Yugoslavia and by supporting Vojislav Kostunica's efforts to effect democratic transition in Yugoslavia. The Macedonians, Greeks, Bulgarians and Turks are also watching. Depending on what happens in Kosovo, the results may have a great demonstration effect in Russia's southern Muslim republics, where Chechnya is just one piece in a larger maze of interlocking Muslim ethnonational actors.

Finally, liberal democracy is more than the sum of institutional arrangements. It is a cultural disposition based on civic tolerance and loyal opposition. In order for liberal democracy to come to the Balkans and to displace ethnopolitical and ethnoreligious loyalties based on the experience of centuries, it will take at least decades of substantial generational replacement.

NOTES

1. See Hugh Mall, 'Introduction', in Hugh Mall (ed.), *Minority Rights in Europe: Prospects for a Transnational Regime* (New York: The Royal Institute of International Affairs, 1994).
2. See Walker Connor, 'Ethnonationalism', in Myron Weiner and Samuel Huntington (eds), *Understanding Political Development* (Boston, MA: Little, Brown, 1987).
3. Both the Albanian and Serbian sides refused to sign the first draft of the settlement agreement until the US persuaded the Albanians to sign with an implicit suggestion that a referendum on independence would be possible in three years. The Serbian side, however, was faced with a new addendum to the settlement agreement, the now infamous Appendix B: 'NATO personnel shall enjoy, together with their vehicles, vessels, aircraft, and equipment, free and unrestricted access throughout the Federal Republic of Yugoslavia including associated airspace and territorial waters. This shall include, but not be limited to, the right of bivouac, maneuver, billet, and

utilization of any areas or facilities as required for support, training, and operations.' See an analysis of Appendix B in Noam Chomsky, *The New Military Humanism: Lessons From Kosovo* (Vancouver: New Star Books, 1999), pp. 106–7. Chomsky's account makes it clear that signing the agreement would effectively force Milošević to give up Yugoslav sovereignty. The agreement signed after the bombing ceased, did not contain Appendix B.

4. Gabriel A. Almond and Sidney Verba, *The Civic Culture* (Princeton, NJ: Princeton University Press, 1963).

5. See Ted Robert Gurr, 'Ethnic Warfare and the Changing Priorities of Global Security', *Mediterranean Quarterly*, 1 (1990), pp. 82–98.

6. See, of course, Max Weber, *The Protestant Ethic and the Spirit of Capitalism* (New York: Charles Scribner's Sons, 1958).

7. See, for example, Robert Heilbroner, *The Great Ascent* (New York: Harper & Row, 1963); W.W. Rostow, *The Stages of Economic Growth: A Non-Communist Manifesto* (Cambridge: Cambridge University Press, 1960).

8. Samuel P. Huntington, *Political Order in Changing Societies* (New Haven, CT: Yale University Press, 1968).

9. See, for example, John S. Earle, Roman Frydman and Andrzej Rapaczynski (eds), *Privatization in the Transition to a Market Economy: Studies of Preconditions and Policies in Eastern Europe* (New York: St Martin's Press, 1993); John S. Earle, Roman Frydman and Andrzej Rapaczynski *et al.*, *The Privatization Process in Central Europe* (Budapest: Central European University Press, 1993); Andras Koves, *Central and East European Economies in Transition: The International Dimension* (Boulder, CO: Westview Press, 1992); Carole Nagengast, *Reluctant Socialists, Rural Entrepreneurs: Class, Culture, and the Polish State* (Boulder, CO: Westview Press, 1991).

10. See Francis Fukuyama, 'The End of History', *The National Interest*, 16 (Summer 1989), pp. 3–18.

11. For an examination of ethnicity and the state in the Asian context see Steven Majstorovic, 'Ethnicity and the New World Disorder: The Malaysian Experience', in Douglas Borer and Mark Berger (eds), *The Rise of East Asia: Post-Cold War Perspectives on the 'Pacific Century' and the 'New World Order'* (London: Routledge, 1997).

12. See The International Institute for Democracy (eds), *The Rebirth of Democracy: 12 Constitutions of Central and Eastern Europe*, 2nd edn (Strasbourg: Council of Europe Publishing, 1996), pp. 55–6.

13. See Michael G. Roskin, *The Rebirth of East Europe*, 3rd edn (Upper Saddle River, NJ: Prentice Hall, 1997); and Joseph Rothschild, *Return to Diversity: A Political History of East Central Europe Since World War II*, 2nd edn (Oxford: Oxford University Press, 1993).

14. See S.K. Zadaci, *Srbije u razvoju medjunacionalnih odnosa i borbi protiv naciolnalizma* (Belgrade: Kommunist, 1978), pp. 122–5.

15. See Todo Kurtovic, *Crkva i religija u socilalistickom samoupravemon drustvu* (Belgrade: Ras, 1978), p. 64.

16. Cynthia H. Enloe, *Ethnic Conflict and Political Development* (Boston, MA: Little, Brown and Company, 1973).

17. Japan, Iceland and, until recently, Germany are exceptions to the general incongruence between the state and nation that is characteristic of the majority of nation-states.

18. For an extended analysis that asserts that nations precede states see Anthony D. Smith, *The Ethnic Origins of Nations* (Oxford: Blackwell, 1986).

19. See, for example, Edvard Kardelj, *Razvoj slovenackog naciolnalnog pitanja*, 2nd edn (Beograd: Kultura, 1958), p. 50; Pedro-Sabrina Ramet, *Nationalism and Federalism in Yugoslavia* (Bloomington, IN: Indiana University Press, 1984); and Alex N. Dragnich, *The First Yugoslavia: Search for a Viable Political System* (Stanford, CA: Hoover Institution Press, 1983).

20. See Samuel P. Huntington, 'The Clash of Civilizations?', *Foreign Affairs*, 72, 3 (Summer 1993), pp. 22–49.

21. See V.P. Gagnon, Jr, 'Serbia's Road to War', in Larry Diamond and Marc F. Plattner (eds), *Nationalism, Ethnic Conflict, and Democracy* (Baltimore, MD: The Johns Hopkins University Press, 1994).

22. See Steven Majstorovic, 'Ancient Hatreds or Elite Manipulation? Memory and Politics in the Former Yugoslavia', *World Affairs*, 159 (Spring 1997), pp. 169–70.

23. Throughout this paper I use the terms ethnic, ethnonational, nation, ethnicity, ethnonationalism and nationalism interchangeably, since all of the warring parties in the former Yugoslavia

have been politicized and mobilized towards the goal of creating nation-states; the difference between an ethnic group and a nation is a matter of semantics. See Walker Connor, 'A Nation is a Nation is a State, is an Ethnic Group, is a', *Ethnic and Racial Studies*, 1 (1978), pp. 377–400.

24. For an indepth discussion of these categories of ethnic analysis in the context of the former Yugoslavia see Steven Majstorovic, 'Ancient Hatreds or Elite Manipulation: Memory and Politics in the Former Yugoslavia', *World Affairs*, 159, 4 (Spring 1997).

25. Thomas L. Friedman, 'Nations at War With Themselves', *New York Times* (2 June 1991), p. E3.

26. Describing ethnicity as an independent variable does not imply a simplistic causal assumption. It is clear that no sociopolitical variables are completely independent or dependent. It is argued here, however, that the force of politicized ethnicity is powerful enough to shape political outcomes in a manner that is largely independent of class structures.

27. For a representative survey of Walker Connor's perspectives on ethnicity see Walker Connor, 'Ethnonationalism'; Walker Connor, 'Eco- or Ethno-Nationalism', *Ethnic and Racial Studies*, 7 (1984), pp. 342–59; Walker Connor, 'A Nation is a Nation is a State'; Walker Connor, 'Nation-Building or Nation-Destroying?', *World Politics*, 24 (1972), pp. 319–55.

28. Connor, 'Ethnonationalism', pp. 204–5.

29. Ibid., p. 206.

30. See Salo Wittmayer Baron, *Modern Nationalism and Religion* (New York: Meridian Books, 1960).

31. See Barbara Hargrove, *The Sociology of Religion* (Arlington Heights, IL: AHM Publishing, 1979), p. 4.

32. See Pedro Ramet, 'The Interplay of Religious Policy and Nationalities Policy in Soviet and East European Politics', in Pedro Ramet (ed.), *Religion and Nationalism in Soviet and Eastern European Politics* (Durham, NC: Duke University Press, 1989), p. 5.

33. Ramet, 'Interplay of Religious Policy', p. 6.

34. See Constantine A. Chekrezi, *Albania, Past and Present* (New York: Macmillan, 1914), pp. 221–3.

35. I spent approximately two weeks in Kosovo during the summer of 1990. It is not an overstatement to suggest that ethnic hostility almost physically permeated the social atmosphere.

36. See Ramet, 'Interplay of Religious Policy, pp. 3–41.

37. See Sabrina P. Ramet, 'Whose Democracy?', *Nationalism, Religion, and the Doctrine of Collective Rights in Post-1989 Eastern Europe* (London: Rowman & Littlefield, 1997).

38. In Serbo-Croatian the word 'yug' means south. Thus, Yugoslavia was the land of the Southern Slavs.

39. See, for example, Ivo Banac, *The National Question in Yugoslavia: Origins, History, Politics* (Ithaca, NY: Cornell University Press, 1984); and Alex N. Dragnich and Slavko Todorovich, *The Saga of Kosovo* (New York: Columbia University Press, 1984).

40. Radovan Mihaljcic, *Kraj Srpskog Carstva* (Beograd: Beogradski Izdavacko-Graficki Zavod, 1989).

41. June 28 (15 June in the Eastern Orthodox calendar) is a critical day in Serbian mythology. This day, called Vidovdan for St Vitus day, commemorates the Battle of Kosovo, the assassination of Austrian Archduke Ferdinand by a Bosnian Serb (Gavrilo Princip) in 1914, and the date of the first Yugoslav Constitution in 1921. Along with Christmas, Easter and the Serbian family saint day (Slava), it is considered the holiest of days.

42. See Konstantin Mihailovic, 'Janicarove uspomene ili Turska bronika', in Djorje Zivanovic (ed.), *Ostrovice* (Belgrade: Srpska Patrijarsija, 1966), pp. 105–7.

43. See Nicholas C.J. Pappas and Lee Brigance Pappas, 'The Ottoman View of the Battle for Kosovo', in Wayne S. Vucinich and Thomas A. Emmert (eds), *Kosovo: Legacy of a Medieval Battle* (Minneapolis, MN: University of Minnesota Press, 1991), pp. 41–60.

44. See Dragnich and Todorovich, *The Saga of Kosovo*.

45. When Serbian soldiers returned to the Field of Blackbirds in the winter of 1912, they crept over the field barefoot so as not to disturb the fallen warriors from the 1389 battle. Certainly, an instance where historical memory seemed to reach mythic dimensions.

46. Thomas Emmert, 'The Battle of Kosovo: Early Reports of Victory and Defeat', in Vucinich and Emmert (eds), *Kosovo*.

47. See Vuk Stefanovic Karadzic, *Narodna srpska pjesnarica* (Vienna, 1815) and *Narodne srpske pjeme*, II (Leipzig, 1823). While doing research in the former Yugoslavia I happened to be in

Belgrade during the summer of 1990. The history, myth, and present circumstances of Serbs in Kosovo were discussed in endless forums. It was clear at the time that Yugoslavia was on a downward spiral that might lead to war.

48. Alex N. Dragnich, *Serbs and Croats* (New York: Harcourt, Brace and Company, 1992).
49. Michael Lees, *The Rape of Serbia* (New York: Harcourt, Brace, Jovanovich, 1992); David Martin, *The Web of Disinformation: Churchill's Yugoslav Blunder* (New York: Harcourt, Brace, Jovanovich, 1990); and David Owen, *Balkan Odyssey* (New York: Harcourt Brace and Company, 1995), p. 9. Owen notes that Serbian resistance leader Draza Mihailovich was exonerated of collaboration charges levelled at him by Tito in a 1946 show trial after which Mihailovich was executed despite protests throughout the world. An American investigation during the Truman administration completely exonerated Mihailovich and he was posthumously awarded the Legion of Merit in 1948, America's highest honour for a foreigner. The award notes Mihailovich's substantial contributions to the allied cause and the rescue of over 500 American pilots by the Mihailovich forces.
50. Bosnian Muslims who sided with the Ustasha formed their own Nazi Handjar Division in World War II. See Alfred Lipson, 'The Overlooked Holocaust: Sephardim in Europe', *Midstream*, October (1993). The Handjar division was revived by the Bosnian government during the recent war, which only reinforced exaggerated Serbian claims of an Islamic invasion. See Robert Fox, 'Albanians and Afghans Fight For the Heirs of Bosnia's SS Past', *Daily Telegraph*, 29 December 1993.
51. See Mark Aarons and John Loftus, *Unholy Trinity: The Vatican, The Nazis, and Soviet Intelligence* (New York: St Martin's Press, 1991).
52. For harsh criticism of the Serbs and the Serbian Orthodox Church see Michael A. Sells, *The Bridge Betrayed: Religion and Genocide in Bosnia* (Berkeley, CA: University of California Press, 1996).
53. See Anthony Knezevic, *A Short History of the Croatian Nation* (Philadelphia, PA: Croatian Catholic Union, 1983).
54. See Eric Hobsbawm, *Nations and Nationalism Since 1780: Programme, Myth, Reality* (London: Cambridge University Press, 1993), pp. 76–7. Hobsbawm claims that although Serbs can make the claim for an unbroken history of national consciousness since medieval times, Croatian consciousness can only be traced to the nineteenth century and chides Ivo Banac for his 'Failure to allow for this adequately [which] makes [an] otherwise excellent discussion less than persuasive on the Croatian aspect', footnote 53, p. 76. Hobsbawm then goes on to suggest that 'mass Croatian consciousness appears to have developed only after the establishment of Yugoslavia, and against the new kingdom, or more precisely the alleged Serb predominance within it', p. 135. Hobsbawm's critique, however, is only applicable from the perspective of the development of modern nationalism. The historical record is clear that Croatian ethnic consciousness certainly predates the nineteenth century.
55. Branka Prpa-Jovanovic, 'The Making of Yugoslavia (1830–1945)', in Jasminka Udovicki and James Ridgeway (eds), *Yugoslavia's Ethnic Nightmare* (New York: Lawrence Hill Books, 1995).
56. See Ramet, 'Religion and Nationalism in Yugoslavia', in Ramet (ed.), *Religion and Nationalism in Soviet and Eastern European Politics*, p. 306.
57. See Dennison I. Rusinow, 'Crisis in Croatia Part I', and 'Crisis in Croatia Part II', *American Universities Field Staff: Southeast Europe Series*, Vol. 19, pp. 4–20 (Part I), pp. 1–17 (Part II); and Ramet, *Nationalism and Federalism*, pp. 104–43.
58. See Richard West, *Tito: And The Rise and Fall of Yugoslavia* (New York: Carrol and Graf, 1994), pp. 300–1.
59. Ramet, *Nationalism and Federalism*, p. 156.
60. Ibid., p. 146. During my research in Yugoslavia in 1990, I encountered quite a few Bosnian Muslims, particularly professionals and political elites, who claimed that they were ethnically Turks and not at all descended from Slavs.
61. See Robert J. Donia and John V.A. Fine, Jr, *Bosnia and Hercegovina: A Tradition Betrayed* (London: Hurst and Company, 1994); Francine Friedman, *The Bosnian Muslims: Denial of a Nation* (Boulder, CO: Westview Press, 1996); Noel Malcom, *Bosnia: A Short History* (New York: New York University Press, 1994); and Mark Pinson (ed.), *The Muslims of Bosnia-Herzegovina* (Cambridge, MA: Harvard University Press, 1993).
62. Although non-native Balkan scholars tend to be less biased than are native scholars, it is often the case that researchers tend to drift toward a Serb, a Croat, or a Muslim perspective. The works

cited above (note 61) are all somewhat Muslimcentric although Donia and Fine are by far the least biased.

63. Donia and Fine, *Bosnia and Hercegovina*, pp. 75–135; Friedman, *The Bosnian Muslims*, pp. 57–116.
64. See Donia and Fine, *Bosnia and Hercegovina*, pp. 13–75.
65. Ibid., p. 78.
66. Ibid., pp. 78–119; Pinson, *The Muslims of Bosnia*, pp. 61–80.
67. See Alija Izetbegovic, *Islamic Declaration,* 2nd edn (Sarajevo: Mala Muslimanska Biblioteka, 1990). In his book Izetbegovic scathingly attacks Kemal Atatürk's secular reforms in Turkey in the early part of the twentieth century and holds up Pakistan as a societal model to be followed. Izetbegovic's party has also come under criticism for its repression of political opposition. See Mike O'Connor, 'The Opposition In Bosnia Faces Terror Tactics', *New York Times*, 17 August 1996. See also Diane Johnstone, 'Izetbegovic: Islamic Hero of the West', *Covert Action Quarterly*, 66 (Winter 1999), pp. 58–61.
68. Susan Woodward, *Balkan Tragedy* (Washington, DC: Brookings Institution, 1995), p. 196.
69. National Public Radio report on 1 July 1994.
70. See Chris Hedges, 'Bosnians Sending Soldiers to Iran for Infantry Training', *The New York Times*, 3 March 1996; Laurent Rebours, 'NATO Seizes Bosnia Terrorist Training Site', *The Associated Press*, 17 February 1996; Kit B. Roane, 'NATO Accuses Sarajevo of Link to Terror Training', *New York Times*, 17 February 1996; and John Pomfret, 'Bosnian Officials Involved in Arms Trade Tied to Radical States', *Washington Post*, 22 September 1996.
71. See Tom Walker, 'U.S. Alarmed as Mujahedeen Join Kosovo Rebels', *The Times* (UK), 26 November 1998; and Chris Stephen, 'US Tackles Islamic Militancy in Kosovo', *The Scotsman*, 30 November 1998.
72. See Chris Hedges, 'Croatian War-Shrine Revives Pain', *New York Times*, 19 May 1996.
73. Richard Boudreaux, 'Pope Beatifies WWII Croat Nationalist', *Los Angeles Times* (4 October 1998); and Alessandra Stanley, 'Pope Beatifies a Croat, Fanning Enmities', *New York Times*, 4 October 1998.
74. These differences in Croatia are often generational and were described to me by Father Frano Doljanin, a Franciscan priest from Split, Croatia, during our work together at the Duquesne University Centre for Conflict Resolution and Peace Studies, spring 1998.
75. David Holley, 'Croatia in Turmoil Over Tribunal Cooperation', *Los Angeles Times*, 9 July 2001.
76. See David Rhode interviewed by Charlene Hunter-Gault on the *PBS News Hour With Jim Lehrer*, 17 November 1995. Rhode, who won a Pulitzer Prize for his Srebrenica investigation, remarked that the Muslims used the safe haven of Srebrenica to launch attacks against Serb villages that resulted in over 2,500 Serb civilian deaths. The Muslim leader responsible for these acts, Nasir Oric, has recently been indicted by the Hague. Of course, Rhode did mention that despite Muslim atrocities around Srebrenica, the massive Serb response had no justification. To further complicate matters, the Bosnian parliamentary member for Srebrenica, Ibran Mustafic, accused the Bosnian government of ordering attacks against Serbs within the UN safe area so any Serb response would lead the Muslims 'into a catastrophe'. See Dario Sito Sucic, 'Bosnian Government, Srebrenica Survivors Divided Over Fall of Town', *OMRI Reports*, Prague, 15 July 1996.
77. See Michael Dobbs, 'Serbian Orthodox Church Criticizes Milosevic Regime', *Washington Post*, 3 January 1997.
78. See Patrick Moore, 'No Room in the Chateau for Artemije', *RFE/RFL Daily Report*, 11 February 1999; and Jane Perlez, 'Serb Monk in Ancient Church Is a Thorn in Milosevic's Side', *New York Times*, 12 October 1998.
79. Milivoj Popovic, 'Kako ce mo mi napred u Kosovo?', *Sprska Borba*, 21 July 1995, p. 6.
80. Dario Sito Sucic, 'Bomb Damages Catholic Church in Sarajevo', *OMRI*, 5 March 1997.
81. Dario Sito Sucic, 'Tear Gas Thrown During Orthodox Christmas Service in Sarajevo', *OMRI*, 8 January 1997.
82. Dario Sito Sucic, 'Serb Mob Attack Muslim Homes, Russian Troops Watch', *OMRI*, 4 March 1997.
83. Vaso Stankovic, 'Opet', *Dnevni Avaz,* 18 July 2001.
84. See Robert L. Hardgrave, *India: Government and Politics in a Developing Nation* (New York: Harcourt, Brace, Jovanovich, 1993), p. 182.
85. Paul Watson, 'Christian Sites Being Decimated in Kosovo', *Los Angeles Times*, 22 September 1999.

86. Ian Fisher, 'Cease-Fire in Macedonia Stops the Guns but Not the Distrust', *New York Times*, 7 July 2001.
87. Ian Fisher, 'U.S. Troops Escort Rebels, Setting Off Riot in Macedonia', *New York Times*, 26 June 2001.
88. Patrick Moore, 'Macedonian Orthodox Church Demands Military Solution', *Radio Free Europe/Radio Liberty Daily Report*, 6 June 2001.
89. Paul Watson, 'Bosnia Goes to Polls 3rd Time Since War', *Los Angeles Times*, 12 November 2000.

11

Religion, Politics and Democracy in Turkey

JOSEPH S. SZYLIOWICZ[1]

INTRODUCTION

Although debates over the relationship between the secular and the sacred have a long history, the topic has gained widespread saliency in recent years, not least owing to the worldwide growth of fundamentalism, especially in the Islamic world. It is obvious that Islam plays an important political role in many Islamic countries. In some, such as Iran, Afghanistan and Sudan, Islamic radicals control the state, in others such as Egypt they represent important opposition elements; in Algeria, they are engaged in a violent struggle for power; in almost every other state with large Muslim populations, Islam has been resurgent as evidenced by debates over the role and interpretation of law and the position of women in the social order.

Turkey has not been immune from these developments even though it differs from other Muslim states because it possesses both a secular and a multi-party system. Atatürk, the founder of the Turkish Republic, was determined to create a modern, Western state and to that end he enacted his well-known reforms – the hat law, the language reform and the substitution of the Arabic alphabet and Islamic law codes and calendar by Western ones. He paid special attention to education, creating a single, unified, secular school system on the same day that the Caliphate was abolished (3 March 1924).

Since then, Turkey has continued to change. It has urbanized rapidly, grown economically at a relatively rapid rate, and established – and maintained – a multi-party system, albeit one in which the military is an influential actor. Thus, one would expect on the basis of what were, until recently, accepted theoretical perspectives on the relationship between modernization and religion, that Turkey today would be, not only nominally but in reality, a wholly secular state.

Yet this is not the case. Turkey has not been immune from the spread of Islamic values and attitudes. It has witnessed a powerful Islamic 'revival' as indicated by a marked upsurge in the number of religious publications of all kinds, in the number of new mosques, in the number of people making the Haj and fasting during Ramadan, and in the number of İmam-Hatip (Prayer Leader and Preacher) schools. Furthermore, beginning in the 1970s an Islamic party succeeded in becoming a member of both left- and right-wing coalition governments, captured the mayorships of Istanbul, Ankara and many other major cities, and formed a coalition government in 1995 with its head, Necmettin Erbakan, serving as Prime Minister. This government fell in 1997 as a result of great pressure from the military that subsequently forced the closure of the Welfare Party, imprisoning many of its leaders and, in January 1998, banning Mr Erbakan and five other leaders from politics for five years. The Virtue Party was promptly formed to contest the 1999 general elections.

The results surprised everyone. The interim Prime Minister, Bülent Ecevit, led his left of centre party, the DSP, to victory with 22 per cent of the vote but the Islamic party saw its percentage of the vote drop from 21 per cent to 15 per cent. The big winner, however, was the ultra nationalist National Action Party (MHP), which emerged as the second largest party, doubling its percentage of the vote to 18 per cent. The big losers were the centre-right parties, the DYP and ANAP, which fell to 12 per cent and 13 per cent respectively. These results did not allay the concerns of the secularist forces, and subsequently the Constitutional court closed the Virtue Party.

Many Turks are pleased with the recent developments for they remain greatly apprehensive about what they perceive to be a religious threat to the future of democracy in their country and support the military's actions. Indeed, the military continues to rank high in public opinion. A few surmise that Turkey could still become another Iran or Algeria and even believe that the Algerian Ambassador to Ankara was correct when he commented that he was watching a rerun of a movie that he had already seen at home. Others, however, view the future differently, arguing that in a democracy there is room for a religious party and that election results demonstrate that democratic institutions and secular values are sufficiently entrenched to ensure their future, particularly if the country continues to develop. Which of these perspectives is correct?

Turkey is an important regional power with a key strategic location. Its character and policies have important implications for developments in the Middle East, Central Asia and Europe. All these developments were followed closely not only within Turkey but in the United States, Europe and other countries as well, for Turkey, with its key strategic location, is an important geostrategic actor. The end of the Cold War and the disintegration of the Soviet Union have enhanced its importance for it possesses historic cultural ties to Central Asia. Thus, it can be a force for stability and a model for a unique Islamic pattern of secular, democratic development. Its troubled relationship with the European Union, which it aspires to join, further enhances its importance as well as the significance of religious and other developments within the state including human rights, civil–military relations and the nature of civil society.

Such issues are not only relevant for policy makers but can help clarify the relationship between Islam and democracy. Have the Islamists suffered only a temporary decline? Or, are there countervailing forces that place limits on the Islamic resurgence? Does the closing of the Virtue Party violate fundamental democratic principles? Can the military continue to block the spread of Islamic political activity without endangering the emergence of a civil society and the continuation of democratic processes?

Answering questions such as these, however, is a complicated task, for each involves concepts and variables that require elaboration and discussion. Accordingly, before turning to a consideration of the Turkish scene, it is necessary to specify more precisely the general context as well as the concepts and variables that will be used in the analysis.

ISLAM AND DEMOCRACY: THEORETICAL ISSUES AND PERSPECTIVES

This topic has generated considerable discussion in recent years but the debate often has been marked by prejudice and stereotypes, which it unfortunately is necessary to address. First, although the term 'Islamic Fundamentalism' commonly is encountered, it possesses Christian roots and carries considerable emotional baggage that makes it offensive to many Muslims. Accordingly, I shall use 'Islamist' to refer to those persons and groups who advocate a greater role for Islamic values and principles in the polity; that is, those who ideologize Islam.

Second, it unfortunately is necessary to emphasize that Islam, as a religion, is no more a threat to democracy, development, international peace and stability than Judaism or Christianity. Certainly many Islamists severely criticize the West and what they consider its corruptions and some engage in violent action to advance their cause but this does not mean that all Islamists are potential terrorists. Jewish and Christian religious fanatics who resort to violence also can be identified – as the massacre in Hebron and the shooting of doctors performing abortions in the United States tragically demonstrate. Nor does it mean that a 'clash of civilizations' is under way or that many devout Muslims do not believe in democracy.

For many, however, Islam is more than a faith, it is also an ideology that advocates a specific form of government, one based upon Islamic principles. Hence, it is important to differentiate between those who regard Islam as a faith by which to live and those who wish to gain control of the state in order to enforce its principles upon the populace. It is particularly with Islamists who are ideologically oriented that many scholars have raised questions about the compatibility of Islam and democracy.[2]

They argue that such factors as the lack of distinction between the secular and the sacred and the subservience of the polity to God make it difficult if not impossible to have a democratic Islamic state. Hence, no moderate Islamic ideology (one that accepts the principles of pluralism and liberalism) can emerge.

If a group believes that it is an agent of God's will, it is morally obliged to enforce their view of what constitutes a virtuous society and polity. Since that view is based on a 'true faith', then issues involving the rights of minorities, who will be allowed to participate and freedom of the press and of association will inevitably arise. Moreover, it will be unwilling to relinquish power because if it does so God's design will be frustrated.

Those who hold this view acknowledge that Islamist leaders make frequent assertions of their commitment to democratic principles and in many countries, including Turkey, they are active participants in the political process. They argue, however, that the Islamists use language and rhetoric to disarm their opponents, that their words are tailored to specific audiences. They believe that the Islamists are determined to achieve political power to establish an Islamic state but, once in power, they will no longer abide by democratic rules and principles.

Other scholars, however, criticize this view on two general grounds.[3] First, they point out that such arguments overlook or at least minimize the many differences that characterize the movements encompassed within the Islamist category. These range from the FIS in Algeria to Hezbollah in Lebanon to Hamas in the West Bank and Gaza to the Islamic Action Front in Jordan to the Hezb-i Islami in Afghanistan and to the Muslim Brotherhood in Egypt and elsewhere to the regimes in Saudi Arabia and the Sudan. Among these, one can identify important variations in structures, goals and strategies and in their orientations towards democracy.

Second, even if a particular group of Islamists who are hostile to democracy gain control of the state, political realities will temper the Islamists' policies. In the modern world, effective governance has become the major determinant of legitimacy and any Islamist government will have to meet the practical expectations of the society if they are to remain in power. Accordingly, they will have to temper their orientation and reach accommodations with other powerful forces in society including the military and the business community, unless they have the ability to impose a harsh authoritarian regime and are willing to sacrifice economic growth, as has occurred in Afghanistan and the Sudan. On the other hand, the Iranian case seems to demonstrate the validity of this argument.

Such differences highlight the importance of conceptual distinctions and the need to examine the assumptions that underlie these perspectives. History does matter and one must consider how it has shaped ideology and its relationship with political behaviour and between the state and its elites and the civil society, the character of the political culture and the role of education therein, and the nature of democracy.

Democracy is obviously the place to begin because it is subject to multiple interpretations and applications, although in the West there is a tendency to overlook the degree to which it remains controversial and contested. Still, there is general agreement that a democratic system must incorporate at least three elements: genuine competition for political power, widespread participation in leadership selection, and the existence of the necessary associated freedoms.[4] However, the actual practice of democracy often differs from these criteria. The rights of minorities are often ignored and the level of public involvement and control is often minimal.

This situation, which is often the norm, has led many scholars to make distinctions among democracies. Often they are divided into those that approxi-mate the above norms – 'institutionalized' or 'strong' democracies and 'delegative' or 'thin' democracies with personalized leadership and little public impact on major decisions. Whether a democracy is 'strong' or 'thin' is determined by several factors – the nature of the state and of the civil society, the political culture, the role of the military and the character of the democratic transition.[5] In considering the Turkish case, we shall keep this fundamental distinction in mind.

States can also be categorized in various ways. One of the most common is whether they are 'strong' or 'weak' in terms of their relation to the civil society. A widespread consensus exists in the scholarly literature that Turkey inherited a strong state tradition from the Ottoman Empire. Essentially a patrimonial state, the Sultan and/or the ruling elites were not constrained (as in the West) by powerful aristocrats or an economically rooted middle class. They possessed the autonomy to define and pursue policies that they believed to be in the state's interest. That tradition profoundly influenced political developments after the creation of the Republic. Atatürk and his successor, İsmet İnonu, forged a state elite that possessed the power to act much like its Ottoman predecessors.

The nature of the democratic transition fundamentally altered this pattern. The decision by the state elite to democratize after World War II led to the emergence of a political elite with its own culture and perspectives that soon brought it into conflict with the state elite, whose social base shrank steadily until it came to comprise only the military plus some intellectuals and bureaucrats.[6]

This development was influenced by the existing political culture – the attitudes, beliefs and values of elites and the mass towards political activities, structures and processes. Although the concept can and has been abused, it nevertheless, if used sensitively by making appropriate distinctions (such as between state and other elites and the general populace), provides a useful tool for understanding political life in any society.[7] For a democratic system to thrive, the political culture must promote 'civility' – the acceptance of diverse views, the legitimacy of opposition and the peaceful settlement of disputes. In the case of Islam, this variable often has been used to explain what is perceived to be a lack of tolerance towards opposition and pluralism and patterns of authoritarianism.[8]

Political culture not only influences political behaviour, it is also shaped by the actions of political actors and structures, especially the state and its elites and the educational system that socializes individuals into an acceptance of particular beliefs and values. Educational policies were a major consideration of Atatürk and the state elites and the question of how the educational system should deal with Islam has aroused heated debate and controversy. Hence, in the sections that follow, I shall discuss the role of education as well as attitudes regarding Islam and democracy.

The power of the state is clearly related to the strength of the civil society. The concept of civil society has gained great currency in recent years because of its perceived role in democratization, especially in regard to the former communist states of Eastern Europe. However, this too is a concept subject to many interpretations and even debates about its utility generally and for the Middle East specifically.[9] Yet there is widespread agreement on the close and positive link between civil society and democracy. As one scholar has pointed out, 'the existence of civil society is central to democracy'.[10] Accordingly, I shall simply define it as the 'space' between the individual and the state – the area where organizations and groups of all types, representing all classes, freely organize to articulate their interests and claims against the state apparatus. I shall not differentiate, as is sometimes done, between 'economic society', 'political society' and 'civil society'.[11]

The effective functioning of civil society depends on two key factors. First, the state must permit the existence of such a space; though, here again, the reality is that states tend to try to limit it and to control the activities therein. Second, the political culture must be supportive; it must promote 'civility'. As is obvious from the above discussion of the relationship between Islam and democracy, many analysts argue that Muslim states do not share this norm because of such factors as the nature of Islam, the absence of a 'reformation', and the lack of legal recognition for corporate bodies.[12] They also believe that the political culture in Muslim states inhibits the development of a civil society because politics is viewed as a 'zero-sum' game.[13]

Clearly, all the concepts discussed above – democracy, political culture, the state and civil society are intrinsically linked and in the sections that follow, I shall apply them to the Turkish case to determine whether the Turkish experience provides any insights into the validity of the conflicting positions outlined earlier. Specifically, I shall discuss:

1. the relationship between the state and Islam,

2. the character of civil society, and

3. the political culture and the functioning of democratic processes in order to assess the consequences and implications of the Islamic revival.

THE STATE, ISLAM AND POLITICAL PARTIES

Atatürk was determined to establish a Turkish state possessing all the attributes of a European one and a populace that culturally would be Westernized. Accordingly, he moved vigorously through a series of dramatic reforms, and the establishment of a single party (CHP), to build a strong state with committed elites. He also sought to develop educational institutions that would socialize the mass of the populace into values and orientations that were radically different from those taught by traditional Islam. This does not mean, however, that he was anti-Islam, as so many have since charged. He wished to eliminate the Islam of the state, with its official hierarchy and ideology, and to replace it with a modern Islam that was solely a personal faith.[14]

Doing so, however, was no easy matter, for there were two kinds of Islam in Turkey – the Islam of the state and a 'parallel' or unofficial Islam that consisted of religious orders, convents and sects. Both of these, in his view, were reactionary forces but he followed different policies towards each. He moved quickly to eliminate the latter whereas he adopted a policy in regard to the former that suggested that he wished to create a new, modern, official Islam.

A 'modern' Islam could help further Atatürk's goals in several ways. It could serve as an element of collective identity against enemies, internal and external, an ideological tool to help enhance legitimacy, and a means of decreasing the influence of centres and groups that, operating outside the purview of the state, produced their own religious ideologies.

But it may well be that Atatürk, committed to producing and diffusing his ideology and values, was following a different strategy. Being a pragmatist, he recognized the strong feelings that the overwhelming majority of the population retained for Islam and its opposition to secularization (as evidenced by the Sheikh Said revolt of 1925 and the Menemem incident in 1930) and understood the need to proceed cautiously in this area.

In any event, by the time of his death in 1939, Atatürk had eliminated Islam from public life but the 'parallel' Islam continued to thrive within the society. The state elites (the intellectuals, the bureaucracy and the military) possessed a positivist, secular orientation, but the majority of the population continued to view Islam as they had always done, as the centre of their lives, as a source of self-identity and as a code of conduct.[15]

Atatürk's successor, İsmet İnonu, decided, after World War II, that the time had come to establish a multi-party system. This decision, it must be stressed, was not the result of the growing power of civil society; rather, it was a function of the new international environment and the ideological commitment of the state elites. It also involved a miscalculation of the ability of opposition parties to organize.[16] Thus democracy, in a real sense, was imposed by the state elites upon the society.

The most important of the new parties, the Democrat Party (DP), realizing how greatly the mass of the society resented the secularization policies that had been followed until now, began to emphasize the issue. For the next two years the press, parties and Parliament debated whether there should be greater religious freedom, including religious instruction in the schools.

Though the DP was defeated at the polls in 1946, the debate over religion continued. Those in favour of religious education argued that such courses would help build morality and serve as a bulwark against a very real threat – the Soviet Union and its ideology. Those opposed contended that it was essential to protect Atatürk's principles. Prime Minister Recep Peker argued that using Islam against communism is like using one deadly poison to cure another. Nevertheless, the majority of the CHP leaders concluded that, in light of the real threat that the DP posed to the CHP government in the forthcoming elections, the time had come to confront the social realities. Since religious feelings remained strong, especially in the countryside where a large number of unofficial schools were teaching obscurantist ideas, it was decided, in 1949, that the state should establish programmes for religious education.

This move did not help the Republican People's Party (CHP), founded by Atatürk, and its defeat in 1950 changed the situation dramatically, for the new DP government was willing to make significant religious concessions. Its policies fell into two categories. The first were designed to lessen the controls that Atatürk had placed over religion – the call to prayer could once again be chanted in Arabic, religious sermons could be broadcast, and mosque construction and repairs were supported. The second involved education, where religious instruction once again became part of the curricula in schools of various kinds.

These measures were widely criticized, especially since many sects that had been forced underground began to come out into the open, the most notorious being the Ticani which publicized its opinion of Atatürk by destroying his statues. The DP's willingness to accede to demands for greater official recognition of Islam in order to retain popular support, especially after 1954 when its popularity suffered owing to economic difficulties, generated criticism as well as debates in Turkey and abroad, of whether a religious revival was under way. Its concessions, however, were never designed to destroy secularism and it prosecuted Ticanis and others who exceeded certain limits.

The importance of these policies lay not only in their substance – a dual system of education was being recreated that would have a negative impact on modernization [17] – but because PM Menderes was creating a new political reality – the political elite began to differentiate itself from the state elites and enter into conflict with them. Increasingly alienated by his populist approach to governance and the absence of coherent economic policies, the state elites, who retained a veto power, felt that the wellbeing of the state was in jeopardy. [18]

The result was a military coup in 1960 that tried to purge the political system of its former political leadership and enacted a new constitution. Democratic processes were restored soon after, but the military's efforts produced little fundamental change. The parties continued to be based on patronage and had little concern for rational policy-making. All governments, especially those led by the Justice Party (AP), the successor to the DP, essentially followed the same policies and viewed themselves as furthering democracy and the state elites as obstructionists. This attitude led to growing and ongoing tension between the state and the political leadership that fed upon itself. These feelings were further exacerbated by the politicians' efforts to gain control of the state apparatus by politicizing the bureaucracy. [19] The result was another crisis in 1971 that the military (which regarded itself as the guardian of the state) resolved through a 'coup by communiqué', and the establishment of a new technocratic government.

In regard to religion, all governments recognized the popular appeal of Islam and generally did not interpret laicism rigidly. In essence a kind of moderate consensus emerged about the relationship between the state and religion, that secularism did not mean hostility to religion and was compatible with Islam as long as the latter was restricted to the moral dimension and did not intrude into political and legal matters.

This consensus was shaken in the 1970s as Islamic forces expanded and also became active in politics. The 1970s were a period of weak coalition governments that proved unable to control a growing anarchy. Essentially the patterns of the 1950s and 1960s re-emerged regarding the organization and orientations of the political parties. This environment proved highly beneficial to those seeking to promote an Islamic ideology and the National Salvation Party (MSP), a new explicitly Islamic party, began to thrive.[20] Although a small minority party, it often held the balance of power between the two main parties, the JP and the CHP and was able to extract a high price for its participation in first, a left of centre government (thus gaining considerable legitimacy) and subsequently a conservative one. Thus, the decade was marked by a 'dramatic escalation of the role of Islam in the state ... (that) definitely represented something new'.[21]

For this and other reasons, the polity became increasingly polarized. A new, violence-prone, right-wing party, the nationalist, secular National Action Party (MHP), founded by Alparslan Turkeş, one of the leaders of the 1960 revolution, engaged in violent struggles with leftists for control of universities and other institutions. As the political situation became ever more marked by assassinations and violent clashes, the military finally intervened once again in 1980.

This time it enacted a major restructuring of the Turkish political scene. As part of this effort it prepared a new constitution which was formally approved by a national referendum in 1982. The document reaffirmed the principles of freedom of conscience and religion but it also stipulates that courses in 'religious culture and morality' would be compulsory in primary and secondary schools (Article 24).

At first glance there seems to be a glaring contradiction between ideology and practice, since this decision was taken by a military regime committed to preserving and strengthening the Atatürk principles, especially that of laicism. A closer examination, however, suggests that this was not the case, that it reflected a continuation of policy whereby the state tried to control Islam and harness it to its own goals. The control dimension is evident in the charge that heretofore all the parties had exploited religion for political purposes, the attempt to suppress various illegal brotherhoods and certain religious publications, its choice of the phrase 'religious culture and morality', and the placing of the Ministry of Education in charge of all religious education, which it promptly expanded.

The underlying motive for the military's actions was essentially the same as that which had influenced previous regimes – the state needed an accommodation with the religious forces and the military wished to enhance the regime's legitimacy. Islam could serve as an integrative force and as a source of morality and ethical behaviour that would insulate the populace, especially the youth, against alien ideologies (now including Khomeinism) and prevent a recurrence of the anarchy of the 1970s, strengthen official Islam against the teachings of the sects, and assist the state in its efforts to find allies and markets in the Middle East.[22]

When the military decided to restore democratic processes in 1983, the political scene was transformed as a new centre-right party founded by Turgut Özal, the Motherland Party (ANAP), won a large victory and re-election in 1987. Özal represented a new type of political leader. He was committed to the free market and to rational economic policy-making, to a non-ideological approach to politics, to an efficient and effective bureaucracy, and to meaningful party platforms. Above all he hoped to unite disparate elements through a 'Turk–Islam synthesis' and his party incorporated liberals, conservatives, nationalists and Islamists who eventually came to constitute two conflicting groups, one headed by Mesut Yilmaz, the secular nationalists, the other the 'nationalist-Islamic'.[23] During his tenure, Turkish foreign policy continued to incline towards the Islamic world, and Islamic banks were introduced for the first time.[24]

Özal's vision, however, could not be maintained, especially when former politicians were permitted to resume their activities and the veteran politician Suleyman Demirel was able to build the True Path Party (DYP), essentially a continuation of the AP (itself the former DP), which he had headed, into a powerful political force that successfully challenged Mr Özal's ANAP for power. Hence, Mr Özal felt compelled to abandon fiscal rigor, stoking the flames of inflation, which led to his defeat in 1991. Former patterns of patronage and clientelism were also restored, reaching a peak in the mid 1990s. When Mr Demirel gained the Presidency in 1993, Mesut Yilmaz emerged as leader of the DYP.[25]

The party that identified itself exclusively with Islam, the Welfare Party (RP), the successor to Necmettin Erbakan's National Salvation Party that had been banned in 1980, contested its first election in 1984, winning 4.4 per cent of the vote. Its share rose to 7.1 per cent in 1987, 9.8 per cent in 1989, 17 per cent in the general election of October 1991, 19 per cent in the municipal election of March 1994, which gained it the mayorships of Istanbul, Ankara and 26 other cities and 21 per cent (the largest share) in the 1996 election. The two centre-right parties, ANAP and the DYP won 20 per cent and 19 per cent of the vote respectively (as compared to 24 per cent and 27 per cent in 1991) and the two centre-left parties, the DSP and the CHP, 15 per cent and 11 per cent (11 per cent and 21 per cent in 1991).[26]

The two centre-right parties proved unable to agree on a lasting formula because of personal rivalries between the two leaders. Then ANAP, headed by Tansu Çiller, who had served as Prime Minister between 1993 and 1995, and who was facing indictment on corruption charges, entered into a coalition with the RP (thus gaining immunity from prosecution), and the RP's leader, Necmettin Erbakan, became the first Islamic Prime Minister in the country's history. Ironically, Çiller had portrayed herself as a strict secularist and had successfully lobbied the European Parliament in December 1996 to implement a customs union in order to strengthen the secularist forces in the country.[27]

The RP moved vigorously to enact its economic and social programme, labelled the 'Just Order'. The RP had committed itself to an anti-monopoly, non-interest-based economy with a tax on production rather than income. This programme was denounced by the business community and by economists for its detachment from the realities of Turkey's economic situation. Most important, the military (which more than ever viewed itself as the protector of the state) began to fear that the RP (or at least important elements within it) was pursuing policies that would enable it to establish an Islamic state at some point in time and it took measures to block such an outcome.[28] I shall return to the role of the military in Turkish politics below.

Here, however, it is necessary to note that its role in the campaign to bring the government down was initiated on several fronts. In the legislature, motions of censure were tabled and efforts made to encourage defections from Çiller's DYP. Eight thousand women demonstrated (February 1997) to protest the government's policies. And the military made its displeasure increasingly obvious. In February, the National Security Council decided to increase compulsory education from five to eight years, a step that was opposed by the RP because of its implications for the İmam-Hatip schools that enrolled students at the middle-school level. It also urged the government to fire extremists and to ban radical TV religious programmes. Mr Erbakan procrastinated. On 28 April 1997, the National Security Council urged Mr Erbakan to abandon policies that promoted the Islamization of Turkish society, especially in the educational sector. It demanded action on its educational programme. When these suggestions were ignored, the military increased its pressure and in June, the General Staff held a number of meetings with judges and prosecutors, academics, labour, business and Turkish and foreign journalists in which it accused the government of 'crimes against the constitution' and declared a boycott of 1,000 Islamic businesses. Finally, Mr Erbakan agreed to resign in favour of his coalition partner, Ms Çiller, hoping that early elections would return him to power with a larger vote. President Demirel, however, in accordance with precedent, chose to ask Mr Yilmaz, the leader of ANAP (the second largest party with 129 seats as compared to 116 for Ms Çiller's DYP), to form a new government. Because of defections, particularly from Ms Çiller's DYP, Mr Yilmaz was able to obtain a vote of confidence.[29] The government lasted until 25 November 1998; an interim government was formed with Mr Bülent Ecevit, the leader of the left of centre DSP, as its head and new elections were scheduled for 18 April 1999. As noted earlier, the outcome was a major surprise, witnessing the decline of the Islamic party and the rise of the chauvinistic MHP.

This historical overview serves to highlight the degree to which the state and its political elites have shaped the role of Islam. It is clearly erroneous to view the state and its elites or the political leadership as hostile to Islam or the state's response as concessions to a growing power that forced itself upon the state. On the contrary, despite a commitment to secularist principles, the state and all political parties sought to use it for their own purposes. Ironically, by doing so they encouraged developments that they later came to regret, for they spurred the growth of Islamic activities of which they disapproved.

One can, however, make an important distinction between the single and multi-party eras. Until the emergence of the multi-party system, the state elites sought to control Islamic forces and to keep them out of public life. With the introduction of democratic processes, this changed so that while the principle of control was maintained, various kinds of Islamic involvement in politics were permitted. One scholar has aptly described this situation as follows:

> Without changing its basic secularist stance, the Turkish state adopted a double discourse: on the one hand, establishing rigid segregation between Islam and the public political realm; on the other, accommodating and incorporating Islamic politics into the system in various ways.[30]

Hence, every government – left-wing, right-wing, military and civilian – has been confronted with pressures to make concessions in the religious area and all did so, albeit for different reasons.

CIVIL SOCIETY AND ISLAM

To understand this accommodation between the state, the political parties and the Islamists, it is necessary to consider the nature of the civil society and the changes that it underwent in this period. Three dimensions are especially noteworthy:

1. the nature of the political parties,
2. the basis of Islam's appeal and its organizational implications, including the structure and character of the religious groups, and
3. the emergence of new economic relationships and groups after 1980.

As noted earlier, Turkey could best be characterized as a strong state that dominates the civil society. Even though new groups emerged as the society modernized, these were essentially coopted by the state and its elites. Nor did the coming of democracy change this pattern, though now it was the political parties organized around patronage that continued to limit the space available for new organizations to gain autonomy and function as independent actors.

All parties share certain characteristics. They are essentially leader-dominated organizations committed to obtaining patronage and are structured along patron–client lines with loyalty an important value. The goal is to secure political office and to use it as a base from which to reward one's followers. They 'tend not to follow the usual pattern of representing long-established interest groups with clearly defined constituencies and local organizations'.[31] Hence, party programmes have little significance, rational policy-making is subordinated to personal needs, and electoral politics revolve around leaders and personalities. The successful politician tends to be rich, well connected, persuasive, a skilled bargainer and focused on his or her own advancement with little concern for policy; ministers are chosen on the basis of loyalty and the strength of their client networks and are dominated by the Prime Minister.[32] This situation has not changed fundamentally over time, so that the political dynamics and the relationship between state and society have remained remarkably stable even though Turkish society has been transformed over the years. Hence, Turkey clearly fits the model of 'thin' democracy discussed earlier.

Turkey has achieved a high level of industrialization and its rates of population increase and of urbanization are extremely high. In less than 30 years, for example, the population of Istanbul climbed from 600,000 to over 6 million. A good part of this migration is housed in large shanty towns that are now decades old and are to be found on the outskirts of every major city. Nor can one ignore the large migration of Turks to Western Europe where they constitute sizable minorities in several countries, notably Germany. And improved communication and transportation permitted traditional preachers and teachers to extend their influence greatly. These developments began under Atatürk but accelerated significantly after World War II, and especially in the 1970s and after.

These changes did not transform state–society relations but, rather than enhancing secularism as theory predicted, strengthened the power of religious orders, sects and brotherhoods and of informal Islam generally. This phenomenon might have been anticipated if theorists had been more sensitive to the importance of traditional relationships and especially the functions that Islam has always served in the periphery.

One such function, traditionally met by religion, is to provide a moral code. However, the development model followed since the days of Atatürk did not produce results that were consonant with Islamic expectations for it has led to a widening of the elite-mass gap and to economic difficulties. The failure to promote 'social justice' led to widespread disillusionment that caused people to turn to Islam.[33] Disenchantment with Western models and institutions have helped spur the Islamic revival in many countries.

Islam's other functions, especially as performed through sects, were also important factors. Having traditionally provided their members, in return for veneration of the leader and acceptance of his teachings, with a wide range of tangible rewards ranging from education to welfare, as well as less tangible benefits such as a sense of meaning and purpose, the religious groups were uniquely positioned to meet the need for such services as physical and psychic dislocations became widespread. Islamic tendencies grew not only in scope, as the periphery was increasingly penetrated, but geographically as well, because the improvements in transportation and communication facilitated their ability to reach new audiences which were to be found in urban as well as rural areas since the cities now included large numbers of 'urban peasants', migrants from rural areas and small towns. And the demand for support and solace from religious groups expanded still further as a wave of Turks migrated to Europe, where they faced not only similar problems to their countrymen in Istanbul or Ankara but also the added difficulty of having to function in an alien culture.[34]

New transportation and communication channels have furthered the internationalization of these groups in other ways as well. The Iranian revolution and the activities of the Muslim Brothers have resonated among Turks. More concretely, links have been established to such states as Saudi Arabia, Iran and Kuwait; these have supplemented, to a significant degree, the resources that various groups receive from their members and have sponsored some of their activities.[35]

The growth of education also fuelled the rise of 'parallel' Islam. The new schools provided a new channel of mobility and generated widespread new expectations and aspirations that often could not be satisfied. Despite the explosive expansion of the regular schools, many rural inhabitants did not possess the necessary economic or psychic resources to acquire an advanced modern education. Furthermore, many recognized the importance of acquiring new skills and knowledge but wished to do so within an Islamic context. Hence, the 'secondary elite' in the provinces (whose members were often affiliated with and supported by various sects) promoted and financed the growth of the İmam-Hatip schools.[36]

They did so by forming associations that raised the funds for the construction and equipment of the schools. Overall, it has been estimated that these associations contribute 87 per cent of these costs, the state only 13 per cent; this figure is somewhat misleading, however, because the teachers and administrators are all on the state's payroll and if such support were withdrawn, the system would not be viable.[37] Nor are their activities limited to these schools, many religious associations are also reaching out to the students enrolled in the regular schools by sponsoring dormitories and kitchens. These organizations have had an explosive growth; by the late 1960s, their number had grown from 1,500 in 1950 to more than 10,000 and has increased many-fold since then.[38] As a result, two ever-growing groups of students from traditional backgrounds acquired a modern education. Some did so in the regular schools, many more through the İmam-Hatip schools that, by the end of the 1980s, had graduated over 150,000 students.[39]

Given the popularity of these schools and the political power of the pious Turks who supported them, no party was willing to oppose their rapid expansion, with important consequences for the growth of fundamentalism, for these graduates have had a profound impact upon intellectual and political life in

Turkey and provide a rich pool for the Islamic movements. Many have gone on to become activists in one form or another, as writers, publishers, editors and teachers, while many more constitute the audience for the numerous books and journals, supporters of the foundations and members of sects and organizations. Overall, there are over 50 journals and newspapers with a circulation estimated at a million. Total readership is obviously much higher.[40] And the Islamists have their own TV channels.

The growth in Islamic activities during these years can be seen in the following data: in 1979, the state published two million copies of 30 religious works; in 1982, 5.7 million copies of 53 such works. The number of students in Quranic schools more than doubled from about 70,000 in 1980 to over 155,000 in 1989. The number of mosques increased from about 55,000 in 1984 to about 65,000 five years later and the number of persons making the pilgrimage increased nine-fold in a decade, from about 11,000 in 1979 to 92,000 in 1988.[41]

These schools also contributed to the emergence of a new intellectual elite, the 'Muslim Intellectuals'.[42] Familiar with Western literature and scholarship, they handle Western concepts and ideas in their works that bring an Islamic perspective to bear upon contemporary ideological and cultural issues. They are a heterogeneous group with many different viewpoints who do have, however, one common bond, 'the Muslim intellectual is sensitive to any attempt to justify Islamic principles from a Western perspective. This, he argues, was the basic mistake of Islamist thinkers of the late nineteenth and early twentieth centuries.'[43] Furthermore, such well-known figures as Ali Bulac, Rasim Özdenören and İsmet Özel share another characteristic – they wish to establish an Islamic order but 'their worldviews can hardly be reconciled with that of an Islamic state'.[44]

These personages have greatly influenced the flow of ideas and concepts in Turkey, for their views are widely disseminated even by the secular media. They frequently are interviewed and participate in numerous debates, discussions and programmes. As a result, dialogues over the place and role of Islam in Turkish life have been taking place between individuals and groups who heretofore never interacted, especially in the universities, which now contain large numbers of students who are sympathetic to the arguments being made by the Muslim intellectuals.

Thus a whole range of new religious associations began to emerge which supplemented the existing brotherhoods and sects. Although Islamic sects and groups have prospered greatly in recent years, it is important to stress that they represent many different approaches to Islam and its role in the modern world. There are many sects and groups – the Suleymanci, the Muslim Brothers, the Kardiri, the Nakşibendi, the Nurcu and the Bektaşi – and there are important ideological and other differences among them. Some are democratic, others reactionary, some apolitical, others call for action, some emphasize tradition, others scripture, some have a positive attitude towards Western technology and institutions, others reject both, still others accept selected technologies.[45] More-over, the position of particular groups is not fixed, and important changes can and do occur. The Nurcu, one of the most important of the radical groups and once quite reactionary, for example, now respect science, are open to new ideas and support Republican values.[46]

The basic division, however, is between such 'neo-traditionalist' Islamic groups as the Nakşibendi and the Nurcu, who regard Islam as a faith and are oriented towards promoting Islam and the Islamic way of life in a peaceful and gradual manner and the 'radicals', who politicize Islam and use it as an ideology that calls for organizing the state and all institutions within it along religious lines. In order to do so they attempt to infiltrate the bureaucracy, the armed forces and the security apparatus and are active within the Welfare Party.[47]

These differences are reflected in their political behaviour. The 'neo-traditionalist' groups tend to be apolitical or to support the established parties, especially the DYP and its predecessors and ANAP.[48] And many deputies are members of religious orders. Özal was known to have links to the Nakşibendi.[49] These groups, however, are themselves sometimes fragmented so that each faction supports different political parties. Some Nurcus, for example, have supported Mr Demirel's parties consistently, others, ANAP, still others, the RP.[50]

The economic sphere has also witnessed major changes, for by the late 1970s the economy had reached a crisis point and it had become obvious that major structural reforms were essential. Accordingly, the traditional import substitution strategy that legitimized government intervention at all levels of the economy was abandoned in favour of a more open export orientation. The private sector had accepted this pattern in return for significant economic benefits that were provided by the state.[51]

Now, radical changes began to sweep through the economy as market forces were unleashed, not always with favourable results as the country's recent economic crises demonstrate. This pattern accelerated throughout the 1980s as Mr Turgut Özal, the architect of the new policy, emerged victorious in the 1983 elections and was re-elected in 1987. In terms of the civil society, business now increasingly became an independent and autonomous actor. Concomitantly, the number of voluntary organizations of all sorts increased tremendously. Between 1980 and 1995 in Istanbul alone, their number grew by more than 150 per cent, from 5,101 to 12,424, and there are signs that this growth is accelerating.[52]

Although this is obviously a promising development, the relationship between the state and such organizations continues to be influenced by the strong state tradition. The state and many political leaders remain wary of such organizations and are, at best, uneasy about the emergence of an effective civil society. In March 1997, for example, TUSIAD, the leading business organization, published a report analysing the state of democracy in Turkey and proposing various reforms. These included reorganizing the political parties, abolishing the National Security Council, placing the military under tighter civilian control, repealing laws that restrict public debate and granting language autonomy to the Kurds. Perhaps not surprisingly, these suggestions were promptly denounced by the political elites and the military.[53] The legal profession encountered similar problems,

the relationship turned out to be a struggle of the bar associations aiming to
maximize their power to influence state policies in line with their interests
and values and an effort on the part of the state to maintain its autonomy
and to minimize interference in its affairs.[54]

Given the prevalence of such attitudes, the emergence of an effective civil society
will be no simple matter.

The weaknesses of the state apparatus and the obstacles that inhibit the
emergence of a strong civil society became particularly evident in the aftermath
of the disastrous earthquake that struck the western part of the country in
August 2000. Corruption had permitted poor construction and misappropri-
ation of funds and resources by Red Crescent officials, the civilian and military
responses were poorly planned, uncoordinated and inadequate, and government
officials showed little empathy for the victims. One analyst concluded that 'these
problems plunged the state into a crisis of legitimacy, as the image of an all
powerful, if not all-benevolent, state was shattered'.[55] Of equal significance,
however, was the state's response to the ways in which the civil society responded
to the disaster. Many organizations (and individuals) rushed to assist the victims,
even forming a Civil Coordination Centre. Early hopes that good would come
out of the disaster proved illusory. The organizations ranged from Kemalist to
Islamist, from political to apolitical, from state affiliated to opponents. As a
result, the early cooperation soon evaporated into rivalry and conflict. This
outcome was facilitated by the state's actions that moved to limit and hinder the
activities of various groups (especially the Islamic ones) through various haras-
sing techniques (in which the military played a part). As a result, the hope that
these groups could unite around a common vision and programme that would
lead to a new kind of civil society proved illusory.[56] Nevertheless, one should
not underestimate the degree to which civil society continues to expand or the
pressures that exist for change. In 1999, for example, the President of TUSIAD,
the leading business organization, reiterated its call for political and economic
reforms.[57]

POLITICAL CULTURE AND ISLAM

Although the changing nature of the political system may have eroded the
dominance of the state somewhat and made it more difficult for the state to
control the civil society and related religious activities, Turkey's institutions are
secular. The state retains responsibility for key sectors, notably education and
law, that were once the purview of the religious establishment and important
sources of its power. And although religious education is now widespread within
the secular schools, the goal continues to be to create and maintain a new
political culture by socializing students into an acceptance of Islam as an integral
part of Atatürk's ideology, on being a good Turkish citizen within a democratic,
secular state.

Socialization occurs both informally through teaching methods and interactions and formally through the curriculum. Although many efforts have been
made to modernize the former, it is generally accepted that traditional authoritarian patterns remain the norm. The impact of such practices upon political
culture remains unclear. Somewhat more data is available concerning the latter
because we possess extensive knowledge of course organization and curricula at
all levels as well as analyses of the textbooks that are used in various courses.

These studies indicate that the texts used for religious instruction have always
stressed secular values.[58] The texts prepared in 1948–49, while the secular
ideology was clearly dominant, surprisingly remained in use until 1983, despite
the great changes that occurred during those decades. In 1956, I examined the
primary school texts and found that they emphasized nationalism and morality.
A good Muslim, for example, was honourable, reliable and respectful of the
rights of others and a loyal citizen. The works used at the higher levels have a
similar orientation; they too teach the basic tenets of the faith and emphasize
individual responsibilities and obligations, especially towards the state, in such
areas as military service and tax paying. Furthermore, Islam is depicted as a
religion that esteems science and technology. The orientation of these works has
been well summarized:

> The objective followed by this education is not so much to form good
> Muslims as to shape, on the basis of a reshaped Islam, good citizens, veritable
> patriots and zealous workers as capable of adapting themselves in their
> private lives as in their social life to the evolution of the modern world.[59]

The orientation of the new works published by the military regime in 1983
(significantly entitled 'Religious Culture and Moral Knowledge') was similar to
that of their predecessors, though they emphasized Atatürk and his ideology far
more explicitly and in greater detail than before. Atatürk is depicted as an
advocate of genuine Islam whose policies are consonant with Islamic teachings.
One middle-school text, for example, stresses, in addition to the usual utilitarian
view, that Islam endorses liberty of conscience and laicism. At the lycée level,
the orientation is similar, although significant attention is devoted to other
religions that are generally depicted as less worthy than Islam.[60] The same
message is promulgated (though according to critics in a heavy-handed and
ineffectual manner) in related courses – the texts used in middle schools for the
history of Turkish revolution and Kemalism and the lycée sociology course, for
example, both stress secularism and Atatürk's acceptance of Islam.[61]

What of the students who study in the religious schools? Some have argued
that there too the emphasis is upon socialization into the official ideology.[62]
Others, however, fear that students are socialized into conservative Islamic
attitudes. Unfortunately, it is difficult to draw specific conclusions because little
research has been carried out in this area, though some data on student
backgrounds and their attitudes are available. Although as many as 75 per cent
may be of rural origin,[63] most students do not come, as one might expect, from

the least developed parts of the country. Nor do they come from the most developed provinces where the large cities are located. Rather, they come from areas that have been modernizing rapidly. They tend to be the sons of farmers, merchants and craftsmen and chose to enrol in these schools because they and their parents approved of the mix of religious and modern subjects. Less is known about their values and orientations. Though they do not appear to be reactionaries, they do hold conservative views concerning women and family relationships (only 8 per cent believed that women can travel alone, 25 per cent that they should be educated). Their favourite courses included, besides Arabic and the Koran, mathematics, physics and literature. Islamic law, Islamic theology, biology and philosophy all were disliked. They did tend, however, to view the world in terms of oppositions.[64]

It is also worth noting that only a small percentage enter the religious professions for which they were trained; an overwhelming majority seek to continue their education, primarily in non-religious areas. Only 10 per cent select a religious faculty, 43 per cent seek admission to law, public administration or international studies, 15 per cent such fields as medicine and engineering. In short, their graduates seek to enter every academic sector and many succeed in gaining admission to the faculty of their choice.[65] The consequences of this development are not clear. They may not be Islamic revolutionaries, but many fear that they are infiltrating the state in order to change its cultural basis to reflect more adequately Islamic values and concerns.[66]

The military certainly shared this view, for one of its key demands, as noted above, involved the reorganization of these schools so that they would admit only older students. Hence, educational issues were largely responsible for the crisis, for Mr Erbakan refused to bow to demands that the religious school system be modified so that students could enrol in these schools only after they had been socialized in nationalist values through middle school. This, and other educational reforms, such as requiring five years of schooling rather than two for enrolment in Koran courses, were subsequently enacted by Mr Yilmaz's government, despite Islamist opposition.[67]

The military's faith in education is justified by the available data which shows that the schools and other socializing institutions have effectively promoted a strong commitment to nationalist values. As early as the 1960s, 50 per cent of a textile factory workforce identified themselves as 'Turks', 38 per cent as 'Muslims'; a rural survey also found nationalism to rank higher than religion. Three decades later, in 1994, 70 per cent identified themselves as 'Turks', 21 per cent as 'Muslim Turks', 4 per cent as 'Muslims'. In 1969, a study of migrant workers showed only a weak relationship between religiosity and theocracy. About 20 years later, only 7 per cent of the respondents in a national survey wished to see an Islamic state based on Islamic law.[68] Such values as popular rule and the tolerance of opposition and minorities, and the multi-party system and its institutions are all widely accepted.

Recent surveys corroborate these findings. One concluded that Turks are religious (fasting and praying) but they are also tolerant of other beliefs and deeply committed to secularism. For example, 75 per cent thought that, in direct contrast to the official position, women should be allowed to wear Muslim headscarves even in government offices but 66 per cent were not offended by miniskirts and almost 80 per cent approved of Atatürk's republican principles.[69] Such data are strengthened by a poll of young Turks that concluded that there was a pronounced discrepancy between religious values and religious faith and practices. This finding strongly suggested that religion occupied 'a specific place within the framework of a secularized world view'.[70] Indeed, it has been argued that young people (and women), especially in urban areas, are a major social force that will block the continuing growth of the Islamists. Nor can one overlook the influential Shiite (Alevi) minority, about 20 per cent of the population.[71]

Anthropological studies in small communities also suggest that republican values have been widely disseminated and accepted. Islam and politics generally are viewed as being part of one ideology – a fundamentalist nationalism. Or, at the very least, republican values coexist uneasily with Islamic moral teachings.[72] Hence, though each may be represented by different elites and have its own rituals, important accommodations have been achieved between them.[73]

In short, there seems to be considerable evidence of a commitment to democracy and to the secular state. Politics and religion are regarded as constituting more or less separate spheres and secular considerations should prevail when selecting someone for high office. Overall, the role of Islam in Turkish political life has been aptly described thus: 'Religion in Turkey appears to be an underlying dimension of membership in the political community, it has a moderate role in political ideology, and finally, it is a source of values which affect political goal-setting and behavior in society.' However, those values (e.g. equality, authoritarianism) cannot be identified with certainty.[74]

ISLAMISTS, THE MILITARY AND POLITICS

How can one reconcile such findings with the appeal of the Islamic party? To answer this question it is appropriate to consider the structure, composition and appeal of this party in more detail. Earlier, I discussed the reasons for the growing Islamic feelings within Turkey. Such sentiments, however, do not necessarily translate into political support for the Islamists because, as I have emphasized, there are numerous religious groups with varying orientations that have traditionally supported other parties such as ANAP and the DYP.

The appeal of the party can be attributed to several factors. First, it is a very well organized and well-financed party that has waged effective campaigns. It carefully tracks voters, provides transportation and takes care of all the administrative details necessary for electoral success. Second, it has been able to mobilize the numerous Islamic organizations that have emerged in recent years (business, labour, youth, women and media) in order to help disseminate its message. Third, that message emphasizes its moderation, its integrity and honesty. These themes resonated well with an electorate that was greatly discontented with the functioning of the political system and its corruption and the performance of the other parties, their divisions and weaknesses. Fourth, disillusionment with the West has grown over its policies in such areas as Bosnia, Kosovo and rejecting Azerbaijan, the withholding of military equipment by the United States and, especially, with the Europeans for their reluctance to accept Turkey as a member of the European Union. The Islamist media has feasted on such events that impact most upon the disadvantaged.[75] Fifth, economic conditions have deteriorated and there is a growing disparity between rich and poor. The party has focused its attention on those who have not benefited from the rapid changes that have swept and continue to sweep through Turkish society. Finally, it has also won widespread support in the Kurdish areas as a protest against the other parties' support of military policies and because it seems to offer the hope of reconciliation through Islam. The appeal of political Islam, in other words, is based, as would be expected from the above discussion of the political culture, largely on instrumental rather than ideological considerations.

The available empirical evidence supports this view. A 1994 survey revealed that only one-third of its vote was religiously motivated.[76] Another analysis suggested that 40 per cent of the vote was based on religious issues and 60 per cent represented a protest vote. Furthermore, half of the 40 per cent were identified as moderates, thus classifying only 20 per cent of its support from radical Muslims. This was extrapolated to mean that perhaps 5 per cent of the population could be considered as militants.[77] Further buttressing such findings are the result of a study of party preferences that concluded that '75 per cent of the Turkish voters have moderate ideological tendencies' and that this tendency has remained constant over time.[78] The results of the 1999 election which saw such a dramatic switch away from the Islamists towards nationalism suggests, however, that pragmatism may lead not to moderation but to chauvinism, though it must be noted that the MHP sought to distance itself from its violent past and to portray itself as a moderate conservative party.

The Islamists have always sought to present a moderate image but there are many different elements within their ranks – Islamic radicals, moderates and even practical businessmen – and there is no consensus on policy although one can point to many radical statements. The Mayor of Istanbul, for example, stated that he would not attempt to impose Islamic dress codes upon women or segregate urban transport.[79] Similarly, the Mayor of Kayseri described the 'Just Order' which deplored the 'order of slavery' imposed by 'Zionism and western imperialism' and called for 'disinfectants' to destroy the 'microbes' of capitalism as 'sheer nonsense'. Moreover, moderate elements made concessions to the militants in many ways.[80] But, when in power, Mr Erbakan toned down his anti-Western, anti-Israel and anti-NATO stance and did not implement various policies that he had previously advocated, accepting, for example, close defence ties with Israel. Hence, analysts differed in their views of the balance of power between the 'young Islamic progressives' and the radical elements. Some argued that moderation was a mask to gain power, still others that the conflict between the moderate and radical elements within its ranks could end either with a split or with the radicals gaining control.[81]

The military drew its own conclusions as to a likely outcome and, as noted earlier, took strong action to weaken the Islamists. It had been concerned about the threat to the Kemalist ideology for some time. As early as 1986, General Kenan Evren, the President, expressed concern about reactionary tendencies in higher education and it soon became clear that the military was following developments closely, although it did not openly express its concern until the Welfare Party's victory in the 1994 municipal elections and, following the party's victory in the 1995 general election, initiated a more active stance that culminated in the decision in early 1997 to demonstrate that it was willing to use force to limit the spread of fundamentalism. It thus achieved its goal of removing Mr Erbakan from office without intervening militarily.[82]

Subsequently it continued to work behind the scenes to weaken the Islamists and their appeal, using the legal system to do so. The public prosecutor sought to ban the party on the grounds of extremism. He cited speeches made by Mr Erbakan, over the years, in which he talked of a 'Jihad' and his refusal to accede to demands made by the National Security Council concerning religious education. The RP leaders denied these charges and argued that a party that is committed to democratic principles and to peaceful change cannot be banned. The Constitutional Court sided with the prosecutor, closing the party, banning Mr Erbakan from politics and sentencing Mr Tayyip Erdoğan, the popular mayor of Istanbul, and a contender for the party leadership, to 10 months in jail.

This was a familiar experience for Mr Erbakan, whose parties had been banned twice before, and a new successor organization, the Virtue Party, was quickly formed. This party, however, suffered from several weaknesses. First, the splits among the Islamists soon led to a leadership struggle and a dispute over policy as Mr Erbakan strove to maintain control from behind the scenes. He fought vigorously to get the party to support a group of deputies who sought to postpone the election because they had not been named to party lists and thus would not be reelected. He did so because, in order to return to open political life, he had to build a coalition to repeal Article 312 of the penal law. Although he eventually prevailed over the 'young Islamists', the struggle weakened the party, making it seem as personality and power driven as the others. They also enabled the military, that made it plain that it wanted the elections to be held as scheduled, to maintain its pressure. The public prosecutor promptly filed charges against the new party on the grounds that it was obviously just the outlawed Welfare Party under a new name.[83] In June 2001, this party too was banned and two of its deputies were expelled from the legislature, although another 100 (the party had 102 out of 580 seats) were permitted to stay in office.[84]

Although the court's decision was handed down well after the election, the legal manoeuvring strengthened a widespread perception that the Islamists were unable to govern effectively. The Party's official leader, Recai Kutan, held little appeal and had a difficult legacy to overcome. Many voters blamed the Islamists for their inept performance when in power since their policies led to an educational reform that limited religious schooling as well as political instability and turmoil.

Only one leader emerged unscathed from the events of recent years – Bülent Ecevit, the interim Prime Minister. Having been out of power for years, he has not been tainted by the scandals that have affected other political leaders. Furthermore, he was remembered for his strong stand on Cyprus, and the capture of the PKK leader, Abdullah Öcalan, enhanced his prestige and popularity. The subsequent terrorist attacks further focused attention on the Kurdish issue and inflamed nationalist feelings. He also possessed a strong base on the left (the rival leftist CHP, led by Deniz Baykal, is quite weak and did poorly in the election).

Accordingly, his victory was no surprise but the election results raise at least two important points that deserve consideration. First, it would be naïve to dismiss the power and appeal of the Islamists. Despite the severe handicaps under which they laboured, they still managed to gain 15 per cent of the vote. Second, the appeal of the MHP can be attributed to a rising nationalism as well as a high degree of disillusionment with the major centrist parties and the functioning of the political system. One can easily view the votes for the VP, MHP and HADEP (a pro-Kurdish party) as signs of alienation with the existing political parties, and if one does so, about 35 per cent of the voters expressed their dissatisfaction with the system. This is obviously not a healthy situation. Furthermore, although the future of the Islamic movement's political activities remain unclear owing to its factionalism, one cannot rule out the possibility that a charismatic leader could emerge to lead a new Islamic resurgence.

Even in the absence of such a development the military continues its hard line against Islam. Fethulla Gülen, the leader of an Islamic brotherhood that operates an extensive network of schools in Turkey, Central Asia and elsewhere, was indicted in 1999 'for planning to establish a theocratic dictatorship' even though Prime Minister Bülent Ecevit, a staunch secularist, has praised him for his charitable works.[85] Eric Rouleau, a former French ambassador to Turkey, explains the military's stance as follows, '[the] pashas … tend to be suspicious of any Muslim activist who is not under state control',[86] and adds to that, 'what exasperates the supporters of the status quo is that (the Islamic party) has made itself the champion of democratizations and human rights, thereby implicitly challenging the political power of the army'.[87]

CONCLUSION

This analysis reveals the extent to which Islam has always been and remains an important element of Turkish identity. But the nature of its role in society has changed dramatically over time as a result of the secularizing reforms of Atatürk and the great changes which have swept over the country since then. Islam has been disestablished though, as has always been the case, and the state continues to control 'official' Islam. Now, however, the challenge is being posed by radical Islamists who have moved from the periphery to the centre.

One reason for the growth of Islam is that the state always sought to control Islam and to use it to promote its agenda, as did all political leaders. But at the same time it was challenged by demands from the periphery, demands that were furthered by newly empowered Islamic groups of all kinds and by a changing international environment. Thus, since 1946, every political party (and the military too), in an effort to utilize Islam to advance specific goals, has been willing to make various concessions. However, important differences in terms of motivation (some have been more driven by short-term electoral considerations or by ideology than others) and scope of policy can be identified.

These concessions did much to promote democratic processes. They permitted the integration of peripheral groups into the polity, led to the dilution of the elite-mass gap, and facilitated the promotion of a democratic secular political culture. At the same time, they created an environment wherein Islamist ideologues could thrive and facilitated efforts to control the growth of civil society.

Turkey's experience is proof that in the modern world secularism does not happen by accident or because of inevitable historical trends. Nor is it an inevitable concomitant of modernization; on the contrary, modernization, because of its strains and dislocations, may well lead people to religion and to assaults on secular values. Secularism is the result of a deliberate political choice, a choice that, if effectively implemented, can lead to the creation of a new political culture which will support a state which espouses such values. And it thrives only if institutions are established that can meet the social, political and economic needs of the populace. If this does not happen, then people will naturally turn to the religious and other organizations that can do so.

For Turkey, the decision to modernize within a secular, democratic framework has yielded precisely this result. On the one hand, it has resulted in the growth of Islamic activities. On the other, barriers have been erected that block the creation of an Islamic state. The Islamist groups have achieved much of their agenda, especially in regard to education and matters of faith, but Turkey today is a complex society upon which it will be difficult to impose an Islamic state that destroys democratic secular values.

There is one fundamental reason for this proposition. Islam can serve as an ideological rallying force only if the state institutions prove ineffective in meeting popular expectations. In the eyes of many, Turkey now stands at a turning point and its leaders confront difficult choices. In the introduction, I identified three major elements that shaped the democratic pattern and the role of Islam therein – the nature of the state, the civil society and the political culture. Further development in each of these, especially the first two, is required, for, as noted above, Islam, like any religion, meets many human needs, needs that become especially acute in times of rapid socioeconomic change. These can be roughly divided into two categories: (1) issues of meaning and morality and (2) issues of economic and social wellbeing. If the appeal of radical Islam is to be stanched or decreased, these needs must be met by the state. This is not to suggest that the state can provide a meaning to life; clearly, that lies in the domain of religion. But the state and its agents can set a moral tone and act in ethical ways. Corruption can be eliminated, social justice promoted, so that the populace will feel that they are living in a state that pursues justice and equity for all its citizens. It also can be a state that is able to devise and implement socioeconomic policies that meet people's expectations. What is required are reforms that will lead to the creation of new patterns of political activity and of a new kind of state, one that is smaller, stronger and imbued with an ideology of service rather than control.[88]

This means that Turkey must confront many difficult issues including widespread corruption, political stagnation, political liberalization, the role of the military and whether it is wiser to continue to try to exclude, isolate and control the Islamists and their organizations or whether a policy of engagement is more compatible with democratic standards. Repression will not eliminate Islamic feelings and tendencies. Nor will it solve ethnic issues; the problem of the Kurds remains to be dealt with even though the PKK has been defeated. And the Cyprus issue requires solution, for the stalemate not only represents a drain on scarce resources but, what is more important, damages one of Turkey's primary foreign policy objectives – European Union membership.

Whether the needed reforms can be implemented is not at all clear though the success of the Islamists has caused much soul searching among the secular elites. Before the financial crises that have gripped the country, one could identify some signs that suggested that at least a beginning was being made. Now, however, the economic situation with its resurgence of inflation, the sharp drop in the value of the currency, and the rise in unemployment does not create the kind of environment that would facilitate attempts to create the kind of state that can accommodate new local and national power centres and nurture the establishment of a dynamic civil society.

Under these circumstances, it is obviously difficult to draw definite conclusions about the future of Islam in Turkey, for the situation remains in flux. It is not premature, however, to suggest that its history provides empirical verification for several important points. First, Islam, including its radical variants, is ever changing, for it responds to changing circumstances. Second, its political role is influenced profoundly by the nature of the state and its institutions; the more solidly established the institutions, the more democratic the political culture, the more legitimate the state, the smaller the risk of violent conflicts involving Islam. In other words, the Turkish experience provides powerful support for those who believe that democracy is the most effective antidote to radical Islam and that Islam and democracy are not incompatible. It is precisely because Turkey has travelled further along the road to democracy than most other Islamic states that it is not likely to undergo dramatic revolutionary change in the future. But, if its democratic future is to be assured, then the secular elites must take the necessary actions to travel still further along that road.

NOTES

1 This chapter is an expanded and updated version of an earlier work published as 'Religion and Democracy: The Turkish Case', in C. Balim-Harding and C. Imber (eds), *The Balance of Truth* (Istanbul: The Isis Press, 2000).
2. Judith Miller, 'The Challenge of Radical Islam', *Foreign Affairs*, Spring (1993), pp. 43–56.
3. Leon T. Hadar, 'What Green Peril?', *Foreign Affairs*, Spring (1993), pp. 27–42.
4. Larry Diamond, 'Beyond Authoritarianism and Totalitarianism', *Washington Quarterly*, Winter (1989), p. 142.
5. Guillermo O'Donnell, 'Delegative Democracy', *Journal of Democracy*, January (1994), pp. 55–69; Richard E. Sclove, *Democracy and Technology* (New York: The Guilford Press, 1995); P. Schmitter and T. Karl, 'What Democracy is ... and is not', *Journal of Democracy*, Summer (1991), pp. 75–88; J. Linz and A. Steppan, *Problems of Democratic Transition and Consolidation* (Baltimore, MD: The Johns Hopkins University Press, 1996).
6. Metin Heper has pioneered the study of the role of the state in Turkey and has in various works utilized this perspective to provide important insights into Turkey's political development. See, for example, his *The State Tradition in Turkey* (Walkington, UK: The Eothen Press, 1985), 'Center and Periphery in the Ottoman Empire', *International Political Science Review*, 1 (1980); and 'State and Society in Turkish Political Experience', in M. Heper and A. Evin (eds), S*tate, Democracy and the Military: Turkey in the 1980's* (Berlin: Walter de Gruyter, 1988), chap. 1.
7. Michael Hudson, 'The Political Culture Applied to Arab Democratization', in R Brynen, B. Korany and P. Noble, *Political Liberalization and Democratization in the Arab World* (Boulder, CO: Lynne Rienner, 1995), specifies the requirements.
8. R. Brynen, B. Korany and P. Noble, 'Introduction: Theoretical Perspectives on Arab Liberalization and Democratization', in *Political Liberalization*, p. 7; see also Michael Hudson, 'The Political Culture Applied to Arab Democratization'.
9. See, for example, John A. Hall (ed.), *Civil Society: Theory, History, Comparison* (Cambridge: Polity Press, 1995); Eva Bellin, 'Civil Society: Effective Tool of Analysis for Middle East Politics?', in *PS: Political Science and Politics*, September (1994), pp. 509–10.
10. A.R. Norton, 'Introduction', in A.R. Norton (ed.), *Civil Society in the Middle East*, vol. 1 (Leiden: E.J. Brill, 1995), p. 8.
11. See L. Laasko, 'Civil Society and the Consolidation of Multi-Partyism', paper presented to the XVIIth World Congress of the International Political Science Association, Seoul, Korea, August 1997, p. 5.
12. A.R. Norton, 'The Future of Civil Society in the Middle East', *Middle East Journal*, 47 (1993), p. 7; see also his 'Introduction', Brynen *et al.*, 'Introduction', pp. 10–11.
13. See also Ernest Gellner, 'Civil Society in Historical Context', *International Social Science Journal*, 129 (1991); John Hall, 'In Search of Civil Society', in John Hall (ed.), *Civil Society: Theory, History, Comparison* (Cambridge: Cambridge University Press, 1995); and Bernard Lewis, 'Islam and Liberal Democracy', *Atlantic Monthly*, February (1993). For a contrary perspective, see Y. Sadowski, 'The New Orientalism and Democracy Debate', *Middle East Report*, 183 (1993).
14. In this and subsequent sections, I draw upon my 'Religious Education and the Future of the Turkish State' (UCLA: Von Grunebaum Center for Near Eastern Studies, Working Paper Series, 1992). See also B. Salmoni, 'Islam in Turkish Pedagogic Attitudes and Education Materials', *The Turkish Studies Association Bulletin*, Fall (2000), pp. 23–62.
15. See Ş. Mardin, *Religion and Social Change* (New York: SUNY Press, 1989) and 'Culture and Religion', in *Towards the Year 2000* (Washington, DC: The Association of American Publishers, 1989); B. Toprak, *Islam and Political Development* (Leiden: Brill, 1981).
16. İlter Turan, 'Stages of Development in the Turkish Republic', in H. Lowry and R. Hattox (eds), *IIIrd Congress on the Social and Economic History of Turkey* (Istanbul: Isis Publishing, 1990);

Ergun Ozbudun, 'Turkey: Crisis, Interruptions, Reequilibrations', in L. Diamond, J. Linz and
S.M. Lipset, *Politics in Developing Countries* (Boulder, CO: Lynne Rienner, 1995).

17. *Din ile İlgili Egitim ve Öğretim Komitesi Raporu* (Ankara: MEB, 1961), cited in T. Alkan, 'The
    National Salvation Party in Turkey', in M. Heper and R. Israeli, *Islam and Politics in the Modern
    Middle East* (New York: St Martin's Press, 1984), pp. 159–60.
18. For a detailed analysis of the nature of the political parties and their relationship to the state,
    see Metin Heper and Fuat Keyman, 'Political Patronage and the State in Turkey', paper
    presented to the XVIIth World Congress of the International Political Science Association,
    Seoul, Korea, 1997.
19. See M. Heper, 'The Strong State and Democracy: The Turkish Case in Comparative and
    Historical Perspective', in S.N. Eisenstadt (ed.), *Democracy and Modernity* (Leiden: E.J. Brill,
    1992).
20. See T. Alkan, 'The National Salvation Party in Turkey', pp. 79–101.
21. David Kushner, 'Turkish Secularists and Islam', *Jerusalem Quarterly*, 49 (1986), pp. 90–1.
22. Ibid.; François Georgeon, 'La politique de l'enseignement en Turquie', *Les Temps Modernes*,
    July/August (1984), pp. 383–5; P. Dumont, 'Les disciples de la lumière: le mouvement Nourdjou
    en Turquie', in O. Carré and P. Dumont (eds), *Radicalismes Islamiques*, vol. 1 (Paris:
    L'Harmattan, 1985), pp. 215–56.
23. J. Salt, 'Nationalism and Muslim Sentiment in Turkey', *Middle Eastern Studies*, January (1995),
    p. 17.
24. Ibid., pp. 18, 20–1.
25. Heper and Keyman, 'Political Patronage', pp. 18 ff.; Andrew Mango, 'Testing Time in Turkey',
    Washington Quarterly, Winter (1997).
26. 'Turkey', *The Economist*, 8 June 1996, p. 5.
27. Alan Makovsky, 'Islamists Take Power in Turkish Coalition', *Policy Watch*, 28 June 1996;
    Mango, 'Testing Time in Turkey'.
28. Heper and Keyman, 'Political Patronage', pp. 24 ff.
29. T. Goltz, 'Double Pyrrhic Victory for Turkey's Military', *Jinn Magazine*, 29 June 1997; Kelly
    Couturier, 'Turkey's Military Gives Ruling Party "Last Warning"', *Washington Post*, 13 June
    1997; Heper and Keyman, 'Political Patronage', pp. 24 ff.
30. U.C. Sakallioglu, 'Parameters and Strategies of Islam–State Interaction in Republican Turkey',
    International Journal of Middle East Studies, 28 (1996), p. 231.
31. *The Economist*, 8 June 1996, p. 6.
32. Heper and Keyman, 'Political Patronage', pp. 11 ff.
33. Mehmet Ozay, *Islamic Identity and Development* (London: Routledge, 1990); Salt, 'Nationalism
    and Muslim Sentiment', p. 25.
34. Ibid., pp. 122–3.
35. R. Cakir, *Ayet ve Slogan* (Istanbul: Metis Yayinlari, 1994); Ozay, *Islamic Identity and
    Development*, p. 123.
36. Mardin, 'Culture and Religion', pp. 163–86.
37. P. Zavier Jacob, *L'Enseignement Religieux dans la Turquie Moderne* (Berlin: Klaus Schwarz,
    1982), 319–20; Faruk Bilici, 'Sociabilité et Expression Politique Islamiste en Turquie', *Revue
    Française de Science Politique*, 43 (1993), p. 49.
38. Ahmet Yücekök, Türkiyede Örgütlenmis Dinin Sosyo – Ekonomik Tabanï (Ankara: Sevinc
    Matbaasi, 1971), p. 133, cited in Dumont, 'L'Islam', p. 353.
39. Zekai Baloglu, *Turkiyede Egitim* (Ankara: Bilmem Matbaasi, 1992), Table 96, p. 136.
40. S. Ayata, 'Traditional Sufi Orders on the Periphery', and A. Gunes-Ayata, 'Pluralism Versus
    Authoritarianism: Political Ideas in Two Islamic Publications', in Richard Tapper (ed.), *Islam
    in Modern Turkey* (London: I.B. Tauris, 1991), pp. 52 and 166.
41. Salt, 'Nationalism and Muslim Sentiment', p. 18.
42. M. Meeker, 'The New Muslim Intellectuals in the Republic of Turkey', in Tapper, *Islam in
    Modern Turkey*, pp. 189–219.
43. Ibid., p. 190. E. Özbudun, 'Antecedents of Kemalist Secularism: Some Thoughts on the Young
    Turk Period', in A. Evin, *Modern Turkey* (Opladen: Leske, 1984), pp. 25–44, provides a useful
    introduction to their ideas.
44. Metin Heper, 'Islam and Democracy', *Middle East Journal*, Winter (1997), p. 41; See also
    Michael Meeker, 'The New Muslim Intellectuals in the Republic of Turkey', in Tapper, *Islam in
    Modern Turkey*, pp. 189–219.

45. A. Saktanber, 'Muslim Identity in Children's Picture-Books', S. Ayata, 'Traditional Sufi Orders on the Periphery', Gunes-Ayata, 'Pluralism Versus Authoritarianism: Political Ideas in Two Islamic Publications', F. Acar, 'Women in the Ideology of Islamic Revivalism in Turkey: Three Islamic Women's Journals', in Tapper (ed.), *Islam in Modern Turkey*; John A. Norton, 'The Bektashi Order of Dervishes', Dumont, 'Les disciples de la lumière', pp. 253–6; see also his 'L'Islam en Turquie, facteur de renouveau?', *Les Temps Modernes*, July/August (1984), pp. 352–6; Sencer Ayata, 'The Rise of Islamic Fundamentalism and Institutional Roots', in A. Eralp, M. Tunay and B. Yesilada, *The Political and Socioeconomic Transformation of Turkey* (Westport, CT: Praeger, 1993), pp. 52–9.
46. See the analyses of Dumont cited above.
47. See Ayata, 'Traditional Sufi Orders', pp. 52–61.
48. Norton, 'Bektashi Order', pp. 81–2; Tapper, *Islam*, p. 11; Dumont, 'Les disciples de la lumière', p. 371; Ayata, Traditional Sufi Orders', p. 224.
49. Salt, 'Nationalism and Muslim Sentiment', p. 19.
50. Ayata, 'Traditional Sufi Orders', p. 55.
51. See my *Politics, Technology, and Development* (London and New York: Macmillan's St Antony's College Series and St Martin's Press, 1991), pp. 208–9; 214 ff.
52. A. Yucekok, I. Turan and M. Alkan, *Civil Societal Organizations in Istanbul* (Istanbul: The Economic and Social History Foundation of Turkey, 1996).
53. S. Kinzer, 'Businesses Pressing a Reluctant Turkey on Democracy Issues', *New York Times*, 23 March 1997.
54. A.A. Ozman, 'Bar Associations in Turkey in the 1980–1991 Period: A Case Study on the Interface Between the State and Civil Societal Groups', *METU Studies in Development*, 23, 54 (1992), p. 557.
55. Paul Kubicek, 'Europe, and Prospects for Political Change in Turkey', *Middle East Review of International Affairs* (MERIA), 5, 2, June (2001), p. 4.
56. Ibid., pp. 5–6.
57. *Financial Times*, 15 June 1999.
58. See J. Szyliowicz, *Education and Modernization in the Middle East* (Ithaca, NY: Cornell University Press, 1973), and *Political Change in Rural Turkey* (The Hague: Mouton and Co., 1962). See also Salmoni, 'Islam in Turkish Pedagogic Attitudes'.
59. Dumont, 'L'Islam', p. 360.
60. Ibid., p. 362; Bilici, 'Sociabilité', p. 54; E. Aslan, 'Ortaögretimdeki Türkiye Cumhuriyeti İnkılap ve Atatürkçülük Ders Kitaplarî', N. Direk, 'Liselerde Sosyoloji', and J. Baysal, 'Din Kültürü ve Ahlak Bilgisi Ders Kitaplari', in S. Ozil and N. Tapan, *Türkiyenin Ders Kitaplarî* (Istanbul: Cem Yayinevi, 1991).
61. Aslan, 'Ortaögretimdeki', pp. 200–2, Direk, 'Liselerde Sosyoloji', p. 234.
62. Dumont, 'L'Islam', p. 363.
63. Jacob, *L'Enseignement*, p. 320.
64. B. Aksit, 'Islamic Education in Turkey', in Tapper, *Islam in Modern Turkey*, pp. 147 ff.
65. Baloglu, *Turkiyede Egitim*, p. 137.
66. Bilici, 'Sociabilité', p. 49; Mardin, 'Culture'.
67. 'Education Minister Explains Implementation of New Law', *BBC Summary of World Broadcasts*, 20 August 1997.
68. Heper, 'Islam', pp. 34–5; see also I. Turan, 'The Evolution of Political Culture in Turkey', in A. Evin, *Modern Turkey* (Opladen, Germany: Leske, 1984), pp. 84–112.
69. 'Political Islam in Turkey', www.turkeyupdate.com/tesev/htm.
70. Social Research Centre, *Turkish Youth*, 98 (Ankara: Konrad Adenauer Foundation, 1999), p, 52.
71. David Shankland, *Islam and Society in Turkey* (Huntington: The Eothen Press, 1999) .
72. David Shankland, 'Alevi and Sunni in rural Anatolia', in P. Stirling (ed.), *Culture and Economy* (Hull: The Eothen Press, 1992), p. 51; the Shiite villagers, on the other hand, are strong supporters of the nationalist ideology, pp. 61–2.
73. R. Tapper and N. Tapper, 'Religion, Education and Continuity in a Provincial Town', in Tapper, *Islam*, pp. 56–83; C. Hann, 'The Nation-state, Religion, and Uncivil Society', *Daedalus*, 71, 126 (1997).
74. I. Turan, 'Religion and Political Culture in Turkey', in Tapper, *Islam*, pp. 47–8, 52.
75. Andrew Mango, 'Testing Time in Turkey'.

76. Heper, 'Islam', p. 35.
77. *The Economist*, 8 June 1996, p. 6.
78. E. Kaylaycioglu, 'Elections and Party Preferences in Turkey', *Comparative Political Studies*, October (1994), p. 422.
79. *The Reuters Library Report*, 2 April 1994.
80. 'Turkey: Faces of Islam', *The Economist*, 17 August 1996.
81. Mango, 'Testing Time in Turkey'; Nadire Mater, 'Fears of Civil Strife After Islamic Victory', Inter Press Service, 7 April 1994; 'Turkey's New Mayors', *The Times*, 4 April 1994; Hugh Pope, 'Victorious Islam', *The Independent*, 3 April 1994; Heper, 'Islam', pp. 35–8.
82. Gareth Jenkins, *Context and Circumstance: The Turkish Military and Politics* (London: International Institute for Strategic Studies, Adelphi Paper #337, 2001) pp. 59 ff.
83. 'Prosecutor Seeks Closure of Virtue Party', *Turkey Update*, 27 March 1999.
84. Douglas Frantz, 'Turkish Court Bans Religious Party', *The New York Times*, 23 June 2001.
85. Eric Rouleau, 'Turkey's Dream of Democracy', *Foreign Affairs*, November/December (2000), p. 108.
86. Ibid.
87. Ibid., pp. 112–13.
88. Ilkay Sunar, 'State, Society, and Democracy in Turkey', paper presented at the conference on 'Turkey and Europe', The Bologna Center of the Johns Hopkins University, 25–6 February 1994, p. 25.

12

Religion and State in Israel:
Another Round of an Ancient Conflict
among the Jews

IRA SHARKANSKY

One of the accomplishments of Zionism was the creation of a nation where Jews could renew ancient arguments about Judaism. While we celebrate Chanukah as a joyous festival of national victory against Greek oppressors, the conflict that gave rise to it was also a civil war between zealous Jews and those Jews who adopted the culture of the ruling Greeks. According to I Maccabees, 2:24–25, the first person killed in the revolt by Mattathias about 167 BCE was a Jew who went to offer sacrifice at a Greek altar. Josephus describes the bloody next chapter in this tale. Then the antagonists were zealous Jews on the one hand, and those who would adopt the culture of the Romans on the other hand.[1] Earlier hints of a similar conflict appear in the Books of Ezra and Nehemiah. They rail against marriages between proper Jews and people of the land whose Jewish character is suspect.[2] It was passages from those books that Rabbi Meir Kahane was likely to quote in his diatribes against the non-Jews of Israel.[3]

Ancient as well as modern Jews have quarrelled about the desirability of religious purity or being cosmopolitan and taking advantage of other cultures. The Books of Jonah and Ruth are cosmopolitan in their perspectives. Jonah describes God's concern even for Nineveh, the capital of the Assyrians. Ruth describes the openness of Judaism to converts, and makes the point that the great grandmother of King David was born a Moabite.[4] The Book of Isaiah expresses both ethnocentric ('Israel will prevail over the nations')[5] and universalistic sentiments ('nation shall not lift up sword against nation, neither shall they learn war any more').[6]

Jewish history has not been continuous. Dispersion and passivity became prominent after the Romans crushed revolts in the first and second centuries CE. The Enlightenment, pogroms, and Zionism of the nineteenth century signify an end to Jewish passivity. The reassembling of a substantial community in the Promised Land seems to have triggered a repeat of ancient antagonisms between the aggressively pious and insular, and the aggressively worldly.

WHY IS THERE CHRONIC CONFLICT AMONG ISRAELI JEWS ABOUT RELIGION IN THE JEWISH STATE?

The nature of Judaism is one of the conditions promoting conflict among Israel's Jews. Judaism is set apart from other major religions by the prominent element of ethnicity. Jewish humanists, agnostics and atheists are no less at home in Israel than the ultra-Orthodox.

A description of Judaic doctrines could begin with the 613 commandments said to be derived mostly from Numbers, Leviticus and Deuteronomy, and developed in the post-biblical Mishnah and Talmud, plus 1,700 years of additional rabbinical commentaries. Religious Jews adhere to these rules when preparing food, choosing their clothes, engaging in economic transactions, performing their prayers, or interacting with a spouse or someone else of the opposite sex. There are likely to be more than 613 combinations of how Jews interpret and observe – or fail to observe – these commandments.

A description of Judaic doctrines might also begin with the sentiments on behalf of freedom, justice, humanism and other universal values in Exodus, the prophets, Psalms, Job and Ecclesiastes.

In sharp contrast to this concern with Judaic doctrines, some commentators assert that there is no Jewish theology. They make the point that the people called Hebrews, then Israelites, then Jews, were not Greeks.[7] By this, they mean that Judaism lacks a primal concern for doctrinal consistency. While this is true, it is only partly true. There were ancient animosities between Greeks and Jews, as well as a seeming lack of concern with doctrinal consistency in the Hebrew Bible,[8] but there was also strong empathy for Greek culture among Jews who 'Hellenized'. Commentators concede some lasting impacts of Greek thought even on documents with Jewish religious significance. Ecclesiastes found its way into the Hebrew Bible with its theme of relativism and its scepticism with respect to faith and justice. It is read in synagogues annually during the festival of Succot.[9]

The ethnic element in Judaism, as well as the lack of Jewish preoccupation with doctrinal niceties, allows the argument that Judaism is what Jews do! Even though there may be only 14 million or so Jews in the world (still below the 17 million prior to the Holocaust), this is enough to array a great variety of doctrines, rituals, legends and customs.

Our primary concerns in this chapter are the Jews and Judaisms in Israel. We leave to others to explicate disputes involving the country's Christian and Muslim minorities. The Jews comprise some 79 per cent of the population, and it is religious disputes among them that are allowed to play themselves out through stages of demand, protest, low-level violence and treatment by political and religious leaders. Conflicts between Jews and Muslims or Christians enjoy less freedom to run their course, insofar as leading political and security figures view them as threatening disaster. The word 'crusade' was coined for an earlier conflict between religious communities in the Promised Land, and its implications are not lost on current policy-makers. In order to keep from provoking Muslims, the police have prevented religious Jews from praying where Solomon and later Herod built their Temples, but where the Muslim Dome of the Rock and Al-Aqsa Mosque have dominated for the better part of 1,400 years.

Here it is appropriate to note that Jewish–Muslim conflict associated with a prominently national dispute involving Israelis and Palestinians seized the headlines in Israel and much of the world in 2000, and still has not let up as this article goes to press. As we shall see in an epilogue to this chapter, violent conflict across national and religious lines served at least temporarily to silence the more conventional disputes about religion among the Jews.

We also leave it to others to explore the fascinating issue of how Judaism has developed, and continues to develop, in different national settings.[10] However, it is worth making the point that diversity within Israeli Judaism is not unique. Research into the religious behaviour of American Jews finds considerable variety even within that one national entity. They are less inclined than adherents of other major faiths in the United States to attend religious services regularly, or to express a belief in God. They are also most likely to express political sentiments of racial equality and civil liberties, and to vote for candidates of the Democratic Party. Among American Jews, however, the Orthodox differ from other Jews on all of these traits.[11]

The American Jewish scholar Jacob Neusner claims to identify eight varieties of Judaism, but a reading of his material uncovers a discussion of at least ten varieties: that which preceded the Judaism of the dual Torah, which Neusner dates from the fourth century CE; the Judaism of the dual Torah; Reform; Orthodox; and Conservative Judaisms; Zionism; Jewish socialism; American Judaism; Israeli Judaism; and a Judaism of 'reversion' which advocates a fresh encounter with the Judaism of the dual Torah.[12] (The dual Torah refers to the written Torah, i.e., the first five books of the Bible, and the oral Torah. The oral Torah is the accumulation of rabbinical commentaries on the written Torah and religious law derived from it.) In writing about the Jewish experience in the United States, Neusner confuses his own concepts by asking if it is Jewishness without Judaism. He calls some efforts of American Jews 'grotesque', but concludes nonetheless that they represent the efforts of Jews to survive, that so far have been successful.[13]

As in other faiths, Judaism endures competing claims of legitimacy by various adherents of orthodoxy and reform. It has no central authority that might resolve disputes. Here and there are ultra-Orthodox congregations that declare individuals to be banned, and forbid contact with them. However, there is now little difference between Judaism and other major faiths with respect to their modern tendency to overlook heresy or blasphemy. Jews who would curse the Lord or violate his commandments do so at the risk of being ignored.

Also contributing to religious dispute in Israel is the multiplicity of national experiences. Most Israeli Jews are no more than three generations in the country. They, their parents or grandparents came from more than 100 countries. Major immigrations came from Eastern Europe, the Balkans, Germany, North Africa, Yemen, Iraq, Iran and a dozen or so sub-regions of what had been the Soviet Union. The diversity crosses the cultural divide between east and west. It includes Slavic faces and blond hair alongside the facial structures and shades of Yemen, India and Ethiopia. The immigrants brought – and their children preserve – differences in ritual and tradition, as well as conflicting sentiments as to the proper role of religion in a modern state.

Within Israel, a substantial ultra-Orthodox community (perhaps 10 per cent of Israel's Jews and 25 per cent of those in Jerusalem) present their own multiplicity of ethnicity (German, Hungarian, Polish, Moroccan) with a preference to isolate themselves from other Jews and from modern education. One anthropologist (himself religious but not ultra-Orthodox) observed a group of ultra-Orthodox 12-year-olds who were highly trained in the exegesis of religious texts. When he asked them to draw a map of Israel, none of the group knew what he meant by a map. None could name Israel's neighbours. One thought that the Philistines were still a problem. When asked to indicate how long it takes to travel from Beer-Sheva to Jerusalem (83 kilometres), several said that the biblical Abraham had done it in three days, and since he had the Lord's help, it must take longer now.[14] One of my own relatives tells what happened while riding a bus in Jerusalem. When the hourly news broadcast reported something about Libya, an ultra-Orthodox man sitting alongside of him asked, 'What is Libya?' 'A country in Africa', was the response. The next question was, 'What is Africa?' A study of ultra-Orthodox women carries the title, *Educated and Ignorant*. It emphasizes the paradoxical contrast between a community that provides its members with intensive schooling and is organized to exclude outside influences or individual initiative.[15]

The nature of the Israeli polity makes its own contribution to the chronic nature of religious dispute. Divisions among the Jews have created a situation where no political party has ever won a parliamentary majority. Part of the explanation for multifaceted political conflict is the vexatious nature of the country's problems. And part is the lack of a strong governing majority that can dictate to a minority. Every government since the founding of the state has been a coalition between parties that seek to advance their own interests and frustrate others, even while they formally govern together. Religious parties have never had as much as 25 per cent of Knesset (Parliament) seats. They have done well in advancing some of their causes and holding back anti-religious efforts. As we shall see, the secular parties have also done well in keeping at bay the prospect of a religious state.

THE AGENDA OF DISPUTE

Points of chronic contention among the Jews of Israel include which aspects of religious law should be enforced by state authorities, and which bodies should have the final say in determining the nature of religious law or its application to individual cases. This cluster of disputes includes prohibitions of work, public entertainment, and transportation on the Sabbath and religious holidays, the availability of non-kosher food, laws governing abortions, autopsies, burials, marriage and divorce, who should be considered a Jew, and who should be given the designation and authority of 'rabbi' to perform marriages, divorces and conversions to Judaism.

From time to time Orthodox or ultra-Orthodox Jews have sought to change the Law of Return, which grants rights to Jews to immigrate to Israel, but does not require a religious definition of who is Jewish (born of a Jewish mother, or converted according to acceptable procedures). The law has provided rights to Jews converted by non-Orthodox rabbis, as well as to non-Jewish spouses, children and other relatives of Jews. The issue reappeared in 1999 when ultra-Orthodox activists claimed that most immigrants from the former Soviet Union were not Jews and posed a threat to the Jewish state.

Claims about religious law have stood in the way of creating a constitution for Israel. One religious position is that a central legal document with high status would challenge the importance of the Torah in Jewish law, and provisions that secular Jews would insist in including would conflict with religious laws concerned with the priorities to be given to Jews, to men and to rabbis as judges of the law. To date the Jewish state has stumbled through a continuous procedure of adopting basic laws, or a constitution in stages, which deal with some of these issues while avoiding others.

What should be the rights and privileges of various categories of Jews? Religious and secular Jews, ultra-Orthodox and non-Orthodox communities, as well as the communities of Jews from North Africa, Asia and Ethiopia each feel that they have been treated unfairly by some other group of Jews. What is the significance of the biblical Land of Israel, and how much of that imprecise landscape should be insisted on in negotiations with Palestinians and other Arabs or bargained away for the sake of peace?

In practice, the disputes touched by religion are more extensive. The diversities within Judaism, the mixture of ethnicity, many doctrines and traditions, and the dominance of Israel's polity by Jews provide every public issue with something of a religious element. Political activists add claims about *Jewish values* to their arguments about social policy and public finance; assert the safety of the *Jewish people* and the *Jewish state* when talking about the budgets for the police and the military; and emphasize the sanctity of the *Land of Israel* when demanding more attention to environmental protection.

DISPUTES AMONG THE RELIGIOUS

Religious disputes among Israel's Jews are not only a matter of the religious versus the secular or the anti-religious. There is enough diversity within Judaism to assure chronic tensions among the Orthodox and ultra-Orthodox. Orthodox and ultra-Orthodox movements unite in seeking to advance religious interests against the secular, but also compete with one another. SHAS (an ultra-Orthodox party of Jews mostly of North African and Asian backgrounds known by its Hebrew acronym) and the Orthodox National Religious Party (NRP) held up confirmation of the government of Prime Minister Binyamin Netanyahu over a dispute as to which of them would get to name the first minister of religions after they had agreed to rotate the position between them after two years. (Israel's prime minister and Knesset serve for a maximum of four years.) Each party feared that the first one to hold the position would commit to its own congregations more than their share of budget allocations and personnel appointments.

Orthodox rabbis have issued contrary rulings as to whether it is permitted under Jewish law to move remains from one grave site to another for the purposes of construction. A newspaper account included in its headline, 'Who Is He in the Eyes of the Burial Societies?' The message was that an ultra-Orthodox rabbi's pronouncement in support of moving remains would not convince the ultra-Orthodox rabbis who operate the burial societies.[16] The continuation of this story produced threats of violence between followers of rabbis taking different positions with respect to the movement of graves, wall posters in religious neighbourhoods that referred to a rabbi who would permit moving the graves as a 'whore', and the hiring of security guards by one group of ultra-Orthodox who felt themselves in danger from another group of ultra-Orthodox.[17]

A Knesset member of the Orthodox NRP said of the rabbi who is the head of the ultra-Orthodox political party SHAS:

> What Rabbi Yosef said was narrow-minded, immoral incitement and is distinctly un-Jewish. He should not be seen as a Torah great, no matter how many pages of the Talmud he knows by heart. His words drip with personal hatred and have nothing to do with an ideological disagreement.

In response, SHAS's Rabbi Yosef was hardly modest in condemning the NRP:

> the NRP's religion can be dumped in the garbage can – it and the NRP both. … This party calls itself a bridge? … It's a bridge all right – a bridge straight to hell for teaming up with Labor. They are both bound for hell.[18]

RITUALIZED CONFLICT WITH NEGLIGIBLE RESULTS

Despite the chronic and intense nature of the disputes, the outcomes of political quarrels about religion among Israel's Jews amount to sound and fury with little significance. They are allowed to play themselves out because they only produce great noise and inconvenience. They have not provoked mass violence or threatened the security of the state. A ritualized scenario begins with a charge by religious or anti-religious activists that there has been a violation of the *status quo*. This accepted policy of no change on matters involving religion is designed to limit disputes, but the *status quo* is ambiguous. The policy of *status quo* accepts conditions that were in place in 1948 when the State was created. But it is silent about activities in cities or neighbourhoods created since 1948, and about technologies introduced after 1948.

When a dispute catches hold there is likely to be an escalation in rhetoric, with speakers for both religious and secular interests proclaiming that the other side is anti-Semitic and has provoked the confrontation by threatening the *status quo*. The routines escalate to street demonstrations with overturned trash dumpsters, fights between religious and anti-religious participants with sticks, stones and fists, mounted police trying to minimize the damage and jailing the most extreme demonstrators for a few hours.

An assessment of several issues that have been prominent during recent years reveals chronic conflict about religion, with sporadic outbursts of public demonstrations, occasional victories by both religious and secular activists, but with neither dominant. Characteristically, policy-makers avoid the impossible. They do not aspire to settle general problems once and for all times. They limit their efforts to finding a way out of a particular episode. Thus, they deal with the issue of a particular instance of Sabbath controversy (e.g., a particular shopping centre whose functioning on the Sabbath provokes religious protests) rather than ruling conclusively what activities will be permitted, and what forbidden on the Sabbath. While limited treatment is possible, although often difficult, the larger goal of fulsome treatment would be more threatening to a religious or a secular posture, and would be likely to escalate religious–secular animosity. A later section will describe this strategy as coping rather than problem solving.

1. In the case of the construction of roads and a new stadium that was opposed by religious activists, the outcomes were delay or alteration in the implementation of policy rather than total reversal. Some roads have been closed to traffic on the Sabbath and Jewish holidays, but others have remained open despite the demands of religious leaders.

2. An issue of 'indecent' advertising in bus shelters comes and goes, with a wave of the burning of shelters having offensive posters, and then an agreement between the advertising company and religious representatives as to what constitutes offence.

3. Laws prohibiting the sale of non-kosher food are enacted but generally not enforced.

4. Demands by non-Orthodox rabbis for recognition and funds for their congregations are viewed as challenges to the Orthodox religious establishment. We will see below that the outcomes have been mixed. The *status quo* remains to provide Orthodox rabbis a monopoly of official functions with respect to marriages, divorces and conversions performed in Israel. There has been

an increase in the number of Reform and Conservative synagogues and schools, with financial support from government and quasi-governmental organizations. The state also recognizes several options that Israeli Jews employ in order to evade Orthodox marriage and divorce.

5. Orthodox and ultra-Orthodox demands to change the Law of Return by inserting a halachic (religious law) definition of who is a Jew have failed against the contrary demands of secular Israelis and overseas non-Orthodox Jews, and more recently the large and vocal communities of immigrants from the former Soviet Union and Ethiopia.

6. On the side of clear secular victories is the opening of restaurants, discothèques, and cinemas on the Sabbath. The municipal by-laws which had kept them closed were ruled to be flawed in a 1987 court decision, and religious politiians have not succeeded in enacting a new measure.

7. There has been a continued expansion of ultra-Orthodox neighbourhoods and increased allocations of public resources to schools and other institutions of ultra-Orthodox communities. Secular politicians charge that religious political parties inflate their demands and receive excessive material rewards by virtue of their importance in governing coalitions. Religious politicians insist that they continue to receive less than their fair share of resources, and what they do receive is the result of legitimate politicking. Absolute truth eludes systematic research. Financial allocations for housing and infra-structure in religious neighbourhoods, and support for religious schools and other institutions come from a variety of ministerial and quasi-governmental budgets, under numerous programme headings. Complex bookkeeping discourages a comprehensive and persuasive record of who gets what.[19]

Behind the particular details of individual disputes is a pattern that repeats itself from time to time. After a period of quiet on the religious front, an issue appears and gains momentum. It can be a demand to close a road on the Sabbath, an objection against offensive advertisements, the sale of non-kosher food, or the discovery of ancient graves at a construction site. There is no obvious reason for an issue's catching fire. Similar events had occurred without exciting the religious. Perhaps one or another religious leader feels a need for publicity in order to help with a squabble within the religious parties, or wants leverage to be used in pressuring the government for funds. What follows is likely to be ritualized demonstrations and counter-demonstrations, threats of religious parties to leave the government coalition, and a cumbersome resolution that satisfies neither religious nor secular activists, but quiets the issue until it surfaces again in different circumstances.

The ambiguous standoff between religious and secular Jews is similar to what was observed during a period in the late 1970s and early 1980s. At that time religious parties controlled the balance of power between the Government and the Opposition. Prime Minister Menachem Begin was inclined to add religiosity to the Jewish nationalist programmes of his Likud Bloc. Religious politicians demanded the cessation of abortions and post-mortems, archaeological digs (which they accused of spoiling ancient Jewish graves), as well as Sabbath flights of El Al Israel Airlines. They wanted the further liberalization of the Army's policy of exempting religious women from service, the definition of 'Who is a Jew?' according to religious law and more money for religious institutions.

The religious camp won some victories, but the sum of their importance remains open to doubt. The Army eased its procedures for exempting religious women from military service. It became the responsibility of a military board to demonstrate that a candidate who claimed an exemption was not entitled, whereas the previous arrangement had put the burden on the claimant to convince authorities that she was entitled to an exemption. El Al ended its Sabbath flights but other Israeli airlines expanded theirs. The criteria for allowing abortions in public hospitals were changed to exclude 'social distress', but the Ministry of Health rejected the demand that a representative of the Rabbinate be included on the boards that applied the criteria to individual cases. Applicants for abortion learned to explain their problem as one of 'emotional distress'. The religious parties did not succeed in changing the Law of Return. Then as more recently, the clearest victory of religious parties was in the pragmatic politics of money. They won increased allocations for religious schools and housing in religious neighbourhoods.[20]

Several problems stand in the way of a systematic, quantitative reckoning of who wins individual confrontations dealing with religious issues, or whether religious or anti-religious interests have been dominant in recent Israeli history. Activists who work for some issues claim that their postures are derived from 'Jewish norms', or would benefit the Jewish state, but they are not making claims that are religious, *per se*. After a dispute begins there may be public quarrels between Orthodox or ultra-Orthodox rabbis as to what is an issue of religious importance, and what is the correct view of the religious interest.

Additional problems derive from judging the outcomes of individual confrontations: how to record success if one side has won the enactment of a law, but where the measure is seldom enforced, or implemented in ways that are criticized by those who supported its enactment, and how to reach a general conclusion when the same general problem (e.g., public modesty, Sabbath observance, the availability of non-kosher food) returns time and again, with variations in the character of the demands and subtle nuances in the ways that issue is resolved, or when individual episodes disappear from the public agenda without a resolution. In light of these problems, the weight of argument is that neither side has won. Religious activists have scored some victories, but so have secular Israelis. It is difficult to weigh the closure of a road on the Sabbath against the opening of discothèques, cinemas and restaurants on the Sabbath. The score is tied, more or less.

THE SPECIAL CASE OF NON-ORTHODOX RELIGIOUS JEWS

The categories of Conservative and Reform Judaism describe most of the Jews in North America. Surveys of Israeli Jews tend not to use these terms. Much of the Israeli population may be unfamiliar with them, or perceive in the words a meaning substantially different than what they signify to Americans.[21] One survey of Israeli Jews found 10 per cent of the population within each of the 'ultra-Orthodox' and 'Orthodox' categories, 29 per cent 'traditional', and 51 per cent secular.[22] Israelis who consider themselves 'traditional' are typically from North African or Asian backgrounds. Many of them observe dietary laws and Sabbath, and wear *kipot* (skullcaps), but are not as rigorous about observances as those who consider themselves Orthodox.

Disputes between ultra-Orthodox and Orthodox Israeli Jews on the one hand, and non-Orthodox religious Jews on the other hand, represent a special case. Most non-Orthodox Israeli Jews are secular. Members of non-Orthodox congregations in the country are heavily populated with American immigrants, or are supported financially and politically by co-religionists in the Diaspora. They are largely outsiders in Israel, and their political problems reflect that status.

To be sure, the conflict between Orthodox and non-Orthodox Judaisms has not split the Jewish community into hermetically sealed camps. The ethnic component in Judaism limits the extent to which the Orthodox and ultra-Orthodox can accuse the non-Orthodox of not being Jewish. On particular issues of relevance to Judaic doctrine, the line-up of rabbis in the two camps is not uniform. We have already seen that some Orthodox rabbis are viewed by their nominal colleagues as falling outside the acceptable realm of orthodoxy. While some Orthodox rabbis are intense in their commitment to Jewish control of the biblical Land of Israel, other Orthodox rabbis are willing to relinquish some of the Land of Israel in return for peace, and many ultra-Orthodox rabbis seem more interested in other religious issues. Rabbis affiliated with Conservative, Reform, or smaller progressive movements differ in their concerns for land and peace. Non-Orthodox rabbis also differ among themselves on other issues of religious law and practice. The lack of simple alignments confuses analysis, but it also prevents an all-encompassing *us* versus *them* and thereby moderates tensions between the various religious movements.

Individual disputes can be grouped into clusters concerned with conversion to Judaism, marriage, divorce and burial, the practise of Reform or Conservative rituals at the Western Wall, and the representation of non-Orthodox Jews on local religious councils. In practice, particular cases may straddle two or three of these categories. A conversion that is not accepted by the Orthodox Rabbinate would prevent marriage to a Jew in Israel, or burial in a Jewish cemetery. For some participants, the status of women is a distinct issue of prime importance. It appears prominently in disputes about rights of partners in divorce proceedings, the rituals permitted at the Western Wall, and the representation of non-Orthodox Jews on local religious councils.

We can describe a conflict as being on either of two levels: an individual case or a matter of general principle. The actual dispute is likely to be a discrete case, such as a person demanding to be registered as a Jew by the Ministry of Interior. At the same time, it can be viewed as part of a larger conflict about a principle, such as the right of non-Orthodox rabbis to perform conversions. Individuals seek to resolve their dispute in a particular forum, most often the local office of a government ministry or the courts. Organizations 'adopting' the case wish to arouse public support for the more general campaign, such as the rights of non-Orthodox rabbis to perform conversions or to authorize marriages. Organizations press their demands on behalf of individuals in ministries and the courts, as well as promote legislation by the Knesset. Due to the power of Orthodox and ultra-Orthodox political parties, the Knesset has not proven to be a hospitable forum for changing the *status quo*.

A decision by a ministry or a court about one individual might not transfer to other cases that seem to be of the same type. Administrators hostile to a ruling might begrudgingly apply it to the case at hand, but not to other cases that are similar. As a result of the weakness of non-Orthodox Judaisms in the Knesset and the bureaucracy, it is not easy to summarize where the country stands on the general lines of argument. Individuals win some claims that fit into the categories of demands made by non-Orthodox Judaisms, but the lack of carry-over to general policy requires separate struggles by other claimants.

Conversion

The issue of conversion to Judaism involves the acceptance or not of conversions performed by non-Orthodox rabbis. The issue has increased in temper during recent years and has occupied a prominent place on Israel's public agenda. One occurrence that has increased the importance of conversion is the mass migration, approaching one million people from the former Soviet Union and Ethiopia, since the late 1980s. A substantial number of non-Jewish spouses and other relatives have come with Jewish migrants. Some of them have shown an interest in conversion, either out of conviction or to facilitate their life in Israel, looking ahead perhaps to their needs for marriage, divorce, or burial. A less sudden occurrence, but one that has been building for some time, is the phenomenon of mixed marriages in the Jewish communities of North and South America.

Marriage is a separate issue of conflict between Orthodox and other Jews, and will be discussed below. However, it is associated with the issue of conversion when the non-Jewish partner is willing to become Jewish. Few mixed couples migrate to Israel from North America. However, mixed marriages and non-Orthodox conversions that occur in the Diaspora figure in Israeli disputes. Israeli Orthodox and ultra-Orthodox campaigns against Conservative and Reform Judaism feature stories of rabbis performing a marriage ceremony along with a Christian priest or minister, perhaps in a church, a rabbi performing a Jewish marriage ceremony involving a non-Jewish partner, or a rabbi performing an easy conversion to Judaism for someone wanting to marry a Jew.

The issues of conversion that sets Orthodox and other communities against one another are the extent of study and commitment demanded of a convert. The conventional Orthodox practice is to discourage conversion, and then to demand a long period of study and a convincing commitment to live a religious life as a Jew. The typical Orthodox charge against non-Orthodox rabbis is that they perform superficial conversions, often as a fig-leaf for a mixed marriage that an Orthodox rabbi would not perform in any case.

As in other cases of dispute between Orthodox and non-Orthodox perspectives, an important element in the issue is the collective status of Orthodox and non-Orthodox rabbis. The practices of individual rabbis get lost in the noise. Individual rabbis in both the Conservative and Reform movements claim to discourage potential converts and then perform only serious conversions. There are also visionary Orthodox rabbis who seem motivated by an intense commitment to produce more Jews. One Orthodox rabbi arranged the migration to Israel of Peruvian Indians he perceived to have a special affinity for Judaism.[23]

Hyperbole is the language of this and other disputes between Orthodox and non-Orthodox rabbis. When combined with convoluted proposals and bureaucratic manipulations, it makes one question the spirituality that is expected to co-exist with religion. According to non-Orthodox activists, proposals in the Israeli Knesset to affirm the sole right of Orthodox rabbis to perform conversions within Israel are said to de-legitimize the Judaism practised by the majority of American Jews.[24] Individual members of North American Reform congregations, who should have no doubt about their status as Jews, have expressed their fear that they would not be recognized as Jews in Israel. At one point, a group of eight Conservative and Reform rabbis chained themselves to the entrance of the Interior Ministry office in Jerusalem, 'because our communities are being held hostage'. The police came but did not take action, and the protesters unchained themselves and left after about an hour.[25]

Marriage

Issues associated with marriage are perhaps the most complicated of those setting Orthodox Israelis against the non-Orthodox. There are religious laws of long-standing indicating who can be married to whom. A man's status as a *kohen* (priest) is important here, as well as a woman's status as a divorcee, and either partner's misfortune to be labelled as a bastard or as a non-Jew. A man with the surname of Cohen or someone with another surname who is known to be a *kohen* cannot be married to a divorcee in Israel, and a bastard cannot be married to a Jew. The status of a bastard differs from Christian traditions that designate a bastard as the child of a couple not married to one another. The child of unmarried parents may not be a bastard in Judaism. Jewish law bestows the status of bastard on the child of a couple who *could not* be married to one another by virtue of one or another prohibition of religious law. Men have more freedom than women in this corner of Judaism. The child of a married man and an unmarried woman is not a bastard. But the child of a man and a woman married to someone else is destined for life as a religious outcast, and the child's descendants inherit the stigma. However, there are provisions that provide room for interpretation, and inclinations among rabbinical judges to find a reason for not deciding that a person is a bastard.

Israeli law gives to Orthodox and ultra-Orthodox rabbis a monopoly of control over the marriage of Jews in Israel. There are enough complexities in both religious and secular laws to occupy an army of experts. As in the case of conversion, Israel's secular courts have expanded the rights of Jews who marry outside of the recognized Rabbinate, but administrative officials are not always forthcoming in applying those rulings to similar cases.

Evasions of the religious rules are easy for someone who is not bound by conscience or family pressure to accept Orthodox rituals. Some couples marry within the requirements of the official Rabbinate, but have a ceremony performed by a non-Orthodox rabbi. Individuals who cannot be married in Israel, or who prefer not to bow to Orthodox procedures, can marry overseas, perhaps by mail, and have Israel's Interior Ministry register them as married. And individuals who wish to thumb their noses at the whole business can live together as a couple, taking advantage of Jewish and secular laws that recognize such unions and grant the partners and their children status and rights with respect to support and inheritance. For some purposes, however, the informal arrangement may not provide the couple with the same rights as individuals who are officially married. Certain mortgages, employee privileges and tax concessions may be available only to individuals who are recorded as married in their identity cards.

Non-Orthodox organizations do what they can to keep the marriage issue before the public. When a *kohen* and a divorced woman were refused a marriage licence by the Israeli Rabbinate, the Reform Union of American Hebrew Congregations arranged their ceremony to coincide with the group's biennial convention in Atlanta, in order to 'bring home to Reform Jews in the United States the problems some Jews have in marrying in Israel'. The organization of American Reform Zionists set out to raise $2 million in a campaign built around the issue of marriages not allowed in Israel.[26]

What Israelis call a 'Cyprus marriage' (which may be performed in any number of countries as well as Cyprus) may be had for the cost of travel, plus a waiting period required by the locale and the fees associated with a civil marriage. Cyprus marriages are recognized by secular authorities in Israel, although clerks opposed to the process may raise questions and cause a couple to begin a lawsuit before the marriage is actually registered. Reform Jewish activists call the procedures insulting and a nuisance. They have cited the costs involved as pricey but not prohibitive.[27]

According to one of the organizations active in the anti-Orthodox camp (the

Council for Freedom of Science, Religion and Culture in Israel), perhaps 20 per cent of Jewish couples marrying in recent years have evaded the official Rabbinate's procedures. For 1994, the Rabbinate recorded 21,000 marriages, while the Central Bureau of Statistics reported over 26,000 marriages involving Jews. An activist with another anti-Orthodox organization (the Israel Religious Action Committee) estimates that an increasing number of Israelis are behaving like couples in other Western countries, i.e., avoiding the entire set of marriage options and simply living together.[28]

Divorce

The way out of marriage bears some resemblance to the way into marriage for those Israelis who object to the Orthodox Rabbinate. Israeli law provides a monopoly in cases of divorce to Orthodox rabbinical courts. The problems for secular and non-Orthodox religious Israelis include Orthodox rules of procedure that provide substantial advantages to the man in a case of dispute. Somewhat less prominent in public discussion, but still troublesome for individuals, are religious rituals associated with divorce, and rabbinical judges who demand another period for reconciliation even when both partners want an immediate divorce.

Israel's secular courts have ruled in favour of divorces granted by civil authorities overseas, and they have issued rulings concerned with financial settlements and child custody. Where religious and secular courts have ruled differently on the same points, the state's bureaucrats have at times followed the ruling of religious courts. In these cases, however, the route remains open to secular courts, and anti-Orthodox movements exist to assist the plaintiffs.

Burial

From one perspective, Israeli burial arrangements are progressive in comparison with other countries. National Insurance pays for a plot and internment. The family of a deceased makes its own arrangements for a memorial stone, and may pay a fee to the burial society if it wants a choice site for a grave, or to reserve a grave site for a spouse alongside the deceased.

Problems focus on the virtual monopoly of Orthodox organizations for the burial of Israel's Jews. The picture resembles that of marriage, insofar as the incidence of troublesome cases has increased with immigrations from the former Soviet Union and Ethiopia.

One problem concerns deceased Israelis who are not Jews, or whose claims to Judaism do not satisfy the Orthodox burial societies that deal with civilians or the Orthodox rabbis who control military burials. Some of these cases have provoked widespread dismay and anger: recent immigrants killed as soldiers, who thought themselves Jewish, whose families suffered as 'Jews' while in the Soviet Union, but who could not be buried in the Jewish section of an Israeli military cemetery; deceased civilians about whom someone 'whispered' to the Rabbinate that they were not really Jewish, and where the Rabbinate insisted on what may become a lengthy investigation; a deceased whose family considered itself Jewish, but who cannot convince the Rabbinate, and whose claim to Judaism keeps the family from turning to a Christian cemetery, or prevents a Christian cemetery from accepting them; a non-Jewish deceased with no connection to a Christian or a Muslim community.

An Israeli who died in December 1997 left behind a record of being born as a Muslim, marrying a Jewish woman, converting to Judaism, then returning to Islam and marrying a Muslim woman. Each of his families quarrelled over the body. A compromise seemed acceptable: he would be buried in a Muslim cemetery close to the boundary of a Jewish cemetery, with interment ceremonies of both faiths. During the day when this was supposed to have been put into practice, the police had to intervene in order to break up a fight between the Jewish and Muslim families.

And as in the case of marriage and divorce, Orthodox burial has rituals that disturb some Jews. They or their family members want their last journey or final resting place to be something of their own design. Israeli practice is to clean and wrap a body in a shroud and to bury without a coffin. Jewish law prohibits cremation, and will not allow the burial among Jews in a Jewish cemetery for non-Jewish relatives of a Jew. As a result, a non-Jew and a Jew who had lived together as man and wife cannot be buried alongside one another in a Jewish cemetery. Some local Orthodox burial societies do not permit non-Hebrew dates or script on gravestones.

Kibbutzim have provided space in their cemeteries for cases where the deceased or family cannot qualify for a religious burial or does not want a religious burial. The privilege can be expensive, US$5,000 per plot, as opposed to no charge for a plot in a cemetery managed by an Orthodox burial society. The limited space of the kibbutzim cemeteries led to legislation enacted in 1996 requiring the establishment of public secular cemeteries not further than 50 kilometres from each settlement. The opposition of Orthodox burial societies and the lack of enthusiasm of local authorities had prevented, as of mid-1998, the selection and preparation of public secular cemeteries. In June 1998, the Ministry of Religions responded to a citizen's suit by indicating that it had appointed a committee to locate a site for the first such cemetery, and some time later a cemetery began operating in Beer-Sheva.[29]

Non-Orthodox Rites at the Western Wall

The issue of religious freedom is perhaps most stark in the case of non-Orthodox Jewish movements that want to perform their rituals at the Western Wall. In practice, this is likely to mean prayers involving men and women together, perhaps with women carrying the Torah and reading from it, with the women adorned with *kipah* (skullcap) and *tallit* (prayer shawl). Other problems affecting individuals directly (marriage, divorce, burial) have room for alternative procedures, however unpleasant. Yet there is only one Western Wall viewed as a remnant of the Temple destroyed by Romans. Efforts have been made to arrange non-Orthodox rituals at what is called the 'little wall', outside the plaza known to world Jewry since it was cleared in 1967. The efforts have so far not succeeded in attracting either the support of the non-Orthodox or the tolerance of the Orthodox.

The problem arises when Orthodox Jews claim that it is a violation of religious law or custom for men and women to pray together, for women to carry the Torah or read from it, or to wrap themselves in a prayer shawl. The Orthodox claim a prior right to pray at the Western Wall, and assert that the sight of women violating law or custom disturbs their prayers.

As in other issues considered here, there is something of a muddle in rulings of Israel's Supreme Court and actual practice. The court has ruled that women should receive police protection for their prayers at the Western Wall on condition that they refrain from reading from the Torah and wearing prayer shawls. On one occasion, police had been stationed near the Wall but did not intervene to protect Reform women from verbal abuse, spitting and shoving. A police spokesman cited the responsibility of the Rabbinate's ushers to keep order at the Wall.[30] In a later episode, the Supreme Court heard a case brought by Reform Jewish women who demanded to pray as they wish (i.e., without restrictions pertaining to reading from the Torah or wearing prayer shawls). Against their petition were Orthodox Jews who did not want their own prayers disturbed by the presence of women doing what the Orthodox viewed as unacceptable. The Court decided that it was not possible to respond positively to the Reform women.[31] During the holy day of Shavuot in 1998 the police escort assigned to protect a group of Conservative Jews allowed to pray in a designated corner of the plaza had to employ force in order to protect the Conservative contingent from some of the many ultra-Orthodox gathered at the wall. On another occasion, during an ordinary weekday when there were few ultra-Orthodox Jews at prayer, the police assigned to protect a group of Reform Jews had little to do.[32]

The same committee that was assigned to deal with the problem of conversions toured the area of the Western Wall in order to find a location where Reform and Conservative Jews might conduct mixed prayers without disturbing the Orthodox and ultra-Orthodox. A newspaper report of the tour described a situation of numerous interests with conflicting demands and antipathies. The problem resembles those of Christians at their holy sites: too many denominations, a history of conflict between them, and sites that are too small to provide satisfaction for everyone.

Reform and Conservative rabbis express their sense of insult at the need to segregate their followers from the area of the Wall that has come to be known since 1967 as Judaism's central holy place. However, they may nevertheless accept a site off to the side alongside an extension of the Wall. When the

Orthodox chair of the committee indicated that this portion of the Wall was no less sacred than the better known segment, one of the non-Orthodox rabbis quipped that the Orthodox Rabbinate could take for itself that portion, and the non-Orthodox would go to the section vacated by the Orthodox Rabbinate. The section offered was also problematic from the perspective of the Antiquities Authority, which indicated that it would not surrender its right to continue archaeological excavations there. And a group of non-Orthodox women who had been demonstrating periodically at the Wall for some time seemed disinclined to accept any compromise. They continued to demand their own prayers in the well-known section of the Wall, including women wearing prayer shawls and reading from the Torah.[33]

The Appointment of Non-Orthodox Members to Local Religious Councils

The appointment of non-Orthodox members to local religious councils is a case of organizational competition with a hope of material payoff. The councils distribute public funds for religious institutions. Membership for non-Orthodox representatives means financial allocations for non-Orthodox synagogues, schools and social services. Appointments to the religious councils are made partly by the municipal councils; members of local political parties are chosen in proportion to their parties' seats on the latter.

Non-Orthodox claimants have won judgements in Israel's Supreme Court that one's identity among the competing streams of Judaism should not disqualify an appointment to a local religious council. Representatives of the left-wing Meretz party on the Jerusalem city council assured themselves maximum publicity by naming a female Reform rabbi as one of its delegates to the religious council. The high court ordered her enrolled as a member of the religious council, but did not order the Orthodox members of the religious council to address her as rabbi, or to accept her demands with respect to budget allocations.[34] In April 1998, the SHAS and NRP minister and deputy minister of religions formulated a legislative proposal that would give them greater control over appointments to religious councils. They were explicit in saying that the legislation would work against the selection of non-Orthodox members to such councils.[35]

Where Things Stand: Who Is Winning?

Non-Orthodox Jewish institutions and programmes improved their standing during the Rabin–Peres governments of 1992–96. For part of the government's term, no Orthodox or ultra-Orthodox party was formally part of the ruling coalition. Representatives of the overtly secular Meretz Party served as ministers of education and culture, and a secular member of the Labour Party served for a while as minister of religions. During this period, the Ministry of Education and Culture added instruction in Conservative and Reform Judaism to religious programmes in Jewish secular schools. The minister of religions opened to public scrutiny the Rabbinate's list of Jews forbidden to marry in Israel. He also demanded that individuals placed on the list on account of one or another provision of religious law be given an opportunity to appeal their designation, and he proposed public funding for them to travel overseas in order to obtain a secular marriage. With the change in government that occurred after the elections of 1996, the Ministry of Education and Culture passed to a member of the Orthodox NRP, and the Ministry of Religions was to be headed in rotation by a member of the Orthodox NRP and the ultra-Orthodox SHAS. With these changes, the Ministry of Education and Culture renewed its stress on traditional Jewish values in teaching programmes on citizenship. Nothing was heard from the Ministry of Religions about public support for Jews travelling abroad for civil marriages.

Meretz gained the Ministry of Education again with the election of Ehud Barak in 1999, but the presence of SHAS, NRP and for a while United Torah Judaism in the same government worked against any wholesale turn to the religious left. As minister of education, Yossi Sarid was preoccupied with protecting the resources of the entire education sector from a budget-cutting Finance Ministry. Sarid spent considerable time on the problems of the SHAS school system. Its substantial deficits and its resistance to accounting reforms produced smaller classes and other conditions superior to those in other schools and smelled of corruption meant to funnel moneys to the legal defence of party leader Aryeh Deri. Meretz eventually left the government coalition and Sarid lost his position as minister of education. After the election of Ariel Sharon as prime minister in 2001, Meretz remained outside of the government. A member of Sharon's Likud party assumed the role of education minister, and focused on increasing the Zionist (nationalist and/or religious) component in Israeli education.

EXPLAINING THE WEAKNESS OF NON-ORTHODOX JUDAISMS
IN ISRAEL

The weakness of non-Orthodox religious Jews begins with their limited numbers in Israel. The overwhelming majority of non-Orthodox Israelis are secular, and show little interest in the religious doctrines embraced by Reform and Conservative Jews. Orthodox and ultra-Orthodox have no provision for female rabbis. As a result, women who call themselves rabbis are unusual. Women who wear religious garments associated with men (*kipah* and *tallit*) are equally unusual. Issues of gay and lesbian congregations, rabbis, or marriages are mostly unknown in Israel, except as they provide material for Orthodox and ultra-Orthodox denunciations of other Judaisms.

A prominent indication of progressive Judaism's weakness is the lack of Knesset representation. Against religious parties that in one form or another have represented Orthodox or ultra-Orthodox movements since Israel's Independence and count 23 Members of the Knesset elected in 1996, there is no party in the Knesset that represents Reform or Conservative Judaism.

Left-wing, secular Israeli politicians would appear to be the most receptive to Reform and Conservative demands. However, some of these have made a point of criticizing the spokespersons of liberal Judaism for being out of touch with political realities in Israel. Former interior minister Haim Ramon and former health minister Efraim Sneh (both members of the Labour Party) have wanted the help of Jews well connected in America with the peace process. They have come away from meetings with leaders of liberal Judaism saying that those people are interested only in their own religious agenda.[36]

According to Ramon, there are only two important communities in Israel, Orthodox and secular, and the others are insignificant. To change that, he said, would require the Reform movement to send several hundred thousand of its members to Israel as immigrants. Reacting to the American flavour of Reform Judaism, Ramon said, 'I don't tell you what to do in the US; don't tell me what to do here.'[37]

POINTS OF COMPARISON

The details of political dispute about religion in Israel differ from those in other countries, but the larger picture is one of international similarities, at least with respect to Western democracies. Surveys reported indicate that 49 per cent of Israelis define themselves as ultra-Orthodox, Orthodox, or traditional; and 79 per cent place themselves on a continuum between 'strictly observant' and 'somewhat observant'. A collection of surveys from 21 countries (not including Israel) suggest that Israel falls within a normal range. For these other countries, between 2 and 82 per cent report that they attend church weekly; between 24 and 81 per cent feel religious; and between 39 and 96 per cent express a belief in God.

On the dimension of government support for religion, Israel also finds itself in company with numerous other countries. To be sure, the various modes of support complicate any effort at systematic international comparison. In Israel as elsewhere, material aid flows from public authorities to religious bodies in several ways. Even in the United States, alongside a claim of separation of Church and state, substantial benefits flow to religious organizations via tax exemptions, as well as direct public support for hospitals, schools, and other institutions affiliated with religious bodies. While there is no established church in the United States, religiosity appears to be the national creed. In Utah, it is Mormon authorities who speak out prominently on issues of public policy, and occasionally seem to influence the decisions of government officials. Elsewhere it may be a Cardinal of the Roman Catholic Church who is prominent in New York, Boston, Chicago, or Philadelphia; and the preacher of a Baptist mega-church in a southern city. Like the rabbis of Israel, however, none of these Christian authorities can be assured of influencing government on a matter of religious importance, or even producing anything close to uniform behaviour among the faithful.

The prominence of a religious symbol on the national flag puts Israel in a group along with the United Kingdom, Finland, Sweden, Norway, Denmark, Iceland, Switzerland, Greece, Australia and New Zealand. The flag of the United States is secular, but coins and currency, as well as the pledge of allegiance, proclaim the importance of God. Perhaps every democracy's list of national holidays is heavily affected by religion, with special prominence for Good Friday, Easter and Christmas, and whatever might be said about the residue of religion attaching to St Patrick's Day, Valentine's Day, New Year, Easter Monday, Boxing Day and Halloween.

The prominence of religious issues on Israel's national agenda also appears to be comparable with the situation in other countries. Topics with elements of religion that have surfaced in other countries include abortion, euthanasia, prayer in schools, the wearing of religious garb in schools or the military, ritual slaughter of animals, the rights of homosexuals, provisions for divorce and birth control, and the status of children born out of wedlock.

EPILOGUE: FROM THE PERSPECTIVE OF 2001

Writing about religion and politics in Israel has been problematic since the onset of Palestinian–Israeli violence that acquired the label of '*Intafada Al Aqsa*' in September 2000. In contrast to a situation that prevailed for the better part of 50 years – in which quarrels among Jews about religious and political issues had a prominent item on the national agenda – there has been a re-emphasis of dispute between Jews and Palestinians, coupled with an onset of violence that threatens a conflict much greater in conceptual and geographical dimensions. Along with this has been a marked lessening of conflict among the Jews.

From an Israeli perspective, mid-summer 2000 was a time of hope verging on euphoria. The government headed by Prime Minister Ehud Barak offered the Palestinian Authority a package of proposals that included control of 90 per cent or more of the territories under dispute, including sections of Jerusalem populated by Arabs and a formalization of what had been *de facto* Muslim control of what Jews called the Temple Mount and Muslims Haram Esh Sharif. That is the Jerusalem plateau that contains the Muslim Dome of the Rock and Al Aqsa Mosque. Jews revere it as the site of Temples built by Solomon, destroyed by Babylon, rebuilt first by returnees from Babylonian exile and then by Herod, and destroyed by a Roman army in the year 70 CE. A substantial number of Jews from Israel and overseas objected to what they viewed as surrender of the national patrimony, but polls indicated – before the onset of Palestinian violence – that a majority of Israelis might well have supported the deal in a referendum.

What emerged from the summer's negotiations was not an agreement but a surge in sectarian violence. The view widespread among Israeli Jews is that Palestinian Authority Chairman Yassir Arafat orchestrated violent demon-strations and gunfire at Jewish soldiers and settlements, neighbourhoods of Jerusalem, and explosions in crowded urban places. Threats of a widening conflict recalled that disputes about holy places in Jerusalem and nearby Bethlehem a millennium ago gave rise to the word 'crusade'. As at that time, the issues were not entirely religious.[38] Competing national movements use religious claims to bolster their claims of legitimacy. Palestinian and Israeli activists have sought to score points against rivals in their own camps by outdoing one another in the articulation of religious sentiments.

Partly on account of his far-reaching offers of concession, and partly on account of Palestinian violence, the Barak government lost its support in parliament. The prime minister tendered his resignation and set out on an election campaign against Ariel Sharon of the Likud party. Missing from the campaign were challenges about almost all of the religious issues that had divided the country's Jews in recent years. Prominent, however, was a religious/ nationalist criticism directed at Barak for his willingness to give up Israeli control over Jerusalem and the Temple Mount.

Both the larger issue of Jerusalem and the more focused issue of the Temple Mount are problematic from perspectives of Jewish doctrine. Their rocketing to the top of the political agenda suggests the service of religious traditions to current political needs as much as their religious importance.

Jerusalem is called the Holy City (in both Hebrew and Arabic), but not all parts of the city are holy sites. Currently about 30 per cent of the population is Arab and 70 per cent Jewish. The two populations largely are separated in neighbourhoods, although there is enough intermingling of blocks, individual plots, and apartments to confound any simple division of the city. While Israeli politicians have spent much of the time since the 1967 war pledging not to re-divide the city, it is clear that Israeli control over Arab sections has been partial. Few Jews visit Arab sections of the city, and there seems to be extensive control by the Palestinian Authority over schools, hospitals and the media, as well as the operation of Palestinian security personnel, in Arab neighbourhoods.[39]

The issue of the Temple Mount/Haram Esh Sharif is, if anything, more difficult to describe and comprehend than that of Jerusalem. The plateau, which comprises perhaps one-sixth of the Old City (which is itself 1 kilometre square) was captured by the Israeli forces during the Six-Day War of 1967. Immediately after its capture, Defence Minister Moshe Dayan ordered the lowering of an

Israeli flag that had been raised on the Dome of the Rock, and conceded *de facto* administration of the area to Muslim religious authorities.

While the Temple Mount figures prominently in the Jewish national memory and religious aspirations, Jewish presence is another matter. The prevailing Orthodox view is that Jews should not visit the site for fear of treading on the location of what was the Holy of Holies, forbidden to all but the highest religious authorities, and only to those who had undergone ritual purification of a kind no longer practised. While it is hoped that God's Temple will once again appear on the Mount, the religious view is that only the Lord and/or his Messiah can build a proper Temple.

With attitudes like this prevailing among religious Jews, it has been possible for Israeli authorities to forbid Jews from entering the site on Muslim holy days, to forbid Jews from praying on the Mount at all times, and to halt the small groups of religious/nationalist extremists who advocate building a Jewish Temple. Israeli security personnel have entered the Temple Mount on several occasions since 1967 on occasions of violent confrontations, but on the vast majority of days the place has been administered by Muslim religious officials.

What changed in the period 2000–2001? The issue of 'sovereignty' on the Temple Mount/Haram Esh Sharif appeared on the agenda of Israeli–Palestinian negotiations, and the working principle of *de facto* control gave way to escalating demands concerned with formal definitions of control. Barak and his negotiators may have misjudged the capacity of the Israeli Jewish population to accept the formal handing over of a site that most of them rarely visited, and which many of the most overtly religious of them never visited. Rabbis and politicians proclaimed the impossibility of ceding sovereignty of the most sacred of Jewish sites. Palestinian officials added to the dispute by claiming control over the adjacent Western (Wailing) Wall, which the Israelis had not included in their offer. After a period of confused talk about differential sovereignty over the surface and the subsurface of the Mount (where the remnants of the Temple might be located) Prime Minister Barak backtracked and claimed that he would never agree to a deal that he seemed to have offered.

Ehud Barak lost a lopsided national election to Ariel Sharon 63 to 37 per cent. In twentieth-century America, only Franklin Roosevelt's victory over Alf Landon was similar to the Sharon landslide in a contest for national leadership. The day after his victory, Sharon prayed at the Western Wall, and reiterated his commitment to maintaining a united Jerusalem under Israeli control.[40]

As this chapter is being finalized some nine months into *Intafada Al Aqsa*, violence between Palestinians and Israelis has become a daily occurrence, but conflict among the Jews about the role of religion in the state has all but disappeared. Sharon's government of national unity stretches from the Labour Party on the moderate left to Likud on the moderate right, and further to Jewish religious and nationalist parties. Almost all the discourse involving Jewish religious and secular politicians concerns Israel's relations with the Palestinians, and most of that focuses on the degree of violence that is appropriate.

NOTES

1. Josephus, *The Jewish War*, trans. G.A. Williamson (New York: Penguin Books, 1970).
2. Ezra, 10.
3. Rabbi Meir Kahane, *Forty Years* (Brooklyn, NY: The Institute of the Jewish Idea, 1983).
4. Ruth, 4:13–22.
5. Isaiah, 54:3–4.
6. Isaiah, 2:4.
7. H. Mark Roelofs, 'Hebraic-Biblical Political Thinking', *Polity*, XX, 4 (Summer 1988), pp. 572–97; and Roelofs, 'Liberation Theology: The Recovery of Biblical Radicalism', *American Political Science Review*, 82, 2, June (1988), pp. 549–66.
8. See my *Israel and Its Bible: A Political Analysis* (New York: Garland Publishing Co., 1996).
9. Robert Gordis, Koheleth: *The Man and His Work: A Study of Ecclesiastes* (New York: Schocken Books, 1968), p. 68; and Mordechai Zar-Kavod, 'Ecclesiastes', in *The Five Scrolls* (Jerusalem: Mossad Harav Kook, 1973), Hebrew.
10. Eliezer Don-Yehiya, 'Does Place Make a Difference? Jewish Orthodoxy in Israel and the Diaspora', in Chaim I. Waxman (ed.), *Israel as a Religious Reality* (Northvale, NJ: Jason Aronson Inc., 1994), pp. 43–74; Charles S. Liebman and Eliezer Don-Yehiya, *Civil Religion in Israel: Traditional Judaism and Political Culture* (Berkeley, CA: University of California Press, 1984); Charles S. Liebman and Elihu Katz, *The Jewishness of Israelis: Responses to the Guttman Report* (Albany, NY: State University of New York Press, 1997).
11. See, for example, Wade Clark Roof and William McKinney, *American Mainline Religion: Its Changing Shape and Future* (New Brunswick, NJ: Rutgers University Press, 1987).
12. Jacob Neusner, *Death and Birth of Judaism: The Impact of Christianity, Secularism, and the Holocaust on Jewish Faith* (New York: Basic Books, 1987); and Calvin Goldscheider and Jacob Neusner (eds) *Social Foundations of Judaism* (Englewood Cliffs, NJ: Prentice Hall, 1990). This book uses BCE (Before the Common Era) and CE (Common Era) as equivalent to the Christian BC and AD.
13. Neusner, 'Judaism in America: The Social Crisis of Freedom', in Goldscheider and Neusner, *Social Foundations*, pp. 130–3.
14. Samuel Heilman, *Defenders of the Faith: Inside Ultra-Orthodox Jewry* (New York: Schocken Books, 1992), chap. 14.
15. Tamar El-Or, *Educated and Ignorant: On Ultra-orthodox Women and Their World* (Tel Aviv: Am Oved, 1992), Hebrew.
16. *Kal Ha'ir*, 29 April 1998, p. 41.
17. *Kal Ha'ir*, 24 July 1998, p. 29.
18. *The Jerusalem Post*, 8 February 1993, p. 2.
19. *Ha'aretz*, 19 April 1995, p. 6.
20. See the author's, *What Makes Israel Tick? How Domestic Policy-makers Cope with Constraints* (Chicago, IL: Nelson Hall, 1985), chap. 4.
21. Don-Yehiya, 'Does Place Make a Difference?, pp. 43–74.
22. *The Jerusalem Post*, 17 January 1992, p. 1B.
23. *The Jerusalem Post*, 25 March 1990, p. 4.
24. *The Jerusalem Post*, 17 June 1997, p. 6.
25. *The Jerusalem Post*, 31 January 1997, p. 20.
26. *The Jerusalem Post*, 11 September 1995, p. 1.
27. *The Jerusalem Post*, 1 November 1991, p. 6.
28. *The Jerusalem Post*, 29 February 1996, p. 12.
29. *Ha'aretz*, 4 June 1998, p. 5.
30. *The Jerusalem Post*, 8 June 1989, p. 4.
31. *Ha'aretz*, 6 October 1995, p. 5.
32. *Ha'aretz*, 9 June 1998, p. 6.
33. *Ha'aretz*, 16 June 1998, p. 4; 20 July 1998, p. 10.
34. *The Jerusalem Post*, 18 November 1996, p. 12.
35. *Kal Ha'ir*, 29 April 1998, p. 35.
36. *The Jerusalem Post*, 9 February 1996, p. 6.
37. *The Jerusalem Post*, 22 January 1996, p. 1.
38. Aharon Ben-Ami, *Social Change in a Hostile Environment: The Crusader's Kingdom of Jerusalem*

(Princeton, NJ: Princeton University Press, 1969). For a history that puts the emphasis on the sanctity of holy places, see Jean Richard, *The Latin Kingdom of Jerusalem*, trans. Janet Shirly (Amsterdam: North Holland Publishing Company, 1979).

39. Ira Sharkansky and Gedalia Auerbach, 'Which Jerusalem? A Consideration of Concepts and Borders', *Society and Space*, 18, 3, June (2000), pp. 395–409.

40. Lee Hockstader, 'Jerusalem is "Individible", Sharon Says', *Washington Post*, 8 February 2001, p. A01. Internet edition.

13

Secularism in India: Accepted Principle, Contentious Interpretation

SWARNA RAJAGOPALAN

The Indian constitution was amended in 1975 to include the term 'secularism' in the official description of the state.[1] In a deeply religious society, it is not the 'sacred' that is problematic, but the meaning of the 'secular'. Accepting the ideal of a secular state, Indians retain the right to interpret the term 'secular' as they see fit – from a state that knows no religion to a state that recognizes all religions equally to a state that while predominantly Hindu, guarantees the rights of other religious groups. This chapter will begin with an account of the relevant constitutional provisions, and then read them through a variety of lenses – 'traditional' and contemporary. In so doing, the chapter will address those issues (for example, rights, federalism and the use of force) that the democratic context of this debate generates.[2]

SECULARISM IN THE INDIAN CONSTITUTION

The circumstances of the transfer of power in 1947 to the government of independent India determined the direction constitution-makers would be predisposed toward in regard to the relationship between religion and the state.[3] First, much of the political leadership that took over the reins of state was educated in the metropolis – England – at the turn of the century and had been socialized in the liberal and social democratic ideas of that time. Jawaharlal Nehru, who was the dominant figure in the early period after the deaths of Mohandas Karamchand Gandhi and Vallabhbhai Patel, wanted free India to attain to its destiny as a modern power befitting its history and size, unencumbered by superstition and blind faith and unfettered by all things irrational – including religion. Although the freedom movement was made up of many ideological strands, from the socialists to those who would revive the past and its glories, from those who used terror to the satyagrahis, it was the

Congress with its catholic platform and its commitment under Gandhi to non-violence to which power was transferred. The ideological predisposition was to favour a 'separation of Church and State'.

This modernist inclination was reinforced by partition. The creation of Pakistan out of Muslim-majority provinces in India was premised on the existence in the sub-continent of two nations, incompatible with each other culturally and politically. The Congress did not accept this theory and therefore, the India that was constituted under their leadership had to reflect such a rejection, not identifying with any particular religious group. Further, in the aftermath of the riots that accompanied the Partition, there was great anxiety that giving any cause for communal discontent against the state would leave room for another bloodbath. What Partition did was to underscore the idea that religion was a primitive and dangerous beast that must be leashed for the social good.

The resulting constitution of India established a sovereign democratic republic in which it was resolved to 'secure to all its citizens: ... liberty of thought, expression, belief, faith and worship',[4] and although this republic is self-consciously devoid of any identification with any religious group, the constitution shows that not for one moment did its authors forget the labyrinthine diversity of the society for which they were meant to speak. The relationship between the Indian state and its citizens, as individuals and as members of groups, is defined in the chapters on Fundamental Rights, Directive Principles of State Policy and Fundamental Duties.[5]

Indian citizens are guaranteed the right to equality before the law. The Indian state is further enjoined not to discriminate against any citizen 'on grounds only of religion, race, caste, sex, place of birth or any of them'.[6] Equality of opportunity is guaranteed in public employment as well, except in the circumstances described by Article 16(5), which provides that officials serving in connection with the affairs of religious institutions or organizations shall be individuals who practise that religion. Article 17 abolishes the practise of 'Untouchability' and makes such practise punishable by law.

Freedom of conscience and religion, to which the Preamble alludes, is secured by Article 25(1) to all citizens. The state is, however, permitted to regulate secular activities associated with religious practice, such as levying taxes associated with property ownership. What constitute activities that are secular or that are non-essential to religious tenet is decided on the merits of each case. The really interesting provision here is 25(2)(b), which provides for 'social welfare and reform or the throwing open of Hindu religious institutions of a public character to all classes and sections of Hindus'. The explanation that follows states that 'the reference to Hindus shall be construed as including a reference to persons professing the Sikh, Jaina or Buddhist religions and the reference to Hindu religious institutions shall be construed accordingly'.[7] Apart from this, all religious sects have the right to establish and maintain religious and charitable institutions, to manage their own affairs in religious matters, to own and acquire movable and immovable property and to administer such property in accordance with law.[8] The state is prohibited from levying taxes for the promotion of any religion and citizens are free to pay or not to pay religious levies of any sort.

In 1863, the Religious Endowments Act was passed with the view of reducing the government's authority to intervene in the management of religious trusts.[9] Under this law, the affairs of religious endowments may be managed by committees set up for the purpose, while the civil courts of the state may intervene to arbitrate disputes. Section 22 of this act prohibits the government or any of its agents from taking charge of or managing the property of religious trusts. In the constitution, both the central and state legislatures are empowered to make laws regarding these trusts and endowments. The Concurrent List (in the Seventh Schedule of the Indian constitution) authorizes both centre and states to make laws on 'Trusts and trustees' (Item 10, List III) and 'Charities and charitable institutions, charitable and religious endowments and religious institutions' (Item 28, List III). In the case of items on the Concurrent List, both central and state governments can legislate on these subjects, but in the event of a conflict, the central law prevails. Article 290A of the constitution, which was added in 1956, provides that the state of Kerala's Consolidated Fund shall pay a fixed sum annually to the Travancore Devaswom Fund to maintain temples and shrines transferred from the State of Travancore-Cochin when it acceded.

The Indian state subsidizes school education on a large scale, and so there are restrictions on religious instruction at state-aided schools. The constitution also affirms the right of minorities to establish their own cultural and educational institutions and these are eligible for funding from the state. Schools wholly funded by the state cannot impart any religious instruction. However, schools established by a religious group that partly are aided by the state may offer religious instruction without making it compulsory. No one may be refused admission to any state-aided educational institution solely on religious, race, caste, linguistic or similar grounds.

Although in religious matters citizens may follow their conscience, the state is enjoined in the constitution to 'endeavour to secure for the citizens a uniform civil code throughout the territory of India'.[10] The constitution also contains instructions for the citizens of India, who must make it their duty to promote communal harmony and a fraternal spirit, 'transcending religious, linguistic and regional or sectional diversities'.[11] Further, the next clause asks citizens to renounce those practices that are derogatory to women.

To summarize, Indian citizens are free to profess, practise and propagate their religious beliefs, and irrespective of those beliefs, are equal before the law and have equal access to government employment. Religious sects may establish educational institutions and seek state assistance, but if they do that they must admit anyone who seeks to be admitted and not compel them to undertake religious instruction. Educational institutions run wholly by the state cannot impart religious instruction. India is thus constituted as a state which neither interferes nor prevents citizens from having one or another religious affiliation.

This 'hands-off' state is entrusted with a task that completely contradicts this characteristic that is so carefully nurtured by all the other provisions. It is charged with providing for social welfare, and also with 'the throwing open of Hindu religious institutions of a public character to all classes and sections of Hindus'. As the constitutional explanation tells us: 'Hindu' must be construed to include Jainas, Buddhists and Sikhs. Further, regardless of its obvious merits, the ban on Untouchability constitutes an intervention in 'Hindu' religious practice, as does the enforced public access to temples. Finally, even as the citizenry are asked to 'value and preserve the rich heritage of our composite culture', there is a provision in the constitution allowing state monies to be paid for the upkeep of the temples and shrines in the erstwhile Travancore region. This raises important questions about the relationship between the state and Hindu religious practice. While the state's authority to legislate or take action on matters relating to other religious groups is delimited by more general laws pertaining equally to non-religious groups, such as laws on the regulation of accounts and trusts, in the case of Hinduism the state is explicitly charged with intervening to alter practices undertaken in the name of religion. As we will see later in the chapter, this ambiguity is an important part of the contemporary debates on the issue of 'secularism' in India. D.E. Smith attributes the need for this intervention to the nature of Hindu society. He writes:

> The chief reason for such state interference is that Hinduism lacks the kind of ecclesiastical organization necessary to set its own house in order; the tremendous urge for effective social and religious reform that characterizes present-day India can only be satisfied by state action.[12]

The question, however, is whether a secular state might act to reform any religion and what part of that religion's thought and practices might it seek to reform.[13]

Following the 1973 Keshavananda Bharati judgment, the idea has been evolving that there is an ideological core to the constitution that may not be abrogated or amended – a theory of the basic structure of the constitution. A series of judgments have suggested different lists of core elements. One of these was by Justice Y.V. Chandrachud, in the *Indira Nehru Gandhi* vs. *Raj Narain* (1975) case:[14]

1. India's status as a sovereign, democratic republic.

2. Equality of status and opportunity.

3. Secularism and the freedom of conscience.

4. The rule of law.

Following a spate of constitutional judgments, the Constitutional (Forty-Second) Amendment passed in 1975 instituted sweeping changes, only a few of which were subsequently repealed. One that remains is the addition to the Preamble of the words 'secular' and 'socialist'. Our interest lies in the former. Prior to 1975, the only use of the word 'secular' in the constitution was in a reference to the secular (as opposed to ecclesiastical or religious) activities of groups. Thus secularism, although a core ideal, was an ideal that was not defined.

So, if secularism is (part of) the core, then what does it mean within and outside of the constitution?

Indians understand this constitutional principle in two ways. The first is *dharma nirapekshata* (impartiality towards all religions) and the second is *sarva dharma samabhaava* (favouring all religions equally). The state that is *dharma nirapeksha* is neutral towards all religious groups. In its studied avoidance of identification, the Indian state seems to simulate this attribute. The state that is *sarva dharma samabhaava* is a state to which all religions are the same. In its equality and cultural rights provisions, the Indian state resembles this ideal. Both are different from the European ideal of secularism that arose as a political expression of the separation of the Church and state. Following the Reformation and the rise of absolute monarchies, the state asserted the priority of its claim to political authority. The authority of the Church was confined primarily to matters spiritual. It is hard to translate this to the Indian cultural context, partly because of India's diversity and partly because there is no single ecclesiastical authority from which secular authority may be wrested. The state is left negotiating an uncertain space between these three ideals, as well as its own historical and intellectual antecedents.

RELIGION AND THE POLITY – A BRIEF HISTORICAL REVIEW

The key to reading the relationship between the polity and religion in subcontinental history is the word *dharma*, used in both Indian interpretations of secularism. What does *dharma* mean? According to A.L. Basham, 'derived from the Sanskrit root *dhr* – to bear, to support, to maintain – the word *dharma* has the literal meaning of that which is established, that is, law, duty, or custom'.[15] Hard to translate exactly in English, it may be said to refer to all matters of law and custom, preferred values and behaviours and to the ethical standards that govern the public sphere.

Statecraft as *rajadharma* is a means whereby the social (*dharmik*) order is upheld.[16] In most periods of Indian history, the maintenance of social order, rather than a territorially contained state, has been the primary purpose of political organization. With marginal variations, this order was understood to be the *varnashramadharma* (social order that ordains specific roles and duties by a person's caste and life-stage) whereby individuals acted according to their castes and their life-stages. As long as individuals did not fail in the performance of these duties, order would prevail and the survival of society (and its polity) was ensured. While the *varnashramadharma* was, basically, a form of social organization, the early literature of India, secular and religious, makes enough mention of it that it implicitly is understood to have some religious sanction. So the purpose of political organization was related to the maintenance of an order sanctioned by one, if dominant, set of 'religious' beliefs.

Apart from the secular texts and commentaries on statecraft, the two great Indian epics (mythological to the scholarly mind, but real to most Indians) are treasure-troves of ideas on politics. In the numerous stories of patronage and protection therein, we find examples of how the ruler related to the religious and the ritualistic. In both Sanskrit epics, the *Ramayana* and the *Mahabharata*, there are innumerable stories of rulers and their sons marching into forests and frontier regions to protect ascetics and their hermitage against threats from 'others', portrayed as demons and monsters. Further, the teachers of princes, who also appear to have the status of counsellors and ministers to the ruler, sometimes hold positions in the army. They also perform critical rituals for the ruling family and are never less than sages – a status that is distinctly religious. Finally, the kings who are praised in the epics, in all of their versions, are those who 'uphold' *dharma*. Sometimes *dharma* means truth – at any cost, sometimes it means performing one's duty, sometimes it means playing by the rules, no matter what those rules are. The performance of ritual and the upholding of this *dharma* formed the link between religion and politics.

Indeed, noted Indologist Ananda Coomaraswamy makes a case for regarding as the central political relationship in the Indian tradition that between those who write, teach and interpret *dharma* (*brahmins*) and those who enforce and guard it (*kshatriyas*).[17] Coomaraswamy and most other writers on Indian political thought argue that the king's power is legitimized through his cooperation with higher offices. Further, when the king becomes over-assertive then he leaves himself open to be overthrown and the polity open to chaos and destruction. The *brahmin*, acting in the name of *dharma*, is permitted, even expected, to do what is necessary to rid the polity of the king who does not uphold *dharma*, and again, in the epics and other Indian stories, we have several instances of what in modern times we would read as religious interference in the secular realm. Thus, if we were to equate the *brahmin* and the *kshatriya* respectively with the 'sacred' and the 'secular' elements in modern politics, then we would say that in its early history, these elements stood in a symbiotic relationship to each other.

The first imperial unification of a large part of the Indian sub-continent, underpinned by force and by administration, occurred under the Maurya kings (c.324–249 BCE). Each of them followed a different faith and the most prominent, Asoka, adapted his chosen path or personal *dharma* to the exigencies of statecraft.[18] Romila Thapar articulates his definition of *dhamma*, the Pali version of this noun, thus:

> The *Dhamma* of Asoka emerges as a way of life incorporating a number of ideals and practices … the practice of virtue can be made common to all men. The *Dhamma* embodying such behaviour transcends all barriers of sectarian

belief. ... In the propagation of his *Dhamma* Asoka was attempting to reform
the narrow attitude of religious teaching, to protect the weak against the
strong, and to promote throughout the empire a consciousness of social
behaviour so broad in its scope, that no cultural group could object to it.[19]

Although Asoka's adoption of *Dhamma* as a policy followed his own
conversion to Buddhism, we know from his edicts on pillars and rocks that he
advocated not merely religious tolerance but also equal respect for the teachings
and teachers of all sects. Asoka is an important figure in India's long history
because he represents one ideal of a good ruler who ruled at a time when India
was already becoming ethnically and religiously diverse.[20]

The centuries that followed saw the full flowering of Brahminic Hinduism
and several states whose rulers were Hindu (although they would have identified
their faith more narrowly) but whose politics did not specifically shun other
practices. Among the better-known kings around the seventh century (CE) was
Harsha,[21] whose reign is amply chronicled by a court writer, Banabhatta, and by
Hsuien Tsang, a Chinese Buddhist monk who travelled the sub-continent. We
have descriptions of his generous gift-giving assemblies where the learned, the
holy and the poor of all communities were given money, land, rice and other
gifts. The point is that these gifts and such patronage in general came out of the
state treasury but served all groups equally.

The founders of the Delhi Sultanate (1206–1526) brought with them the
political traditions of central and west Asia.[22] It was the custom of these regions
that the *khutba* (the Friday sermon at the mosque) was read in the name of the
Caliph who was the head of the Islamic community at large, holding secular and
some spiritual power. This signified that the local ruler was in fact a deputy of
the Caliph. Rulers who wished to assert their sovereignty would have the *khutba*
read in their names. In the Delhi Sultanate polity, the degree of subordination
of the ruler to the decree of the Islamic clergy, the *ulema*, and the whims of the
aristocracy varied widely from the independence of a Balban, Allauddin Khilji
or Muhammed bin Tughlaq to the relative weakness of a Razia Sultan,
Ferozshah Tughlaq or Ibrahim Lodi.[23] In principle, all the rulers were subordinate to the Caliph but in fact, they asserted their independence to the extent
that they were able. Subordinate as they were to the Caliph, they were under
great pressure to implement the political ideas and doctrines of Islam in the land
of non-believers that they had conquered. This included special taxes and in the
case of some rulers, iconoclasm.

The identification of the rulers and their rule with one religion must be seen
in light of the fact that they were a minority and it was a minority religion that
received official patronage and protection. Accustomed to invasion and immigration, the local elite learned how to carve a place for itself in the new order,
learning the new languages and the ways of the new rulers. This period saw the
rise of a new synthesis between the cultures of the settlers from central and west
Asia, and the culture of the Indian sub-continent. This is most visible in the

arts and literature of the period, including the devotional literature in Indian languages and the new camp language, Urdu. Bhakti and Sufi teachers and poets learned from each without sectarian barriers and forged the basis of contemporary Indian culture.

The Sultans of Delhi were not the only Muslim rulers of India in this period. Their repeated campaigns in the Deccan peninsula had seen the rise of smaller kingdoms that were ruled also by Afghan and Turkish settlers – the rulers of the Bahamani and the Deccan Sultanates.[24] In this setting was born the kingdom of Vijayanagara,[25] whose character was defiantly Hindu. Like the Maurya Empire before it, the story of the founding of this kingdom is that a Brahmin teacher groomed and advised his protégés to establish themselves at Hampi. Vijayanagara flourished as a self-consciously Hindu island in a Muslim sea. Nevertheless, accounts of interstate relations in the Deccan in this period suggest that in Vijayanagara's relations with other states, realpolitik rather than religion determined the relation.

The Mughals followed the Delhi Sultans and under them the synthesis of Indic and Turko-Afghan (as well as Hindu and Muslim) cultures reached its apogee. The Caliph was nominally the sovereign and the Shariat, the law of the state. While the first two Mughal emperors did not depart much from the Delhi Sultans in the relationship that obtained in theory between the state and Islamic law, things changed under Akbar.[26] Akbar's state has been described as secular,[27] but in fact, it was not secular in the Western sense in that the state was not separated from religion. Quite the contrary – Akbar sought to fuse ideas and practices from all the religions he encountered and to replace the awkward equation of Islam and the state with an ideology or religion, even, designed expressly to glorify the emperor and, in that fashion, the state. *Sulh-i-kul* was a policy of tolerance for all religions. Akbar's heterodoxy lost him the support of the conservative *ulema*. The new Sufi sects were growing in power and popularity, however, and Akbar and his successors drew their support from that source instead. His son Jehangir's reign witnessed incidents of religious persecution. Aurangzeb, the last of the great Mughals, was a conservative Sunni and reversed the syncretist and catholic atmosphere of the court. Under his dispensation, the old taxes were re-imposed on non-Muslims and the state moved closer to the old orthodoxy that it had seen prior to Akbar.

The Mughal Empire under Aurangzeb was both at its pinnacle and beleaguered by regional rebellions. The most significant of these in the period of Aurangzeb's life was that by the Marathas under Shivaji. Shivaji went on to establish an independent state and while he has now been appropriated by those who would treat India as a Hindu state, his kingdom continued the sub-continental tradition of treating all religions equally.[28]

Thus we see that historically, politics has always borne some relation to religion in the sub-continent. In a manner of speaking, the protection that it has accorded religiously sanctioned or defined social orders has been the same in every polity or political tradition discussed above. The difference has been in two things: first, whether the polity protects and patronizes all religions and sects equally, and second, what the degree of diversity was in society. Arguably, in the latter case, the greater the diversity – not just as numbers of different sects, but how much they differ from each other – the more inevitable it was that the polity would favour one group over others. It was easier for those kings who had to patronize equally the many sects of Hinduism, Buddhism and Jainism alone than it has been thereafter. This is partly because they are products of the same intellectual evolutionary process. The basis of the polity itself has been one or the other ethical or social order. In the next section, we will see how ideas about this relationship have changed in the last two centuries.

COLONIAL AND CONTEMPORARY VIEWS – THE PLACE OF RELIGION IN THE POLITY

The colonial state was the first Indian state to keep its distance from matters religious, in the sense that it was not identified with any religion. However, the colonial state, acting under the direction of Governors-General like Bentinck, intervened in religious and social practice in a way that no political dispensation had ever done in the past. The enterprise of reforming Hindu religious practice (along with that of imparting Western education) was the first act by a state of intervention in the social order. Traditionally, the state had remained sub-ordinate to society and the colonial state reversed this pattern of domination. The abolition of Sati and Thuggee, the influx of missionaries and the intro-duction of legislation and policy that undermined or rejected traditional Indian practices (such as Dalhousie's Doctrine of Lapse, which derecognized the practice of adoption by childless kings) are some examples of this interventionist state. Hinduism, as the exotic other to their Protestant Christianity, attracted the most 'reform' by its new secular rulers.

Indians from all sects responded to this reform programme in a variety of ways, common to most of which was some examination of their own identity as Indians.

Two categories of movements made up the anti-colonial experience of Indians.[29] The first category of movements adopted elements from Western religions in their reforming zeal – rejection of idolatry (Brahmo Samaj), selection of one or another book as the fundamental text (Arya Samaj), establishment of clerical orders (Ramakrishna Mission) – and co-opted ideas from the West with regard to the status of women and the caste system. It should be noted that organizations like the Arya Samaj also had a strong revivalist strain in their doctrine and that this actually built on what has been characterized as 'borrow-ing'. The second category of movements began by petitioning the colonial government for greater inclusion of Indians in their administration and ended up by asking for an independent nation-state. The rhetoric and practice of South Asian nationalism[30] showed the influence of the liberal ideas of Mill and

Bentham in the petitions for more representation and for greater involvement by the government in public welfare, the dialectical materialism of Marx and Engels in the economic critiques of colonialism, the ideas of Thoreau and Ruskin in Gandhi's techniques of resistance and the nationalism that had swept through Europe in the nineteenth century in the growing demand for self-determination. European domination was, ultimately, hoisted by its own petard!

The contemporary debate in India about the meaning of the term 'secular' is to be seen in light of this historical and intellectual background.[31] Today, the debate features three voices: the Hindutva-vadins,[32] the 'left-liberal' response to *Hindutva* and those who contest the terms of the debate.

Hindutva is an idea that is translated most accurately as Hindu-ness.[33] This is a quality that those who are not Hindu by faith may possess, and indeed do, according to the ideologues of this now prominent school, as long as their lifestyle and culture is Hindu. The argument is that there is an innately 'Hindu' quality to the practice of any religion once it makes its home in the Indian sub-continent. Therefore, it is to be expected that non-Hindus, as much as Hindus, should regard India as their *'pitr-bhoomi'* (fatherland) and their *'punya-bhoomi'* (holy land). When Hindutva-vadins call India a Hindu nation, their ideology states that the term 'Hindu' is to be understood as the attribute of 'Hindu-ness' and not 'Hinduism', to put it awkwardly. In effect, it has been understood, by their followers as well as their detractors, to mean that, as Hindus are the majority, and as Pakistan is a Muslim nation, so should India come right out and identify as a Hindu one.

The political platform of *Hindutva* has multiple planks – minority appeasement, majority assertion and nationalism are three rubrics under which they may be classed. The campaign against special status for Kashmir and separate Personal Laws for religious minority groups fall under the rubric of minority appeasement. The argument is that the Indian state has been 'pandering to' the minority communities, most objectionably to Muslims, and that it therefore favours them. Thus, the claim to secularism by the Indian state is a cover for its partiality to the minorities. The majority which has been enslaved and marginalized since the first arrival of Muslim raiders in 1017 CE, must now reclaim its temples and assert its right to dominance within the Indian polity. There is a rhetoric of a 'thousand years of slavery' and the generation of a 'minority complex' among the majority community. 'The Muslims have four wives and do not plan small families, and therefore, their population will overtake ours', often heard among middle-class supporters, is an example of this. The secularism of the Indian state is the weak-kneed response of a Hindu élite which has forgotten how to assert itself. Secularism is a sign of weakness. True secularism lies in the brand of nationalism that the Hindutva-vadins propagate. It is a nationalism that is openly identified with the majority community and its hegemonic culture and it is a strident nationalism *vis-à-vis* the rest of the world. It is also a nationalism with some irredentist elements, particularly with regard to Pakistan. The Bharatiya Janata Party, which headed the government that decided to conduct tests of India's nuclear capabilities, is the political front of the Hindutva-vadins.

All that remains of Nehru's secular, socialist, modernist legacy in the discussions of secularism is the opposition of a fragmented and politically disparate array of 'secularists' – known to their Hindutva-vadin antagonists as 'pseudo-secularists'. (Note that both schools appear to place a normative value on being secular.) Although the founders of the Indian republic were largely of this school, its present proponents have failed them on a number of counts. Notwithstanding their early 'incumbent' advantage with a favourable constitution, they allowed the terms of the debate on secularism to be set by the Hindutva-vadins. Through the decades, they have reacted to the Hindutva-vadi organizations, be they the Rashtriya Swayamsevak Sangh (National Volunteer Workers Association) or RSS, the Jana Sangh or the Bharatiya Janata Party (BJP).

Scholars of this description, most notably a collection of historians from Delhi, have marshalled evidence to counter the claims made by communal groups, especially the Hindutva-vadins.[34] Political parties that have used communities as 'voting blocs' are held responsible for the communal political climate. The Congress, which is even today the largest of India's secular/ 'secular'[35] parties, in its eagerness as ruling party to win and retain the electoral support of minority groups, has supported the most conservative elements of these groups without regard to internal changes and dissension therein. In the Shahbano case in the 1980s, the government stepped in on the side of conservative readings of Islamic divorce law that place women at a disadvantage, in the face of both a judicial pronouncement otherwise and disregarding more liberal opinion within a diverse community of Muslims. When the government acts in this fashion, it essentializes the minority community in ways that violate their rights. This leads some writers to argue that the guarantee of minority rights must be predicated on the dominant group within the minority promising the same within. It is also pointed out that the centrist and leftist parties have not taken the trouble to match the mobilization efforts or the public education efforts of the Hindutva-vadins. The result is that the constitutional idea of secularism is not a negotiated one, nor one that appears open to negotiation, only interpretation.[36] Rather than act on this by framing the issue in positive terms, some activists have reacted by dismissing, banning, opposing, critiquing, lamenting and disputing the arguments raised by their 'other'. They have failed to initiate any of the discussion on their own. Further, giving credence to the criticism of the Hindutva-vadins as well as those who are dissenters from the debate itself, the left-liberal school has equated religion with the use of religion as politics, and directed a good part of its opposition to religion, and Hinduism in particular. Flawed as Hinduism may be, this is not a sound political stratagem in a country which, Hindu, Muslim, Christian or otherwise, is populated largely by devout citizens! Opposing Hindutva by condemning caste, idol worship, superstition, polytheism or the abuses of religious leaders is like combating AIDS with the Green Revolution – both affect public health in their own way, but the one does not provide the cure for the other. It appears as though members of this school have completely lost touch with the reality of the society that they live in, a fact that their opponents have used skilfully.

Both the Hindutva-vadins and the left-liberal school have this in common – they are modernizers who view the state as an important instrument of society. They differ on the role of religion in this modernist vision. For the Hindutva-vadins, religion is a tool for political mobilization. For the left-liberal school, it is an unspeakable condition of the human mind that must be terminated in the interests of modernity. For both sides, the state is an important agent in the modernization process. For the Hindutva-vadins, it is the vehicle for the realization of mass aspirations. For the left-liberal school, it is the symbol of all that is scientific.

Observing both sides of this debate, some scholars have begun to dispute its very terms. Ashis Nandy is the best-known interlocutor of this position.[37] Nandy is an influential voice in the intellectual community in South Asia. He argues that in these times, religion is faith and religion is ideology. The whole debate about secularism arises from the failure to understand that everyday tolerance has arisen from the practice of religion as faith. From Nandy's work, we understand that it is the association of the state with all that is secular and scientific and the relegation of faith to the private realm, by what I characterize as the left-liberal school and he calls the secularists, that leaves the state vulnerable to the use of religion as ideology. He associates the rise of religious violence with the consequences of the modernization process. Nandy's critique of the debate over secularism is thus also a critique of modernity and its trappings, including the state. Thus:

> it is from non-modern India, from the traditions and principles of religious tolerance encoded in the everyday life associated with the different faiths of India, that one will have to seek clues to the renewal of Indian political culture ...
>
> The moral of the story is this: the time has come for us to recognize that instead of trying to build religious tolerance on the good faith or conscience of a small group of de-ethnicized, middle-class politicians, bureaucrats and intellectuals, a far more serious venture would be to explore the philosophy, the symbolism and the theology of tolerance in the various faiths of the citizens and hope that the state systems of South Asia may learn something about tolerance from everyday Hinduism, Islam, Buddhism, and/or Sikhism, rather than wish that ordinary Hindus, Muslims, Buddhists and Sikhs will learn tolerance from the various fashionable secular theories of statecraft.[38]

SECULARISM AND DEMOCRACY

What is the relationship between the debate over the meaning of secularism and democracy in India? 'Secularism' is not merely a component of the basic structure of the Indian constitution; for Indians of almost any political predisposition, it is a predicate of Indian identity. This is especially so because the equation of Indian identity with secularism provides to Indians a formidable other in the non-secular Pakistani state. Therefore, it is terribly important to Indians that India be seen as a secular state. The problem, as we have seen, arises because it is hard to see what that actually entails. On the other hand, the negotiations over the meaning of secularism and its proper consequences for the political system cannot but impinge on the workings of democracy. Five issues illustrate this.

The Constitution of India directs the state to create a uniform civil code, but permits the continued operation of religious codes of personal law with regard to members of minority communities, as a mark of religious freedom. The government has undertaken, however, the reform of Hindu personal law. This is construed as the imposition upon Hindus of a civil code while other communities remain exempt. The consideration of these questions is complicated by those pertaining to the rights of minority groups within each community. If all communities are permitted to follow their own personal laws, then who is to protect minorities within each community, including women? On the other hand, if a uniform civil code is to come into operation, what is the degree of consensus that is required to give it legitimacy? Who should represent the various communities in the framing of such a law and how might it reflect and guarantee each group's beliefs and identity? All these are questions that a democracy must consider.

Under the Indian constitution, policing is a subject over which the individual states (provinces) have jurisdiction. When riots break out, the local police are called into break them up. A problem well documented is that when this happens repeatedly, the police, who are after all part of the same setting, lose their detachment from the situation. They take sides in the fighting, bringing to bear upon the other group the access to violent means that they exercise on behalf of the state.[39] The group they turn on is further alienated. This raises one set of problems. If the state's enforcement agents are communalized in this fashion, then who is to protect the civil rights of the citizens against the violence of the state? Bombay, a city proud of its cosmopolitan culture and effective government, witnessed such a process through the 1980s, culminating in the police excesses of the December 1992 riots.[40]

When the local police become partisan, they become ineffective, and the next step is the deployment of paramilitary and, then, military forces. In the 1992–93 riots in Bombay, the army was deployed and tanks rolled down Bombay's busiest commercial streets. This expands the scope of the communalization problem because now these forces can lose their distance from the local situation if they are deployed too often. (It also has consequences for their military effectiveness but that is not relevant to this discussion.) The other problem it creates is that of the erosion of state autonomy. Each time the local police fails and the central government has to send in forces, control over the local situation passes to the higher level of government. The state government loses autonomy and it also loses credibility. In states whose constitutions provide for centralized decision-making during crises, the increasing frequency with which local authority fails and is supplanted by military and central decision-making, erodes the democratic structure of the state. Further, the grounds for such 'security' emergencies may sometimes be rather specious, but resistance to them is weak, as the frightening alternative appears to be rioting and chaos.

The election into office of a party such as the Bharatiya Janata Party (BJP) raises another issue. The BJP represents the Hindutva-vadin voice in this debate, but is prevented from explicitly pursuing this part of its agenda because several of its coalition partners, whose support is essential for its continuance in office, are ideologically opposed to it. Nevertheless, as a cadre-based party, the BJP leadership has to communicate with and respond to its rank-and-file,[41] as well as the other organizations in the Sangh Parivar, the 'family' of Hindutva-vadin organizations to which the party belongs, and these appear to exert an equal and opposite pressure on the government.

Since 1997, there have been several incidents of violence against Christians – an unprecedented number since the BJP-led government came to power in 1997, according to the United Christian Forum for Human Rights.[42] One prominent incident was the brutal killing of an Australian missionary and his young son. The government's response was to set up a commission of inquiry that exonerated the Sangh Parivar, notwithstanding police and eyewitness evidence linking the organizer of the killing with the Parivar.[43] Where culpability is not an acceptable finding, who is to bell the cat? The government has no credibility in this matter. Unable to ensure justice, the government is reported to have considered measures such as declaring 1999 the Year of Christ[44] or suggesting a national debate on conversion[45] which is an evocative issue for the Sangh Parivar. Clearly, the BJP members in the government are responding to two different constituencies – their coalition partners and other outraged Indians on the one hand, and their fellow-Hindutva-vadins on the other. Given that most analysts expect the era of coalition governments to last a while, we have to consider the bizarre consequences that such political arrangements, democratically arrived at, will have for debates on identity – national, communal and other. If unable to move in any particular direction, coalition governments simply blunder through, trying to appease whoever they can along the way, the stage is set for terrible confrontation and conflict.

Finally, even as 'minority appeasement' is one of the grievances of the Hindutva-vadins, a recommendation by the National Commission for Minorities that Hindus should be granted minority status in six states does enjoy their support. While the Commission's rationale for this relates to protection and representation, for the Sangh Parivar, it carries the additional benefit of depriving national minorities of their special protections in states where they do in fact constitute a majority. Affirmative action questions, or 'reservations' in the Indian context, are a very sensitive subject in an economy where jobs are scarce and expanding public-sector (including administrative) quotas hold immense threat and promise to young people whose futures depend largely on those jobs. Minority status holds much greater incendiary potential, affecting as it does the status of entire communities that in the sub-continental context number millions. One of the hardest tasks of any democratic state, like India, is to delicately balance the historical imperative of meaningfully expanding inclusion against all the cross-cutting, corollary, accidental exclusions that follow. In an era of coalition governments, this is even harder.

All of these are questions that scholars interested in the creation, strengthening and sustenance of democratic institutions must raise. Debates over a fundamental marker of collective identity are often acrimonious and violent, and the temptation to silence voices in the debate sometimes hard to resist. This is the lesson that Indians are learning as all appearances of consensus over the relationship between religion and the polity have frayed in the 1980s and 1990s.

SUMMARY CONCLUSION

The sweeping surveys in this chapter of constitutional provisions, historical interpretations and relatively contemporary ideas on the relationship between religion and the polity show two things. First, Indians have always considered there to be a relationship between their larger belief-systems and the principles and practice of politics – be it through the maintenance of an ethical or social order or the adherence to the Shariat or the creation of tolerant and syncretist faiths to serve the ends of the polity. Second, in contemporary times, the wide divergence of interpretations of the commonly accepted ideal of 'secularism' in fact illustrate this very history as much as they suggest the unsuitability of a 'separation of faith and state' secularism in the Indian context. Insofar as the religion–polity relationship has consequences for the democratic political system, it is important too that the meaning of 'secularism' and other key values be negotiated and discussed, and any consensus on these meanings constantly reviewed. Indians who will participate in this discussion must abandon intransigence and an unwillingness to listen to unpalatable positions, because the middle ground essential to every democratic resolution and its review can be charted only by so doing.

NOTES

1. I would like to acknowledge with gratitude Seema Gehlaut's careful reading and critique of an earlier version of this chapter.
2. In the last ten years, there has been a proliferation of writings on the questions of secularism and the problem of the religion–politics relationship in South Asia. Some important works have been: Sarvepalli Gopal (ed.), *Anatomy of a Confrontation: The Babri Masjid-Ram Janmabhumi Issue* (New Delhi: Penguin, 1991); K.N. Panikkar (ed.), *Communalism in India: History, Politics and Culture* (Manohar, Delhi, 1991); Tapan Basu, Pradip Datta, Sumit Sarkar, Tanika Sarkar and Sambuddha Sen, *Khaki Shorts and Saffron Flags*, Tracts for the Times 1 (Hyderabad: Orient Longman, 1993); Gyanendra Pandey (ed.), *Hindus and Others: The Question of Identity in India Today* (New Delhi: Viking, 1993); Rajeev Bhargava (ed.), *Secularism and its Critics* (Delhi:

Oxford University Press, 1998).

3. Caveat: I have some reservations about the terms 'Hinduism' and 'religion' and their use in conjunction with each other. On the other hand, because these words are used to mean that large body of sometimes unrelated, sometimes contradictory, always connected beliefs and practices and the people associated with it, even in the constitution discussed here, I will conform to the same.

4. *The Constitution of India*, Preamble.

5. Some of the same ground is covered in D.E. Smith, 'India as a Secular State', in Rajeev Bhargava (ed.), *Secularism and its Critics* (Delhi: Oxford University Press, 1998), pp. 177–233.

6. *Constitution*, Article 15(1).

7. *Constitution*, Article 25, Explanation II.

8. *Constitution*, Article 26.

9. I am grateful to New Delhi-based lawyer, Nitya Ramakrishnan, for the information in this paragraph.

10. *Constitution*, Article 44.

11. *Constitution*, Article 51(e).

12. D.E. Smith, 'India as a Secular State', pp. 213–14. This article was first published in 1963.

13. Marc Galanter, 'Secularism East and West', in Bhargava, *Secularism and its Critics*, pp. 238–9.

14. Subhash C. Kashyap, *Our Constitution: An Introduction to India's Constitution and Constitutional Law* (New Delhi: National Book Trust, 1994), pp. 256–7.

15. A.L. Basham, *The Origins and Development of Classical Hinduism* (Oxford: Oxford University Press, 1989), p. 102.

16. The next few paragraphs draw on Swarna Rajagopalan, 'Security in the Ancient Indian Political Tradition', unpublished paper, 1994. Important sources include U.N. Ghoshal, *A History of Indian Political Ideas* (Oxford: Oxford University Press, 1959), and Charles Drekmeier, *Kingship and Community in Early India* (Stanford, CA: Stanford University Press, 1962).

17. Ananda K. Coomaraswamy, *Spiritual Authority and Temporal Power in the Indian Theory of Government*, edited by K.N. Iengar and R.P. Coomaraswamy (New Delhi: Indira Gandhi National Centre for the Arts and Oxford University Press, 1993), p. 1.

18. The early reign of the third Maurya king, Asoka (c.273–232 BCE), was marked by great violence. However, he is said to have felt great remorse upon the carnage his army wrought in Kalinga and upon his conversion to Buddhism, he followed a policy premised on *Dhamma*. His pillar and rock edicts speak of these events and also set out both his precepts and his practices.

19. Romila Thapar, *Asoka and the Decline of the Mauryas* (Oxford: Oxford University Press, 1963), pp. 180–1.

20. Independent India retains Asoka's lion capital and Dhamma Chakra as symbols of the Indian state.

21. Harsha (606–46 CE) was the only prominent member of a dynasty (Pushpabhuti) in the Indian plains. He is familiar to us through the chronicles mentioned above and also his own literary efforts. In an era of rapid political changes, therefore, his forty-year reign and its achievements stand out.

22. The Delhi Sultanate is the collective name given to four dynasties that successively ruled large tracts of north India between 1206 and 1526. These were the Mameluk, Khilji, Tughlaq and Lodi dynasties.

23. Razia Sultan (1235–40) and Balban (1266–87) were members of the Mameluk dynasty. Although Razia Sultan was a competent ruler, she could not survive the intrigues and manipulations of her courtiers. Balban was one of those who conspired to overthrow her, and in his time, the king's pre-eminence was asserted through the introduction of court ritual and the ruthless use of espionage and force. Allauddin Khilji (1296–1316) expanded the reach of the Delhi Sultanate to the southern tip of the sub-continent, ruling his empire competently but autocratically. Muhammed bin Tughlaq (1325–51) sought to expand the empire once again, and his reign was marked by great (if unsuccessful) innovation and extreme cruelty. He tried to move the imperial capital to the Deccan and to introduce a token currency. Both were disastrous efforts. His cousin Ferozshah Tughlaq (1351–88) was an excellent civic administrator but his religious orthodoxy and paring down of the state's coercive apparatus reduced the autonomy of the state. Ibrahim Lodi (1517–26), the last Delhi Sultan, inherited a declining empire and in his time, both the Portuguese in the south and the king of Kabul (Babur, the first Mughal emperor of Delhi) in the northwest found their way into India.

24. The Bahamani kingdom was founded in 1347 by a disgruntled rebel from Muhammad bin Tughlaq's Deccan entourage. At its zenith, it covered a large area of western India, and held its own with varying success until 1538. It gave way to five Sultanates in the Deccan, led by former Bahamani governors, in Bijapur, Golconda, Ahmadnagar, Bidar and Berar. Within 150 years, these states were annexed to the Mughal Empire.

25. From 1336 to 1672, the four dynasties that ruled Vijayanagara maintained an important peninsular bulwark against the expansion of the Delhi-based empires of the north. In so doing, they set up a parallel state/interstate system in south India.

26. In 1526, Babur defeated the last Delhi Sultan to capture the throne of Delhi. Except for a brief interregnum when his son lost the throne to an Afghan general, the Mughals held Delhi and most of India unchallenged from then until 1707. Akbar's reign (1556–1605) is marked by territorial expansion, political consolidation, diplomatic successes, artistic accomplishment, administrative reform and intellectual experimentation. His son, Jehangir, occupied the Mughal throne from 1605 to 1627 and was succeeded by his son, Shah Jehan (1628–58), who is best known for having commissioned the Taj Mahal. His son, Aurangzeb (1658–1707) presided over the Mughal Empire at the pinnacle of its power and the beginning of its decline.

27. Satish Chandra, *Historiography, Religion and State in Medieval India* (New Delhi: Har-Anand Publishers, 1996), p. 215.

28. Shivaji, who campaigned against the Mughals in the mid-seventeenth century, was coronated in 1674 and died in 1680, has become an interesting figure in the debate on secularism. He is the chief protagonist in local school history texts in Maharashtra, portrayed as a champion of regional interests. However, in the texts written by the central educational board, his nationalism is questioned, as it undermined the imperial unity of India under the Mughals. Finally, in recent years, he has been claimed by the Hindutva-vadins and reviled by secularists for establishing what he called 'Hindavi Swaraj', although accounts of his administration suggest that it was not a Hindu state.

29. See chapter 1 of my dissertation, 'National Integration: The State in Search of Community', University of Illinois at Urbana-Champaign, 1998.

30. The use in this section of 'South Asia' in place of 'India' takes cognizance of the fact that the people of the Indian sub-continent, while still bound by geography and some shared history, were beginning to seek different avenues of self-determination. Thus, all of the thinkers and visionaries discussed form part of the same ideological heritage of the present, although they would place themselves differently within that heritage.

31. This debate is represented comprehensively in Bhargava, *Secularism and its Critics*.

32. The 'Hindu fundamentalists' or the 'Hindu right-wing' of Western press accounts are more accurately described as Hindutva-vadins, a term that draws on their own ideology. Arguably, you cannot have fundamentalists in a belief-system characterized by the lack of a single, unique set of commonly held beliefs and a book. Likewise, the term 'Hindu right-wing' does not capture the distinctive use that this school makes of the term 'Hindu'. This understanding is based on writings by ideologues from this school and their own publications.

33. This section draws on insights and notes from archival and field research conducted on the Bharatiya Janata Party and the larger ideological movement to which it belongs in June–August 1990 in New Delhi. The project also entailed a study of other major parties in the Indian political system. The author was then working with the Centre for Policy Research on a Ford Foundation project on 'Problems of Governance in South Asia'. The research was directed by Dr Bhabani Sen Gupta, who drew on it in the book he authored, *Problems of Governance in India* (Delhi: Konark, 1996), which was one of five country studies produced under its aegis.

34. For instance, Gopal, *Anatomy of a Confrontation*, and Satish Chandra, *Historiography, Religion and State in Medieval India* (New Delhi: Har-Anand Publications, 1996).

35. The word 'secular' is so charged with meaning on either side that to use quotes or not, around it, indicate bias. I therefore, use both versions of the word, separated by a '/' to indicate that both are used and not without truth!

36. For instance, Bipan Chandra, 'Communalism and the State: Some Issues in India', in K.N. Panikkar, *Communalism in India*, pp. 132–41; and Akeel Bilgrami, 'Secularism, Nationalism and Modernity', in Bhargava, *Secularism and its Critics*, pp. 380–417.

37. Ashis Nandy, 'The Politics of Secularism and the Recovery of Religious Tolerance', in Veena Das (ed.), *Mirrors of Violence: Communities, Riots and Survivors in South Asia* (Delhi: Oxford University Press, 1990), pp. 69–93. In recent years, Nandy's oeuvre has invited a great deal of

commentary and discussion. See, for example, 'Plural Worlds, Multiple Selves: Ashis Nandy and the Post-Columbian Future', *Emergences*, 7/8 (1995–96), a special issue on his work. The Bhargava volume includes other important critiques, those of T.N. Madan, Akeel Bilgrami, Partha Chatterjee and Stanley Tambiah among them.

38. Nandy, 'The Politics of Secularism', pp. 85–6.
39. See P.R. Rajgopal's path-breaking studies on violence in India: *Communal Violence in India* (New Delhi: Uppal Publishing House, 1985), and *Social Change and Violence* (New Delhi: Uppal Publishing House, 1986).
40. See Dileep Padgaonkar (ed.), *When Bombay Burned* (New Delhi: USPD, 1993).
41. At the December 1999 National Council session of the BJP, a contentious passage stating that the BJP agenda in government was no more, no less than the agenda of the National Democratic Alliance coalition that it leads, found its way into the final declaration. In other words, the BJP government will not pursue any Sangh Parivar issues that are outside this coalition agenda. A senior party official is quoted as saying that this document was binding on 'every BJP worker'. Neena Vyas, 'Identity Crisis Dogs the BJP', The Hindu on indiaserver.com, 14 January 2000, wysiwyg://4/http://www.the-hindu.com/stories/0114000b.htm, accessed 14/1/00.
42. George Iype, 'Concerned Vajpayee Faces Minority Upsurge', Rediff On The NeT, 3 December 1998, www.rediff.com/news/1998/dec/03vhp.htm, accessed 14/1/00.
43. Walter Fernandes, 'The Wadhwa Commission report', The Hindu on indiaserver.com, 11 September 1999, www.indiaserver.com/thehindu/1999/09/11/stories/05112523.htm, accessed 16/1/00.
44. George Iype, 'Government May Declare 1999 as the Year of Christ', Rediff On The NeT, 28 December 1998, www.rediff.com/news/1998/dec/28christ.htm, accessed 14/1/00.
45. UNI, 'No Move to Ban Conversions, says Vajpayee', Rediff On The NeT, 18 January 1999, www.rediff.com/news/1999/jan/18conv.htm, accessed 1/14/00.

Notes on Contributors

John Green is Professor of Political Science and Director of the Ray C. Bliss Institute of Applied Politics at the University of Akron, Akron, Ohio. Smidt, Kellstedt, Green and Guth have worked collaboratively on a variety of research endeavours, including *The Bully Pulpit: The Politics of Protestant Clergy* and *Religion and the Culture Wars: Dispatches from the Front.*

Adrian Guelke is Professor of Comparative Politics and Director of the Centre for the Study of Ethnic Conflict in the School of Politics, Queen's University of Belfast. He is the author of *South Africa in Transition: The Misunderstood Miracle* (1999), *The Age of Terrorism and the International Political System* (1995) and *Northern Ireland: The International Perspective* (1988).

James Guth is the William R. Kenan, Jr, Professor of Political Science at Furman University, Greenville, South Carolina. Smidt, Kellstedt, Green and Guth have worked collaboratively on a variety of research endeavours, including *The Bully Pulpit: The Politics of Protestant Clergy* and *Religion and the Culture Wars: Dispatches from the Front.*

Lyman Kellstedt is Professor of Political Science, Wheaton College, Wheaton, Illinois. Smidt, Kellstedt, Green and Guth have worked collaboratively on a variety of research endeavours, including *The Bully Pulpit: The Politics of Protestant Clergy* and *Religion and the Culture Wars: Dispatches from the Front.*

Steven Majstorovic is Assistant Professor in the Department of Political Science at the University of Wisconsin–Eau Claire. He teaches courses in Western and Eastern European Politics, Russia and the NIS, and Culture and Politics. He has a particular research interest in the relationship between ethnonational identity and democratic transition in Eastern Europe, and in ethnic minority politics more generally.

Horst Mewes teaches political theory in the Department of Political Science at the University of Colorado, Boulder, where he is Associate Professor. His main interests lie in the area of modern democratic theory, with emphasis on the problematic relations between private and public liberties in liberal democracies. His most recent articles have been on facets of the theories of citizenship and on Hannah Arendt, John Adams, Tocqueville and Adam Smith.

Adamantia Pollis is Professor of Political Science, New School University, and Visiting Professor at the Graduate Center, City University of New York. She recently co-edited the volume *Human Rights: New Perspectives, New Realities*. In addition to her research and writing on theories of human rights and globalization and human rights, she has published extensively on issues pertaining to Greece and Cyprus, in particular the construction of ethnic identities.

Swarna Rajagopalan was Singh Visiting Lecturer in South Asian Studies at Yale University during 2001–02. She received her Ph.D. from the University of Illinois, and was a post-doctoral fellow at Michigan State University's James Madison College from 1998 to 2001. Other than articles and book chapters, she has written *State and Nation in South Asia* (2001) and co-edited *Re-distribution of Authority: A Cross-Regional Perspective* (2000).

William Safran is Professor of Political Science and Director of the Center for Comparative Politics at the University of Colorado, Boulder. Among his books are *Veto-Group Politics* (1967), *Ideology and Politics* (1979) and *The French Polity* (5th edn, 1998). He is co-author of *Politics in Western Europe* (3rd edn, 2001) and editor of *Identity and Territorial Autonomy in Plural Societies* (2000). He is editor-in-chief of *Nationalism and Ethnic Politics*.

Ira Sharkansky is Professor of Political Science and Public Administration at the Hebrew University of Jerusalem. His recent books include *Israel and Its Bible*; *Rituals of Conflict*; *Ambiguity, Coping and Governance*; *The Politics of Religion and the Religion of Politics* and *Politics and Policymaking: In Search of Simplicity*.

Corwin Smidt is Professor of Political Science and Director of the Paul Henry Institute for the Study of Christianity and Politics at Calvin College, Grand Rapids, Michigan. Smidt, Kellstedt, Green and Guth have worked collaboratively on a variety of research endeavours, including *The Bully Pulpit: The Politics of Protestant Clergy* and *Religion and the Culture Wars: Dispatches from the Front*.

Josephine E. Squires is Assistant Professor of Political Science at Fort Hays State University. Her fields of interest include issues of personal and group identity in the context of regional integration and the relationship between peace, war and identity. She has conducted research in several European Union member states.

Joseph S. Szyliowicz is Professor in the Graduate School of International Studies, University of Denver, specializing in issues of sustainable development. He has received several awards for his scholarship and is the author of numerous articles and books dealing with Turkey and the Middle East including *Politics, Technology, and Development* (1991).

Ray Taras is Professor of Political Science at Tulane University in New Orleans. He received his MPhil from Essex University in 1974 and his doctorate from the University of Warsaw in 1981. His books on Poland include *Ideology in a Socialist State: Poland 1956–1982* (1984), *Consolidating Democracy in Poland* (1995) and *Democracy in Poland* (2002). He serves on the Board of Directors of the Polish Institute of Arts and Sciences in America.

Víctor Urrutia Abaigar is Professor of Sociology at the University of the Basque Country (Bilbao). He received his Ph.D. in Sociology from the University of Deusto-Bilbao. He served as Director-General of the Ministry of Religious Affairs (1994–96).

Index